iBroadway

Jessica Hillman-McCord
Editor

iBroadway

Musical Theatre in the Digital Age

Editor
Jessica Hillman-McCord
Department of Theatre and Dance
State University of New York at Fredonia
Fredonia, NY, USA

ISBN 978-3-319-64875-0   ISBN 978-3-319-64876-7 (eBook)
DOI 10.1007/978-3-319-64876-7

Library of Congress Control Number: 2017951523

© The Editor(s) (if applicable) and The Author(s) 2017
This work is subject to copyright. All rights are solely and exclusively licensed by the Publisher, whether the whole or part of the material is concerned, specifically the rights of translation, reprinting, reuse of illustrations, recitation, broadcasting, reproduction on microfilms or in any other physical way, and transmission or information storage and retrieval, electronic adaptation, computer software, or by similar or dissimilar methodology now known or hereafter developed.
The use of general descriptive names, registered names, trademarks, service marks, etc. in this publication does not imply, even in the absence of a specific statement, that such names are exempt from the relevant protective laws and regulations and therefore free for general use.
The publisher, the authors and the editors are safe to assume that the advice and information in this book are believed to be true and accurate at the date of publication. Neither the publisher nor the authors or the editors give a warranty, express or implied, with respect to the material contained herein or for any errors or omissions that may have been made. The publisher remains neutral with regard to jurisdictional claims in published maps and institutional affiliations.

Cover credit: Alengo/Getty Images

Printed on acid-free paper

This Palgrave Macmillan imprint is published by Springer Nature
The registered company is Springer International Publishing AG
The registered company address is: Gewerbestrasse 11, 6330 Cham, Switzerland

For Doug, Ellie and Hannah

Acknowledgements

I wish to give a heartfelt thank you to each of the authors in this collection for their insight and diligence throughout the stages of this process, and to Elizabeth Wollman for bringing the diverse strands of inquiry together so perceptively in her afterword.

Inspiration for this topic came from multiple panels at the Association for Theatre in Higher Education (ATHE). Thank you to the members of the Music Theatre/Dance focus group for their always enlightening work. Henry Bial and Bud Coleman also gave crucial early feedback on the direction of the project.

Thanks to my colleagues and the administration at the Department of Theatre and Dance at the State University of New York at Fredonia for their support and for the sabbatical leave which allowed the project to come to fruition. My students in the department are an always invigorating and renewing presence, and their ideas helped spark some of the lines of inquiry in the book. Thanks especially to Gretchen Martino for her intensive research assistance and work on the index. Thanks also to Jo Ann Norris for help with the title.

Robert Hillman gave ever-sharp editorial feedback on this project. Thanks and love always to he and Betsy Hillman, whose support made a life spent engaging with musical theatre possible. Finally and most importantly, thank you to Doug McCord without whose love and unending support (not to mention insightful editorial eye) this project, and any other, would be impossible.

Jessica Hillman-McCord

Contents

1   Musical Theatre in the Digital Age   1
Jessica Hillman-McCord

Part I   Creating Musicals and the Digital

2   Connection in an Isolating Age: Looking Back on Twenty Years of Engaging Audiences and Marketing Musical Theatre Online   17
Laura MacDonald

3   The Digital-Age Musical: Sighting/Siting Musicals Defined by High-Tech Content, Themes, and Memes   43
Pamyla Stiehl

4   Ghosts in the Machine: Digital Technology and Screen-to-Stage Musicals   73
Amy S. Osatinski

Part II   Audiences and Performers in the Digital Age

5   Let's Misbehave: Cell Phone Technology and Audience Behaviors   95
Kathryn Edney

6	Digital Fandom: *Hamilton* and the Participatory Spectator Jessica Hillman-McCord	119
7	No-Object Fandom: *Smash*-ing Kickstarter and Bringing *Bombshell* to the Stage Kirsty Sedgman	145
8	"You Can't Stop the Tweet": Social Media and Networks of Participation in the Live Television Musical Ryan Bunch	173
9	Digital Technology, Social Media, and Casting for the Musical Theatre Stage Nathan Stith	207
10	Keeping the Celebrity Flame Flickering: Reality Television Celebrities on Broadway and Fan Interaction Through Digital Media Emily Clark	233

Part III Digital Dramaturgy, Scholarship and Criticism

11	The Advantages of Floating in the Middle of the Sea: Digital Musical Theatre Research Doug Reside	261
12	Recanonizing "American" Sound and Reinventing the Broadway Song Machine: Digital Musicology Futures of Broadway Musicals Sissi Liu	283
13	Rise Again Digitally: Musical Revivals and Digital Dramaturgy on Broadway Bryan M. Vandevender	309

14 The Ever-Evolving World of Twenty-First Century
    Musical Theatre Criticism   331
    Bud Coleman

15 Looking Backward, Looking Forward: An Afterword   351
    Elizabeth L. Wollman

Index   359

Notes on Contributors

Jessica Hillman-McCord is an Associate Professor in the Department of Theatre and Dance at the State University of New York at Fredonia, USA, where she teaches musical theatre performance, acting, Meisner technique and musical theatre history. Her articles have appeared in *TDR: The Drama Review*, *Studies in Musical Theatre*, and *Theatre Topics*, among others. Her book, *Echoes of the Holocaust on the American Musical Stage*, was published in spring 2012. She is also a professional actor, director, and choreographer and a member of Actors Equity Association. She has a B.A. from Cornell University, New York, and an M.A. and Ph.D. from the University of Colorado at Boulder.

Ryan Bunch is a scholar of musicals and the cultures of childhood. His research on musical adaptations of *The Wizard of Oz* has been published in *Studies in Musical Theatre*. He studied musicology at the University of Maryland, USA, and is currently pursuing a Ph.D. in the Department of Childhood Studies at Rutgers University-Camden in New Jersey, USA, where he also teaches in the Department of Fine Arts.

Emily Clark currently works as a Visiting Instructor of Theatre Arts at Marymount Manhattan College, New York City, USA, where she teaches numerous courses in the musical theatre program, directs, and choreographs. She is a Ph.D. Candidate in Theatre at the City University of New York Graduate Center. Her primary fields of study are musical theatre and celebrity.

Bud Coleman is Roe Green Professor of Theatre at the University of Colorado Boulder, USA, and former Chair of the Department of Theatre & Dance. A former dancer with Les Ballets Trockadero de Monte Carlo, he has directed and choreographed many musicals. In September 2008, he directed and choreographed the musical *Company* in Vladivostok, Russia, and was selected to be a 2009–2010 Fulbright Lecturer in Japan. With co-editor Judith Sebesta, he published *Women in American Musical Theatre: Essays on Composers, Lyricists, Librettists, Arrangers, Choreographers, Designers, Directors, Producers and Performance Artists* in 2008. Coleman and Pamyla Stiehl co-wrote *Backstage Pass: A Survey of American Musical Theatre* (2013).

Kathryn Edney earned her Ph.D. in American Studies at Michigan State University, Michigan, USA, and has published articles on American musical film and on race and American musical theatre. At Regis College in Weston, Massachusetts, USA, she teaches in the undergraduate Department of Humanities, serves as Graduate Program Director for the MA in Heritage Studies, is Associate Dean for Academic Assessment, and oversees Academic Computing.

Sissi Liu is a Ph.D. Candidate in Theatre and a Presidential Research Fellow at the Graduate Center, City University of New York. Her articles and reviews are published and forthcoming in peer-reviewed journals such as *Studies in Musical Theatre, Performance and Spirituality, Slavic and East European Performance, Puppetry International,* and an edited volume *Routledge Handbook of Asian Theatre*. Currently she is finishing her doctoral dissertation titled "Wukongism, or Monkey King Consciousness: Kungfu/Jazz and the Performing of Asia/America." She is a classically trained pianist and composer, whose compositions and orchestrations have been read and performed by professional musicians at the Juilliard School. She is a recipient of the doctoral Interactive Technology and Pedagogy Certificate.

Laura MacDonald is Senior Lecturer in Musical Theatre at the University of Portsmouth, UK. Her articles and reviews have appeared in *Studies in Musical Theatre, The Journal of American Drama and Theatre, New England Theatre Journal, Theatre Research International, Theatre Journal,* and *Theatre Survey,* and she is preparing a monograph investigating the making and marketing of long-running Broadway musicals. She has held research fellowships at the Shanghai Theatre Academy in China (funded by the Arts and Humanities Research Council) and at Ewha Womans University in Seoul, South Korea (funded by the British Council's Researcher Links program).

Amy S. Osatinski is an Assistant Professor of Theatre at the University of Northern Iowa, USA. Her research interests include contemporary theatre and musical theatre, specifically the intersections of contemporary theatre, popular culture, and technology. She is also a director, designer, and performer whose credits include directing the Denver regional premiere of *Spring Awakening*. In addition, she is a dedicated theatre educator who created a performing arts training program in partnership with the Parker Arts and Cultural Center for Inspire Creative, a non-profit arts organization in Parker, Colorado.

Doug Reside is the Curator of the Billy Rose Theatre Division at the New York Public Library (NYPL) for the Performing Arts, New York City, USA. Prior to joining NYPL, he served on the staff of the Maryland Institute for Technology in the Humanities at the University of Maryland, USA. He has published and spoken on topics related to theatre history, literature, and digital humanities, and has managed several large grant-funded projects on these topics. He is especially interested in the use of digital forensic tools to study the creative process. He received a Ph.D. in English from the University of Kentucky, USA.

Kirsty Sedgman is a lecturer and researcher at the University of Bristol, UK, studying theatre audiences. Her book *Locating the Audience: How People Found Value in National Theatre Wales* was published by Intellect in 2016, and her articles have appeared in publications ranging from *Studies in Theatre and Performance* to *The Stage*. She is currently working on a three-year British Academy postdoctoral research fellowship investigating audience engagement with the Bristol Old Vic theatre through time.

Pamyla Stiehl is an Assistant Professor of Directing and Musical Theatre at University of Montana, USA. She previously served on the faculties of University of St Catherine (Saint Paul, Minnesota, USA) and University of Denver, Colorado, USA as well as adjunct faculty at University of Colorado at Boulder, where she received her M.A. and Ph.D. She is a professional director, choreographer, actor/singer/

dancer, as well as the co-author of *Backstage Pass: A Survey of American Musical Theatre* (2014).

Nathan Stith is an Assistant Professor in the Department of Human Communication and Theatre at Trinity University in San Antonio, Texas, USA. He earned a Ph.D. in Theatre from the University of Colorado Boulder and is a member of Actor's Equity Association. In addition to teaching acting, speech, and musical theatre courses, he also regularly directs plays and musicals in both academic and professional theatres. As an actor, he has appeared in national tours of *Jesus Christ Superstar* and *Romeo and Juliet*, *Cyrano de Bergerac* at the Metropolitan Opera, and regional theatres throughout the county.

Bryan M. Vandevender is a director, dramaturg, and musical theatre historian. He holds an M.A. in Performance Studies from New York University and a Ph.D. in Theatre from the University of Missouri. He is currently an Assistant Professor in the Department of Theatre and Dance at Bucknell University, Pennsylvania, USA. His publications have appeared in *Studies in Musical Theatre*, *Theatre Journal*, *Theatre History Studies*, and *The Palgrave Handbook of Musical Theatre Producers*.

Elizabeth L. Wollman is Associate Professor of Music at Baruch College, New York, USA, and serves on the doctoral faculty in Theater at the City University of New York Graduate Center. She has written extensively on the postwar American stage musical and its relationship to mass media, gender and sexuality, and the cultural history of New York City. She is the author of the books *The Theatre Will Rock: A History of the Rock Musical, from* Hair *to* Hedwig (University of Michigan Press, 2006), *Hard Times: The Adult Musical and 1970s New York City* (Oxford University Press, 2013) and the forthcoming *A Critical Companion to the American Stage Musical* (Methuen/Bloomsbury, 2017).

List of Figures

Fig. 7.1	US viewers (millions) for NBC's *Smash*	149
Fig. 7.2	Geographic location of commentators on sampled YouTube videos	154
Fig. 11.1	McLane layered PSD file, *Gigi*	265
Fig. 11.2	McLane layered PSD file, *Gigi*, detail	266
Fig. 11.3	*Sunday in the Park with George* emulation by Shannon Schweitzer	268
Fig. 11.4	A scenic design by Mikiko Suzuki MacAdams	270
Fig. 11.5	A scenic design by Mikiko Suzuki MacAdams, detail	271
Fig. 11.6	Graph of Broadway's professional networks	272
Fig. 11.7	Graph of long-running Broadway shows for Michael Keller, detail	272
Fig. 11.8	Transcribing programs using Ensemble	274

CHAPTER 1

Musical Theatre in the Digital Age

Jessica Hillman-McCord

The Internet and other digital technologies have fundamentally shifted our moment-to-moment existence, changing the way we examine the world and the ways we shape, remember, and share our experiences. Our phones or computers, and the worlds they link us to, are omnipresent at almost every waking moment. Within this author's lifetime, in the technologically developed world,[1] we have passed from one way of life into another, vastly different one. Previously, we used home phones, or that cultural dinosaur, payphones, to communicate. Now not only do we have a phone in our pocket at all times, phone calls often feel slow, we'd rather text. Twenty years ago, we sent each other physical letters; now we message or send videos through endless social media sites. We played records, then tapes, then CDs (and briefly laser discs) on physical equipment; now we stream music on multiple devices. We researched using books, encyclopedias, or newspapers; now we can satisfy the smallest query in a moment, on our phones. We contacted friends via phone calls and letters; now we have vast networks of hundreds or thousands of digital "friends" or "followers" who we can blast news to with a click of a button. We read about the lives of celebrities in fan magazines or

J. Hillman-McCord (✉)
Department of Theatre and Dance, State University of New York at Fredonia, Fredonia, NY, USA
e-mail: hillmanm@fredonia.edu

© The Author(s) 2017
J. Hillman-McCord (ed.), *iBroadway*,
DOI 10.1007/978-3-319-64876-7_1

newspaper stories; now we can "follow" as many celebrities as we would like and receive minute-to-minute updates about their personal lives. That's only the beginning. It is, in a vast understatement, a new world. And the pace only quickens.

As a highly popular art form, musical theatre has always acted as a mirror to society. Unsurprisingly then, the form also reflects the ways we react to sweeping technological change. From its historical beginnings, overlapping with the adoption of electric lighting, all the way to today's social media marketing, musical theatre has been impacted by innovation and technology. The digital revolution has fundamentally altered the way musicals are marketed, admired, reviewed, researched, taught, and even cast.

As Elizabeth Wollman explains in her afterword to this volume, musical theatre's relationship to technological change has been fraught throughout its history, mirroring the discomfort and fear society as a whole has exhibited in response to the march of innovation. From the invention of photography, to radio, to film, to television, and all the way to the Internet, the public has reacted with combined terror and passionate fascination. Musical theatre's overall response to the digital revolution can best be described as a cautious arm's-length embrace.

In the first hundred years of its existence, commercial musical theatre functioned on one basic model. With the advent of digital technologies, every musical theatre artist and professional has had to adjust to swift and unanticipated change. Now producers and marketers manipulate the web and social media in order to reach and develop audiences in constantly shifting ways. Scholars make use of digital devices and archives in their research and pedagogy, altering the way they teach the form to a new generation of technologically driven students. Casting directors consider social media reach when choosing whom to cast, and therefore both Broadway celebrities and younger actors looking to build careers must develop and curate their own digital profiles. Designers make use of computer-aided design, or CAD, allowing more flexibility in their artistic process, and also frequently utilize digital scenery, causing audiences to perceive their work in new ways. Dramaturgs employ web technologies to grant context and educate audiences who have grown to expect digital integration. Traditional print media criticism has begun to disappear; in the digital age anyone can declare himself or herself a critic. Audiences and fans engage with musicals in fresh and innovative ways, for musicals now have "postmodern presence." They reach audiences across the globe through both sanctioned means (official websites and Internet marketing), and illegal trading of bootleg performance videos. Attending a live musical is now only a fraction of the experience a fan may have with a musical.

Due to the commercial nature of the musical theatre form, musicals offer a more potent test case to reveal the implications of the digital age than other theatrical art forms. For although the resultant financial pressures might encourage stasis, avoiding change will ultimately prove futile. Musical theatre must transform with the times and strive to meet the challenges of our modern world. Rather than merely reflecting technological change, musical theatre scholarship and practice can lead the conversation about art in the digital age.

Current Scholarship

There has been no full-length work exploring digital culture's fundamental and defining impact on musical theatre. Scholars are only beginning to discover the multifaceted effects of the digital world on musical theatre. Although pioneering works have examined the intersections of the digital world with straight theatre, none have focused on musical theatre, where the implications are particularly significant, both commercially and artistically.

Theatre scholars' response to the digital has continued to rapidly change along with societal attitudes towards technology. Matthew Causey's work, as one example, demonstrates that evolution. Causey has continued to engage with the digital, beginning in 2006, with *Theatre and Performance in Digital Culture*, which asked how theatre can respond to science and technology's "colonization of the body," and how the individual can produce effective theatre in the face of this "regime of embeddedness."[2] Causey's concerns reflected a period where many scholars warned of the potential perils the digital posed to the live theatre. For example Michael Kustow, in *Theatre@Risk* (2000), cautioned of the extensive dangers theatre faces in the digital age, in a world "tidied by information technology."[3] By 2015, Causey demonstrates a shift away from earlier fears, returning to the now more normalized subject. He now argues, "Now that the shock of the virtual has subsided toward a 'new-normal' of computational interference in all areas of life, it is an advantageous moment to reflect on the passage through the virtual and back to the real."[4]

As Pamyla Stiehl puts it in Chap. 3 of this book, "[o]ther theatre theorists and scholars have further explored the phenomenon of mediatized theatre, often focusing on models of reception, production, contextualization, cultural hegemony, phenomenology, semantics and semiotics."[5] Through the myriad lenses she mentions, the majority of theatre scholarship on the digital discusses the implications of incorporating multimedia into performance, in volumes such as *Multimedia Performance* (2011),[6] and *Virtual Theatre: An Introduction* (2004).[7] Amy Osatinski touches on similar questions in Chap. 4 of this book, when she examines digital "magic" in screen-to-stage musicals. Despite the extent of work on multimedia performance, fewer scholars have examined how the digital touches more practical elements of the form, from ticket sales, to audience behavior, to scenography, to fan engagement. This is one of the spaces this book aims to fill. While there are technical manuals that of course address changing technologies for the various areas of theatre, including scenography, lighting and sound, and even several works on the use of digital technologies to teach theatre students (such as *Theatre in Cyberspace: Issues of Teaching, Acting and Directing* (1999) by Stephen Alan Schrum), these books do not bring all areas together holistically. They discuss practical elements of media and online culture for theatre practitioners, but also include little to nothing specific to musical theatre.

In "Theater is Media: Some Principles for a Digital Historiography of Performance," Sarah Bay-Cheng points out that "all history is media"[8] and that the way that we study theatrical history has been distinctly impacted by digital technology. Other scholars have also taken on this subject, such as Maggie B. Gale and Ann Featherstone in their "Researching Digital Performance: Virtual Practices."[9] In this book, Sissi Liu and Doug Reside engage with the implications of digital research specifically concerning musical theatre, through both musicological and social history lenses.

Other scholars have taken up disparate perspectives in response to the digital. Bill Blake examined the lay of the land in *Theatre and the Digital* (2014). He offers a useful overview of current scholarship then examines specific performance art based case studies. Nicola Shaughnessy argues that digital natives' brains may actually be different, and that the plasticity of the brain means that children who grow up in the digital world may actually perceive that world differently.[10] Very recently, in 2017,

Eirini Nedelkopoulou examines the implications of liveness in the age of the digital.[11] A crucial theoretical construct which has shifted dramatically in response to the digital, liveness is by necessity examined in several chapters in this book, including Chap. 3 by Pamyla Stiehl, Chap.4 by Amy Osatinski, and Chap. 8 by Ryan Bunch.

Even with the multiplicity of approaches mentioned above, very few scholars writing about theatre and the digital mention musical theatre, despite that art form having statistically the largest popular audience and therefore arguably the greatest potential impact on culture at large. A few scholars do mention musicals, for instance John H. Muse discusses *Next to Normal*'s (2009) use of a "Twitter play" during its Broadway run in his chapter "140 Characters in Search of a Theater: Twitter Plays."[12] Laura MacDonald also examines these Twitter plays in the context of producers' use of social media marketing in Chap. 2 of this book. Amy Petersen Jensen, in *Theatre in a Media Culture* (2007), incorporates several musicals into her larger discussion of how "theatre has reconfigured itself to access the economic and cultural power of the media, and the extent to which mediatization undermines theatrical creativity."[13] Patrick Lonergan has a section on *Once: The Musical* in his book *Theatre and Social Media* (2016), a work where he discusses social media itself as a performance space.[14] Similar questions to those Lonergan raises, regarding fans' performance of online identity and their subsequent marketing value to commercial musicals, are explored in Chaps. 6, 7, and 8 of this book. While the abovementioned works that include musical theatre scholarship offer useful beginnings, this book bring its full attention to the specificities and peculiarities of the musical theatre form, on its own, and as a whole. It is time to explore all of these issues in terms of technology's specific impact on the musical theatre field, where the digital world currently interacts with commercial and artistic demands on a daily basis.

Organization of This Volume

Chapters in this volume cover a vast array of topics. To showcase the breadth of areas where the digital revolution impacts musical theatre, the book is split into three sections covering thematic areas. Chapters in each section act as case studies demonstrating the current state of musical theatre's intersections with digital technology.

Part I: Creating Musicals and the Digital

Musical theatre authors, designers, and producers must all grapple with changing technologies on the way to creating and selling their product. Librettists, lyricists and composers must decide if modern digital era material resonates with them when choosing new topics to musicalize. Designers must employ a host of digital tools to facilitate their design process. Digital magic may also take center stage, visually through scenic and light design, and aurally through sound design. Producers must utilize digital tools to promote their shows and, once they have succeeded, to sell and distribute tickets.

In our first chapter of this section, Laura McDonald traces the history of Internet branding and audience development. She places digital technologies in the context of the early history of producorial innovation and adaption to technology, from the first discount ticket booth, through the early adoption of the web, to today. This historical grounding offers perspective on current innovative uses of social media and technological outreach, such as the 360° Facebook videos used by *Hamilton* and *The Lion King*. Given that the commercialism of the Broadway musical has been central to its understanding by both critics and scholars, the producer's perspective offers crucial context for the rest of these chapters.

In Chap. 3, Pamyla Stiehl concludes that, despite a few exceptions, most musical theatre to reach Broadway has not yet truly engaged with the digital world as central to its themes or topic. Instead, musical theatre largely looks to the past for material. (The current Broadway success *Dear Evan Hansen* (2016), discussed in the conclusion of this book, does engage extensively with millennial social media culture, but seems to be the exception that proves the rule.) In lieu of other commercial Broadway musicals that engage with the digital, Stiehl discusses the world of new-media musical theatre examples as a reflexive performance site. These short musicals, which take digital culture as their subject matter, are written largely for YouTube, such as AVByte's "Twitter—The Musical" and "Facebook—The Musical." These works not only have immense viewership, but further complicate the traditional definition of a "musical."

Lastly in this section, in Chap. 4, Amy Osatinski examines the design world, specifically the way that digital technology has enabled movie magic to be translated into stage magic in contemporary screen-to-stage musicals. One of the most obvious and lamented trends in recent musical theatre has been the conversion of films into ready-made, ready to promote, musical theatre. These musicals can often be less artistically complex and more derivative, and Osatinski examines three of the most critically dismissed: *Ghost: The Musical* (2011), *Dirty Dancing: The Classic Story Onstage* (2006), and *Rocky: The Musical* (2014). In addition to critical disdain, these have in common their use of digital technology to bring moments from films to life on stage. Why might these musicals feel the need to translate pivotal moments from the films? And why might audiences crave such a direct nostalgic filmic reexperience? In order to answer these questions Osatinski engages with critical frames such as Marvin Carlson's theory of "ghosting," and multiple perspectives on the idea of liveness.

Part II: Audiences and Performers in the Digital Age

The artists and business people discussed in the first section must make active choices in order to engage modern audiences. In our second section we take the perspective of the people who make up those audiences. Audience Studies and Fan Studies are lenses through which we can view the other side of the musical theatre experience. Part II examines the way audiences behave (or misbehave) inside the theatre due to the accessible technology of the cell phone, as well as the way they engage with musicals (both staged and televised) once they have left the theatre. The chapters in this section also engage with fan scholar Henry Jenkins' idea of "convergence culture," where fans seek out information about their fan object across multiple media platforms, from the Internet to the stage.

Several of the chapters in Part II grapple with a recent musical theatre trend: the conjunction of television and musical theatre. From the popularization of musicals via *High School Musical* (2006) and *Glee* (2009–2015), to the return to the televised live musical first popularized with *Peter Pan* (1955) and *Cinderella* (1957), television has been a crucial part of the expansion of the musical theatre fan base and a pivotal factor in making musical theatre "cool" again. While televised musical theatre offers enough rich topics for analysis to fill its own book, here we include chapters that examine the digital activities fans pursue in reaction to these televised musicals.

Several chapters in this section also examine musical theatre fans' active engagement online. Community formation offers one of the central pleasures of fandom. Communal fan activities discussed in these chapters range from reassembling the central musical *Bombshell* from the backstage television show *Smash* (2015), to making *Hamilton* fan art, fan fiction, or fan videos, to hate-tweeting during televised live musical broadcasts. Online fan interaction offers one of the most crucial elements to building future audiences and hopefully bringing those audiences into the live theatre.

In Chap. 5, Kathryn Edney focuses on the cellular phone, perhaps the most central technology of the current day. She contends that audience behavior expectations have radically shifted in the smartphone-enabled world, as evidenced by numerous recent and highly publicized controversies, such as the much-shared video of Patti LuPone confiscating a spectator's cell phone mid-performance. This "summer of the cellphone" in 2015 brought these questions to mainstream attention, and encouraged debate across media. In addition to the impact of cell phones on live audience behavior, which Edney places in the crucial historical context of the theatrical highbrow/lowbrow distinction, the cell phone offers a portal for much of the social media behavior addressed in other chapters.

In Chap. 6, I discuss *Hamilton* (2015) as an example of how the Internet affects the musical theatre fan dynamic. The Internet has not only further intensified fans' traditional personalization process with musicals, but also fundamentally altered that relationship. I trace the kinds of "fan culture" created and circulated via the Internet, and discuss features of the way fan communities function in the digital era. Fans value intensive knowledge about a musical, and share, compete, criticize, debate, and perform that knowledge. Digital media has radically intensified the reach of these fans. The ability of the Internet and social media to facilitate fan community formation has dramatically shifted what it means to be a musical theatre fan, as well as how fans relate to each other.

In Chap. 7 Kirsty Sedgman also takes a close look at how fan communities function. Using the example of *Bombshell*, a musical that does not (thus far) exist outside the fictional universe of the television show *Smash*, Sedgman describes how fans engage in practices that may bring non-existent meta-texts to life. *Smash* fans created a successful Kickstarter campaign in order to fund a concert performance of *Bombshell* and have hopes of subsequently bringing the show to Broadway. Their real-world results model the ways in which modern fans harness the power of the digital world. The fans she discusses, like the *Hamilton* fans discussed in Chap. 6, create new texts in order to pay tribute to, or add to, the fan object's universe.

In Chap. 8, Ryan Bunch examines the phenomenon of the live televised musical "events" which resurfaced with NBC's production of *The Sound of Music Live!* in 2013. He discusses fan communities, shedding light on a darker side of fan culture, the phenomenon of "hate-tweeting," or "fan-tagonism." These fans are not necessarily devotees of the particular show being televised, but are nonetheless passionate in their response. Gleeful negativity has been a feature of much of the response to these events, but Bunch also examines the largely positive embrace of *The Wiz* (2016) in the context of the #blacklivesmatter movement. Such live events offer a perfect example of convergence culture, where live theatre, television, and the Internet coalesce, creating something larger and more complicated than any of these media alone.

The impact of the digital world on the day-to-day life of the actor has been quite dramatic. The final two chapters in this section examine a wide spectrum of professional actors, from those just beginning their careers to musical theatre stars. While the distance between these levels of success may seem extreme, both struggling actors and celebrity musical performers must meet similar digital challenges. All actors must market themselves online. Actors still on the audition circuit, which includes all but the most rarefied celebrities, must contend with digital means of getting a coveted audition slot. Whether or not an actor has the opportunity to be seen live partly depends on their digital impact. More strikingly, the digital world creates questions regarding the construction of online identities. How do actors' "real" selves differ from their constructed identities, and how can the digital version help sell their "product?" The line between one's personal life online and one's professionally constructed social media personality is now fascinatingly blurred.

In Chap. 9, Nathan Stith interviews casting directors and actors to learn how digital tools change their processes, and how performers' social media presence affects their marketability. Their answers are enlightening, if somewhat frightening to those who would like to believe that talent alone determines casting decisions. This chapter begins a fascinating exploration of identity formation online. Consciously constructed personas and careful choices as to where and how one uses social media have become an ever more crucial element of actors' career-building process. This new territory, in addition to affecting actors' and casting directors' day-to-day experiences, raises questions that intersect with fan studies, media studies, and larger philosophical questions of identity formation.

In Chap. 10, Emily Clark continues to engage with these themes by exploring a very particular subset of celebrity Broadway musical theatre performers, namely those who emerged from reality television casting contests. Two very different winners of this new casting model, Laura Osnes, who won the role of Sandy in the 2007 production of *Grease*, and Bailey Hanks, who won an MTV contest to assume the role of Elle Woods in *Legally Blonde*: The Musical, have had highly divergent careers since they first appeared on Broadway. Their varying levels of post-television success are at least partly due to Osnes' social media and digital savvy in creating her "girl-next-door turned Broadway Diva" persona. Online, popular musical theatre performers must tread a delicate line between connected and distant, between humble actor and "star," and between friend and diva. Perceived accessibility plays a pivotal part in celebrity success, or lack thereof.

Part III: Digital Dramaturgy, Scholarship, and Criticism

The final section of this book examines questions of research, scholarship, and criticism germane to scholars in the musical theatre field and beyond. Readers of this book may be scholars or come from outside the academic world, but questions that musical theatre teachers and researchers face in the digital age are fascinating regardless of one's subject position.

In Chap. 11, Doug Reside explores how musical theatre scholars utilize the digital world and summarizes how musical theatre fits within the digital humanities. He offers an introduction to the kinds of digital tools scholars may now access. In the more traditional scholarly world, digital research methods are sometimes met with fear or caution, but Reside points out the myriad uses of such research instruments, and their impact, which adds greatly to the kinds of information scholars now have at their fingertips. More traditional research methods simply cannot offer this intensive level of data, and resultant methods to analyze it. Reside's own work examining Jonathan Larson's floppy disks and what they may tell us about his writing process on *Rent* (1996)[15] offers a striking example of the kinds of research open to us in the digital world.

In a companion chapter, Sissi Liu takes on questions of digital research specific to the musicological field in Chap. 12. Liu explains how new digital tools have changed the way we can study musicals' scores. Liu also questions whether a computer or "song machine" could create a musical theatre hit without human authorship, and Liu discusses *Beyond the Fence* (2016), the fascinating attempt already made. In order to create a digitally authored musical, one would need to utilize all levels of data from the most successful musicals, or the "canon." Liu therefore offers a method of explaining or defining the canon digitally. By doing so she outlines various new data driven ways to analyze musical theatre.

Bryan Vandevender examines similar questions in Chap. 13, through the lens of dramaturgy. Through interviews with major non-profit and commercial theatre dramaturgs, he describes new digital tools and methods utilized in their work. Dramaturgs may use similar digital methods as scholars or teachers, but to a different end. Their job is to reach out to popular audiences and to give them context for the productions they attend. How can major New York City theatres such as Roundabout Theatre Company and Lincoln Center Theater reach audiences digitally, and how does that ultimately change their bottom line? Vandevender examines how digital tools can expand the theatregoers experience with musical theatre, and thus encourage future theatre going.

In the book's final chapter, Bud Coleman discusses the shift away from the theatre critic as a professional journalist and towards Internet criticism. This chapter raises crucial questions of how "quality" can be ascertained in an increasingly democratic online world where paid experts are dwindling in numbers and self-professed "experts" are to be met with caution. The very existence of the traditional theatre critic is increasingly in danger of obsolescence. The new world of social media and blogging reviews demands attention in order to understand its potential impact.

Afterword

In the afterword, Elizabeth Wollman examines how societal distrust has always led the first wave of reaction towards any new technology, and places these individual musical theatre examinations in their overall context. She concludes that theatre scholars always return to the power of live theatre, even in the face of monumental technological change.

Looking Towards the Future

Fourteen chapters admittedly cannot begin to encompass the full expanse of musical theatre's changing responses to the digital world. Examples of a few of the topics not considered in detail here include the impact of digital music sales on cast albums (the "iTunes effect"), the use of digital tracks to back up live performance, and the impact of the digital on other design and technical areas, including lighting and sound. Although the chapters included here are by no means comprehensive, they offer snapshots of the current state of various fields, and do the vital work of beginning a critical discussion.

Like any research on contemporary matters, it is hard to keep up with the dizzyingly fast technological changes that continue to occur even as I write these words. Because scholars often focus on the past, distrust of change can lead to a gap in analysis. We have many histories of musical theatre, but insufficient scholarship situating musicals in today's world. This is a disservice. We need to freeze-frame this moment in order to record for posterity how this art form has responded to technological change. Analysis of this very moment can help scholars and readers pause to process our current cultural and societal values, as well as offer a model on how we will continue to adapt. Digital technology will persist in influencing our world until the next, as yet unseen, breakthrough. We need to understand how the arts, and in particular the musical, this unique mix of artistic and commercial popular culture, adjust to a new world. Predictions about the future may prove right or wrong, but one thing is certain, musical theatre will continue to adapt, as the digital defines the ways we move into the future.

Notes

1. I refer to a specific population who encounter the digital on a daily basis. Figures show that, as of February 2016, economically developed countries such as South Korea, Australia, Canada, and the USA led the world in Internet users, at rates from 94% in South Korea to 89% in the USA. The least developed countries, such as Ethiopia, had rates as low as 8%. The global median was 67%. (http://www.pewglobal.org/2016/02/22/internet-access-growing-worldwide-but-remains-higher-in-advanced-economies/).
2. Causey, *Theatre and Performance in Digital Culture*.
3. Kustow, *Theatre@Risk*.

4. Causey, *The Performing Subject in the Space of Technology*.
5. Stiehl, Chap. 3.
6. Klich, Rosemary and Edward Scheer eds. *Multimedia Performance*. London: Palgrave Macmillan Press, 2011.
7. Giannachi, Gabriella. *Virtual Theatre: An Introduction*. London: Routledge Press, 2004.
8. Bay-Cheng, "Theater is Media."
9. Kershaw, Baz and Helen Nicholson, eds. *Research Methods in Theatre and Performance*, Edinburgh: Edinburgh University Press, 2011.
10. Shaughnessy, Nicola. *Applying Performance: Live Art, Socially Engaged Theatre and Affective Practice*. London: Palgrave Macmillan, 2012.
11. Nedelkopoulou, Eirini "Reconsidering Liveness in the Age of Digital Implication," in Reason, Matthew and Anja Mølle Lindelof, eds. *Experiencing Liveness in Contemporary Performance: Interdisciplinary Perspectives*. London: Routledge Press, 2017.
12. Bay-Cheng, Sarah, Miriam Felton-Dansky and Jacob Gallagher-Ross eds. "Digital Dramaturgies," Special Edition of *Theater* 42:2 (2012) Duke University Press.
13. Jensen, *Theatre in a Media Culture*.
14. Lonergan, Patrick. *Theatre and Social Media*. London: Palgrave Macmillan Press, 2016.
15. Reside, Doug. "'Last Modified January 1996': The Digital History of Rent." *Theatre Survey*, vol. 52, no. 2, 2011, 335–340.

References

Bay-Cheng, Sarah. "Theater is Media: Some Principles for a Digital Historiography of Performance." *Theater* 42(2): 27–41, May 2012.

Causey, Matthew. *Theatre and Performance in Digital Culture: From Simulation to Embeddedness*. London: Routledge Press, 2006.

Causey, Matthew, Emma Meehan and Néill O'Dwyer, eds. *The Performing Subject in the Space of Technology: Through the Virtual, Towards the Real*. London: Palgrave Macmillan Press, 2015.

Jensen, Amy Petersen. *Theatre in a Media Culture: Production, Performance and Perception Since 1970*. London: McFarland & Company, Inc., 2007.

Kustow, Michael. *Theatre@Risk*. London: Methuen Drama, 2000.

PART I

Creating Musicals and the Digital

CHAPTER 2

Connection in an Isolating Age: Looking Back on Twenty Years of Engaging Audiences and Marketing Musical Theatre Online

Laura MacDonald

Two decades after the first Broadway musical theatre tickets were sold online in 1996, the marketing of musicals has become even more sophisticated, with long-running, hit musicals from *Wicked* (2003) to *The Lion King* (1997) and *Hamilton* (2017) shifting or supplementing their in-person rush ticket lotteries with digital ticket lotteries, run through apps such as TodayTix. With a few swipes on a smartphone, theatregoers can toss their name into a digital hat and be notified whether or not they have secured discounted tickets to that evening's performance, and all without venturing to the Times Square or West End theatre districts. Broadway was not always an early or swift adopter of digital technology and online platforms (and London has typically lagged behind New York). But since musicals began launching their own websites, the Internet has fulfilled a range of functions for the musical theatre industry and its consumers.

L. MacDonald (✉)
University of Portsmouth, Portsmouth, UK
e-mail: laura.macdonald@port.ac.uk

© The Author(s) 2017
J. Hillman-McCord (ed.), *iBroadway*,
DOI 10.1007/978-3-319-64876-7_2

More than simply disseminating production information or digitizing a traditional print advertising campaign, musical theatre producers have found a wide and complicated range of uses for web platforms. From communicating ticket availability, offering tickets for sale, engaging with fans, and connecting musical theatre creators with their audience, these platforms have expanded the potential reach of musical theatre marketing. In this chapter I outline the growth of online marketing to demonstrate how far the musical theatre industry has come in harnessing demographic data and celebrating fans' commitment to particular musicals, to create and sustain global, online communities of musical theatre spectators. Theatre's "communities, by the active choice of assembling to attend plays, are more apparent as groups to themselves and to others than are the more abstract literary communities," Marvin Carlson points out, and this chapter investigates the engagement, capture, and visibility of such assemblies once they shifted to online platforms.[1]

Like any other consumer product, Broadway musicals have a brand experience to offer and online marketing is increasingly consumers' first point of engagement with a musical brand. The Internet is also the place where musical theatre consumers will continue to engage long after attending an ephemeral live performance, and their Instagram selfies at the theatre or fan performances on YouTube are far more valuable to a musical brand than a Playbill left on a coffee table at home. The group nature of theatre going Carlson privileges has thus intensified online. "The pressure of audience response can coerce individual members to structure and interpret their experience in a way which might well not have occurred to them as solitary readers," Carlson notes, and musical theatre fans have a myriad of opportunities to coerce fellow fans and spectators, whether through likes, retweets, YouTube comments, or blog posts, to commit to a particular, perhaps more emotional and public experience of musical theatre.[2] The byproduct of this publicized experience, I suggest, is the extension of a musical's brand.

The online brand experience begins the storytelling that ticket buyers will experience at the theatre, and social media platforms allow musical fans and spectators to participate in musical theatre marketing, promoting individual musicals through online activities and helping marketers to expand a community of ticket buyers. Carlson laments the limited scholarship investigating "what an audience brings to the theatre in the way of expectations, assumptions, and strategies which will creatively interact with the stimuli of the theatre event to produce whatever effect the performance has on an audience and what effect the audience has on it," but now the Internet provides a site through which to collect audience expectations, interactions, and effects.[3] Online musical theatre marketing may offer some stimulus, but it also facilitates interaction, and values the effect of theatre *and* audience, in ways not previously possible or visible, which this chapter seeks to map. Whether for theatre geeks or tourists, preteens or musical theatre queens, musical theatre marketing increasingly provides connection in the isolating age of twenty-first century life lived online.

Timeless Advertising and Ticket Sales Strategies

While tickets for plays and musicals have always been available for sale at theatre box offices, in 1894, Joe Leblang started selling discounted tickets to Broadway shows in his small tobacco shop on West 30th Street. Leblang had gotten into the discounting business as a result of marketing. Broadway press agents offered shopkeepers like Leblang free tickets in exchange for displaying theatre posters in their windows. Leblang agreed, but started to resell his free tickets, and those of other shopkeepers, eventually formalizing the business as the Central and Public Service Theatre Ticket Office. He later followed the theatres north to Times Square, installing his cut-rate ticket business in the basement of Gray's Drug Store between 42nd Street and 43rd Street.[4] Leblang's staff shouted out the ticket prices, which were reduced the closer it came to show time. Leblang also expanded to selling tickets by mail and by telephone. After his death in 1931, his family continued to run the business, which evolved into a premium ticket brokerage.

Leblang's innovation, born in the nineteenth century, illustrates key strategies that Broadway marketers continue to employ in the twenty-first century. Marketing Broadway shows must be as much about advertising the show itself as it is about offering opportunities to purchase tickets, and Leblang was the middleman, between the producers and the audience, the role musical theatre marketing still plays today. His move north to Times Square, to be near both the product, and his customers, illustrates marketing's crucial position—to be intimately connected to the product, while also reaching outside the market to recruit more customers. Leblang reacted to new technologies like the telephone, incorporating it into his business, just as musical theatre producers would gradually incorporate the Internet into their marketing campaigns.

Leblang's successor, the Theatre Development Fund's half price TKTS booth, was established in 1972 in a trailer in Times Square and is now permanently established there under an enormous red staircase. The TKTS booth is at the center of Broadway's largest advertisement—Times Square, with all of its billboards advertising musicals. Even the simplest Broadway marketing campaigns, such as *The Phantom of the Opera*'s (1988) mask logo, will at a minimum indicate a telephone number and web address for purchasing tickets—simultaneously selling the musical's brand and actual tickets.

For decades producers had relied on traditional print campaigns in newspapers and magazines, posters and billboards in public places (including on the sides of buses), and radio spots. Harold Prince suggests that he and his producing partners made a mistake with their treatment of the musical *West Side Story* (1957) during its run on Broadway. Having relied on a traditional print advertising campaign and the media coverage expected for a hit show, by 1959, Prince and his co-producers thought they had run out of an audience. Trying to keep the show running until the national tour launched, they lowered prices and introduced a two-for-the-price-of-one policy—and promptly sold out. "We had run out of one audience and into another," Prince explains. "Ticket prices were too high even then for a substantial segment of our audience which indeed is interested in going to the theatre."[5] Ticket pricing, Prince believes, must demonstrate an awareness of a show's different audiences in order to sustain longer runs. But without data on purchasing habits and demographics, he and his co-producers were isolated from their theatregoers, limited to rough, instinctive choices. Such isolation led many producers to focus on developing a musical's hit show status through title recognition, and blunt, imperative suggestions to join a particular community of theatregoers who were in the know and keeping up with Broadway trends.

Pippin (1972) and other musicals experimented with television ads in the 1970s, and credit cards and computerized ticketing brought new efficiencies to ticket sales. With demographic studies conducted from the 1970s onwards by the League of American Theatres and Producers (now The Broadway League) as well as by individual producers, more information was available on theatregoer demographics, including their media preferences, which producers used to purchase more targeted advertising. But although research data could reveal which television programs a prospective ticket buyer might be watching and what newspaper she might be reading, such media buys did not facilitate an active or meaningful relationship between a musical and a theatregoer.

Broadway musicals had long addressed the theatregoer directly, whether in print ads or through television commercials and radio ads—slogans or voiceovers addressed "you," and used the imperative mood to invite or insist that "you" come to the theatre. *"Dancin'. Dancin'. Dancin'.* Come and see *Dancin'*, a new musical song and dance entertainment," a television commercial voiceover commanded, introducing the new musical in 1978.[6] Production numbers from musicals such as *Grease* (1972) and *Sweeney Todd* (1979) were not only staged for the camera when television commercials were filmed, but often featured performers looking directly at the camera, as if to break the fourth wall of the television. This attempt at direct engagement was nevertheless mediated, and while television advertising led to measurable increases in ticket sales, it was not even a simulation of the intense connection live performance facilitates for audiences. A *Cats* (1982) commercial in the 1990s anticipated the engagement theatregoers would enjoy in the future thanks to Internet platforms. Rather than showing performance excerpts, the commercial targeted family audiences. Filmed outside the Winter Garden theatre, the ad included shots of children and fans getting their faces painted, hugs from actors in their costumes, autograph sessions, and a testimonial from a parent who had seen the production nine times.[7]

AMERICA AT THE END OF THE MILLENNIUM

In the mid-1990s, as the Internet was becoming increasingly accessible, many New York City-based companies harnessed the new interactive technology and its myriad communication efficiencies to move their offices to cheaper suburban locations and allow employees to experiment with telecommuting. Ironically, the vacant real estate in Midtown was quickly filled by the most creative people in information technology, who sought both the inspiration of other creative types in Manhattan, as well as proximity to their clients.[8] Renting just a few thousand feet but requiring services and power 24 hours a day, seven days a week, "[f]or landlords, the onslaught of the interactive technology companies is a mixed blessing," Claudia H. Deutsch reported in *The New York Times* in 1995. But new media firms were otherwise undemanding and favored quirky, characterful buildings. Typically small companies, they did not demand the standard amenities of the corporate world such as air conditioning or raised floors.⁹ Realtors saw an emerging market despite initially low rents being paid. Manhattan's Silicon Alley was not only intersecting geographically with the Great White Way, but would help to bring Broadway to the World Wide Web.

Playbill On-Line, a theatre news and listings forum run by the publishers of *Playbill*, launched in 1994 on the Prodigy information service (a platform providing paying subscribers with access to a network of online services). From 1995 onwards, news was posted directly on Playbill.com. Playbill On-Line forums were also launched that year on America Online, Compuserve, and Apple eWorld. Reporting that summer on the debate over Glenn Close's and Betty Buckley's Norma Desmond character in *Sunset Boulevard*, (1994) Ben Brantley suggested: "Check out the Broadway message boards on the Internet or drop in at the sort of piano bar where the patrons know every lyric from 'Flora, the Red Menace,' and you'll get some feeling for it."[10] As intimate as a piano bar and as likely a venue for theatre news and gossip, the Internet was quickly establishing itself with industry insiders and fans alike. Newsgroups such as rec.arts.theatre.*, and email listservs focused on musical theatre discussion topics such as Stephen Sondheim, were also established in the early 1990s and similarly provided opportunities for musical theatre fans to connect online.

The year 1995 came to a close with the launch of reallyuseful.com, a site for Andrew Lloyd Webber fans, that along with providing information on his musicals, sold merchandise not even available at the souvenir stands in theatres.[11] Online access to exclusive content would become a mainstay of musical theatre marketing on the Internet. Reflecting on Playbill.com after its first year, managing editor Robert Viagas suggested Playbill On-Line, "empowers an often-forgotten segment of theatre: the audience. With theatre people from across the U.S. and around the world sharing ideas and feelings in a way never before possible, who knows what 1996 will bring?"[12] The year 1996 brought the launch of another website for audiences, TalkinBroadway.com. Along with providing theatre listings and reviews for Broadway and beyond, the website gave audiences and fans a platform with its extremely popular theatre discussion boards, All That Chat. Both Playbill.com and TalkinBroadway.com helped fans connect with their favorite musicals, but also with each other, to share their passion for Broadway shows. The year 1996 also brought Broadway ticketing online, as the Shubert Organization created the domain Telecharge.com, and Ticketmaster introduced an online service, to sell tickets and provide Broadway show information.[13] The ticket agency Theatre Direct International, then owned by Cameron Mackintosh, also launched a website, primarily providing information on Broadway, Off-Broadway, and London productions, with tickets available for purchase by email and telephone.[14]

As online platforms were introduced to sell tickets online in 1996, and fans gathered to exchange their views, the groundbreaking Off-Broadway musical *Rent* transferred to the Nederlander Theatre, a Broadway house. With the musical's fan community of *Rent*-heads in mind, the musical's producers, Jeffrey Seller and Kevin McCollum, introduced new pricing and ticketing strategies at the physical box office. Their decisions anticipated producers' future awareness of and engagement with fan communities via online platforms. Recognizing that $67.50 tickets were prohibitively priced for younger fans of the musical, and that the musical itself advocated for starving artists and young bohemians, *Rent*'s producers began selling the first two rows of seats at $20 each, to ticket buyers visiting the box office the day of the performance. The *Rent*-heads began lining up the day before performances, camping out overnight on 41st Street, to secure the rush tickets. A crowd outside a theatre box office is usually a good advertisement for a hit show, but within a year, concerned over young fans' safety (drugs were being sold by and to people on the line[15]) and seeking to ensure fair distribution of the discounted tickets, the musical's producers revised the policy and introduced Broadway's first ticket lottery whereby any theatregoer could put her name in a hat for a chance at cheap tickets the day of the performance.[16]

Other hit musicals followed suit, and ticket lotteries became a new normal on Broadway. More than developing a new ticketing strategy however, Seller and McCollum recognized theatregoers and fan communities in a way that had never been seen before by the industry. The *Rent*-heads' affection for *Rent* specifically, rather than musicals generally, made them valuable as ambassadors for the musical. Offering them affordable access to the musical facilitated their ongoing, long-term engagement with the show, both as repeat ticket buyers (who could potentially graduate to full-priced tickets) as well as passionate, knowledgeable promoters of the show. "The die-hard fans of the show who helped sustain its run, self-named Rentheads, formed Internet groups based on, among other things, the camaraderie that resulted from ticket buying on the street; the number of times people had seen the show, in how many cities and countries; and quizzes devoted to all the lyrics and music of the show," Tamsen Wolff explains. "This community's delight in the show was bound up in their lived experience of going to the theatre and in their understanding of themselves as an extension of the show's characters."[17] From *Rent* onwards, harnessing fans delight became a more and more central part of marketing campaigns, and a task greatly facilitated by the Internet.

When *Les Misérables* launched lesmis.com early in 1997, *The New York Times* suggested it "may be the theatre's most ambitious Web site."[18] The website was created by the web design firm T3Media, which was also responsible for designing sites for the Really Useful Group and the Tony Awards, among other members of the Broadway community. Beyond serving as a portal for practical information such as cast bios, lesmis.com provided audio and video clips, a cafe for chatting with other fans, news updates, and a quiz with prizes. More unique content allowed site visitors to "study the issue of bread prices in 19th-century France," or ask the musical's composer, Claude-Michel Schönberg, "how to pronounce Rue du Bac. He will answer out loud. That's 'Roo duh Bahk,' peasant."[19] A website for Schönberg and Alain Boublil's *Miss Saigon* (1991) followed that summer, featuring a gift shop, discussion forum, history of the musical, a quiz, cast lists, and synopses of the story in English, German, and Dutch (the languages the musical was being performed in around the world at the time the website was built).[20] More significantly, the homepage was branded with the musical's iconic helicopter scene and logo, and visitors could click through to purchase tickets, confirming one of the key advantages for a musical in establishing a web presence. In less than six months, show websites were becoming the new normal, as Playbill.com's report on the *Miss Saigon* website concluded by pointing readers to a central button for accessing other shows' sites.

But in 1997 it was not only new musicals that were beginning to benefit from the forums for engagement the Internet was increasingly supporting. On October 1, the Rodgers and Hammerstein Organization announced that its website was under construction by T3Media, the company that had already created websites for *Miss Saigon*, *Les Misérables*, the Really Useful Group, and the Tony Awards. Rnh.com was "intended to be an informative, entertaining and up-to-date resource for both the casual browser and serious customer alike," providing practical information on the musicals in its licensing catalogue, as well as information on productions and an interactive database. "With any luck, this website will never be finished," the press release noted, already anticipating the kind of dynamic activity websites could support. Launching the website was compared to an out-of-town tryout, with the expectation of "a very long run."[21] The launch coincided with the television broadcast of a new production of *Cinderella*, and as *The New York Times* reported, "The Web site is carrying video sequences from the new production plus scenes from the original 1957 'Cinderella,' starring Julie Andrews, which has never been rebroadcast or released on home video."[22] The musical theatre industry was already recognizing that the Internet could host additional content and could be a venue for adding value, granting musical theatre fans access to otherwise inaccessible material like archival videos.

Traffic to rnh.com became newsworthy itself, prompting the Rodgers and Hammerstein Organization to issue a press release in January 1998. The site had received more than 60,000 dedicated visitors in its first week, and was selected as a "Cool Site of the Day" by Infinet, an industry review panel. "Oscar Hammerstein II once said that the most important word in theatre is 'collaboration,' and that the ultimate collaboration is between a performer and his audience," the press release enthused. "Likewise, our website is nothing but another blip in cyberspace without you, its hoped-for visitors."[23] As a licensor rather than a producer, the Rodgers and Hammerstein Organization is not in the business of selling tickets, but nevertheless recognized at this early stage in the history of musical theatre on the Internet that it was a valuable venue for capturing large numbers of musical theatre fans, and cultivating their engagement with musical theatre.

The official websites for individual musicals may offer a range of opportunities for spectators to engage with the musical before and after attending a performance, but the primary function of such sites is always to facilitate ticket purchases. Maintaining an online presence allows producers to gather extensive data on prospective ticket buyers based on web traffic and click throughs. George Wachtel, the president of Audience Research and Analysis and a pioneer in the audience demographic research that began in the 1970s, noted in 1997 that although savvy marketers and ad agencies "recognize the need for good, hard, reliable data … much of the theatre industry remains mom and pop." Wachtel suggested: "It's probably the companies like Disney and Livent that will push the industry along."[24] When Disney premiered *The Lion King* later that year at the New Amsterdam Theatre, the reviews were ecstatic. Disney sold more than $2.7 million in tickets the day after opening, at that time the largest one-day ticket sale in Broadway history.[25] But with performances sold out for the rest of the year, Disney worried potential ticket buyers might give up on seeing the show without even trying to secure tickets. Communicating ticket availability for *The Lion King* and managing ticket buyers' expectations (to limit the potential for hostility towards the hit show) would be an ongoing job for Disney in years to come, and one handled increasingly online.

Discount Codes, YouTube, Blogs, and Social Media: Twenty-First Century Tools

By 2000, online entertainment ticket purchases were becoming far more common, and *The New York Times* Technology section was previewing new websites and providing event listings for live web chats with writers, artists, and other creative types ready to share their process with web surfers.[26] Email blasts distributed discount codes for almost all Broadway shows except the biggest hits, and variable pricing—where theatregoers have paid a range of prices for comparable seats in the same section of the theatre—became a new standard on Broadway. TKTS and ticket lotteries persisted, but Broadway marketers were beginning to embrace the very low-cost facility of emailing theatregoers directly regarding discounts—and sometimes at the last minute. Ken Davenport, producer of the Off-Broadway hit *Altar Boyz*, was especially creative with his email blasts, and would send thank you emails to theatregoers "on behalf of Matthew, Mark, Luke, Juan and Abraham," including a discount code for a return visit or to circulate to friends (along with positive word-of-mouth).[27] Such emails also encouraged theatregoers to visit a musical's website where they might become even more engaged with the show via quizzes, fan groups, and newsletters.

In the wake of 9/11, online discounting and variable pricing played an important role in luring theatregoers back to Times Square. Central discount sites such as Broadwaybox.com also began collecting codes from a range of sources, allowing theatregoers to price compare and consider multiple shows. Simultaneously, premium ticket services such as BroadwayInnerCircle.com and Telecharge.com Premium Seating could guarantee tickets to popular, sold-out shows, to anyone willing to pay—in 2003, premium tickets on these sites cost between $150–240.

Shopping for souvenirs online at sites like TheatreMania.com also began to extend musicals' brand presence even further. "Theatre lovers who can't bask in the footlights can turn to TheatreMania.com, a new Web site devoted primarily to Broadway and Off Broadway theatre productions," Shelly Freierman reported, hinting at the growing role the web might play in the lives of fans who could not attend live performances, whether due to geography, finances, or lack of ticket availability.[28]

Though websites were considered essential for every Broadway musical in the early years of the twenty-first century, for long-running musicals, these sites needed to be updated as online technologies developed and evolved. The first *Hairspray* (2002) website was designed using Adobe Flash multimedia technology, which supports animation and interactive content and helped to tell the musical's story to the site's visitors. But given the musical's more than six-year-long run on Broadway, eventually *Hairspray*'s website needed to be updated to reflect the more current look and feel of the show. Digital marketing specialist Steve Tate worked on the redesign and recalls: "The flash site was more focused around the town and community of *Hairspray* while the redesign turned the focus more visually on the lead character of Tracy."[29] Because the website redesign coincided with the release of the musical's film adaptation, it was important for the producers to have a site that visually matched the Broadway production. The iconic artwork of Tracy's face therefore became the first entry point of the site. Tate explains how most websites were abandoning Adobe Flash as a design format because of bugs. "We were looking for quicker load times and a way to direct the consumer to either the Broadway production or the National tour."[30]

Beyond designing websites, online marketing specialist Situation Marketing (now known as Situation Interactive) opened Broadway producers' eyes to the broader marketing presence a musical could establish online, through banner ads, search engines, and more. In 2006, collaboration between online and traditional marketing teams generated *Hairspray*'s "Big Bopper Dance Topper" dance contest, in partnership with *Ladies Home Journal* magazine and its website, LHJ.com. Contestants submitted videos of themselves dancing to a song from the musical to Hairspraythemusical.com. Ten finalists were chosen and online voting took place over the course of several months, featuring critiques by members of *Hairspray*'s cast and creative team. The winner, Leslie Goshko of Tulsa, Oklahoma, was flown to New York for rehearsals with the musical's dance captain, and performed on stage at the

February 24, 2007 matinee.[31] The online video dance contest was held in 2006, the same year YouTube began a phenomenal period of growth leading to its purchase by Google.

Covering *The New York Times*' theatre beat in 2006, reporter Jesse Green observed that the use of Internet marketing tools had "reshaped the way the theatre reaches its audience."[32] Recruiting theatregoers to share a particular musical via their own social media networks (as *The Color Purple* did in the summer of 2006) helped smaller shows like *The Wedding Singer* (2006), as well as new shows, especially those appealing to a younger demographic more susceptible to viral marketing.[33] Still, Green reported that new musicals' web campaigns in 2006 were allocated just 3–5% of a production's marketing budget. A decade into musical theatre's continuing run on the Internet, Damian Bazadona, the founder of Situation Marketing, explained the long-term consequences of online musical theatre marketing. "If you lived in Missouri 10 years ago, even if you saw a number from a Broadway musical on the 'Today' show and loved it, what would you do?" Able to monitor just how many people are clicking on show websites over their lunch breaks, Bazadona could predict the subsequent listening to other songs, signing up for information about a future tour or even the planning of a trip to New York to see the show in question. "By opening up an instantaneous channel for those with casual interest, the Web may develop the future audience."[34] With new platforms like YouTube and MySpace rapidly increasing their users, more and more channels supporting instantaneous engagement with musicals were available for online marketing pioneers like Bazadona to capitalize on.

A new musical long in development, *Spring Awakening*, arrived from Off-Broadway at the end of 2006. Steve Tate was working for Situation Marketing and recalls Bazadona suggesting he upload video of the song "Bitch of Living" to YouTube. The video sharing platform was so much in its infancy that Tate searched online with no luck for U Tube, not knowing what he was even looking for.[35] Lead producers Ira Pittelman and Tom Hulce recognized *Spring Awakening* was a new kind of musical and would need progressive marketing to reach a new audience. A music video of "Bitch of Living" had been shot at the musical's Off-Broadway home, the Atlantic Theater Company, and became the centerpiece of the Broadway marketing strategy. It was featured on the website, in banner ads and on all of the production's social media channels. The use of up-to-the-minute online and social media tools helped to foreground the musical's youthful energy, rather than its nineteenth-century European setting. Capturing the young audience who had made *Rent* and *Avenue Q* (2003) successful became a central goal for the online marketing campaign. From 2006–2010, spanning its Broadway run and first national tour, *Spring Awakening* was not only a part of the early days of YouTube, Facebook, MySpace, and Twitter, but also a crucible for experimentation with these new tools for marketing musical theatre online.

Online video was such an integral part of *Spring Awakening*'s run on Broadway that a blog, Totally Trucked, was launched in 2008 to promote the national touring company using online video. Because the cast of the musical was so young, fans connected easily to them as peers, seeing themselves in the young performers, which made video an ideal online marketing tool. Then-trendy flipcams were used by the tech-savvy tour cast to shoot video, and the online marketing team relayed content requests from fans. Designed using the Blogger platform, Totally Trucked also housed photos and written posts, and along with the videos, this content was regular pushed to all the key social media channels. The blog's YouTube channel was such a success that it was nominated in the digital media website Mashable's Open Web Awards for "Best Brand Use of YouTube."[36]

It was perhaps a logical next step for online marketing to stage an adaptation of a Broadway musical on Twitter, and what better musical than a contemporary show created in the age of social media? In the spring of 2009, *Next to Normal* began publishing tweets, a line from one character at a time. Several times a day, for 35 days, @n2nbroadway dispatched more of the musical. A week into the Twitter performance, the production's account had 30,000 followers, and by the final utterance, 145,000 followers. Adapted by the musical's librettist and lyricist Brian Yorkey, the tweets were sent by the characters in the moments they don't speak on stage, creating a digital musical theatre hypertext. "It's telling the story of the show," Yorkey explained, "but telling it from a lot of different perspectives. It was the show — but a new multiangle way of thinking of it."[37] The performance tweets were enough to clinch a ticket purchase for many followers, and theatregoers appreciated the thoughtfulness and subtlety of the Twitter musical. Though the social media performance ended the day of the Tony Awards, a Twitter Q&A continued between the production and its followers. Tony nominations certainly contributed to a rise in ticket sales for *Next to Normal*, but Bazadona was confident that the Twitter performance was also a factor.[38] His company had also been renamed, appropriately, Situation Interactive, reflecting a shift in focus away from marketing to more sustained, active engagement with consumers—engagement that, as the Twitter performance demonstrated, can generate sales.

Bazadona's firm continued to design interactive online experiences for theatregoers to engage with their favorite musicals. A 2009 revival of *Hair*, originating at the Public Theater's New York Shakespeare Festival, began filming the post-show dance parties on stage at the Al Hirschfeld Theatre, using a high-definition video camera attached high up at the theatre's balcony level. The filming began in February 2010, one of the more challenging times of the year for any Broadway show, when cold, messy weather keeps tourists away from New York City and New Yorkers away from the theatre. The dance party videos, however, uploaded to hairbroadway.com, could be downloaded to Facebook pages or shared via email and Twitter. Theatregoers could tag themselves in the videos, proudly circulate their brief moment on a Broadway stage, and create buzz for the revival.[39] A couple of months into the video dance parties, New York City mayor Michael Bloomberg joined in, generating more buzz, but potentially with an older generation of theatregoers who might even remember the musical's first outing on Broadway.[40]

Introducing a new, interactive seating map in 2010, Disney allowed ticket buyers to select their own seats for *The Lion King*. Tracking customers' choices, Disney learned that theatregoers would often choose better, more expensive seats.[41] By 2011, variable ticket pricing for musicals was being replaced by dynamic pricing, as Disney introduced an algorithm able to recommend the highest price a theatregoer might pay for every single seat in the Minskoff Theatre where *The Lion King* continued to run. The software tool analyzed data from the musical's (at that point) 11.5 million audience members, to recommend the prices ticket buyers might reasonably be expected to pay at specific kinds of performances, such as weeknights in the off-peak winter season, or prime holiday performances such as Christmas. While other musicals used algorithms to increase ticket sales during busy holiday weeks on Broadway, Disney's careful and constant refining of ticket prices made it possible for *The Lion King* to become the top grossing show on Broadway in 2013, the first time for the production since 2003.[42] Not only does Disney assess consumer willingness to pay, but lionking.com is location-aware so makes sure ticket purchasers are offered the nearest production of *The Lion King*. Any questions a ticket buyer might have are likely covered in the Ticketing Questions FAQ section, and a carefully marked calendar page indicates what performances still have great seats available.

Dramaturgical Online Musical Theatre Marketing

With online marketing and audience engagement well established as key elements in successful campaigns for musicals on Broadway, the precise strategies and a musical website's deployment of the production's dramaturgy are increasingly what help new shows stand out, and long runs keep running. Just as the *Hairspray* website redesign discussed above used the main character's head as an entry point into the online world of the musical, beyond providing practical information and facilitating ticket purchases, musical theatre websites have typically begun to develop consumers' engagement with the musical. Years into its run, *The Book of Mormon* (2011) has vast critical and fan response to mine for pull quotes, but nevertheless uses animated miniature Mormons and the musical's doorbell branding to introduce these positive responses on the website, hinting to site visitors about the musical's playful, tongue-in-cheek depiction of a Mormon mission. But *Mormon* marketing has been sophisticated since the musical opened.

To celebrate the animated television series *South Park*'s 15th anniversary on the air, in 2011, its broadcaster, Comedy Central, sponsored the Year of the Fan, an experiential marketing campaign featuring an exhibit, real versions of snack food from the series, and *South Park* avatars for fans to upload to social media pages, all designed to bring the animated series to life for its fans.[43] *The Book of Mormon*, written by *South Park*'s creators, Trey Parker and Matt Stone, had coincidentally opened on Broadway that year. Rather than simply celebrate the new musical's hit status, its marketing has been tailored to its fan base, taking a leaf from the *South Park* marketing book. Instead of quoting excellent reviews in print and online marketing campaigns, *Mormon* producers used social media comments from fans. Emailed news blasts managed expectations, communicating not only the next stops for the two national touring companies, but also building anticipation by announcing when tickets would go on sale for later tour stops. Using the #loveMormon hashtag or following the @BookofMormon Twitter account could alert fans to opportunities to win tickets, and the in-person box office lottery was explained in detail.[44] A similar campaign was run when *The Book of Mormon* opened in London in 2013, and stood out in the West End

As the production extended its Broadway run again, and then announced an open-ended run, the marketing team sought to communicate the contemporary relevance of a turn-of-the-twentieth-century story. Traditional campaigns were still run using billboards and bus ads, but *Newsies* had been harnessing social media from the outset, aware of the high-tech, mediatized context of its Fansies' twenty-first-century lives. Cast member Andrew Keenan-Bolger already produced his own web series and so contributed a series of backstage *Newsies* videos that showcased the high-energy choreography while reinforcing the musical's one for all and all for one ethos. This approach easily appealed to Fansies, whose unity and determination helped to motivate Disney, but also resonated with a broader audience living through the Occupy Wall Street protest movement. Fansies contributed to the marketing of *Newsies* by circulating memes, GIFs (the compressed file format that supports image sharing), and tweets that helped to grow an even larger community of *Newsies* fans.[48] To recognize the Fansies' role in the musical's success, Disney produced limited-edition trading cards for each cast member to autograph and distribute. Fansies could obtain these at the stage door if they had retrieved the correct "code words" from social media to connect in person with *Newsies* cast members.[49]

Connecting with a musical's cast, whether at the stage door or through social media platforms, is one of the most authentic and satisfying means of engaging with a musical for fans seeking to capture and hold on to the live performance experience. As a result of *Newsies*, Disney has a more sophisticated understanding of the power of online marketing when led by cast members and designed to maximize opportunities for audience engagement. Amy Osatinski explains: "After the success of *Newsies* on social media, DTP adjusted its digital marketing plan for all shows. Every company of each production now has a cast member who is designated as the show's 'Social Media Captain.' The Captain is responsible for capturing video and still images and posting them to the show's Instagram account."[50] Having refined the kinds of experiments *Spring Awakening* made with video and social media, and having taken online ticketing to a new level of responsiveness to the market, Disney has mastered online marketing in the twenty-first century.

Situation Interactive also continues to stretch the creative potential of new technologies on social media platforms. In advance of previews for the 2015 musical theatre adaptation of the film *School of Rock*, the company partnered with Facebook to help *School of Rock* "become the first brand to utilize paid 360° video posts on their platform."[51] The interactive video of the song "You're in the Band" allows viewers to look at any part of the scene (filmed in a New York City classroom)—just like watching a musical in the theatre. As paid media, it was filmed and edited by Situation Interactive as a marketing initiative, and paid for by Andrew Lloyd Webber and his producing partners based on the number of times consumers chose to watch the video. This kind of Pay Per Click advertising, in contrast to a campaign made using traditional video footage of the musical in performance, viewed passively by a consumer, is increasingly popular because of its potential to provoke continued engagement with the product or experience being marketed.[52]

Released on YouTube's TrueView, the video platform's choice-based channel where users choose to watch ads (and are thus considered more proactive), the *School of Rock* music video reached consumers who were primed to continue their engagement through the purchase of a ticket to the musical. The video received one million views within three days, generated a 550% spike in traffic to the musical's website the week the video was launched, and a 160% spike in traffic to the musical's ticketing website that week.[53] *The Lion King* followed within a month, releasing a 360° music video of "The Circle of Life," produced by Total Cinema 360.[54] Unlike the *School of Rock* music video, simulating the world of the musical by using a real classroom, "The Circle of Life" music video was filmed in the auditorium and on stage at the Minskoff Theatre where *The Lion King* performs, as if to emphasize the theatricality of live musical performance in contrast to the platform through which a potential theatregoer might be accessing the video.

Navigating an interactive musical theatre performance, like connecting with Disney musical cast members, has the potential to intensify theatregoers' engagement with musicals, and make musicals desirable commodities in new and exciting ways. The 1.2 million YouTube views the *School of Rock* video generated in under a week will certainly have led to quick ticket purchases.[55] Building on the concept album—a marketing strategy originally pioneered by *School of Rock*'s composer and producer Lloyd Webber—another twenty-first-century musical sought to introduce prospective ticket buyers to the potential live musical theatre experience via an intimate online experience. Months before her new musical even began previews, Sara Bareilles, the singer-songwriter who scored the musical *Waitress*, (2016) released a concept album on iTunes.[56] *What's Inside: Songs From Waitress* features Bareilles singing all the songs written for the musical's female characters.

Joined by the musical's lead actor Drew Gehling on two duets, Bareilles also performed the concept album in a concert live streamed by the search engine Yahoo's Live Nation channel. Featuring diner stools, a checkerboard floor, and a sign for "Joe's Pie," (and thus bringing the musical's dramaturgy online), the concert at New York City's City Center venue was staged as an effort to encourage her established fan base to engage with her music on Broadway, extending the musical's reach beyond traditional theatregoers.[57] Though *Waitress* is adapted from a 2007 independent film hit, the musical's lead producers, Barry and Fran Weissler, recognized the value of digital marketing initiatives. As Barry Weissler explained: "It's absolutely essential that we reach beyond the metropolitan area to national and international [audiences]."[58] No doubt with the value of national and international reach in mind, Bareilles addresses the camera and greets the fans viewing the live stream. With viewers watching from as far away as Brazil and the Philippines, and comments on YouTube after the concert uploaded there enthusing "I wish I could see the musical," Bareilles' online outreach effort has very likely contributed to *Waitress*' healthy grosses since opening.[59]

Conclusion

The convergence of advertising, ticketing and the fan experience on platforms such as WeChat and Weibo has led the growth and expansion of China's young but ambitious musical theatre industry, where producers and marketers are perhaps even leaping ahead of Broadway. The majority of musical theatre marketing and ticketing in China occurs via smartphone apps, and savvy Chinese theatre marketers have recognized that as with any product in China, speed and access are of the essence. Musical branding, whether for large scale productions such as *Man of La Mancha* (2016) or more intimate productions such as *Thrill Me* (2016), seek to position musicals in their potential ticket buyers' daily lives, sometimes through video ads in convenience stores and on subway platforms, but primarily through social media campaigns, which may include banner ads but also informational articles generated by the producers to educate the Chinese audience. Fan buzz is also recirculated by the producers through their official social media channels, but exclusively online (rather than through print marketing). Pre- and post-show photo opportunities are facilitated at performance venues, generating more content for fans to circulate on social media.

But even the largest potential musical theatre market in the world is limited, like Broadway, by the number of seats in theatre auditoriums. Despite the vastness of the Internet, any musical will always have a finite number of tickets available for sale. Decades after television commercial voiceovers used the imperative to command viewers to purchase tickets for a musical, online marketing uses similar phrasing, commanding readers of email blasts to purchase tickets now, watch videos, and win tickets by entering contests. The limited stock of tickets thus makes the swift purchase even more urgent, as the release of *Hamilton* (2015) tickets has demonstrated. In the case of *Hamilton*, online fan engagement has often been focused around ticket availability and pricing, indicating how closely entwined musical theatre marketing, ticketing, and fandom can become thanks to the Internet.[60]

As this chapter has established, over the last two decades new technologies and platforms have made marketing musical theatre online a central element of Broadway business strategies. The consumer's *experience* of a musical has expanded, encompassing a range of interactions from the first impression of an online ad, to a ticket purchase, attendance at the live event and post-show engagement via social media. Consumers demand greater connection in an increasingly digital world, and so online musical theatre marketing strives to offer authentic points of engagement with musicals through their online platforms, whether through vlogging actors, fan selfies, or interactive online performances. This connection consequently recruits theatregoers as ambassadors for musicals, continuing to market musicals on behalf of their producers.

Theatre audiences scholar Kirsty Sedgman (see Chap. 7) questions any assumption that audiences succumbing to intimate engagement with musicals have been taken in by the commercial forces of Broadway. "Rather than seeing musical theatre as a 'pleasure machine', churning out joy for the masses, we might therefore ask how every theatrical encounter can be considered a custom-built experience. This approach better enables us to study how theatrical pleasure is handmade every time, as audiences craft it for themselves."[61] Online musical theatre marketing invites spectators to craft such experiences, but also to personalize them, knowing the personalization may contribute to further extending a musical's appeal and building desire for ticket purchases.

Musical theatre fans active online increasingly seek out this kind of filtering and organization of their engagement with a musical, using hashtags like #fansies or #hamilfans and reacting ecstatically if the musical's official social media accounts recirculate their comments. Being acknowledged on a musical's official social media channels seems to elevate fans' sense of their engagement, as a personal encounter, but, crucially, one witnessed by the online audience of many other fans. And it is precisely *because* of that online audience that a musical's social media team will reach out to recognize fans—that recognition helps to grow the fan community's affection for the musical and thereby increase future ticket sales.

Musing in *The New York Times* in 1995, architectural critic Paul Goldberger suggested, "cyberspace has a presence as real and as full of promise as the lights of Broadway. It is monumental and noble and intimate, all at once. It is able to do all that real architectural space can do and more."[62] Goldberger identified just what makes musical theatre and the Internet such a perfect match—all the promise and dreams musical theatre's emotion-filled songs and dances encapsulate can be sampled via musicals' web presence. Official show websites and social media channels simultaneously facilitate intimate one-on-one encounters with a musical as well as connection with the previously imagined community of like-minded fans. Theatre news sites and fan forums subsequently fan the flames of musical theatre worship.

Goldberger predicted that the mix of anonymity and intimacy provided by the Internet "may be the most startling gift of the computer to social culture at the end of the 20th century."[63] Decades later, Sedgman discusses the fulfillment of this prediction—the "processes by which audiences seek to forge connections—between themselves and performers, and between themselves and their fellow spectators—through posting descriptions of affect and engagement online."[64] Focusing specifically on twenty-first-century fans who view spectacular production numbers from the Tony Awards broadcast (Broadway's largest television commercial) via the online video platform YouTube, Sedgman confirms the potential the Internet continues to provide for such intimate encounters with musicals. But as personal and emotional as much online engagement with musicals has become, this gift of the computer to social culture is not only a gift to musical theatre audiences. It is a significant gift to the musical theatre industry, an industry very much alive at the beginning of the millennium, a fabulous invalid no more.

Notes

1. Carlson, "Theatre Audiences," 85.
2. Ibid.

3. Ibid., 97.
4. Stevenson, "OP-ART".
5. Prince, *Contradictions*, 39.
6. gottagodisco, "Bob Fosse's "DANCIN" Commercial 1978." Accessed September 22, 2016, https://www.youtube.com/watch?v=nrjveIOycIE.
7. BrooklynCelluloid, *Cats on Broadway Fan Appreciation Commercial*, accessed September 18, 2016, https://www.youtube.com/watch?v=fYrSKkB3U4M.
8. Deutsch, "On Electronic Highway".
9. Ibid.
10. Brantley, "A Broadway Battle".
11. Marks, "On Stage, and Off".
12. Playbill, "The Year in Review: 1995".
13. Canedy, "Tickets on Sale!".
14. Levere, "Business Travel".
15. Hodges, *On Broadway*.
16. MacDonald, "Rent Changing".
17. Wolff, "Theatre," 134.
18. Grimes, "On Stage, and Off".
19. Ibid.
20. Lefkowitz, "Miss Saigon Attains".
21. Rnh, "R&h On-Line<".
22. "Footlights".
23. Rnh, "Now Playing At A Computer Near You".
24. Grimes, "On Stage, and Off".
25. Lyman, "On Stage and Off".
26. Freierman, "NEWS WATCH".
27. Green, "Producers Use the Web".
28. Freierman, "NEWS WATCH".
29. Tate, "Hairspray Website".
30. Ibid.
31. Jones, "Oklahoman Wins Hairspray Dance Contest".
32. Green, "Producers Use the Web".
33. Ibid.
34. Ibid.
35. Tate, Personal Interview.
36. Ibid.
37. Newman, "It's Broadway Gone Viral".
38. Ibid.
39. Healy, "'Hair' to Help Facebook Generation".
40. Hetrick, "Bloomberg Lets His Hair Down".
41. Healy, "Ticket Pricing Puts 'Lion King' Atop Broadway's Circle of Life".
42. Ibid.

43. Elliott, "Campaign Marks 15th Season of 'South Park'".
44. *The Book of Mormon.* "News from The Book of Mormon".
45. Healy, "Good Tweets Are Nice, But Group Sales Fill Seats".
46. Cerniglia, "Dramaturgical Leadership and the Politics of Appeal in Commercial Theatre," 208–12.
47. Qtd. in Cerniglia, *Newsies: Stories of the Unlikely Broadway Hit*, 119.
48. Ibid., 121.
49. Ibid., 125.
50. Osatinski, "Disney Theatrical Productions: Anything Can Happen If You Let It," 423.
51. Situation, "Driving Views for Innovative Content – School of Rock 360".
52. *Think with Google.* "Broadway's School of Rock Hits the Stage with a 360° YouTube Video".
53. Ibid.
54. Lee, "Watch 'The Lion King's' 360-Degree Music Video for 'Circle of Life'".
55. Situation, "Driving Views for Innovative Content – School of Rock 360".
56. Lee, "Marketing Musicals in the Digital Age".
57. Ibid.
58. Ibid.
59. pianojames111, "Sara Bareilles—What's Inside—Songs From Waitress [Full Concert]".
60. See Chap. 6 in this volume on *Hamilton* fandom.
61. Sedgman, "What's Bigger than a Standing Ovation?," 50.
62. Goldberger, "DESIGN NOTEBOOK".
63. Ibid.
64. Sedgman, "What's Bigger than a Standing Ovation?," 39.

Bibliography

Brantley, Ben. "CRITIC'S NOTEBOOK; A Broadway Battle: Stars vs. Spectacle." *The New York Times*, August 28, 1995, sec. Theatre. http://www.nytimes.com/1995/08/28/theatre/critic-s-notebook-a-broadway-battle-stars-vs-spectacle.html.

Canedy, Dana. "Tickets on Sale! But Is the Show a Dud?," *The New York Times*, November 10, 1996, http://www.nytimes.com/1996/11/10/business/tickets-on-sale-but-is-the-show-a-dud.html.

Carlson, Marvin. "Theatre Audiences and the Reading of Performance." In *Interpreting the Theatrical Past: Essays in the Historiography of Performance*, edited by Thomas Postlewait and Bruce McConachie, 82–98. Iowa City: University of Iowa Press, 1989.

Cerniglia, Ken. "Dramaturgical Leadership and the Politics of Appeal in Commercial Theatre." In *The Routledge Companion to Dramaturgy*, edited by Magda Romanska, 208–12. London and New York: Routledge, 2014.

———. *Newsies: Stories of the Unlikely Broadway Hit*. Annotated edition. New York: Disney Editions, 2014.

Deutsch, Claudia H. "On Electronic Highway, Manhattan Is A Destination." *The New York Times*, July 23, 1995, sec. Real Estate. http://www.nytimes.com/1995/07/23/realestate/on-electronic-highway-manhattan-is-a-destination.html.

Elliott, Stuart. "Campaign Marks 15th Season of 'South Park.'" *The New York Times*, July 14, 2011. http://www.nytimes.com/2011/07/15/business/media/campaign-marks-15th-season-of-south-park.html.

"Footlights." *The New York Times*, October 28, 1997. http://www.nytimes.com/1997/10/28/theatre/footlights.html.

Freierman, Shelly. "NEWS WATCH; Can't Get to Broadway? Get a Glimpse Online." *The New York Times*, March 16, 2000. http://www.nytimes.com/2000/03/16/technology/news-watch-can-t-get-to-broadway-get-a-glimpse-online.html.

Goldberger, Paul. "DESIGN NOTEBOOK; Cyberspace Trips To Nowhere Land." *The New York Times*, October 5, 1995, sec. Home & Garden. http://www.nytimes.com/1995/10/05/garden/design-notebook-cyberspace-trips-to-nowhere-land.html.

Green, Jesse. "Producers Use the Web to Romance Audience and Bring Them Back," *The New York Times*, July 9, 2006, http://www.nytimes.com/2006/07/09/theatre/09gree.html.

Grimes, William. "On Stage, and Off." *The New York Times*, February 28, 1997. http://www.nytimes.com/1997/02/28/theatre/on-stage-and-off.html.

Healy, Patrick. "Good Tweets Are Nice, But Group Sales Fill Seats." *The New York Times*, April 19, 2011, sec. Theatre. http://query.nytimes.com/gst/fullpage.html.

———. "'Hair' to Help Facebook Generation Spread the Love." *The New York Times*, February 1, 2010. http://www.nytimes.com/2010/02/02/theatre/02hair.html.

———. "Ticket Pricing Puts 'Lion King' Atop Broadway's Circle of Life." *The New York Times*, March 17, 2014. http://www.nytimes.com/2014/03/17/theatre/ticket-pricing-puts-lion-king-atop-broadways-circle-of-life.html.

Hetrick, Adam. "Bloomberg Lets His Hair Down." *Playbill*, April 9, 2010. http://www.playbill.com/article/bloomberg-lets-his-hair-down-com-191422.

Hodges, Drew. *On Broadway: From Rent to Revolution*. New York: Rizzoli International Publications, 2016.

Jones, Kenneth. "Oklahoman Wins Hairspray Dance Contest, Appears in Feb. 24 Performance," *Playbill*, February 23, 2007, http://www.playbill.com/

article/oklahoman-wins-hairspray-dance-contest-appears-in-feb-24-performance-com-138771.

Lee, Ashley. "Marketing Musicals in the Digital Age: Sara Bareilles' 'Waitress' Reaches Beyond Broadway." *The Hollywood Reporter*. Accessed December 15, 2016. http://www.hollywoodreporter.com/news/sara-bareilles-waitress-marketing-musicals-838412.

———. "Watch 'The Lion King's' 360-Degree Music Video for 'Circle of Life.'" *The Hollywood Reporter*. Accessed December 15, 2016. http://www.hollywoodreporter.com/news/lion-king-circle-life-360-841951.

———. "Watch 'School of Rock' Musical's Innovative Music Video." *Rolling Stone*, October 14, 2015. http://www.rollingstone.com/music/news/watch-school-of-rock-musicals-innovative-interactive-music-video-20151014.

Lefkowitz, David. "Miss Saigon Attains Its American Dream – A Website." *Playbill*, July 10, 1997. http://www.playbill.com/article/miss-saigon-attains-its-american-dream-a-website-com-70940.

Levere, Jane L. "Business Travel; Hilton Is Expanding Its Program That Allows Guests to Swap Hotel Points and Airline Miles," *The New York Times*, March 27, 1996, http://www.nytimes.com/1996/03/27/business/business-travel-hilton-expanding-its-program-that-allows-guests-swap-hotel.html.

Lyman, Rick. "On Stage and Off," *The New York Times*, November 21, 1997, http://www.nytimes.com/1997/11/21/movies/on-stage-and-off.html.

MacDonald, Laura. "Rent Changing 'Rush' Ticket Policy," *Playbill*, July 10, 1997, http://www.playbill.com/article/rent-changing-rush-ticket-policy-com-70938.

Marks, Peter. "On Stage, and Off," *The New York Times*, November 10, 1995, sec. Theatre, http://www.nytimes.com/1995/11/10/theatre/on-stage-and-off.html.

Newman, Andrew Adam. "It's Broadway Gone Viral, With 'Next to Normal' Via Twitter." *The New York Times*, August 16, 2009. http://www.nytimes.com/2009/08/17/technology/Internet/17normal.html.

"Now Playing At A Computer Near You," January 1, 1998. http://www.rnh.com/news/739/Now-Playing-At-A-Computer-Near-You.

Osatinski, Amy S. "Disney Theatrical Productions: Anything Can Happen If You Let It." In *The Palgrave Handbook of Musical Theatre Producers*, edited by Laura MacDonald and William A. Everett, 413–26. Basingstoke: Palgrave MacMillan, 2017.

pianojames111. *Sara Bareilles - What's Inside - Songs From Waitress [Full Concert]*. Accessed December 15, 2016. https://www.youtube.com/watch?v=E4oOMYXtnq0.

Playbill. "The Year in Review: 1995." December 29, 1995. http://www.playbill.com/article/the-year-in-review-1995-com-100637.

Prince, Harold. *Contradictions: Notes on Twenty-Six Years in the Theatre*. New York: Dodd, Mead & Company, 1974.

Rnh.com. "R&h On-Line," October 1, 1997. http://www.rnh.com/news/756/N_000219.

———. "Now Playing At A Computer Near You," January 1, 1998, http://www.rnh.com/news/739/Now-Playing-At-A-Computer-Near-You.

Sedgman, Kirsty. "'What's Bigger than a Standing Ovation?': Intimacy and Spectacle at the Tony Awards," *Studies in Musical Theatre* 10.1 (2016): 37–53.

Situation. "Driving Views for Innovative Content – School of Rock 360." Accessed October 17, 2016. http://www.situationinteractive.com/project/driving-views-for-innovative-content-school-of-rock-360/.

Stevenson, James. "OP-ART; Lost and Found New York," *The New York Times*, March 8, 2008, sec. Theatre, http://query.nytimes.com/gst/fullpage.html.

Tate, Steve. "Hairspray Website," E-mail, November 21, 2016.

———. Personal Interview, July 13, 2014.

The Book of Mormon. "News from The Book of Mormon," Email, November 19, 2013.

Think with Google. "Broadway's School of Rock Hits the Stage with a 360° YouTube Video." Accessed December 15, 2016. https://www.thinkwithgoogle.com/case-studies/broadway-school-of-rock-hits-stage-with-360-youtube-video.html.

"Watch 'School of Rock' Musical's Innovative Music Video." *Rolling Stone*, October 14, 2015. http://www.rollingstone.com/music/news/watch-school-of-rock-musicals-innovative-interactive-music-video-20151014.

Wolff, Tamsen. "Theatre," in *The Oxford Handbook of The American Musical*, ed. Raymond Knapp, Mitchell Morris, and Stacy Wolf. Oxford: University Press, 2011.

CHAPTER 3

The Digital-Age Musical: Sighting/Siting Musicals Defined by High-Tech Content, Themes, and Memes

Pamyla Stiehl

In the fall movie season of 2015, commercials and promos saturated media outlets, publicizing the latest film by renowned screenwriter Aaron Sorkin: *Steve Jobs*. Replete with tabloid controversies spurred by contrarian high-tech voices disputing the depiction of the visionary Apple guru, the film garnered mainstream media buzz while inciting voyeuristic interest in the high-tech era and all it entails. Whether the film merited such hype is not the issue. *Steve Jobs* evinced a current pop culture, film/television phenomenon of digital-age exploration and exploitation. Predating *Steve Jobs* was Sorkin's 2010 Academy Award-winning *The Social Network* (chronicling the legally disputed invention of Facebook) as well as auteur Spike Jonze's critically acclaimed 2013 art-house hit *Her* (a fantastical love story between a man and his computer's operating system). Such content is not limited to the big screen, however. On cable television, HBO offers the popular *Silicon Valley* (2014)—a backstage look at the dramatic machinations inherent in

P. Stiehl (✉)
University of Montana, Missoula, MT, USA
e-mail: pamyla.stiehl@mso.umt.edu

where musicals' use of online marketing and social media was still catching up to Broadway.

Stephanie Lee, President of Group Sales Box Office, a group ticket agency operating since 1960, suggested in the wake of Facebook and Twitter buzz for musicals in the 2010–2011 season that her knowledgeable agents, armed with firsthand details from watching performances, were far more valuable to group leaders than often anonymous social media reports. "Facebook is a way for shows to tout themselves and then hope fans will post on the site so buzz can go viral. That's a great tool, but the buzz from all these shows can become deafening," Lee observed. "We've found that on Broadway group buyers still want an agent they know who can tell a hit from a flop."[45] Lee may be defending the traditional mode of promotion and ticketing she offers, but her dedication illustrates the industry's awareness of the breadth of its demographics and thus the necessity of offering a range of marketing and ticketing options. One surprise Broadway hit from Disney, however, only made it to Broadway *because* of buzz, much of it anonymous and on social media.

Disney's *Newsies*, a flop film musical in 1992 but a cult favorite on video and DVD, was nevertheless at the top of the request list with musical theatre licensor MTI, since the company began handling Disney titles in 2004—even though there was no stage version to be licensed.[46] Original composer Alan Menken teamed with Jack Feldman to expand it for the stage, but it wasn't until Harvey Fierstein came on board to write the libretto that the musical began advancing through Disney's development process. A production at the Paper Mill Playhouse in New Jersey was scheduled for 2011 in order to finalize a version of the musical for licensing. During the brief run, fans of the film made pilgrimages and began organizing themselves on social media channels as "Fansies," to campaign for a transfer of the production to Broadway. When a limited twelve-week Broadway run was announced for 2012 and tickets went on sale, Disney Theatricals executive vice president and managing director David Schrader recalls: "You could see the transactions and the chatter going at the same time. We could see them interacting on Facebook and Twitter—and they actually bought tickets."[47] Schrader was witnessing what Damian Bazadona had predicted years earlier—that channels providing information facilitating instantaneous communication around a musical could generate ticket sales. The process had simply become much, much faster.

today's techy universe—while USA Network boasts the award-winning *Mr. Robot* (2015), journeying into the underground world of hacking and cyber-vigilantism. Moving past cable offerings, network television's megahit *The Big Bang Theory* proved revolutionary when it debuted in 2007, focusing on the complications of high-functioning physics and mathematical "nerds" whose everyday entanglements with life and love occur against a high-tech backdrop of online gaming, blogging, coding, and social media platforms. Further exploitation of the digital revolution is evidenced by a critically lauded sixth-season (2015) episode of what is arguably this decade's most popular and acclaimed domestic sitcom: *Modern Family*. The much-publicized episode, titled "Connection Lost," presents an entire storyline through the main character's interfaces with her Mac laptop as she uses FaceTime, iMessage, and other digital media applications to monitor and manage family crises (innovatively, the episode was shot using iPhones and iPads).

Given the above examples, a crucial question should be raised: Where is *musical theatre*'s equivalent to film and television's nascent body of work that provides twenty-first-century audiences with heroes, antiheroes, and supporting characters who not only live in the digital age but whose stories are defined by and dependent upon the content and context of their high-tech habitations? In 1999, theorist Philip Auslander explored the omnipresence, as well as the power, influence and hegemony, of mass media and mediatized forms as they shape and inform live performative events in a mediatized society. Specifically, he asserted that mediatization "is now explicitly and implicitly embedded within the live experience" and that it "is the cultural context in which live performances are now inevitably situated," summating that "mediatization is not just a question of the employment of media technology; it is also a matter of what might be called media epistemology."[1] In short, Auslander argued that mechanically distributed content, mass media forms/methods and technologically habituated audiences merge to create a mediatized cultural consciousness that affects, underpins, contextualizes, and validates all art forms in the modern era. The resultant "media epistemology" suggests that the contemporary way of knowing the world has become almost fully dependent upon a technological, media-driven landscape. Auslander's argument, when applied to today's culture, would most likely prioritize digital media forms as primary components in this mediatization paradigm. And given Auslander's assertion of a new "media epistemology," epistemologies are also fostered and fomented by explicit content which, in terms of high-tech subject matter, is currently lacking in musical theatre librettos, narratives, and themes.

Other theatre theorists and scholars have further explored the phenomenon of mediatized theatre, often focusing on models of reception, production, contextualization, cultural hegemony, phenomenology, semantics, and semiotics. For instance, in *Theatre in a Media Culture* (2007), Amy Petersen Jensen employs Auslander's theory as she works to "identify the influence of media on the culture of American theatre in the narrow terms of production and reception."[2] Similar to Auslander, she sees mediatized spectators and an increasingly digital culture converging to incite a reception paradigm in which contemporary theatre audiences filter, contextualize, and ultimately read live stage material through their mediatized cultural lenses. Specifically, Jensen postulates that "the American consumers' collective interaction with media has created a 'participatory spectator' who … has learned to advance theatrical narratives beyond the threshold of the theatre space into their own private space."[3] While Jensen speaks in theoretic terms, addressing the negotiated and contentious "narratives" residing and competing within the mediated site of the theatre spectator's body, there remains a need to concretely sight and site the literal narratives delivered to that spectator from the musical theatre arena via its textual canon. Thus, this chapter seeks to uncover and trace this overlooked subject matter.

Theoretical interrogations and investigations of theatre mediatization (such as those by Jensen) have also necessarily addressed and unpacked the many ways in which live theatre works to serve mediatized audiences' cultural, artistic, and commercial expectations and desires. Such explorations often survey concrete topics such as theatre publicity and marketing, production staging, design, and technology, as well as external, influential socio-cultural media forms. These subjects, as they pertain to musical theatre and the digital age, are discussed in detail by other authors in this book. This chapter is concerned, however, with what has not, to date, been explored and surveyed in terms of musical theatre [digital] mediatization. Specifically, where are the culturally viable themes, memes, and narratives delivered and connected explicitly through textual content to a digital-age, mediatized audience?

Of course, one might answer that mainstream, commercial musicals often tend to look backward, with many of the genre's hits and landmark works set in past historical periods, often dependent upon models of historicity and nostalgia. One need only survey the most prevalent works of musical theatre's Golden Age, from 1927's *Show Boat* (and 1943's *Oklahoma!*) to 1964's *Fiddler on the Roof*, to see the predominance of backward-looking, nostalgic content, context, and thematic material. And the beat goes on, with the postmodern age adding recycled commodities to the "backward" paradigm. In a 2000 *New York Times Magazine* interview, Stephen Sondheim lamented: "You have two kinds of shows on Broadway—revivals and the same kind of musicals over and over again ... It has to do with seeing what is familiar. We live in a recycled culture."[4] In 2007, Jensen asserted that nostalgia serves as "an engine of commerce for theater producers ... More and more, the resource they rely on—the commodity they choose to sell—is nostalgia."[5] Today, a majority of popular works on Broadway and touring nationally are still firmly rooted in the past, reliant upon nostalgia and recycled material. Examples include screen-to-stage productions such as *Anastasia* and *Charlie and the Chocolate Factory*; revivals such as *Chicago* and *Hello, Dolly!*; sung-through mainstays such as *The Phantom of the Opera*; jukebox hits such as *Jersey Boys* and *Beautiful: The Carole King Musical*; book musicals such as *Wicked* and the postmodern sensation *Hamilton*.

Nonetheless, throughout the nascent twenty-first century, a number of musicals have smartly incorporated high-tech allusions in their overall books and scores. Yet, the works are, in reality, neither driven by nor founded on such topics. In many ways, such contemporary musicals may represent theorist Marvin Carlson's definition of "airy nothings" (in terms of high-tech textual content), "brought into a world of objects" through a process that "must be inevitably conditioned by the artistic tools of the artist's own culture and by the ways the culture defines and interprets artifacts." In this oblique and semiotic model, such works cannot help but represent "manifestations of cultural experience, a way of being in the world," that is, the artistic rendering simply reflects and signifies its digital-age environs and culture.[6] Such musicals may reference and surround their plots with a digital "way of being in the world" and their audiences may infer high-tech narrative substance, but the works actually deliver negligible constitutive or concrete textual content to this effect. In addition, numerous contemporary productions have exploited digital scenic/lighting/sound designs and high-tech visual/aural stage environments (as documented and explored elsewhere in this book), situating the musicals within high-tech milieus and giving pretense that the staged works are digital age, while the actual content of their librettos are loosely, or not at all, concerned with such subjects.

Thus, given the overall lack of musicals that predominantly deal with the digital revolution, one might question whether Broadway has dropped the cyber ball. Further, are there other venues taking up the cause and content? A handful of digital-age productions have been workshopped in the Broadway vicinity, enjoying temporary runs in new works festivals (such as The New York Musical Theatre Festival and NYFringe), while others have premiered on regional stages across America and abroad. Most have been produced with hopes of obtaining the brass ring of future Off-Broadway or Broadway development and engagement. Unfortunately, for their creators, such hopes have not materialized, as there has been no surge of digital-age musicals on the Great White Way.

On the other hand, the limited number of such musicals on the live stage does not suggest that other, more progressive channels have not exploited and embraced high-tech material. For the past decade, Internet "mini-musicals," reflexively and satirically centered on cyber subjects, have gone viral, with spectatorship for popular online productions topping the million-viewer mark soon after their postings. Such online works employ "wink and nod" navel-gazing, having been created for the Internet about the Internet. As a number of these videos—sometimes described as YouTubsicals—have "blown up" on YouTube and other sites, the phenomenon has also further complicated the traditional definition of a "musical." Yet, they ascribe to and reinscribe the traditional format, sound, and aesthetic of the canonical musical (i.e., they may be works delivered through a revolutionary platform about revolutionary subject matter, but their overall form, sound, and structure is anything but revolutionary in terms of the musical theatre genre). In this manner, they may provide potent signposts and roadmaps for live digital-age musicals aspiring to mainstream theatrical relevance and audience appeal, given their synergy between digital-era content/consciousness and traditional, commercial musical form/structure.

Locating the Digital-Age Musical on Broadway: Past to Present Sightings

Why is the digital-age musical a scarcity on Broadway today? Before critiquing the present, it is always wise to survey the past, looking for clues that can point to fomenting moments and glimpses of digital-age potential in musical theatre's history, thereby portending contemporary sightings. Within the canon, there exists an age-old "dialogue" between technological advancement and human progression. A significant early example is "Hey There" from *The Pajama Game* (1954), the Golden Age classic that tackles industrial-age issues of unions, strikes, and labor/management conflicts (while centering upon the timeless theme of conflicted romance), with music and lyrics by Richard Adler and Jerry Ross, and book by George Abbott and Richard Bissell. The entire premise (and gimmick) of the number is based on a technological advancement of the age—the dictaphone—by which an echoing refrain of Sid's recorded voice is sung back to him, to which he replies and argues, ultimately singing a duet with his virtual, audio self. Other examples from the twentieth-century musical theatre canon are not as blatant but variously represent incorporations of technology in the modern musical; albeit they are rare and often atmospheric and suggestive, rather than pointed and central. For instance, in 1970, a landmark musical concerned itself with issues of human conflict and anxiety as played against the milieu of industrialized modernity: *Company*. With music and lyrics by Stephen Sondheim and book by George Furth, the musical mostly deals with the characters' examinations of and searches for fulfillment in interpersonal relationships (e.g., marriage). However, one number, "Another Hundred People," foreshadows themes of the virtual, digital age. In this song, a character laments the lack of human contact in her everyday existence, which includes fleeting relationships made through socially distant connections and the inability to reach others on an authentic, intimate level when relying on relayed messages and phone services as opposed to face-to-face communication (a complaint often hurled today at the social media networking revolution).

In the 1990s, various rock musicals, given their edgy, contemporary sensibilities, incorporated the burgeoning technological revolution as part and parcel of their thematic, dramatic and/or theatrical renderings, while foreshadowing digital memes and themes later exploited by twenty-first-century successors. Specifically, 1993's successful Broadway rock opera *Tommy* (words and music by Peter Townshend) features and narratively builds upon the iconic song "Pinball Wizard." This number highlights the show's protagonist, the eponymous deaf, dumb and blind youth who has "plugged into" the pinball machine, isolated from distractions and becoming one with the game, ultimately achieving cult celebrity status. Through Tommy's journey, one might see vestiges of today's online gaming culture, that is, modern-day "Tommys" living alternate lives as avatars and establishing communities and fandom as they negotiate and battle in fantastical, virtual worlds, isolated from day-to-day realities. This model includes a new generation of "e-athletes" who compete in collegiate and professional video game competitions (e.g., "League of Legends" events and ESPN-sponsored eSports championships). The import of the gaming ethos is simply suggested by *Tommy* (secondary to its much larger themes), but the topical content (i.e., gaming/virtual reality quests) potently introduces one of the few areas popularly exploited by current digital-age musicals in the regional and alternative musical theatre community.

Tommy was not the only rock musical of the 1990s to suggest the dawn of a new cyber era. When composer/lyricist/librettist Jonathan Larson's *Rent* debuted on Broadway in 1996, it not only signaled a renaissance of the rock opera but also brought a digital-age mindset and attitude to the Main Stem. High-tech subject matter may not be the focus of the musical, but *Rent*'s characters—modern-day Alphabet City bohemians—exist in a world highly informed by the technological advances of the 1990s and communicate via its channels, using its lingo. A peripheral character, such as filmmaker Mark's mother, is solely a virtual, voicemail presence, while Mark, himself, obsessively uses his camera as a lens by which he records and engages his "reality," often avoiding genuine human contact. His video projections highlight the show's dramatic arc, punctuating the real-life journeys of the characters, as well as a new age in which their struggles for love, dignity, and survival are mediated and mediatized. This plot device presages a contemporary climate in which social media platforms such as Facebook, Twitter, Snapchat, and Instagram provide high-tech users with a redefined means of "immediate" and "personal" communication, as well as a new filter by which to view and interact with "live" captured moments, whether or not such mediations, be they monumental or mundane, merit such capture. Further, the paradigm foreshadows the reflective and self-absorbed video culture of the digital age, from selfie to YouTube. The musical also criticizes and unpacks such brave-new-world paradigms, given that performance artist Maureen's *pièce de résistance*, "Over the Moon," decries the oppression of living in "cyberland." The number is satirical, but its railed accusations against the crimes of high-tech hegemony should not be dismissed lightly, given that many of the characters of *Rent* are not only marginalized but are in the process of being destroyed, figuratively and literally, by the contemporary zeitgeist, on the cusp of the millennial digital revolution.

Alongside the edgy rock musicals, a few conventional musicals began incorporating high-tech content into their librettos, often in an attempt at relevancy as the twentieth century drew to a close. Specifically, the long-running Off-Broadway and regional hit by librettist/lyricist Joe DiPietro and composer Jimmy Roberts—*I Love You, You're Perfect, Now Change* (1996)—is a concept musical that surveys modern-day romance and relationships. Yet, it contains a social dating video segment—"The Very First Dating Video of Rose Ritz"—in which a character bears her soul on videotape, only to be asked to repeat the recording. This musical theatre scene not only heralded the online dating revolution, but its virtual relationship/romance premise would be extracted and expounded as the sole content for numerous digital-age regional musicals in the next decade.

Citing the above-listed mainstream works as digital-age musical forerunners may seem a bit of a stretch. Nonetheless, the surveyed works are illustrative in various respects. While twentieth-century canonical musicals are rarely situated in their current times and often look backward, there exists a group of musicals, especially those placed in present-day milieus, that play with ideas of technology and the import of a burgeoning new age in which human connection is mediated and even harmed by technological advances. Yet, such anxieties have not found their way to the twenty-first-century crop of mainstream works; for today's *au courant* Broadway musical is seemingly comfortable with the questions and conundrums raised by its predecessors. In short, the new millennial musical on the Main Stem may specifically reference the digital age, but "reference" is the key word; for no current mainstream hit is specifically concerned with or revolves around the actual world of the high-tech revolution and digital age. Instead, the digital/online paradigm is simply a relevant reference point—a matter of fact—with its components and context used as background chatter, often oblique, fleeting, or simply impressionistic. An exception is "The Internet Is for

Porn," found in *Avenue Q* (2003), which speaks to and shares a communal joke with its audience of Generation Xers and millennials while targeting the Internet, possibly, because the subject still seemed novel and deserving of pointed, isolated treatment when the production debuted. In this Tony Award-winning musical (music and lyrics by Robert Lopez and Jeff Marx; book by Jeff Whitty), the intentionally sophomoric manifesto, sung by Trekkie Monster, eulogizes the carnal joys found online, much to the dismay of his more idealistic friend, Kate, who argues in favor of the intellectual and informational uses of the Internet. In the end, Trekkie enlists his "guy pals" in definitively winning the dispute as they extoll masturbation and harmonize in their "porn" chants and cheers, drowning out Kate's highbrow point of view.

Beyond *Avenue Q*, most contemporary musicals have atmospherically incorporated the cyber age into their librettos' contexts, rather than setting the age as defining content/subject, with certain terms becoming part of the accepted lexicon, finding their way into lyrics and dialogues. For instance, googling, texting, iPhones, trending, tweeting, friend requests and Twitter "blow ups" are various drive-by references in the librettos and scores of Broadway musicals such as *Bring It On: The Musical* (2012), *First Date* (2013) and *If/Then* (2014). Further, the four characters of *[title of show]* (2008) variously quote Internet chat board comments and reference Broadway.com's "showcial" site throughout the production. While these references paint tech-savvy worlds and portraits of young, contemporary characters traversing online landscapes, the characters are no longer battling the revolutionary changes and questioning the new frontiers. Instead, they simply inhabit the new realities, with little more than a sideways glance at or mention of the impact of such technology on their lives.

A crucial exception to this paradigm has recently landed on Broadway, setting critics swooning and generating great commercial box office income while using the digital landscape as a potent backdrop and plot driver. *Dear Evan Hansen* (2016) tells the story of a socially awkward and marginalized high school senior, Evan Hansen, whose therapeutic "letter to self" is seized by a troubled school bully who later commits suicide. The letter is found with the dead teen and seemingly suggests that he and Evan were close friends. Evan perpetuates the lie to comfort the deceased teen's grieving family; and through emails and social media, his deception goes viral, turning Evan into a hero of sorts as he struggles to reconcile his newfound popularity with its fraudulent circumstances. With a book by Steven Levenson and score by Academy Award-winning collaborators Benj Pasek and Justin Paul (*La La Land*, 2016), the musical has proved to be a critical phenomenon and socio-cultural touchstone, winning six Tony Awards, including Best Book, Best Original Score, and Best Musical. The show also features a digital world on stage, as the scenic design is heavily dependent on screen projections of social media posts by designer Peter Nigrini. Although *Dear Evan Hansen*'s plot and theme do not center on the digital revolution, per se, the musical is singular in that its content moves past using digital platforms as throwaway mentions but integrates them as crucial aspects of Evan's dramatic journey. Further, while *Dear Evan Hansen*'s commercial and critical success in the mainstream market is a certainty, it is anyone's guess whether this theatrical model will be further explored by future Broadway musicals. One might also question whether it is the human story at the center of the musical that is most responsible for its tremendous cultural impact, as opposed to its digital environs. In any case, the work is currently an outlier—but possible harbinger—in its treatment of social media and the digital-era milieu on Broadway.

Searching Beyond Broadway: Regional, Festival, and International Digital-Age Musicals

If examples of renowned musicals on the national stage (e.g., Broadway) centered on digital-age themes are rare, there have been original works developed, workshopped, and produced by regional theatres that put high-tech content front and center. Most of the works have been highly touted in their local markets, with hopes voiced by authors and critics alike that the shows eventually find homes on Broadway, resulting in national exposure and artistic longevity, while possibly cementing a place in the musical theatre canon. No such regional production has made this leap to date, which may be more reflective of Broadway's conservative leanings and audience preferences than the merit of the shows themselves. Yet, a sampling of such shows should be examined and could prove instructive, as they represent how the high-tech zeitgeist has informed the overall twenty-first-century musical theatre landscape and suggest how certain topics, plots, memes, archetypes, and aesthetics have been used to frame and construct what could be defined today as a "digital-age musical."

One of the earlier and most *outré* musicals rooted in and defined by digital-age content and environs debuted in the Midwest in 2006. *Google: The Musical*, written by brothers Charlie and Drew Hammond (composer and librettist/lyricist, respectively), premiered as a one-act work at various Minnesota festivals (e.g., Minnesota Fringe Festival and the Guthrie Theater's Fringe Encore). The show found a fan base, meriting further development and productions by regional theatres and universities such as University of Wisconsin–Marathon County, with a full-scale work eventually staged in November 2010. The musical's storyline presents an apocalyptic world in which Google (personified as a female dominatrix) controls all information and, thus, the minds and actions of all humans. Tired of trivial and lazy Internet searches, Google vindictively goes offline. Chaos ensues. Humans become zombies, desperate to feed on other human brains for information, necessitating that a heroine—the last librarian on earth—team with a video-gaming savant, a tech support "geek," and an elderly book lover to defeat the zombies and bring Google back online. They succeed in their quest, paradoxically returning the world to a Google-controlled status quo. Given its postmodern element of shrewd cynicism, irony, and comedy, *Google*'s narrative also exemplifies a shifting contemporary attitude regarding the Internet and its major players, as noted by theatre blogger William McGeveran in 2006: "There was a time when Google's stripped down homepage, efficient search engine, and 'Don't Be Evil' slogan made [Google] seem fresh and friendly. If this show is any indicator, those days have ended."[7]

Overall, McGeveran enjoyed the show's concept, as did his fellow bloggers in cyberspace, yet most dismissed or disparaged the music component of the production. Nonetheless, there were high hopes for the musical. Chronicling the work's development at the time of its premiere, local performing arts critic Eric Brandt placed *Google* within the workshop "tradition that dates back to the legendary genesis of *A Chorus Line*." He then exhorted: "Just maybe, a Broadway producer will take note and the Hammonds will have hit the big time!"[8] To date, this prognosis has not materialized, but it reflects prevailing sentiments surrounding other regional and workshop digital-age musicals following in *Google*'s footsteps.

One such musical receiving local fanfare but limited national exposure debuted the same year as *Google*, finding a home on the West Coast. *Internet Dating: The Musical* (2006) premiered at Hollywood's art/

works Theater (a 99-seat professional venue)—the brainchild of composer/librettist/lyricist Ron Weiner whose television writing credits include *Arrested Development* and *Futurama*. In Weiner's libretto, Jenny, a likeable and lonely 31-year-old woman futilely searching for a mate, is talked into online dating by her two sassy, cyber-savvy female workmates. Through the anonymity and creative license of the Internet, she encounters a bevy of suitors masquerading behind misleading profiles, while missing the potential for real-life romance with her secretly arduous male co-worker. Of course, all works out happily in the end, but only after her disastrous and laughable Internet courtships come to farcical life on stage. The 10-member chamber musical received overall positive reviews for its timely content and humor, with its music garnering mixed reviews. While Daryl H. Miller used an emoticon in his 2006 *Los Angeles Times* review to affirm the musical's romantic and whimsical spins that put "a ☺ face on audiences," he proved more measured in his assessment of the score. Addressing a song roster that includes "Did You Read My Profile?" and "Google You," Miller enjoyed *Internet Dating*'s pastiche score, "inflected with '50s doo-wop, Latin rhythms, vintage Burt Bacharach, and the pop sounds of new Broadway," but summated that, although functional, "the tunes won't win the Tony for best score any time soon."[9] *Internet Dating* also offers a significant glimpse into the pitfalls of a musical firmly rooted in and dependent upon the high-tech era and its defining aspects: that the digital age is constantly changing and ever fluid. Lori Peters, contributor for *Splash Magazine*, succinctly points up the inherent problem with content that seems current and "oh so smart" at the time of the regional/workshop production's debut, only to seem dated or even antiquated by the time the show reaches a mass audience. Peters ponders: "Where is eHarmony in this charming calamity of love online?" She further notes that the show was mostly "reminiscent of the early days of the naughty Internet," concluding that, as a solution to the constant flux of digital-age tropes, "the musical should just be firmly set in the '90s for its audience."[10] Does this suggest that digital-age musicals cannot help but become high-tech period pieces in the short span of a decade (or less)? Or, to keep their relevancy and efficacy, should they be constantly updated and revised? Negotiating and reconciling such questions may be crucial to the viability of the digital-age musical.

While traditional musical theatre has often been characterized as a romantic vehicle defined by the relationship meme of "boy meets girl;

boy loses girl; boy wins girl," the digital-age musical has significantly exploited this material, while placing the content within a cyber context/platform. Following *Internet Dating*, another popular regional musical dabbled in similar territory. *OMFG! The Internet Dating Musical* (2011) premiered at San Francisco's Oberlin Dance Collective (ODC) Theater. *OMFG!* was the result of a three-year collaboration between composer/ODC artist-in-residence Christopher Winslow and local Bay Area homoerotic poet/performance artist Gavin Geoffrey Dillard (librettist/lyricist). The five-person show was framed by its creators as a San Francisco "cyber" love story, with its plot revolving around a lonely man and woman in their mid-forties who turn to the Internet to find romance.[11] The lovelorn characters meet in an online chat room, posing behind fictional profiles, but their online romance ultimately resolves in a fruitful "F2F" (face-to-face) relationship. Most critics appreciated the libretto's satiric spirit and wit; however, *OMFG!*'s eclectic pop/rock/blues score only merited a lukewarm reception. Entertainment blogger Anna Pan also provided a pointed argument that goes to the heart of not only *OMFG!* but many other digital-age musicals in terms of librettos that contain critiques of the Internet and social media, often containing postmodern satire and snarky comment, but also burdened with the task of celebrating these same high-tech milieus and subject matter:

> The ensemble members sing, "I've tweeted and texted and Facebook'd my hours away" and they eventually confiscate the leads' laptops. Is the "deep moral" of the show that reliance on technological advancement is evil? That doesn't make much sense, seeing as Brandon and Heather would have never met if they didn't go on the dating site.[12]

As the digital-age love/relationship musical attempted to find theatrical footholds in regional markets across America, the fringes of Broadway also saw promising works centered upon similar themes and content. For example, *#LoveStory*, an entry in 2015's The New York International Fringe Festival (FringeNYC), navigates territory analogous to that of *OMFG!* and *Internet Dating*. The full-length musical has music and lyrics by Mark Oleszko and Bethany Mayes, respectively, and a book by Sophie Frankle, Mayes, and Oleszko. The show's publicity blurb states: "In the digital age, finding love should be as easy as sushi delivery, right? Not really. With the assistance of three friends and her own bravado, Zoe gets a one-of-a-kind crash course in love in the twenty-first century."[13]

Its premiere, almost a decade after *Internet Dating*, suggests that there is still much fodder found in digital-age romance. Also significant is the use of the now-omnipresent hashtag in the title, somewhat cementing a musical theatre presence of high-tech lingo that may become commonplace as the twenty-first-century "hashtag generation" has perpetuated and normalized such terms in today's culture/art dialogue.

While the above examples represent cyber-age romantic musicals on American regional or New York City fringe festival stages that have yet to win national exposure, another work in this thematic vein originated across the pond, only to be similarly thwarted in its Broadway aspirations. In addition to its British roots, *Like Me—The Social Media Musical* (2014) also differed from the abovementioned musicals in its aggressive use of social media and online, crowdfunding sites for commercial promotion, development, and investment. When purveying the burgeoning future of the digital-age musical, there may be questions posed and lessons learned from a production such as *Like Me*, given its reliance on Internet platforms, only to see underwhelming results.

With music and lyrics by Garry Lake and a book by Jon Smith, *Like Me* is an intimate four-hand musical that premiered as a workshop production at London's Courtyard Theatre in October 2014, followed by a reworked version at Waterloo East Theatre in April 2015. After self-funding the show for three years, the creators embarked on an aggressive cyber fundraising campaign through Indiegogo to mount a New York investor showcase, scheduled for July 2015. Per the Indiegogo site, the show centers on four young adults (two men, two women) of contrasting personalities and career aspirations whose lives intersect in real life, as well as through "tweets, pins, selfies, posts, and status updates," while looking "for love, for validation and, ultimately, for themselves in a cyber world populated by thousands of 'followers' and 'friends'."[14] Smith also employed his LinkedIn site to recruit investors, advocating for alternate channels that could bypass "corporates and established producers."[15] In corresponding media blurbs, the authors lamented the "tough, old" theatre world, dominated by "behemoths such as *Phantom* / *Les Mis* / *Wicked*," summarizing that the arena needs more diverse "shows that explore topics more relevant to audiences, especially in the digital age."[16] Their efforts caught the attention of the mainstream media. On May 3, 2015, BroadwayWorld.com spotlighted *Like Me*, providing a link to the creators' Indiegogo campaign and reporting that the work was slated for a summer preview.[17] Further exploiting the Internet as a marketing platform, *Like Me* has its own Wikipedia entry, as well as numerous filmed studio performances of songs posted on YouTube. The overall production did not appear before real-life audiences in the venues and markets aggressively solicited, however, as its creators fell far short of the $32,140 capital they needed to crowdfund the showcase. The musical's "world premiere" has yet to be realized or even jumpstarted. Given that *Like Me*, with its heavy Internet presence, could not find a significant live audience and venue, one might question the power of social media and other online platforms to bypass traditional production avenues and players. Possibly, if today's digital-age musical seeks to enter mainstream markets and win new audiences, they may still need to play by the "tough, old" rules.

Moving beyond social media and its reconfiguration of interpersonal relations and romance in the digital era, other twenty-first-century regional and fringe musicals have more broadly addressed the themes, content, and persons that shape and define the cyber age. These works take a more holistic view of the new frontier, while framing such high-tech stories as quests or stories of human evolution pitted against a newly digitalized and tech-driven world. A pithy metaphor for such digital-era quests is the modern world of computer gaming. While some twenty-first-century experimental or fringe works include video gaming as part of their more expansive high-tech libretto content (especially in terms of musical quests by characters who battle in cyber lands), others have been developed completely around such virtual gaming content and aesthetics, while simultaneously employing the nostalgia factor of traditional musical theatre. To wit, the 2014 season of FringeNYC saw the successful staging of not one but two musicals revolving around such subject matter. First, *Jump Man*, written by Samuel Pitt Stoller, is a full-length musical satire of the Mario Brothers video game, in which Mario and Luigi heroically combat a crime wave in their Brooklyn neighborhood. Concordantly, *King of Kong: A Musical Parody* (music by David Schmoll and lyrics/libretto by Amber Ruffin and Lauren Van Kurin) is a musical adaptation of a 2007 documentary that garnered a cult following, parodying the tale of two men battling to reign as the high-score champions of the popular 1980s video game Donkey Kong.

In the same year, another festival musical exploited the "quest" meme, but took its themes and dramatic exploits beyond gaming to a more fully developed story of humanist struggle against an immersive and intrusive digital backdrop. *WikiMusical* (2014)—book and lyrics by

Frank Ceruzzi and Blake J. Harris; music by Trent Jeffords—enjoyed a sold-out run at the Pearl Theatre Company (PTC) Performance Space during July 2014 as an official New York Musical Theatre Festival (NYMF) selection. On their production's website, the creators describe their virtual-age satire as an "epic tale of two estranged brothers, Peter and Kurt Oglesby, who return to their childhood home for Christmas Eve and ... are magically zapped inside the Internet," framing their misadventure as a classic quest, similar to "*The Wizard of Oz, Alice and Wonderland,* and *The Phantom Tollbooth* (with a dash of *Tron*, a sprinkling of *Super Mario Bros.*, and a hint of *Avenue Q*)." Thematically, the production illustrates "how our preoccupation with the virtual world has affected our ability to live in the real one."[18] The musical's prologue presents Peter and Kurt as wide-eyed, hopeful youths transfixed by their magical Christmas gift of a Gateway computer; however, the action truly starts once they reunite as hostile, embittered young adults, their family in shambles and dreams shattered. Looking for answers, they once again log into the childhood Gateway computer, virtually entering into a riotous cyber voyage that forces them to work together to return to reality. Upon the production's debut, numerous critics applauded Ceruzzi and Harris' libretto for its creative application of Internet tropes and techy comedy, including Stagebuddy.com reviewer Aviva Woolf, who singled out the cast of colorful cyber characters encountered by Kurt and Peter (e.g., blogger Jacqui, Internet mascot Kitten McMitten, Skeeter the Twitter bird, Emoticon, Princess LOL, and the sinister, power-hungry Spam King).[19]

Alongside the complimentary reviews given to the smart libretto, *WikiMusical*'s score also received overall positive notices. Deirdre Donovan, in her 2014 Curtainup.com review, noted that the songs musically serve the funny, creative, and successful cyber-age themes and storyline, especially novelty numbers such as "Search Engine Crash" and "Mean Is the New Nice."[20] If there is any hope of a canonical future for a digital-age musical, it lies in its potential to speak to a broad demographic. In this respect, *WikiMusical*'s prospects are mixed. On one hand, Donovan heralded the show as the most "*au courant*" of the NYMF season, reflecting "the pulse and texture of our technological age," while noting its timeless allusion to "The Prodigal Son."[21] Woolf, similarly positive in her assessment of the libretto and score, somewhat pigeonholed the work in terms of its appeal and audience demographic, however, noting that "many of the jokes are obviously designed for those who were raised and currently residing on the Net." Thus, she recommended the work for the audience member "who can speak in meme, loves fantastical quests or has ever resented their own flesh and blood while connecting more with technological devices."[22]

Of course, such tech-savvy mindsets have become the growing norm as the digital age increasingly dominates everyday life in the new millennium. The question is how long it will take Broadway to catch up and exploit this contemporary development. Looking to films that have capitalized on the high-stakes, angst-ridden tales of digital-age pioneers (e.g., *The Social Network* and *Steve Jobs*), there may be correlative promise for musicals that are grounded in similar biographies. Such works may not only espouse cutting-edge, high-tech sensibilities, but also provide great storytelling, while reflecting age-old rags-to-riches trajectories that have traditionally prevailed in numerous mainstream musicals. One work in this category is *The Agony and the Ecstasy of Steve Jobs: The Musical* (2013) by composer/lyricist/librettist Tim Guillot, based on the 2011 performance piece by monologist Mike Daisey. Guillot's production musicalizes Daisey's autobiographical work in which he critically examines his own ambivalence toward Apple, its founder (Jobs), and its products, recounting his trip to Foxconn (Apple's Chinese factory), where he purports to have seen factory abuses firsthand. Daisey's polarizing account came under scrutiny and censure as critics questioned its authenticity during the run of his one-man show; he subsequently revisited and rewrote the work in 2012. At the same time, Daisey made his play available to a worldwide market, free of license and royalty. Capitalizing on this development, Guillot's musical theatre version debuted in July 2013 at Capital Fringe in Washington, DC, receiving highly positive reviews for all aspects of the production.

At Guillot's hand, Daisey's one-man show grew into an intimate five-person chamber musical. Conceptually, Guillot felt it would be "a fun twist to have the actor who plays Mike also play Steve Jobs;" thus, the lead character assumes both roles in his adaptation.[23] The remaining four cast members play all auxiliary characters (e.g., Steve Wozniak, John Sculley, Sun Danyong, a Foxconn guard, etc.), while also serving as a contemporary Greek chorus, questioning and occasionally censuring Jobs, as well as the entire Apple revolution. As detailed by DCMetroTheaterArts.com reviewer Nicole Cusick, the chorus sings that Jobs is a real "visionary asshole," while two female ensemble members "flirt with Jobs and, at the same time, judge him, representing the enlightened person's moral dilemma when it comes to reliance on the 'Cult of Mac.'"[24] Indeed, the musical includes an overall cultural commentary as to how modern society (epitomized by Mike) likes its "shit" (i.e., high-tech gadgets) but has mixed feelings as to the human costs entailed in the creation and manufacture of such devices. As evidenced by other digital-age musicals, however, *Agony/Ecstasy* may still be limited in its appeal. Upon its debut, Washington DC critic Travis Andrews singled out the "like my shit" line in the libretto as a complete summation of the musical adaptation, asserting, "If you find that line funny, this [musical] is for you. If you don't, skip it."[25] Other critics were not so narrow in their assessment, seeing great potential in the musical as a whole, especially noting the worthy score. BroadwayWorld.com's Jennifer Perry cites Guillot's stylistic diversity and "mostly rock-based compositions" as "broad reason enough to see the show." In the end, she provides a promising assessment that the musical, with its potent biography and timely theme, may have legs beyond a fringe/festival audience and find a place in the musical mainstream.[26]

To date, however, there is only one digital-age musical that can credibly claim to have Broadway in its sights: *Nerds* (2007). Along with *Agony/Ecstasy*, this satiric musical, chronicling the rise of Bill Gates and Steve Jobs, uses high-tech biographies and historical accounts to define the current digital era. Most important, the show may actually see a hard-won Broadway debut (according to various 2015–2016 media reports); yet, it still struggles at the gate. Originally titled *Nerds://A Musical Software Satire*, the production began as a 2005 entry at NYMF and was subsequently reworked and given its world premiere by the Philadelphia Theatre Company (PTC) in 2007, receiving Barrymore Awards for Outstanding Original Music and Outstanding New Play. In 2008, *Playbill* announced that the musical, with its title shortened to *Nerds*, was slated for a fall Broadway premiere.[27] The run did not materialize; and after Jobs' cancer death in 2011, the creators put the show on hold and reworked it once again. Evincing the paradox of the digital-age musical (timely in its day, outdated shortly thereafter), prominent Philadelphia critic Howard Shapiro chronicled *Nerds*' bumpy progression in his 2013 blog:

> When the Philadelphia Theatre Company had a hit on its hands [2007], Jobs' health was no issue, and *Nerds* was on its way to Broadway … Production lagged, though, and after Jobs' illness became public, no one

with any sense would attempt a New York version of a wacky show that hilariously dives into the sea change that Jobs and Gates engineered and then turned into a tidal wave."[28]

With an expanded cast (eleven members), five new songs, and lyric/libretto tweaks, *Nerds* (version 2.0) aggressively moved into a pre-Broadway tryout phase in 2013, starting with limited engagements at North Carolina Theatre and a revival at PTC. Furthering this trajectory, the production moved to New York City. *Nerds* enjoyed a concert version at 54 Below in 2014, followed by two Manhattan workshop productions in April 2015, with BroadwayWorld.com stating that the show "seems to be aiming for a summer or fall 2015 debut on the Great White Way."[29] To date, such plans have again stalled (a scheduled Broadway opening for April 2016 was cancelled in March, even though rehearsals were in process). The creators seem cognizant that further delay increasingly complicates the material's contemporary relevance and reception. Speaking with prominent Philadelphia theatre critic Jonathan Takiff in 2013, Allen-Dutton admitted: "We've learned to make our revisions in pencil."[30] Concurrently, Takiff asserted that the PTC production seemed "stylish enough to transfer 'as is' to a small Broadway house" but also warned that "if their [*Nerds*'] New York producer pals don't act fast, the show might have to be revised again."[31]

Despite recent roadblocks, a Broadway future for *Nerds* still appears feasible. Unlike aforementioned digital-age musicals, *Nerds*' creators and contributors boast serious industry pedigrees. Libretto and lyrics are by Jordan Allen-Dutton and Erik Weiner (veteran, award-winning writers of cable television's *Robot Chicken* and Off-Broadway's *The Bombitty of Errors*), while Hal Goldberg composed the pop-infused, diverse score. Additionally, the show's various incarnations have employed a roster of established Broadway and television talent; for example, Casey Hushion, Philip William McKinley, and Andrew Goldberg (past directors); Josh Bergasse and Joey McKneely (past choreographers); Charlie Pollock, Wesley Taylor, Darren Ritchie, and Diana DeGarmo (past cast members). The combined work paid off. *Philadelphia Inquirer*'s foremost music critic David Patrick Stearns lauded the 2013 PTC production, defining it as "generation-defining … visually hot and musically adept, filled with one knockout, high-velocity number after number." He applauded *Nerds*' use of "surgical precision (something like *How to Succeed in Business* meets *Urinetown*)" to portray "Silicon

Valley's confluence of hippie socialism and rampant capitalism, nailing such underlying themes as the cost of dreams [and] the emptiness of revenge."[32] Concordantly, Shapiro positively compared the show to "a frantic cartoon," summating that "the dumber it [*Nerds*] becomes, the smarter it is, because it finds a way to be subtly serious about success and ambition."[33] North Carolina Theatre's pre-Broadway tryout also merited qualified praise from local critic Susie Potter: "With a little honing, [*Nerds*] could easily meet its goal of being the next Broadway smash hit."[34]

In short, the highly praised chamber musical spotlights (and spoofs) computer geeks and techy culture as it traces Gates' and Jobs' career paths and industry revolutions through three decades. Beginning in the mid-1970s, Gates initially appears as a bullied nebbish nerd in stereotypical form (oversized glasses, social awkwardness, singing "I Am Just a Nerd") and ultimately evolves into a power-grabbing tyrant, partnered by Paul Allen. Jobs is the "cool" nerd, a pot-smoking hippy and rebel with a messianic complex and huckster/shaman side, partnered by Steve Wozniak. Their parallel journeys develop into rivalries (replete with a light saber duel in Act I's climactic closer, "Battle of the Century"), while both men transform from digital dweebs to cultural and technological icons (and pop stars), experiencing professional and personal triumphs, failures and reversals along the way. The show's music not only reflects history, but also explores and defines the characters. Goldberg's score ranges from rock to 1980s' pop, musical theatre, and rap. In a 2013 interview with INDYWeek.com's Tom Elrod, Goldberg explains: "We define Jobs as a rock star in a lot of ways, so that comes through musically. Whereas, Gates, he starts off in more of a traditional musical theater way, which is nerdy."[35]

While the musical irreverently portrays and unpacks the legend and legacy of the Gates/Jobs phenomenon, it more broadly aims to deliver a universal message about the revenge and rise of geeks in the digital age, as well as the engendered social/culture revolutions and repercussions. It is seemingly fortunate that *Nerds'* content is contextually broad, for the profiles of the two protagonists, as well as their industry, have changed significantly since the musical's debut. And as Allen-Dutton told Takiff in 2013, he ponders further necessary revisions, asking: "What's Apple to do next?"[36] Regardless, various critics have asserted that *Nerds* can weather the sea of change that thwarts other such digital-age musicals. Specifically, Stearns ended his review of the musical with the following perspective and prediction: "Their respective transitions—Gates into philanthropy and Jobs into the hereafter—needed to decisively settle in before this story could be told with the irreverent freedom (and New York production money) it now enjoys. As it stands, this show may well maintain relevance long after iPads are outdated."[37]

Exploring Cyber Frontiers and Templates: YouTubsicals and the Digital-Age Musicals of AVByte

Given the trajectory and Broadway potential of *Nerds*, it is significant to note that the production is an anomaly in terms of the digital-age musical on the national stage. The work shows promise—but not proof—that musicals with sole high-tech content/focus can find a broad, mainstream audience. In fact, *Nerds* (and *Dear Evan Hansen*) may be the exceptions that proves the current rule—Broadway has yet to fully exploit the digital age as fertile ground for commercial musical development. But maybe live theatre, especially Broadway, is the wrong place to look when searching for the cyber era conveyed through a musical libretto and score. A more relevant and telling, albeit convoluted, site for digital-age musicals may be actual digital-age platforms. Specifically, there exists a plethora of online musical satires with high-tech subject matter at their core. Many of these works are termed "YouTubsicals," and a lead player in this forum is AVByte—the YouTube brainchild and channel of brothers Antonius (composer) and Vijay (filmmaker) Nazareth.

The Nazareth brothers formed AVByte in a postmodern, technological era ripe for their YouTubsical products. The new millennium saw a flood of satirical digital "musicals" created for the Internet, many of which went viral. A landmark work in this field is 2008's *Dr. Horrible's Sing-Along Blog*. This independent, low-budget online musical was co-written by venerated Hollywood writer/director Joss Whedon, his brothers Zack Whedon and Jed Whedon (composer), and writer/actress Maurissa Tancharoen in an effort to circumvent and counter the 2007–2008 Writers Guild strike. The production originally aired on the *Dr. Horrible* website in July 2008 in three sequential episodes (hosted on Hulu). The entire musical was later offered on iTunes, Amazon, and Netflix and enjoyed a special DVD release, for which the writers provided additional material. *Dr. Horrible* stars Neil Patrick Harris as the eponymous blogging evil-doer who is continually thwarted in both his anarchist villainy and bumbling romance with pure-hearted Penny by an arch nemesis, Captain Hammer. The musical not only found a wide fan base but garnered critical praise and awards, including a 2009 Creative Arts Emmy Award.

In addition to *Dr. Horrible*, numerous YouTube videos found great popularity by playfully musicalizing unlikely subjects; for instance, "*Breaking Bad*: The Middle School Musical" and 2011's mash-up trailer of *Fiddler on the Roof* and *You Got Served*, not to mention the 2015 mockumentary behind rock band Coldplay's fictional attempt to produce *Game of Thrones: The Musical* (over 14 million views). Importantly, however, none of these works center upon digital-age content, that is, actual high-tech topics, platforms, aesthetics, language/memes, and characters. Instead, such musical theatre satires are broad in their comedic reach (and even though *Dr. Horrible* is framed as an Internet blog post, it is a traditional musicalized melodrama, with an uber-villain storyline). AVByte is singular, however, in that it has created a specific canon of digital-age topics delivered through a format that speaks to tech-savvy audiences, possibly providing design templates for fully realized live works that could similarly lampoon and celebrate life in the cyber age.[38]

The Nazareth brothers originated AVByte in 2011; and in 2013, the channel was selected for "YouTube Next Up" (YouTube's development program that chooses only 30 channels per season out of the thousands online for individualized mentoring and tech support). Antonius and Vijay are millennials who collaborate closely, composing and producing a plethora of 2-minute musical works that lampoon a wide range of current trends and topics. Composer Antonius received his Bachelor's degree in music in Germany at age 13 (the youngest German to do so) and dropped out of New York University (NYU) after one semester to found AVByte with Vijay. In an interview with NYUlocal.com's Hannah Orenstein, Antonius noted that he "grew up watching Gene Kelly movies," but "never thought about musical theatre as being contemporary."[39]

Indeed, AVByte's works, which the brothers call "mini-musicals,"[40] evince a throwback quality in terms of form, structure, and style, while the team also brings "Old Hollywood" sounds to the twenty-first century through tongue-in-cheek applications, targeting such subjects as Instagram, Tumblr, Facebook, Twitter, and Google. Having gone online in 2011, AVByte established its fan base in 2012 with one of its first digital-centric YouTubsicals: "New Instagram: The Musical." The YouTube production begins with a short slapstick scene in which a girl falls down concrete stairs and a friend gleefully takes and posts an Instagram photo of her bruised and swollen, yet pathetically smiling, face. The narrative then broadens to include a variety of chipper millennials who variously sing the work's vocal refrain—a peppy, melodic hook that rhapsodizes over the joys of Instagram and picture-taking on iPhones and Androids. The musical structure alternates between solos, duets and small harmonic groups; and the lyrics comprise ironic, affirming sentiments (how Instagram makes one's life look "cool"), simple rhyme schemes, and rapped patter by characters who excitedly list the many Instagram filter options. The production's "choreography" is relegated to stylized mimicry and tongue-in-cheek reenactments, while the segment ends with a sardonic moment in which a reappearing character in a Batman costume takes a "duck face" selfie in a public bathroom mirror.[41]

"New Instagram" merited over a million views, catching the attention of the VlogBrothers, another pair of online writing/producing brothers (Hank and John Green) who create and host a popular blog channel on YouTube. VlogBrothers then collaborated with AVByte on the YouTubsical hit: "Tumblr: The Musical" (2012), which has over 2.5 million views to date. The video both jeers and cheers the microblogging platform, using a heavy dose of sarcasm and inside humor. Featuring Hank and an ensemble of AVByte regulars (including an ingénue actress spoofing Ariel from Disney's *The Little Mermaid*), the YouTubsical revolves around a chorus segment that lauds Tumblr. The score relies on a simply melody and a catchy refrain, replete with cutesy wordplay (e.g., "tumbling down Tumblr"). Appearing in front of computers or cavorting outdoors, the cast also takes swipes at Tumblr's accessibility, lazy authorship (repostings), and mainstream appeal (e.g. the fact that Barack Obama uses Tumblr causes Ariel to gripe that the platform is now "lame").

After "Tumblr," AVByte's channel subscriptions grew steadily and the mini-musical enjoyed a few well-received live performances (enacted by the original video performers) at conventions such as LeakyCon (2014), possibly signaling the live stage potential of an AVByte digital-age musical. In 2013, the company premiered "Facebook—The Musical," which currently boasts over 4.4 million views, sitting atop their digital-age mini-musical catalogue. The libretto (loosely speaking) and dramatic action center upon five actors who eagerly check their Facebook pages on varying devices in numerous indoor/outdoor settings, acting out their lines. The number's chorus riff is mainly built around two notes, set to a driving 2/4 tempo, and pattered lyrics that express the obsessive need to check Facebook (i.e., actors sing that they are "hooked" on the site and must keep hitting "refresh" to see updates). Cheerily parodying social media addiction, the singers conclude that there is no end to this cyclical online activity; it is simply the "Facebook way!" While "Facebook" alternates between a frantic chorus and interjected *Sprechstimme* (lines spoken to the music), the work also contains more melodic variation than previous AVByte productions, including modulated bridges and waltz interludes that extol and list Facebook components and pleasures (along with a winking admission that the site may have a slight problem with privacy). In the end, a lone actor loses the will to shut down his laptop and joins the ensemble who affirms the "Facebook way" in counterpoint, and then harmony, arms opened wide to their virtual audience.[42] This compositional structure is a hallmark of AVByte's mini-musicals, as their musical themes are often divided, countered, and then harmonized in a "big build," resolving in a final choral flourish.

Given the above AVByte examples, as well as subsequent works such as 2013's "Twitter—The Musical" (approximately 3.9 million views) and "Google Is Your Friend—GIYF the Musical!" (views topping 2.2 million), one can draw some conclusions as to the YouTubsicals' identifying characteristics and comprehensive significance, while posing some pertinent questions regarding the future development and overall promise of the digital-age musical. The aforementioned mini-musicals are reflexive in that they center on social media or digital platform crazes but slyly comment on their glitches, in both technical and social/personal terms. Although mostly positive and jingoistic, the works often good-naturedly nip a bit at the hand that feeds them (the cyber sphere), while their virtual audiences seemingly relish this aspect. Further, the works' manic, zealous presentations obliquely manage to satirically highlight and censure the obsessive or "cult" aspect of the digital age. Redefining the "musical" to suit a cyber audience/venue, the AVByte YouTubsicals quickly and efficiently strike a familiar, communal, and aesthetic chord. Nonetheless, one must ask how such productions qualify as "musicals." While the scores evince bright Broadway sounds and the loose librettos suggest narrative problems or themes, further development of such material is not possible due to the limitations of the YouTube production format, not to mention the attention span and expectations of AVByte's target audience. Characters are archetypes, lyrics are memes, topics are reflexive, music is "sing-along-tastic," and choreography is derivative or expositional, all designed to enlist the viewer (i.e., "we are just like you, albeit we're singing and dancing"). Most importantly, the works circumvent the "live" constitution of traditional theatre.

Categorizing their works as "musicals," the AVByte team has redefined and condensed the form, in all its complexity, to one virtual production number (although a typical production number in a musical runs almost two minutes longer than their mini-musicals). Is this the best example of musical theatre for a new generation that may apply this hyper-condensed, digitalized form and definer to the actual genre—a live art form that boasts dramatic narratives and character developments/relationships through multifaceted and evocative scores, librettos, and dance? A simple answer is "of course not." A more nuanced response, however, necessitates looking at how AVByte has exploited the high-tech revolution through a musical theatre lens (or vice versa). Their hit YouTubsicals have possibly introduced many online viewers to the concept of digital-age musicals. Whether this is a good or bad thing, in terms of the purity and defining characteristics of live musical theatre, could be and should be much debated; but it does suggest that there is an audience for digital-age material in musical theatre guise. In 2013, Bob Brown, Network World.com contributor, devoted an entire article to the AVByte works, summating, "While I'd like to see *Annie*, *Bye Bye Birdie*, and the rest of those overplayed musicals go the way of MySpace (oh, it's still around?), it looks like tech-themed musicals are here to stay. At least on YouTube."[43]

Given today's cyber zeitgeist, Brown suggests that AVByte's body of work (and similar online satires) could be seen as harbingers, possibly inducing commercial entities to invest in the legitimate live staging of similar topics and embrace a likewise postmodern, reflexive—yet affectionate and knowing—treatment of tech material.[44] In the same article, Brown traces the influence of the YouTube phenomenon to live theatre works, specifically referencing *Google*, *Agony/Ecstasy*, and *Nerds*, concluding that "there might not be a Tony Award" in the productions' futures, but they represent "a step forward" in terms of "converting tech subjects into musicals."[45] Only time will tell. High-tech material is currently being cultivated on a diverse theatrical landscape (e.g., regional stages, festivals, workshops, alternative and virtual venues). It is up to a new generation of musical theatre makers and consumers, however, to determine whether such content can translate to mainstream success and forge a place in the musical canon. The ultimate test may be whether the works can attract audiences in numbers that sway mainstream musical theatre artists and producers to more seriously consider the timely subject matter as worthy of Broadway investment. Only then may the digital-age musical reshape the genre, truly defining the times in which we live.

Notes

1. Auslander, Philip. *Liveness: Performance in a Mediatized Culture*, 31–32.
2. Jensen, Amy Petersen. *Theatre in a Media Culture*, 2.
3. Ibid., 4.
4. Rich, Frank. "Conversations with Sondheim," 40.
5. Jensen. *Theatre in a Media Culture*, 87–88.
6. Carlson, Marvin. *Theatre Semiotics: Signs of Life*, 111.
7. McGeveran, William. "*Google*: The Musical."
8. Brandt, Eric. "UWMC Preview of *Google*: The Musical."
9. Miller, Daryl H. "Review of *Internet Dating: The Musical*."
10. Peters, Lori. "*Internet Dating: The Musical*: Love on Your Laptop."
11. Oberlin Dance Collective. "ODC Theater Presents *OMFG! The Internet Dating Musical*."
12. Pan, Anna. "*OMFG! The Internet Dating Musical* Will Make You LOL."
13. "*#LoveStory*."
14. "*Like Me—The Social Media Musical*."
15. Smith, Jon. "*Like Me—The Social Media Musical*: Crowd Funding Its Way to Broadway."
16. Smith, Jon and Gary Lake. "The World's First Social Media Themed Musical ... Funded by Social Media."
17. "*Like Me—The Social Media Musical* to Hold Investors Showcase on Broadway."
18. "*WikiMusical*."
19. Woolf, Aviva. "Review of *WikiMusical*."
20. Donovan, Deirdre. "A *CurtainUp* Report: The New York Musical Theatre Festival (NYMF)."
21. Ibid.
22. Woolf. "*WikiMusical*."
23. Guillot, Timothy. "Capital Fringe: *The Agony and The Ecstasy of Steve Jobs*: The Musical."
24. Cusick, Nicole. "Capital Fringe Review: *The Agony and Ecstasy of Steve Jobs*: The Musical."

25. Andrews, Travis. "*The Agony and Ecstasy of Steve Jobs*: The Musical."
26. Perry, Jennifer. "*The Agony and Ecstasy of Steve Jobs*: The Musical Premieres at Capital Fringe."
27. Jones, Kenneth. "Producers Want to Download *Nerds* Musical into a Broadway Theatre."
28. Shapiro, Howard. "*Nerds*, the Newly Downloaded Nerds.2 Version."
29. "Charlie Pollack, Wesley Taylor, Lauren Molina, Patti Murin and More Lead *Nerds* Labs in NYC this Week."
30. Allen-Dutton, Jordan. "*Nerds* Rules in a Rocking, Rollicking Send-Up."
31. Ibid.
32. Stearns, David Patrick. "Title Aside, *Nerds* Has It All."
33. Shapiro. "*Nerds*, the Newly Downloaded."
34. Potter, Susie. "*Nerds* Offers an Evening of Giddy Theatregoing Fun."
35. Goldberg, Hal. "*Nerds*, a New Musical about Steve Jobs and Bill Gates, Premieres in Raleigh."
36. Allen-Dutton. "*Nerds* Rules."
37. Stearns. "Title Aside."
38. It should be noted that AVByte is not the first or only online channel to produce digital-age YouTubsicals (e.g., CollegeHumor's 2009 "Web Site Story"—an online dating satire with a score that applies revised lyrics to *West Side Story* score excerpts). However, AVByte established a viral reputation for producing musicals in this vein.
39. Nazareth, Antonius. "NYU's Future Most Notable Alumni: The AVByte Brothers Are YouTube Heroes."
40. Ibid.
41. Nazareth, Antonius and Vijay Nazareth. "New Instagram: The Musical."
42. Nazareth, Antonius and Vijay Nazareth. "Facebook—The Musical."
43. Brown, Bob. "Make It Stop! 'Facebook—The Musical' and More."
44. Further proof of this trend and reflective of the AVByte YouTubsical aesthetic is "Millennials: The Musical" (2016)—brainchild of Dwayne "The Rock" Johnson and Lin-Manuel Miranda (who also provided the score). Debuting on Johnson's YouTube channel, replete with a mockumentary that chronicles the musical's pseudo stage development, this YouTubsical is unique in that it is positioned and filmed as a "live" stage musical. It details the travails of a millennial, Crystal, who loses her smartphone and, in a panic, enlists the help of her "hunky" neighbor, Jack—a luddite who still uses a flip phone—to find it. While the production is more a satire of millennial life and cringe-worthy cultural trends than a digital-centric musical, a great deal of its plot revolves around the mismatch of a tech-obsessed girl and tech-ignorant boy. In musical theatre fashion, the two incompatible millennials fall in love and both decide to adjust their lifestyles to cement their relationship. The production may be seen

as *Grease* transported into the digital age and further suggests that such YouTubsical material could find a legitimate home on the live Broadway stage.
45. Brown. "Make it Stop!"

Bibliography

"*#LoveStory.*" *FringeNYC*. Accessed January 12, 2016. http://www.fringenyc.org/basic_page.php?ltr=num.

Allen-Dutton, Jordan. Interview with Jonathan Takiff. "*Nerds* Rules in a Rocking, Rollicking Send-Up." *The Philadelphia Daily News*. *LexisNexis*. December 6, 2013. http://lexisnexis.com/lnacui2api/.

Andrews, Travis. "*The Agony and Ecstasy of Steve Jobs: The Musical.*" *DCTheatreScene*. Last modified July 12, 2013. http://dctheatrescene.com/2013/07/12/the-agony-and-ecstacy-of-steve-jobs-the-musical/.

Auslander, Philip. *Liveness: Performance in a Mediatized Culture*. New York: Routledge, 1999.

Brandt, Eric. "UWMC Preview of *Google: The Musical*." *Examiner*. Last modified April 23, 2010. http://www.examiner.com/article/uwmc-theatre-preview-of-google-the-musical-google/.

Brown, Bob. "Make It Stop! 'Facebook—The Musical' and More." *Network World*. Last modified June 7, 2013. http://www.networkworld.com/article/2167067/uc-voip/make-it-stop–facebook–the-musical/.

Carlson, Marvin. *Theatre Semiotics: Signs of Life*. Bloomington: Indiana UP, 1996.

"Charlie Pollack, Wesley Taylor, Lauren Molina, Patti Murin and More Lead *Nerds* Labs in NYC This Week." *BroadwayWorld*. Last modified April 16, 2015. http://www.broadwayworld.com/article/Charlie-Pollack-Wesley-Taylor-Lauren-Molina-Patti-Murin-and-more-lead-Nerds-labs-in-NYC-this-week/.

Cusick, Nicole. "Capital Fringe Review: *The Agony and Ecstasy of Steve Jobs: The Musical.*" *DCMetroTheatreArts*. Last modified July 12, 2013. http://dcmetrotheaterarts.com/ 2013/07/12/ capital-fringe-review-the-agony-and-ecstasy-of-steve-jobs-the-musical-by-nicole-cusick.

Donovan, Deirdre. "A CurtainUp Report: The New York Musical Theatre Festival (NYMF)—*WikiMusical.*" *CurtainUp*. July 19, 2014. http://www.curtainup.com/nymusicfestival2014.html.

Dormehl, Luke. "iDreamed a Dream: Philly Theatre Mounts *Steve Jobs the Musical.*" *Cult of Mac*. Last modified December 6, 2013. http://www.cultofmac.com/257195/idreamed-a-dream-philly-theatre-mounts-steve-jobs-the-musical/.

Goldberg, Hal. Interview with Tom Elrod. "*Nerds*, a New Musical about Steve Jobs and Bill Gates, Premieres in Raleigh." *INDY Week* (blog).

Last modified January 19, 2013. http://www.indyweek.com/artery/archives/2013/01/19/nerds-a-new-musical-about-steve-jobs-and-bill-gates/.

Guillot, Timothy. Interview with Meghan Long. "Capital Fringe: *The Agony and The Ecstasy of Steve Jobs: The Musical.*" *DCTheatreScene.* Last modified July 6, 2013. http://dctheatrescene.com/2013/07/06/capital-fringe-the-agony-and-the-ecstasy-of-steve-jobs-the-musical/.

Jensen, Amy Petersen. *Theatre in a Media Culture.* Jefferson, NC: McFarland, 2007.

Jones, Kenneth. "Producers Want to Download *Nerds* Musical into a Broadway Theatre." *Playbill.* May 23, 2008. http://playbill.com/news/article/producers-want-to-download-nerds-musical-into-a-broadway-theatre/.

"*Like Me—The Social Media Musical.*" *Indiegogo.* Accessed September 8, 2015. https://indiegogo.com/projects/like-me-the-social-media-musical/.

"*Like Me—The Social Media Musical* to Hold Investors Showcase on Broadway." *BroadwayWorld.* Last modified May 3, 2015. http://www.broadwayworld.com/article/LIKE-ME-THE-SOCIAL-MEDIA-MUSICAL-to-Hold-Investors-Showcase-on-Broadway/.

McGeveran, William. "*Google: The Musical.*" *Harvard Law* (blog). March 2, 2007. http://blogs.law.harvard.edu/inforlaw/2007/03/02/google-the-musical/.

Miller, Daryl H. "Review of *Internet Dating: The Musical.*" *Los Angeles Times. Plays 411.* April 29, 2006. https://www.plays411.net/newsite/review/play_reviews.asp?show_id=557.

Nazareth, Antonius. Interview with Hannah Orenstein. "NYU's Future Most Notable Alumni: the AVByte Brothers Are YouTube Heroes." *NYU Local.* Last modified February 28, 2013. http://nyulocal.com/on-campus/2013/02/28/nyus-future-most-notable-alumni-the-avbyte-brothers/.

Nazareth, Antonius and Vijay Nazareth. "Facebook—The Musical." *YouTube.* June 3, 2013. https://www.youtube.com/watch?v=Y2JhpNbe2Io.

———. "New Instagram: The Musical." *YouTube.* April 16, 2012. https://www.youtube.com/watch?v=-waJH21UJ5M.

Oberlin Dance Collective. "ODC Theater Presents *OMFG! The Internet Dating Musical.*" odcdance.org. Accessed June 3, 2015. https://odcdance.org/performance.php?param=68.

Pan, Anna. "*OMFG! The Internet Dating Musical* Will Make You LOL." *Miss A®.* Last modified July 14, 2011. http://askmissa.com/2011/07/14/omfg-the-internet-dating-musical-will-make-you-lol.

Perry, Jennifer. "BWW Reviews: *The Agony and Ecstasy of Steve Jobs: The Musical* Premieres at Capital Fringe." *BroadwayWorld.* Last modified July 21, 2013. http://www.broadwayworld.com/washington-dc/article/BWW-Reviews-THE-AGONY-AND-ECSTASY-OF-STEVE-JOBS-THE-MUSICAL-Premieres-at-Capital-Fringe-20130721.

Peters, Lori. "*Internet Dating: The Musical*: Love on your Laptop." *Splash Magazine*. Accessed August 5, 2015. http://www.lasplash.com/publish/Los_Angeles_Performances_116/Internet_Dating_The_Musical_Love_on_your_laptop.php.

Potter, Susie. "*Nerds* Offers an Evening of Giddy Theatregoing Fun." *Triangle Arts and Entertainment*. January 21, 2013. http://triangleartsandentertianment.org/2013/01/nerds-offers-an-evening-of-giddy-theatre-going-fun/.

Rich, Frank. "Conversations with Sondheim." *New York Times Magazine*. March 12, 2000.

Shapiro, Howard. "*Nerds*, the Newly Downloaded Nerds.2 Version." *Shapiro on Theater* (blog). *NewsWorks*. Last modified December 5, 2013. http://www.newsworks.org/index.php/local/shapiro-on-theater/62611/.

Smith, Jon. "*Like Me—The Social Media Musical*: Crowd Funding Its Way to Broadway." *LinkedIn*. Last modified May 19, 2015. https://www.linkedin.com/pulse/like-me-social-media-musical-crowd-funding-its-way-broadway/.

Smith, Jon and Gary Lake. "The World's First Social Media Themed Musical … Funded by Social Media." *Medium*. Last modified May 14, 2015. https://medium.com/@sanseng/the-world-s-first-social-media-themed-musical-funded-by-social-media/.

Stearns, David Patrick. "Title Aside, *Nerds* Has It All." *The Philadelphia Inquirer/Daily News*. December 6, 2013. http://www.philly.com/philly/columnists/david_patrick_stearns/20131206/.

"*WikiMusical*." WIKIMUSICAL. Accessed June 3, 2015. http://www.wikithemusical.com/about/.

Woolf, Aviva. "Review of *WikiMusical*." *StageBuddy*. July 21, 2014. http://stagebuddy.com/reviews-wikimusical/.

CHAPTER 4

Ghosts in the Machine: Digital Technology and Screen-to-Stage Musicals

Amy S. Osatinski

In recent years many musicals have created distinctive and often iconic brands, utilizing the Internet to market those brands. In Hollywood, many films, both new and old have done the same, often on a much larger scale. Recently, the digital brands of many films have crept onto the stage as adaptations of popular films have proliferated on Broadway. These screen-to-stage musicals utilize digital technologies not only to tell the stories of the film on which they are based, but often to recreate iconic moments from the films with the utmost fidelity to the originals. The mediatization of contemporary culture has led fans to interact with beloved movies on multiple platforms, expanding the reach of those films into every part of American life, including the theatre. The contemporary theatregoer lives in this mediatized world, which often leads to a new way of thinking about live performance. In her 2007 book, *Theatre in a Media Culture*, Amy Petersen Jensen observes:

> The American consumers' collective interaction with media has created a 'participatory spectator' who, influenced by interactions with media forms,

A.S. Osatinski (✉)
University of Northern Iowa, Cedar Falls, IA, USA
e-mail: aosatins@yahoo.com

© The Author(s) 2017
J. Hillman-McCord (ed.), *iBroadway*,
DOI 10.1007/978-3-319-64876-7_4

has learned to advance theatrical narratives beyond the threshold of the theatre space into their own private space.[1]

In contrast to Jensen's assertion that spectators seek to move narratives from public space to private space, contemporary spectators, seeking material connections with live performance, often move narratives from private space to public space, seeking to connect with beloved films in a tangible way. One way that producers are providing that connection is the recycling of familiar material in the form of screen-to-stage musicals. Theatregoers come to these shows having already interacted with the properties in their own private space, and desire a more visceral connection with the stories and characters.

Digi-themed musicals may not have taken over the Great White Way, as we see in Chap. 3 of this volume, but digital technology has. Digital scenography allows the creators of musicals to explore stories and stagings that may have been impossible before, including many screen-to-stage musicals. Over the last twenty years, dozens of commercial musical stage adaptations of films were produced. Many of these musicals used advances in technology to make the leap from screen to stage. By transitioning known titles across mediums, these musicals recycle iconic characters and moments from their source material and are often, in the words of Marvin Carlson, "ghosting" the films on which they are based. In his 2008 book, *The Haunted Stage: The Theatre as Memory Machine*, Carlson notes that theatre "has always been concerned not simply with the telling of stories but with the retelling of stories already known to its public … [involving] the dramatist in the presentation of a narrative that is haunted in almost every aspect."[2] Digital technology often aids in the manifestation of these apparitions not only by providing a haunted narrative, but also evoking nostalgic apparitions of the time periods in which the films were released.

While traditional scenographic techniques can conjure the ghosts of iconic films, advances in digital scenography have led to stage productions that can both literally and figuratively evoke the material on which they are based. It is not only easier to create multiple locations on stage by utilizing light-emitting diode (LED) screens; it also adds a cinematic quality to the projected locations, blurring the line between stage and screen. The digital world from the screen is echoed on stage in ways that wood and canvas simply cannot replicate.

There are two significant ways that screen-to-stage musicals are employing digital technology. First, many adapted musicals are utilizing technology in order to solve practical problems with putting a film on stage. Films that heavily rely on special effects, or that are animated, often have important sequences that cannot be staged without a certain amount of technological magic. Next, many screen-to-stage musicals use digital scenography to recreate iconic moments, settings, and images from the well-known films on which they are based. This chapter will discuss three screen-to-stage musicals that have employed digital technologies in these ways: *Ghost: The Musical* (2011), *Rocky: The Musical* (2014), and *Dirty Dancing: The Classic Story on Stage* (2006).[3]

Transferring a film to the stage poses a unique challenge. The audience is often simultaneously aware of the original source that was adapted and of the live performance being presented. In the 2008 edition of his book, *Liveness: Performance in a Mediatized Culture*, Philip Auslander discusses the expectations of concertgoers who are familiar with a music artist's music videos. He mentions that producers want to replicate the videos as closely as possible because "the audience comes to the show expecting to see what it has already seen on television."[4] The same can be said of the audiences that attend screen-to-stage musicals. Often they are most interested in a personal, live interaction with a beloved film, rather than the enjoyment of a completely new work of art. Although traditional scenographic techniques could be employed to transfer many films to the stage, digital technologies offer opportunities for fidelity to the source material that non-digital techniques simply cannot match. The ability to use cinematic content in screen-to-stage musicals brings the stage shows closer to the films on which they are based.

The use of digital technologies in screen-to-stage musicals often leads to productions that are more focused on the spectator's experience while watching the musical than on the quality of the musical itself, in order to provide the desired experience. Theatregoers come to many screen-to-stage musicals to experience the live incarnation of the source material, rather than to have a transcendent musical theatre experience.

Auslander notes, "within our mediatized culture, whatever distinction we may have supposed there to be between live and mediatized events is collapsing because live events are increasingly either made to be reproduced or are becoming ever more identical with mediatized ones."[5] Here Auslander is referring to live concerts; however, the same is true of theatre. Live theatre in recent years, much to the chagrin of many critics and theatre purists, has turned to the digital to remain relevant and profitable. This fact is evident in contemporary commercial theatre in two respects. First, the end goal of most commercial theatre is to have licensed productions after an initial commercial run, making reproduction a goal in many shows' creations. Next, many theatrical productions, especially musical productions, are reproductions of known film titles. Commercial theatre is concerned with making money, and reproduction can often lead to profit.

As budgets continue to expand, producers become more cautious about the projects they are willing to back. Many producers have turned to familiar titles to draw in audience dollars. This trend has led to an influx of musicals based on popular and well-known films. In his column for *The New York Times*, "The Staggering Cost of Broadway," Patrick Healy states:

> Bigger-scale musicals tend to cost $10 million to $15 million these days. (The hit musical *The Book of Mormon* cost about $9 million). The most lavishly produced musicals are even higher: DreamWorks has confirmed that *Shrek the Musical* cost $25 million to mount on Broadway, while the producers of *Spider-Man: Turn Off the Dark* have confirmed that the show cost $75 million to stage.[6]

In Carla Hay's 2004 article, "Movies Inspiring New Round of Musicals," entertainment lawyer Jay Cooper notes, "musicals don't have an afterlife like movies do. If a musical flops, it's over"[7]. There is no recouping investment dollars by selling DVDs; if the show closes the money is lost. This fact has led to many producers turning toward pop culture titles to attempt to negate some of the risk of producing on Broadway. In his 2001 text, *The Haunted Stage: The Theatre as Memory Machine*, Marvin Carlson asserts that "recycling in theatre arises from the fact that this art, in order to survive, must attract an ongoing public."[8] This desire for familiarity in order to attract audience dollars has led to an influx of stage adaptations of films.

The screen-to-stage musical is not new. As long as there have been movies, there have been musicals based on movies. However, recent years have seen a rise in the number of stage musicals based on films, especially well-known and highly successful films. From January 1, 2010 to December 31, 2015, a total of 84 original musicals (not revivals) played on Broadway. Of those 84 musicals, 31 of them were based on films.[9] In contrast, in the middle of Golden Age of musical theatre,[10] there were far fewer movie adaptations. From January 1, 1950 to December 31, 1955, there were 79 original musicals played on Broadway. Of those 79 musicals, only five of them were based on films.[11] In addition, contemporary screen-to-stage musicals are often based on blockbuster films or cult classics. Take for example, *Rocky* (2014), based on the hit film from 1976; *The Lion King* (1997), based on the Disney animated blockbuster from 1994; and *Hairspray* (2002), based on the John Waters cult classic from 1988. Audiences are already intimately familiar with these films and simply announcing the title generates momentum, buzz, and ticket sales before the show opens.

The growing trend toward the recycling of the familiar has led to an interesting tension between the live and the mediatized. Marvin Carlson (2001) posits:

> There appears to be something in the very nature of the theatrical experience itself that encourages ... a simultaneous awareness of something previously experienced and of something being offered in the present that is both the same and different, which can only be fully appreciated by a kind of doubleness of perception in the audience.[12]

This phenomenon is evident in the contemporary screen-to-stage musical, where seeing iconic moments and characters from beloved films come to life on stage enthralls audiences. This duality is seen in the cheers that erupted from the audience during *Rocky: The Musical* when the title character drinks a glass of raw eggs or punches a frozen side of beef. These moments ghost the original film and remind spectators of the connection between the film and the live production; therefore, the audience cheers the ghost of the film rather than the action on stage. Carlson points out one important aspect of dramatic recycling: "it encourages audiences to compare varying versions of the same story, leading them to pay closer attention to how the story is told and less to the story itself."[13] This fact works in the favor of many screen-to-stage musicals that are more concerned with the audience's experience watching the show than with the show itself. In many screen-to-stage musicals, digital technologies play a major role in creating the desired audience experience.

Ghost: The Musical

On April 23, 2011, *Ghost: The Musical* opened at the Lunt-Fontanne Theatre.[14] A transfer from London, the show was the stage version of the 1990 film of the same name. The Academy Award Best Picture nominated film tells the iconic story of Sam and Molly, a couple deeply in love. Sam is killed after refusing to give his wallet to a mugger. After his death, through the use of a medium, Oda Mae Brown, Molly is able to communicate with Sam. The film, and subsequent musical, required the ghosts to walk through walls and pass through objects, presenting a daunting staging challenge.

Ghost: The Musical required so many special effects that the production hired an illusionist, Paul Kieve, who was responsible for creating original magic effects for the production.[15] One of the key elements of the plot of the movie (and the musical) is the fact that the main character, Sam, is a ghost and, as such, possesses ghostly abilities. Though the production team for *Ghost* was very tight-lipped about the actual technologies and methods used to create the theatrical illusions, it is certain that state-of-the-art projection technologies were used. For example, toward the middle of the show, the "Subway Ghost" teaches Sam how to move objects. Magically, Sam passes his hand through what appears to be a 3D projected image of a soda cup in one moment, and then sends the real version of that same cup flying across the stage in the next. Without the use of high-powered, digital projection technology, this effect would not be possible.

Another of Kieve's illusions was employed when Sam (the ghost) exits his and Molly's apartment by passing through a closed door. Earlier in the scene another character used the door and closed it behind him, then, by means of a 3D projected magic trick, Sam walks through that same closed door. In reviewing footage of this effect, it appears that either the door becomes a three dimensional projected image and the actor moves through it, or the actor becomes a holographic projection and his image is what walks through the door, not the actor himself.

This digital wizardry serves a dual purpose in the transfer of the title from screen to stage. First, the precision of the equipment and its ingenious use produces an illusion that is so close to the filmic reality of its source that one cannot help but be awestruck by the beauty and magic of these moments. Next, the use of digital projection, in these instances and in others, brings the stage version closer to the film version by using real, projected imagery, rather than fabricated, theatrical reproductions.

Although the creation of apparitions on stage is the most striking use of digital technology in *Ghost*, the show also utilized a series of moveable digital walls. These giant LED screens were an integral part of the production and were used in several ways. First, the LED walls were used to indicate location several times in the show. At times the walls became literal images of the locations where scenes take place, such as an office or a city skyline. The scene in the subway car plays behind the walls, which had the ability to become semi-translucent, and the motion of the train was created using the LED screens in front of the actors. The screens were also used during the major dance numbers in the show and were filled with projected images of dancers doing the same choreography as the live dancers on stage.

Ghost: The Musical employed state-of-the-art digital technology to evoke iconic and important moments from *Ghost* the film. Though the story could have perhaps been told in another way to negate the need for theatrical magic tricks, audiences had certain expectations, which the stage show had to meet. Many in attendance at the show wanted to experience the beloved film live in front of them, magic and all. This is evidenced in several of the user reviews of *Ghost: The Musical* posted on *Yelp* during its run. On December 14, 2012, Irene C. from Fort Lee, NJ posted: "I remembered this movie came out when I was just a teen, and now I am in my 30s and I still love this story so much and the musical is even better than the movie."[16] On August 9, 2012, Sally W from New York, NY posted: "IMHO [in my humble opinion] this show didn't measure up to the movie for me."[17] James W. from New York, NY noted: "*Ghost the Musical* is a great rendition of *Ghost* the movie. I was a bit apprehensive as to how they were going to create the illusions of the ghosts, but they did it."[18] These reviews clearly show that some theatregoers were interested in how the show would recreate the film. Some were thrilled with the experience, and others were disappointed. As ironic as it may be, *Ghost: The Musical* was expected to ghost the film on which it was based with as much fidelity as theatrically possible. Marvin Carlson notes:

> Recycling today often serves to call the attention of the audience to the constructedness of the theatrical performance, to its status as a product not

spontaneously appearing but consciously assembled out of preexisting elements, many of them already known to the observers.[19]

As is clear from the aforementioned *Yelp* reviews, many audience members already knew the story, characters, and images of *Ghost: The Musical*, and their expectation of the show was tied more to its relationship with the preexisting material than to its merit as a musical.

Although *Ghost* employed ingenuity in its use of digital technology, pushing the boundaries of what had been done on stage before, the show was not well received by critics. Charles Isherwood of *The New York Times* wrote a scathing review challenging the show for its focus on spectacle rather than drama. Isherwood complains, "The show relies mostly on elaborate video imagery, modestly ingenious special effects and the familiarity of its ectoplasmic romance to entertain."[20] He called it "a thrill-free singing theme-park ride" and "a dreary digital spectacle." He also stated: "it is ... flavorless and lacking in dramatic vitality."[21] Isherwood continues:

> Video wallpaper plays a major role in the production, with Sam and Molly's love scene blown up to Times Square billboard scale, and images of busy New Yorkers caroming around the streets amplifying the formless gyrations of Ashley Wallen's choreography. Nifty special effects by Paul Kieve are used to show how Sam learns (from a rapping ghost he meets in the subway ...) to break through the life-death barrier and make objects move ... These high tech flourishes lend the show the feel of one of those sensory-bath, movie-inspired rides at the Universal Studios and Disney theme parks.[22]

The theme-park ride, spectacular, in-your-face use of theatre magic and technology combined with the title's appeal, may be the reason why the show ran for five months despite widespread disdain from critics like Isherwood and the less than exemplary quality of the show's book and score. Isherwood's reaction points to the larger critical dismissal of many screen-to-stage musicals, partly because there is a bias against recycled material on Broadway by the Broadway establishment, and partly because, like many other screen-to-stage musicals, *Ghost: The Musical* focused attention on the magic of the show at the expense of the libretto. *Ghost: The Musical* and other shows like it focus on spectacle rather than substance, a trend that many establishment critics like

Isherwood disdain. Though the technical magic of the show was impressive, Isherwood felt that it was a gimmick and was not enough to cancel out the less impressive book and score.

Ghost was also nominated for three Tony Awards: One for Da'Vine Joy Randolph for Best Actress in a Featured Role for her portrayal of Oda Mae Brown, one for Rob Howell and Jon Driscoll for the scenic design, and one for Hugh Vanstone for the lighting design.[23] Although the show did not win any of the awards, nomination in two technical categories points to the artistry and innovation employed in staging the iconic film. *Ghost: The Musical* could not have been successfully staged without the use of state-of-the-art digital technologies.

Rocky: The Musical

Based on the award winning 1976 film, *Rocky: The Musical* opened at the Winter Garden Theatre on March 13, 2014 after a tryout in Hamburg, Germany. With a score by Broadway veterans Lynn Ahrens and Stephen Flaherty, and Sylvester Stallone collaborating on the book, producers were hopeful that the iconic film could become an iconic musical. Though the show only ran for 180 performances, far fewer than hoped, *Rocky: The Musical* did successfully recreate the film on stage and according to Peter Marks of *The Washington Post*, delivered, "the most exhilarating sports choreography you're likely to experience in the theatre."[24]

The film, *Rocky* (1976), is an American classic. It is a film whose story, characters, and events are beloved and immediately recognizable to audiences. In order to recreate the events of the film, and to transform the theatre into the various iconic locations, video designer Dan Scully and video programmer Ben Keightley utilized state-of-the-art digital technology. Scully and Keightley used a variety of digital tools; first, a large digital server was employed to house and run the video content for the musical. Next, two large video walls were flown into the space to display media reports and live interviews during the musical.[25] The content displayed was a combination of prerecorded digital video news reports about Rocky and Apollo Creed in the lead up to the fight, and live interviews with the two boxers. The screens were paired with a live feed of reporters interviewing both Rocky and Creed on stage and the images of the interviews were played in real time. This use of digital video and digital screens replicated the media reports from the film and helped to move the plot forward toward the final fight, while simultaneously ghosting the media presence in the film.

Video was not only used to represent the media, but digital screens were also used to create the fish tanks in the pet shop where Adrian, Rocky's love interest, works. 24 screens attached to the scenic unit for the pet store were used to simulate fish tanks.[26] These digital aquariums served as electronic apparitions, evoking memories of the scenes from the film that took place in the pet store.

The film also contains an iconic sequence that follows Rocky as he trains for the final fight. One of the most memorable moments from the film is the famous montage of Rocky running through the streets of Philadelphia, that concludes with him running up the steps of the Philadelphia Museum of Art, which are now known as the "Rocky Steps." Recreating these locations required some digital magic. In order to stage the montage, the show utilized "an array of Christie and Panasonic projectors"[27] to simulate not only the locations from the film, but also the movement of Rocky through those locations. The projected images moved as Andy Karl, the actor playing Rocky, ran either in place or in slow motion. At the end of the sequence, stairs were brought in that he ran up while the façade of the Philadelphia Museum of Art was projected onto video screens behind him. Thus, Rocky's triumphant ascension of the steps on stage is haunted by memories of its celluloid counterpart.

In addition to the montage, perhaps the most challenging and iconic moment to stage was the final fight between Rocky and Apollo Creed. Rather than simply bringing out a set piece to simulate the boxing ring on the stage, behind the proscenium, the theatre was transformed into a boxing arena for the final bout. Director Alex Timbers notes: "I wanted the audience to feel like they were really at a boxing match. And so, the set designer and I pitched this idea, we wanted the boxing ring to push out into the auditorium."[28] Prior to the fight, patrons seated in the first eight rows of the theatre were escorted out of their seats onto the stage where a set of bleachers was erected. Once the audience members were moved, the boxing ring was brought in and pushed out onto an extension of the stage that moved over the top of the now empty rows of the house. The audience members in the rear and side orchestra were also encouraged to get out of their seats and surround the ring.

Once the ring was lowered, a large jumbotron was also brought in above the ring for the final fight. The jumbotron had digital video screens on all four sides and displayed a live feed of the fight from the various cameras on stage as well as above the ring. Video designer Dan Scully notes: "The video [was] about providing the audience this view of the action that you can't get normally sitting in a theatre seat."[29] By using the digital video and screens, the audience was transported from the Winter Garden Theatre to the boxing arena. The combined effect is a hybrid viewing experience unlike anything else ever staged on Broadway. The fight felt like a sporting event rather than a theatrical event, and by physically moving the audience into the configuration of a boxing match, the line between audience member and participant became blurred, heightening the excitement of the experience. Adding to this transformation was the use of the jumbotron above the action. The meticulous fight choreography was displayed via live feed on the digital screens. Therefore, the choreography had to play not only to the audience members, none of whom were less than ten feet away, but also in close up on screen. The flawless execution of the fight and its magnification via digital means furthered the hybridity of the theatrical event, leaving audiences with a visceral experience of athletic combat combined with the more passive experience of seeing a musical. Audience members attending *Rocky: The Musical* not only viewed a ghostly representation of the film, they were able to participate in that representation. Without the use of digital video, the scene would have been far less successful and far less exciting.

Unlike many other digi-centric musicals, the last scene in *Rocky: The Musical* combined digital technology with game-changing, innovative staging. The configuration of the audience and the relationship of the actors and the spectators shifted during the performance. This shift, in combination with the use of digital video, led to the ingenious finale of the show. Neither element on its own would have been as successful without the other, leading one to wonder if there are perhaps more inventive ways of using digital technologies to recreate films that might lead to productions that find critical success. *Rocky: The Musical* not only managed to ghost *Rocky* the film; it also ghosted the experience of attending a live sporting event. Spectators attending the musical witnessed the story and characters come to life live in front of them, and experienced the excitement of the film's final fight firsthand by taking an active role in the action. Several critics noted the success of the fight, including Ben Brantley of *The New York Times* who stated, "Admittedly, it's a hell of a fight, a brutally balletic coup de theatre that shakes up the joint in more ways than one."[30] In her review, Marilyn Stasio of *Variety* explains:

> The fight itself is a brilliant piece of staging, all the more so because it's also seen in closeup detail on the giant video screens of the Jumbotron ... The fight clocks in at about 20 min, but by that time everyone in the house is so caught up in the spectacle that nobody's counting.[31]

Although *Rocky: The Musical* did not have the longevity or financial success that its producers had hoped, the show employed state-of-the-art video technology to successfully recreate the film for the stage. Although other iconic moments from the film, like Rocky drinking raw eggs or boxing a side of beef, may have elicited cheers from the audience, the silent star of the musical was the digital technology that transported the audience from the theatre to the world of the film.

Dirty Dancing: The Classic Story on Stage

On April 13, 2006, the *Daily Mail* reported that the West End production of *Dirty Dancing: The Classic Story on Stage* was completely sold out for the first two months of its run, over six months before it was to open, bringing in a record-breaking £3 million. The show hit the West End in October 2006, after a highly lucrative run, having sold over a million tickets in Australia.[32] The stage adaptation of *Dirty Dancing* had a significant task to complete; it not only needed to work as a live musical, but it also needed to please an audience filled with patrons who wanted to see the film meticulously recreated on stage. Emma Brockes of *The Guardian* notes that the show "benefit[s] from a double-whammy of nostalgia: for the age of innocence in which it takes place, and for the state in which most people first saw it, as children."[33] The show is simultaneously ghosting the film on which it is based, the time in which it is set, and the time in which the original film was released. By evoking ethereal memories of the film, *Dirty Dancing: The Classic Story on Stage* not only recreated iconic moments from the film, purposely ghosting its source material, but its blatant references to the film also evoke childhood memories of viewing the movie for many audience members. In order to successfully ghost the film, the show employed digital technologies.

The film *Dirty Dancing* was released in 1987 and tells the story of Frances "Baby" Houseman who travels to Kellerman's Resort in the Catskills with her family for three weeks at the end of the summer in 1963. Over the course of those weeks, Baby meets Johnny, a dance instructor at the resort, falls in love, and transitions from a girl to a woman. The film is an American cult classic and a childhood staple for many Generation Xers and millennials.

The scenic design for the show utilized several large screens that are moved into various configurations depending on the scene. The video screens enabled the recreation of exact locations from the film. For example, the scenes that took place in the employee housing at Kellerman's Resort were performed in front of a projected backdrop of the location from the film. The rows of cabins, complete with wooden steps, were immediately recognizable. The same is true of the iconic scene between Baby and her father that happens on the porch of the dining hall; the video backdrop looked exactly like the porch overlooking the lake from the film. While viewing the show, one couldn't help but remember these scenes from the film, and this ghostly presence featured prominently and deliberately in the scenic design. Though a painted backdrop could have been used to evoke the locations from the film, the digital scenery has a cinematic quality that painted scenery lacks. The water in the lake ripples and the lights seem to reflect off the digital water. The use of mediatized scenery adds to the feeling of interaction with the film, making it seem as if the audience has not just entered the world of the film, but the film itself.

The video screens were also used to ghost the feeling of iconic moments by recreating the visual landscape of the film, transporting viewers. Toward the beginning of the show (and the film), Baby helps one of the employees carry watermelons to the room where the staff is having a dance party. It is the first time that the audience sees the "dirty dancing" that the film/show is named for, and in the film the cinematography allows us to feel the sweat and passion of the dancers. In the stage show, after uttering one of the film's most famous lines, "I carried a watermelon," the audience experienced the dirty dancing for the first time with Baby, as gyrating bodies were artfully projected on the large video screens while the cast danced downstage. The use of this video technology allowed not only fidelity to the film, but also for the audience to feel like they were experiencing the moment along with the characters on stage. The film was ghosted literally in the scenery through the visual imagery that matches the film, while it was ghosted abstractly in the way it evokes the audience's memories of the film.

Digital projection was again used in the second act to recreate the famous montage of Baby and Johnny rehearsing. When the two characters leave Kellerman's to practice, a scrim was dropped in front of the stage. In the film Baby and Johnny rehearse the infamous lift that they are to perform in their routine in two locations that are difficult to recreate on stage, a field of tall grass and a lake. In the stage version, a high-powered projector was used along with the aforementioned scrim to simulate both locations. The field and the lake were projected onto the scrim, and then Baby and Johnny are lit through the scrim. This technique gives the effect of the two of them being in the field and the lake, as only the lit part of their bodies was visible, and the rest appeared to disappear into the projected location. For the sequence in the lake, a splashing sound effect was used every time that Johnny drops Baby into the lake, much to the delight of the audience.

Dirty Dancing: The Classic Story on Stage was by no means a triumph of the musical form, but it was well received by audiences both in the West End and on tour in the United States. Lyn Gardner of *The Guardian* points out:

> [Audiences] might not be disappointed if what they are looking for is a *straightforward frame-by-frame* recreation of the movie experience, because that is pretty much what is on offer here in an evening which is less full-blown musical and more a play with a musical soundtrack.[34]

Dominic Cavendish of *The Daily Telegraph* notes:

> In all key respects, the stage version resembles a carbon-copy of the film. That not only means that the most often quoted lines of dialogue—'I carried a watermelon' and 'Nobody puts Baby in the corner'—are there, as expected, but that almost every exchange is lifted verbatim from the script ... You can accuse director James Powell of a lack of imagination or just providing great customer service.[35]

By utilizing digital technology to recreate the iconic moments of the much-beloved film, *Dirty Dancing: The Classic Story on Stage* gave audiences exactly what they wanted. The show provided an opportunity for patrons to live the film that they had so enjoyed and to feel as if they were a part of the action at Kellerman's in the summer of 1963. By deliberately recreating iconic images and moments from the film, the creators of *Dirty Dancing: The Classic Story on Stage* capitalized not only on the popularity of the film, but also on the memories that the film's fans have of viewing the film as children. The show was able to simultaneously ghost the film and its fans' childhoods. Though the production was by no means a triumph of the musical form, its draw was in the ability of ticketholders to experience live the film that featured so prominently in their own pasts. Fans of the film were able to live *Dirty Dancing* along with Baby and Johnny as the characters and locations come to life in front of them, with the help of digital technology.

Conclusion

Our modern instant-gratification-obsessed, ultra-connected yet somehow disconnected society has led to short attention spans and fickle audiences. One way that commercial musical theatre has responded is by focusing more on the experience of watching a musical than on the merits of the musical itself. Many screen-to-stage musicals, including the three discussed in this chapter, offer a clear example of this phenomenon. The producers of these shows, and many others, sought to capitalize on the desires of contemporary audiences to have tangible experiences with familiar narratives. In contemporary culture, often audiences seek to engage with media on a more visceral level. Fans of many films that are adapted into stage shows want to have a live interaction with those films and often expect the stage version to be a carbon copy of the film version.

This expectation has led to the intentional ghosting of these films on stage. In order to sell tickets, often screen-to-stage musicals take advantage of the "doubleness of perception"[36] that Carlson asserts exists in contemporary theatregoers. These musicals are bringing that doubleness to the forefront and marketing it. Musicals that ghost films are now being intentionally created, rather than arising by theatrical accident. This means that production elements are often specifically designed to evoke the material on which the shows are based, and in order to successfully recreate these iconic images, theatre is turning to the digital.

In his July 2011 *Vanity Fair* article, James Wolcott notes: "Broadway purists may deplore the influx of movie-spinoff musicals in recent years, wishing someone would turn off the popcorn machine and let more imaginative brainstorms blow through."[37] Wolcott is voicing the sentiments of much of the Broadway establishment who for years have dug their heels in, asserting that contemporary screen-to-stage musicals are of low quality and are only out to make a buck, rather than to create artistically viable works of theatre.

The three shows discussed in this chapter are examples of the type of shows the Broadway establishment deplores, as the dramatic elements of all three shows are decidedly underwhelming. These three shows, however, represent advances in technological spectacle, which some might argue is as worthy of praise as outstanding dramatic material. It cannot be denied that watching Sam walk through the once solid door in *Ghost: The Musical* is awe inspiring, or that reliving the iconic moments of *Dirty Dancing* live elicits a delightful feeling of nostalgia, or that the final fight in *Rocky: The Musical* pushed musical theatre for a moment into a new realm of active spectatorship. In attempting to draw in digital age audiences, producers have turned to technology to excite and engage. As theatrical technology continues to advance, the experience of attending a live musical will continue to evolve. Digital technologies have opened doors to new ways of approaching musical theatre, and perhaps someday soon more digi-centric musicals will pair the excitement of a mind-blowing experience with the solid foundation of an award worthy libretto.

Notes

1. Jensen, *Theatre in a Media Culture*, 4. In this volume, chapters by Hillman-McCord and Stiehl also utilize Jensen's work.
2. Carlson, *The Haunted Stage*, 17.
3. Refers to the opening date in London, as the show did not have a Broadway run, but rather a US tour.
4. Auslander, *Liveness*, 34.
5. Ibid., 35.
6. Healy, "The Staggering Cost of Broadway," Arts Beat: Culture at Large.
7. Hay, "Movies Inspiring New Round," 5.
8. Carlson, 166.
9. "Internet Broadway Database."
10. The Golden Age of musical theatre refers to the period between 1943 and 1964.
11. "Internet Broadway Database."
12. Carlson, 51.
13. Ibid., 27.

14. "Internet Broadway Database."
15. "*Ghost the Musical.*"
16. Irene C., *Yelp* Review. December 14, 2012. https://www.yelp.com/biz/ghost-the-musical-new-york.
17. Sally W., *Yelp* Review. August 9, 2012. https://www.yelp.com/biz/ghost-the-musical-new-york
18. James W., *Yelp* Review. July 24, 2012. https://www.yelp.com/biz/ghost-the-musical-new-york
19. Carlson, 173.
20. Isherwood, "In a Broadway Afterlife," review of *Ghost: The Musical*, sec. C, 1.
21. Ibid.
22. Ibid.
23. "Search Past Winners," Tony Awards.
24. Marks, "Theatre Review: 'Rocky'," review of *Rocky: The Musical*.
25. "*Rocky the Musical* Debuts," 50.
26. Ibid.
27. Ibid.
28. "Rocky Broadway: The Anatomy of a Knockout" video file.
29. Ibid.
30. Brantley, "Swinging at Fighters and Serenading," review of *Rocky: The Musical*, sec. C, 1.
31. Stasio, "Broadway Review: Rocky the Musical," review of *Rocky: The Musical*.
32. "Dirty Dancing Is Box Office Hit." *Daily Mail.*
33. Emma Brockes, "The Time of Our Lives," sec. G, 2.
34. Gardner, "First Night Once More."
35. Cavendish, "The Time of Your Life."
36. Carlson, 51.
37. James Wolcott, "Pop Goes the Great White Way."

Bibliography

American Theatre Wing. "Search Past Winners." Tony Awards. Accessed February 9, 2016. http://www.tonyawards.com/p/tonys_search.

Auslander, Philip. *Liveness: Performance in a Mediatized Culture.* 2nd ed. London: Routledge, 2008.

Brantley, Ben. "Swinging at Fighters and Serenading Turtles: 'Rocky,' the Musical, Brings Songs to a Film Story." Review of *Rocky: The Musical*, New York, NY. *The New York Times*, March 14, 2014, sec. C, 1. Accessed June 27, 2016. http://www.nytimes.com/2014/03/14/theater/rocky-the-musical-brings-songs-to-a-film-story.html?ref=theater&_r=0.

Broadway League. "Internet Broadway Database." Internet Broadway Database. Accessed September 11, 2017. http://www.ibdb.com.

Brockes, Emma. "The Time of Our Lives - Revisited: From Footloose to Dirty Dancing, the West End Has Fallen in Love with 1980s Musicals. But, Asks Emma Brockes, Is Anyone Ready for This Nostalgia Trip?" *The Guardian* (London, England), April 13, 2006, sec. G, 2. Accessed February 23, 2016. Business Insights Global.

Carlson, Marvin. *The Haunted Stage: The Theatre as Memory Machine*. Ann Arbor: University of Michigan Press, 2001.

Cavendish, Dominic. "The Time of Your Life, Again. First Night." *The Daily Telegraph* (London, England), October 25, 2006.

"Dirty Dancing Is Box Office Hit." *Daily Mail*. Accessed February 23, 2016. http://www.dailymail.co.uk/tvshowbiz/article-382954/Dirty-Dancing-box-office-hit.html.

Gardner, Lyn. "First Night Once More Round the Dance Floor - But It's Less a Musical More a Soundtrack: *Dirty Dancing* Aldwych London 2/5." *The Guardian* (London, England), October 25, 2006, 15. Accessed February 23, 2016. ProQuest.

"Ghost the Musical." Accessed February 26, 2016. http://www.ghostontour.com.

"Ghost the Musical New York." *Yelp*. http://www.yelp.com/biz/ghost-the-musical-new-york.

"Glen Keane." Internet Movie Database. Accessed February 4, 2016. http://www.imdb.com/name/nm0443855/?ref_=ttfc_fc_wr14.

Hay, Carla. "Movies Inspiring New Round of Musicals." *Billboard*, July 31, 2004, 5. Accessed February 26, 2016. ProQuest.

Healy, Patrick. "The Staggering Cost of Broadway." Arts Beat: Culture at Large. Last modified July 21, 2011. Accessed February 26, 2016. http://artsbeat.blogs.nytimes.com/2011/07/21/the-staggering-cost-of-broadway/.

Isherwood, Charles. "In a Broadway Afterlife, Time Goes by So Slowly." Review of *Ghost: The Musical*, New York, NY. *The New York Times*, April 24, 2012, sec. C, 1. Accessed July 19, 2016. http://www.nytimes.com/2012/04/24/theater/reviews/ghost-the-musical-at-the-lunt-fontanne-theater.html?_r=0.

Jensen, Amy Petersen. *Theatre in a Media Culture: Production, Performance, and Perception since 1970*. Jefferson, NC: McFarland, 2007.

Lassell, Michael. *Tarzan: The Broadway Adventure*. New York: Disney Editions, 2007.

Lee, Jeff. Interview by the author. New York, NY. June 12, 2015.

Marks, Peter. "Theatre Review: 'Rocky': A Musical Thrilla That's Vanilla." Review of *Rocky: The Musical*, New York, NY. *The Washington Post*, March 13, 2014. Accessed April 26, 2016.

"Rocky Broadway: The Anatomy of a Knockout." Video file. YouTube.com. Accessed February 16, 2016. https://www.youtube.com/watch?v=fVy-O9KziFs.

"*Rocky the Musical* Debuts on Broadway with Video Assist." *Projection, Lights & Staging News* 15, no. 4 (May 2014): 50.

"Search Past Winners." Tony Awards. Accessed July 19, 2016. http://www.tonyawards.com/p/tonys_search.

Stasio, Marilyn. "Broadway Review: Rocky the Musical." Review of *Rocky: The Musical*, New York, NY. *Variety*, March 13, 2014. Accessed June 27, 2016. http://variety.com/2014/legit/reviews/broadway-review-rocky-the-musical-1201132095/.

Viagas, Robert. "Long Runs on Broadway." *Playbill*. Last modified February 24, 2016. Accessed February 26, 2016. http://www.playbill.com/article/long-runs-on-broadway-com-109864.

Wolcott, James. "Pop Goes the Great White Way." *Vanity Fair*, July 2011. Accessed February 26, 2016. http://www.vanityfair.com/culture/2011/07/musicals-201107.

PART II

Audiences and Performers in the Digital Age

CHAPTER 5

Let's Misbehave: Cell Phone Technology and Audience Behaviors

Kathryn Edney

It is perhaps by now a truism in theatre history that the expected behaviors of Western audiences during theatrical performances have, over time, become highly regulated. As Lawrence Levine noted in his landmark 1988 book *Highbrow/Lowbrow*, American audiences became "well behaved" during the nineteenth century as part of larger social and cultural battles involving class, race, and gender. Immigrants, people of color, and those of the lower classes might yell at the actors on the stage and otherwise behave rudely, but white, native-born, middle-and upper-class Americans knew that in order to appreciate culture—and what constituted culture was carefully defined—one must be silent during performances and applaud only at the right moments.[1] Conflicting ideas about proper theatre etiquette, and discussions over whether or how to best enforce that etiquette, is nothing new within the United States.

In the twenty-first century, what is new is the impact of mobile cell phone technology on particular types of audience behaviors. Thus, while in America much of the twenty-first-century rhetoric surrounding how to best manage—and stamp out—bad theatre etiquette mirrors

K. Edney (✉)
Regis College, Weston, MA, USA
e-mail: kathryn.edney@regiscollege.edu

© The Author(s) 2017
J. Hillman-McCord (ed.), *iBroadway*,
DOI 10.1007/978-3-319-64876-7_5

the rhetoric of the nineteenth century, how audiences behaved in theatres prior to the ubiquity of the cell phone was typically quite different from their behaviors now. That difference is primarily one of engagement, and what it means to be present at a live performance as an audience member. As Caroline Heim notes, "in the communal space called a theatre auditorium [people] come together to play a role—that of audience," while Richard Schechner theorized that the root of theatre lies in its exchange of stimuli. By definition, theatre is relational. Regardless of genre, there is always a specific set of obligations and expectations within a series of relationships between actors and actors, between actors and audience, and between the individual members of the audience as they come together.[2] However, cell phone technology has changed how audience members perform as an audience. The stimuli being exchanged are not always necessarily located within the performance space. Commercial Broadway theatres in general and musical theatre as a genre in particular have had difficulty in effectively managing and adapting to the changes in relationships as they exist within the space of the theatre brought about by cell phone technology.[3]

There is a fundamental difference between bad behaviors erupting in direct *response* to a performance, and manifesting bad behavior *in spite* of a performance. In other words, booing a performer is not the same as texting a friend, because texting disrupts the encounter between audience and actors, and between individual members of the audience themselves.[4] Cell phones connect individual users to a world outside of the one created on the stage; booing, however disruptive, is an encounter between voices and bodies.[5] The outside connection established by the cell phone distances and distracts members of the audience both from the live performance and from other audience members. When an individual member of the audience absents himself/herself from the performance, the community formed within the space of the theatre is transformed from a shared space to a fragmented, individual one.[6] The transformation distances the user of the technology from the temporarily formed community of spectators who come together with the common purpose of watching a performance. Depending on the use to which the cell phone is put, there is also the real potential of distracting other, technology-adjacent audience members, as well as the performers on the stage.

There are of course non-technological ways of being mentally absent while physically present when attending a performance. Members of an audience can evince bad behavior in spite of a performance by whispering to each other, flipping noisily through the program, or by falling asleep. These are all very clear indicators of an individual disengaging from the live performance. But it is still the case that cell phone technology fragments audience communities into its component parts ruthlessly and, effectively, it is this atomization that differentiates twenty-first-century audience misbehavior from nineteenth- and early-to-mid-twentieth-century audience misbehavior.

Scholars such as David Savran, Dan Rebellato, and Laura MacDonald have variously discussed the importance of considering the global impact of musical theatre.[7] There are clear pitfalls in considering musicals to be a uniquely "American" genre when, for example, China is not only hosting English-language versions of *My Fair Lady*, but also producing Chinese-language jukebox musicals based on popular Chinese films Americans will likely never see.[8] The evolution of "American musicals" into the globalized "American-style musicals"—or "American/Broadway-style musicals"—implicates audience studies. Audiences located far from the Great White Way in New York City may have quite different or limited ideas regarding what constitutes Broadway-style musical theatre. And within the limited frame of audiences for musical theatre is the broader context of culturally specific expectations for audiences' behaviors. Cell phone use in these other cultural contexts for musical theatre performances thus might well play out in ways that are quite different from the norm in the United States.[9]

This chapter focuses on the impact of cell phone technology on audience behaviors attending live musical theatre performances in the particular culture of the United States.[10] Thus, it will first provide a brief history of the cell phone in the United States, and survey the literature regarding the ways in which this technology has, in broad terms, altered human behaviors and interactions. The ability for an individual to detach from her/his immediate surroundings using a mobile phone is well researched by scholars. Next, a more popular history tracking *Playbill*, the *New York Times*, and other news outlet anecdotes on the use of cell phones in New York City theatres within the context of musical theatre performances will be discussed. Particular emphasis will be paid to the reactions and rhetoric from actors, producers, and directors as they have attempted to negotiate the changing landscape of audience behaviors brought about by cell phones. The chapter will conclude with an analysis of notable contemporary examples of transgressive audience behaviors in the United States from the "summer of cell phones" in 2015.

A Brief History of the Cell Phone in the United States

Although cell phones were first commercially introduced into the US market in 1985—by twenty-first century standards these early iterations were large, clunky, and unwieldy—they did not become popularly widespread until around 1995.[11] After another ten years, by 2005, the number of cell phones surpassed the number of landline telephones, and now, in 2016 it is almost impossible to imagine contemporary American life without mobile phone technology. As many scholars have noted, the near-universality of cell phone usage, regardless of age, gender, race, or income, has had fundamental effects on how Americans work, play, and communicate with one another. While certainly there are distinctions between how different groups use their phones, with age being a key determinant in those differences, it is nonetheless the case that not owning a cell phone is an increasingly rare phenomenon within contemporary American society.[12]

With ubiquity of cell phone ownership and use comes implicit standards for the use of that technology. Cell phone etiquette—both inside and outside of theatres—can be a highly contentious issue. Concerns about the appropriateness of cell phone usage range from using cell phones in order to document police brutality, to taking "selfies" in front of the 9/11 Memorial in New York City, from texting-while-walking down a busy sidewalk, to answering a cell phone call in the middle of a live performance. Not surprisingly, in a 2013 report on cell phone etiquette, the Pew Research Center noted that:

> About three-quarters of all adults, including those who do not use cellphones, say that it is "generally OK" to use cellphones in unavoidably public areas, such as when walking down the street, while on public transportation or while waiting in line. At the same time, the majority of Americans do not think it is generally acceptable to use cellphones in restaurants or at family dinners. Most also oppose cellphone use in meetings, places where others are usually quiet (such as a movie theatre), or at church or worship service.[13]

However, while 95% of respondents did not believe it was acceptable to use a cell phone at places where people are generally quiet, the report makes no mention of the types of actual usage in such venues. Indeed, the authors of the report themselves acknowledge that the term "cell phone use" was left undefined in their survey, and could encompass anything from texting quickly and unobtrusively, to a long voice conversation, to livestreaming a football game.

What is meant by the phrase "cell phone use" is malleable and highly dependent on the user. However, it is also the case that regardless of the purpose to which Americans put their cell phones, numerous studies have demonstrated that for twenty-first-century users, going without a cell phone results in the user feeling lost, vulnerable, or naked.[14] Cell phone users rely on their phones to feel connected—to their families, their place of work, their friends, and to the larger world—thus being temporarily unable to use their cell phone has come to be equated to a significant loss, such as that of a limb.[15] While not having the cell phone within easy reach is construed as a hardship, it is also the case that social norms prohibiting the use of cell phones, everything from the request to turn off phones during a performance to public service announcements noting that texting while driving is more dangerous than driving drunk, can result in similar feelings of loss and disorientation.[16] Ironically, the need to be connected to the outside world through cell phones necessitates that users disconnect from their immediate surroundings, regardless of what those surroundings are.[17] This absenting has profound implications for audience behaviors, and the constitution of the audience as an audience, in theatres. In the case of musical theatre performances, which in part rely on audiences bridging the ontological gaps between a show's narrative and its song and dance numbers, the impact of cell phones on audiences is significant.

Cell Phone and Theatre

It is difficult to precisely ascertain when the first instance of cell phone disrupting a live performance was reported. During the rise of the cell phones over the 1990s, newspapers such as the *New York Times* began featuring articles about the impact these devices were having in the workplace—with an emphasis on the overstressed man of business—but very quickly stories shifted their focus to broader lifestyle issues. Articles from 1999 reflecting on cell phones in public life frequently referred to an audience-actor encounter that occurred during a performance of the *Death of a Salesman* revival:

> Brian Dennehy was startled to hear a cell phone ring near the end of the second act. Even more disturbing was to hear the phone being answered, and a woman in the audience clearly saying, 'It's almost finished,' and going on to make dinner plans.[18]

Dennehy subsequently stopped the show. The Dennehy incident seemed to stick in the minds of reporters and was often referred to between 2002 and 2003 in relation to other more recent incidents of actor/audience confrontations. The longevity of the story concerning how *Death of a Salesman* was interrupted is perhaps not surprising. It was one of the earliest reported examples of disruptive cell phone use—and the subsequent strong actor reaction to that use—that reporters could harken back to when, in the early 2000s, the New York City Council was considering making the use of cell phones in performance venues illegal.[19]

Broadly speaking, arts organizations—museums, theatres, and orchestras—have found that mobile technology combined with the Internet have facilitated the public's involvement with, and investment in, their organizations.[20] Cell phone technology, and the use of social media made possible by the technology, allow for wider forms of public engagement with the arts at multiple levels, from fundraising to tweeting. However, in terms of audience behaviors within arts organization venues, it is important to note that 40% agree with the statement that digital technology is:

> 'negatively impacting audience members' attention spans for live performances,' including just 9% who strongly agree this is the case [...] One other impact is cited prominently by many of these organizations: 37% of respondents strongly agree (and another 34% somewhat agree) that 'digital distractions such as ringing cell phones and audience member texting are a significant disruption to live performances.'

Significantly, one anonymous respondent noted, "The audience has already moved from 'arts attendance as an event' to 'arts attendance as an experience.'" The implication is that an event is communal and shared with others, while an experience is more narrowly constructed as personal. Individuals who construct a performance as an experience are therefore less likely to consider themselves as part of an audience, and more likely to disrupt what is meant to be a communal event.

Running alongside, but rarely intersecting, concerns over audience behaviors are discussions about decreasing interest in live theatre, especially in terms of young people and people of color, and how to best use technology in order to increase audiences for live theatre. The very technologies and platforms that can distract members of the audience from the live performance occurring in front of them are the very technologies used to promote those performances and bring audiences into the theatre.

There is thus a very real tension within arts organizations between the need to engage their public—and their potential public—by using mobile and other technologies, while at the same time needing to regulate the use of those same technologies by that public within the four walls of the cultural institution. Cell phones, and the access those phones give its users to platforms such as Twitter, Instagram, SnapChat, Facebook, and myriad others, are validated and encouraged outside of the performance space when it helps promote an upcoming event or the organization more broadly.[21] For example, in acknowledgment of the desire of patrons to document their theatrical experience, some theatres now carefully regulate and allow the photography of sets just prior or just after a performance. In addition, as Stacy Wolf notes, (predominantly female) fans of musical theatre use Instagram, Snapchat, YouTube, and Twitter as a means of celebrating their favorite musicals by extending their experience of the live performance into virtual spaces.[22] And yet during the performances themselves, cell phone technology is more often than not portrayed as an intrusive enemy in relation to the performing arts that must be repelled like an invading army.

The theatre space, and the audience and actors within that space, are thought to be sharing a communal and ephemeral experience. In contrast, "cell phones seem to prioritize communication with distant people over those sharing one's space."[23] Thus, a key disjuncture between the ontology of the live theatre experience and the ontology of the cell phone is what it means to be present.

But there is another disconnect between engaging with theatre and engaging with cell phone technology: "at heart, the mobile concept is about being in control—as a separate and distinct individual. This is the basis of mobilizing the concept of communication—that it's an activity undertaken by an individual, over which that individual seeks control."[24] In a formal theatrical venue, while communication between audience members and actors takes place, it is, broadly speaking, not a conversation or dialogue in the typical sense.[25] To be a member of an audience, one generally gives up a certain amount of individuality and control; it is relatively rare for members of the audience to hold conversations with the actors while they are performing on the stage. While in the past, audience members might have coughed as a means of regaining that sense of self,[26] now the cell phone—and the ways in which it has become a naturalized extension of day-to-day interactions with others—can serve as a more forcible, and performative, reclaiming of individual control.

There are several ways in which the reclaiming of control by the audience from the standard mode of communication within a theatre is manifested by individual audience members: recording the performance; communicating (through texting, talking, tweeting, on the phone etc.) during the performance; watching something other than the performance; neglecting to power off the cell phone; and, more recently, using the technology of the mobile device to interfere with the performance.

In February 2003, the New York City Council passed a law making it illegal to use cell phones "during public performances, including plays, movies and concerts, and in galleries and museums. The Council's vote of 38 to 5, with 2 abstentions, was the first in the nation restricting cellphone use in public performances."[27] Those who elected to use their cell phones in public performance venues would be fined $50 for doing so. The City Council vote overrode then-Mayor Michael R. Bloomberg's veto of the measure, who had worried that the law would be completely unenforceable.[28] The law, the first of its kind in the nation, was touted by proponents as having the potential to increase the quality of life for New Yorkers by silencing cell phones. Proponents of the law argued that a law regulating cell phone etiquette was a necessity in the face of so much rudeness; a glaring screen or a noisy ringtone should not spoil anyone's enjoyment of a cultural experience. Barbara Janowitz, speaking on behalf of the League of American Theatres and Producers, went so far as to argue that as a result of a ringing cell phone "the damage to the art created on stage is palpable."[29] All of this is the language of control, and contains echoes of nineteenth-century concerns regarding "proper" understanding of cultural events, albeit without the explicitly attendant Anglo-American (male) need to enforce dominance over other racial/ethnic groups who were "infiltrating" theatres. In the twenty-first century, the rhetoric of attracting younger audiences to theatres clashes with the need to strictly regulate the behaviors of these audiences. Issues of class, age, and generational divides, however, most definitely thread through Playbill.com, Broadway.com, the *New York Times*, and other outlets featuring "cell phone horror stories." Perhaps the most significant change is the marriage of the term "entitlement" to that of the term "uncivilized" as applied to younger patrons. This marriage of terms points to the generational divides that exist in terms of cell phone usage and attitudes toward that use identified by the Pew Research Center.

Nineteen months after the cell phone ban was enacted, the *New York Times* ran a follow-up story on the impact the ban was having on cell phone usage in cultural venues. The short news essay is long on anecdotes, and short on hard data, concluding that not only were average citizens not aware of the ban, many theatre owners (inclusive of movie theatre owners) were unaware of it as well.[30] The long-term impact of the ban has not, as of yet, been studied; however, based solely on the resurgence of new stories and Twitter rants regarding audience behaviors, it would seem that the use of cell phones in New York City's theatres has not significantly decreased in the thirteen years since the ban was introduced.[31]

Anecdotally, it does appear that audience members are more and more likely to use their cell phones in the theatre, even while simultaneously, members of the audience believe that when other people use cell phones in a theatre, it is annoying and disruptive. In May 2015,[32] Goldstar, an online company which sells full- and discounted-price tickets to a diverse array of live performances, conducted an online survey of over 1000 of their members in order "to gain a little clarity on some of the biggest live entertainment etiquette questions and concerns."[33] The results of the survey—whose questions on etiquette covered everything from how to negotiate seat armrests to the use of cell phones—were widely reported in July of that year. Intentionally or not, the release of the report more or less coincided with a number of high-profile occurrences of breaches of theatre etiquette.

When asked, "do you turn your phone off completely" only 3.7% of the respondents answered, "leave my cell phone on—I need to stay connected." The remaining respondents were almost evenly split fifty-fifty between those who turned off their phones completely, and those who set it to silent/vibrate.[34] Similarly, when asked "is it OK to take photos or videos during a show?" 71% declared "Never ok" with 28% admitting that documenting a performance was acceptable if done "discreetly."[35] As with the Pew Center's survey, when the Goldstar survey asked participants about their biggest live theatre "pet peeve," cell phone use was one of the answers, but the type of use was not defined. Thus, while 40% of respondents believed that cell phone use was second only to people who talk during a performance (44%) in terms of annoyance levels, it is not clear into which of those two categories survey respondents would have placed someone talking on the cell phone.[36]

One of the more telling results of the survey was in terms of following a theatre's "house rules" for behavior: 23% of respondents answered that they did not know such rules existed, while 15% never followed the rules at all.[37] Since "house rules" typically include an admonition to refrain from using cell phones and other electronic devices, the lack of awareness of these rules might, in part, explain why audience members use their phones as a matter of course during a performance. How rigorously Goldstar administered their survey is not known, and it is, of course, a limited sample. But broadly speaking, these results align with the research conducted by scholars who examine the impact of cell phone technology on public life. In general, there is theoretical agreement among Americans that using a cell phone in a situation that typically has low levels of participatory action (e.g., an orchestra performance or live theatre) or is perceived to be quiet, solemn, or sacred (e.g., church services) is rude.[38] However, at the level of actual, situated behaviors the agreement breaks down. In other words, when I tweet during a performance I do so discreetly and so I am not being disruptive; it is the person five rows down from me texting who is the problem.[39]

In terms of the use of cell phones in movie theatres, Hassoun notes that the movie industry deploys three interrelated techniques to ameliorate the bad behaviors of its audiences when it comes to cell phones: "surveillance, intervention, and self-regulation."[40] Within the context of live theatre, the subtext of "shame" could be added to Hassoun's list of regulatory techniques. Or, as the anonymous announcer prior to the Goodman Theatre's 2016 production of the musical *War Paint* proclaimed, if a cell phone rang during the performance, the owner of the phone would be subject to "public humiliation."[41] Within the context of a musical that explores issues of class and appearance, such an announcement can be received by audiences with good grace and humor. However, since the co-star of *War Paint* was Patti LuPone, an actress known both for her implacable stance against cell phones in the theatre and for her ability to castigate audience members who interrupt a performance, the announcement has the potential to contain the weight of a very real threat capable of being enacted.

As the above suggests, one of the primary modes of bad audience behavior facilitated by mobile cell phone technology is forgetfulness. People neglect to turn off their phones (or to switch it into "silent" mode). This type of etiquette breach is passive, rather than deliberate, although it can lead to other, more active forms of bad behavior. If the phone rings, and a patron turns the phone off—regardless of the time it takes to dig the phone out of a pocket or handbag—that might be considered to be one level of bad behavior. If a phone rings during a performance, the audience member answers the phone, and then proceeds to hold a conversation, that is a different level of misbehavior because it enacts a disengagement from the community formed within the theatre, and an engagement with a community outside of the theatre. Another form of deliberate and active separation from the communal experience of the theatrical space is texting/tweeting/emailing during a performance. As a silent activity,[42] texting might seem less obtrusive than talking on the phone or conducting a whispered in-person conversation. However, the process of disengagement from the theatre space is not lessened, and the now familiar glow from the cell phone screen in the context of a darkened theatre is potentially no less distracting to other audience members or performers.

In terms of texting and other forms of silent communication that can take place when using a cell phone, playwrights, directors, producers, and actors have, in some cases, begun to incorporate texting into productions. Everything from "tweet seats" designated for audience members so that they may tweet about the production, to plays which incorporate texting and tweeting as a deliberate form of audience participation, are being experimented with by playwrights and production teams.[43] These modes of incorporating cell phones and refashioning unproductive audience behavior to productive audience behavior, however, do not work for every production. While such practices open up discussions about the role of technology in the United States more broadly, and within American theatres very specifically, they have not as yet provoked a wave of change in theatre venues or documented changes in audience behaviors.

"Summer of the Cell Phone": Case Studies

"As far as theater goes, the past few months could plausibly be dubbed the summer of the cellphone." So ran the first sentence of an online article published in *The Atlantic* in August 2015. Indeed, the summer of 2015 saw a number of high-profile instances of cell phone-enabled bad audience behaviors.[44] Perhaps the most notorious of these instances occurred on July 2, 2015, in an event that highlighted another cultural shift triggered by the advent of the cell phone and the need among users to be connected to the outside world at all times. A new sense of entitlement permits anyone to recharge their phones by "borrowing" electricity from available outlets in any public space, such as a bar, a coffee shop, or even a theatre. Sarah Stiles, a cast member of the play *Hand to God* (2015) tweeted on that night: "A guy jumped on the stage and plugged his phone into the fake outlet on our set just before we started. @HandtoGodBway #fullmoon or #idiot?" The following day, fellow cast member Marc Kudisch tweeted a general remonstrance to potential audience members regarding theatre etiquette: "Dear general audience, an electrical socket that's a part of the set of the play is NOT for you to charge your iPhone.....just an FYI....."[45] The initial event, which went far beyond the usual story of an audience member answering his or her phone in the middle of a performance, made national headlines. These headlines were further stoked by a press conference held by the offending patron who attempted, with little success, to explain his actions to the satisfaction of enraged theatregoers: "I saw the outlet and ran for it [...] That was the only outlet I saw, so I thought, 'Why not?' I was thinking that they were probably going to plug something in there on the set, and I figured it wouldn't be a big deal if my phone was up there, too." His phone needed charging because he had been receiving phone calls from "girls" all day.[46]

There are multiple ways through which to interpret this particular, and extreme, example, of bad theatre behavior on the part of an audience member. One interpretative mode is an examination of the rhetoric deployed by various news outlets when describing the event and the man involved. As alluded to above, the descriptions are highly gendered and frequently referenced his age (19 years). That he was a member of a college lacrosse team also tended to be a means through which his maleness and youth were highlighted. There are also hints of class derision on the part of some stories, which place his enrollment in a community college up against his "idiotic" behavior and his unfamiliarity with the conventions of theatre etiquette. He was often implicitly framed as a "dumb jock," who had no common sense or ability to see beyond his own (presumably) very narrow, life experiences.

Attempting to recharge a cell phone using a stage prop is an extreme version of both bad theatre etiquette and pure ignorance on the part of an audience member. More typical are the types of behaviors faced by musical theatre icon Patti LuPone during that same "cell phone summer." As with the Brian Dennehy incident from a few years earlier, LuPone's reactions to cell phone use during theatrical performances— and musical theatre performances in particular—are really what caught the attention of the media. The mere use of a cell phone in a theatre by audience members is not in and of itself news- or note-worthy; however, the reaction of a star performer to that cell phone use is.[47]

LuPone is a key figure through which media engage with audience cell phone use, and a key moment from the history of that engagement is January 10, 2009, a moment which continues to reverberate through to the present day. During a performance of the song "Rose's Turn" from the revival of the musical *Gypsy*, LuPone noticed a member of the audience taking her picture with his phone. Her direct confrontation with the spectator, coupled with her request that he be thrown out of the performance—all captured on a cell phone and uploaded onto YouTube—made headlines; again, the main thrust of the reporting was on LuPone's reaction.[48] In June that same year, when LuPone again confronted a member of the audience for similar behavior, Dave Itzkoff from the *New York Times* "ArtsBeat" chastised the actress for her reaction: "Just when we were starting to remember Patti LuPone as a luminescent if detail-oriented theatre star—and not, say, the sort of person who brings an entire show to a halt when she catches an audience member snapping photographs of her—she goes and does it again."[49] Descriptions of her anger in both cases implicitly evoked the figure of the diva. According to many commentators, her reaction was in fact an overreaction; LuPone disagreed. In a letter to the editors regarding the June incident, LuPone characterized her response to these incidents as a mode of protecting not only her artistic rights as a performer, but also as protecting other members of the audience.[50]

The example of the apparent "extreme" nature of each of LuPone's reactions to audience misbehavior is further complicated by popular media rhetoric around the meanings of theatrical performances. For example, in 2016, the wireless cell phone provider AT&T combined threadbare ideas accentuating cultural and gender divides between the lowbrow (sports) and highbrow (theatre/ballet) with the discourse regarding audience etiquette for an online campaign promoting its services. The advertisement featured a man checking sports scores on his phone while attending the ballet; clearly he had been forced to attend the venue by his female companion.[51] This advertisement came on the heels of a summer of audience misbehaviors, prompting an exchange between the Twitter accounts of Playbill.com and ATT.com, as well as a statement from Patti LuPone expressing her great displeasure, and a video response from the cast of the musical *Avenue Q*.[52] Of course, the fact that the man in the AT&T advertisement clearly had no interest in being a member of the audience perfectly captures his disengagement with his immediate surroundings by using his mobile device.

That the advertisement had him ignoring his physical presence as an audience member at one kind of performance venue for a virtual presence as an audience member at a performance of a different kind—where it is within the bounds of etiquette to use a cell phone—highlights the complex territories audience members must negotiate depending on the types of performances they elect to attend.

Conclusion

Schechner asked: "What happens to a performance when the usual agreements between performer and spectator are broken?"[53] Schechner's question was posed hopefully and in terms of those moments when audience participation in theatrical events transforms the theatrical into something else, perhaps something greater (although purists of the stage might have disagreed with him):

> It is hard to talk about participation because participation is not about 'doing a play' but *undoing* it, transforming an aesthetic event into a sodal event—or shifting the focus from art-and-illusion to the potential or actual solidarity among everyone in the theater, performers and spectators alike.[54]

What Schechner describes as an "undoing" of a production is a reformation of the audience and performers into a new kind of community, "a solidarity" brought about by the disruption of the theatrical event through audience (over-) engagement. Cell phone technology, however, disrupts the theatrical event through audience disengagement, or, perhaps more accurately, through under-engagement.

However, as discussed in a Twitter forum sponsored by Howlround, an online commons for practitioners of the performing arts, one reason an audience member might take out the cell phone is precisely because the performance itself is not engaging or does not engage audiences—especially younger audience members—in ways that they expect.[55] Some theatres have therefore instituted "tweet seats" and some recent plays, such as 2016's *Privacy* starring Daniel Radcliffe, encourage live tweeting during performances as a way to constructively shape audiences' need to be attentive to their cell phones into activities that help recreate a sense of community.[56] Unless a production takes the form of immersive theatre—such as the 2012 production *Babble*—such artistic incorporations of the audiences' technology into the diegesis of a production's narrative are still relatively rare.[57]. Contemporary musical theatre libretti have yet to make that leap, perhaps because the built-in tension between the narrative arc of a show, and the songs which interrupt that narrative, might not bear that additional disruptive element.[58] Further, perhaps because of the genre-defining disjunctions between narrative and music, the history of American musical theatre within the United States is dominated by shows emphasizing the creation of a utopia based on community and typically represented by a chorus of voices singing together in harmony in the same place and time. Cell phone usage constructs utopia and community in a fundamentally different mode; the use of one during the performance of a musical theatre production suggests that there is a widening generational division over the meanings of community and utopia, and how to best achieve these goals.

Of course, it might eventually still be the case that over time, as audience demographics change, the cell phone will become essential to the enjoyment of being a member of the audience for a musical theatre performance. A 2016 study in the *Journal of Personality and Social Psychology* found that when people took photos of "experiences"—whatever those experiences might be where photo-taking was an acceptable social norm—that engagement with, and enjoyment of, the experience increased.[59] Contrary to popular wisdom, those who took photos were more likely to pay attention to what they were experiencing because "taking photos generally requires attention being directed *toward* the experience one wants to capture."[60] Musicals, from *Show Boat* (1927) to *Hamilton* (2015), have historically played a role within popular culture in helping Americans define themselves as a community. If musical theatre professionals decide to embrace the use of cell phones by their audiences and, perhaps, the ethos of immersive theatre as well, this might further change the tenor of what constitutes "good theatre etiquette." The community that previously was disrupted by cell phones could perhaps be reconstituted by embracing audience "misbehavior" and the potential new community formed by the cell phone.

Notes

1. Levine, *Highbrow/Lowbrow*, 195. A similar phenomenon marked the rise of film-going culture in the United States during the twentieth century. For recent examination of the history, and the place of "second screens" (i.e. cell phones) among the movie-going public, see: Hassoun, "Engaging

Distractions." The most obvious, and perhaps the most important, difference between the use of cell phones in movie theatres during a screening versus cell phones during a performance is that the actors in a live performance have the potential to react in real time to the use of a cell phone, while the actors on a movie screen cannot. In terms of the ways in which cell phone use is regulated in live theatre, this difference is crucial.

2. Heim, *Audience as Performer*, 2. Schechner, *Environmental Theatre*, xxiii. Schechner discusses other relationships, which are not relevant to this essay.
3. Of course there is a distinction between successfully using cell phones to promote a performance, as discussed in Chap. 2, and incorporating cell phone technology within a performance; this chapter focuses on audience behaviors within the theatrical space.
4. Heim, *Audience as Performer*, 3. Heim might argue that texting during a performance falls within a new "repertoire" of audience behaviors, and as such qualifies as encounter/presence; my argument is that while cell phone use is now part of the audience repertoire, it serves to distance and distract rather than promoting cohesion and engagement.
5. Rebellato, "Booing," *Contemporary Theatre Review*, 11.
6. Campbell, "Perceptions of Cell Phone Use in Public," 70.
7. For example: Laura MacDonald and William Everett's *The Palgrave Handbook of Musical Theatre Producers*; Dan Rebellato, *Theatre and Globalization*; David Savran, "Broadway as Global Brand," *Journal of Contemporary Drama in English*.
8. Laura MacDonald, "The Sound of Musicals in China," *American Theatre*, 25 April 2017.
9. Nickerson, Isaac, and Mak, "Multi-National Study of Attitudes about Mobile Phone Use," make it clear that there are significant national differences in perceptions regarding when and how cell phones are used. For example, "perceptions of the prohibition of texting in theatres differ across countries with Italy agreeing with such prohibition, and the US and Finland disagreeing" (553).
10. In his 2015 article, "The Passive Gaze and Hyper-Immunized Spectators: The Politics of Theatrical Live-Broadcasting," Daniel Schulze examines the interactions European audiences have with theatrical performances when they are broadcast live within movie theatre venues, and calls for more research into this particular subset of musical theatre audiences. In the United States, musicals such as *Newsies* and *She Loves Me* have also been live-broadcast to movie theatres, while live television productions of classic musicals, such as *The Wiz* as discussed in Chap. 8, are experiencing a small boom.
11. Hanson, *24/7*, 2. Based on a database search of the *New York Times* between 1975 and 2000, it appears that the first *New York Times* article featuring the term "cell phone" was in 1992: Lewis, "Smaller, Lighter, Stronger, Cheaper."

12. According to the Pew Research Center, in "Mobile Technology Fact Sheet," as of 2014, 90% of American adults owned a cell phone, with few significant differences in terms of race, gender, or education level. Only age demonstrated the greatest difference, and even then just in terms of those adults over the age of 65, with a reported cell phone ownership at 74%.
13. Rainie and Zickurh, "Americans' Views on Cell Phone Etiquette."
14. For a sampling of these studies, see the review of the literature section in: Pinchot, Paullet, and Rota, "How Mobile Technology is Changing Our Culture," 41.
15. de Souza e Silva, "Interfaces of Hybrid Spaces," 31.
16. de Souza e Silva, "Interfaces of Hybrid Spaces," 42–44.
17. "Users avoid what is close at hand but unfamiliar and reach instead for the familiar but spatially remote." Law, McNeish, and Gray, "Base Station Fears," 321.
18. Louie, "If the Phone Had a Cord, You Could Strangle the User." Laurence Fishburne experienced a similar disruption, also in 1999, during a performance of *The Lion in Winter* when a cell phone rang for an extended period of time. Fishburne confronted the offending audience member to general audience appreciation, signified by an extended ovation. Wallis, "Noises Off."
19. McKinley and Christian, "Hark, Hark, That Tweet is No Lark. It's Illegal"; Gans, "Stanley Tucci Admonishes Audience." It is also the case that Dennehy became an outspoken critic of mobile phones in general. In recollecting the 1999 incident in 2003, he recommended the death penalty for cell phone users. Rome Neal, "Cell Phone Battle Turns Bitter," http://www.cbsnews.com/news/cell-phone-battle-turns-bitter/ 6 August 2003.
20. The thoughts and quotations in this paragraph are drawn from Thomson, Purcell, and Rainie, "Arts Organizations and Digital Technologies."
21. See Laura MacDonald's chapter in this volume regarding how producers use cell phone technology to promote sales.
22. Wolf, "Musical Theatre Studies," *The Journal of American Drama and Theatre*, http://jadtjournal.org/2016/03/23/musical-theatre-studies/. Chaps. 2, 6, 7 and 8 of this volume also explore this phenomenon.
23. Katz and Wang "Cell Phone Culture."
24. Myerson, *Heidegger, Habermas and the Mobile Phone*, 20.
25. There are of course many views of the kinds of communication, and "talking back" that occurs within the context of a traditional theatrical, or musical theatre, performance.
26. According to a study cited by Burland and Pitts, "Prelude," 2, "people cough twice as much during [concert music] performances than they do in everyday life." It is not too difficult to extend this thinking to theatrical performances.

27. McKinley and Christian, "Hark, Hark, That Tweet Is No Lark. It's Illegal."
28. Goldman, "NYC Votes to Curb Annoying Use of Cell Phones."
29. Forlano, "Cell Phone Ban."
30. Reeves, "Despite Cellphone Ban in Theaters, Dialing Continues."
31. A popular interest story published in 2007 is apparently the only "long term" report on the impact of the law. The consensus seems to be that there was no discernable difference in cell phone use in theatres. However, given the overall rise in the use of cell phones since the law went into effect, some believed that the law has had a positive impact on audience behavior. Simonson, "Things that go Chirp in the Night." There are, of course, anecdotal reports concerning cell phone usage in theatres. According to one author: "I can honestly say that within the last four years there have only been a handful of shows where I did not experience a cell phone making some kind of cringeworthy noise!" Alicia Samuel, "Let it Ring One More Time!"
32. "Please Take our Etiquette Survey and Enter to Win an Apple Watch."
33. Carrillo, "Theater Etiquette Pet Peeve?"
34. Carrillo, "Theater Etiquette Conundrum: Phone Off or On Vibrate?"
35. Carrillo, "Theater Etiquette Conundrum: Are Photos Ok?"
36. Carrillo, "Theater Etiquette Pet Peeve?"
37. Carrillo, "Theater Etiquette Conundrum: Obey House Rules?"
38. There is less agreement over whether or not using a cell phone during a rock concert is rude, presumably because the noise levels and level of participation manifest themselves differently than at an orchestra performance.
39. According to the Goldstar survey, 89% of their respondents view texting or tweeting during a performance to be unacceptable. (To be very clear: the author always turns her phone off when attending live theatre performances.) Carrillo, "Theater Etiquette Conundrum: Phone Off or On Vibrate?" In the United Kingdom, a 2013 Ticketmaster survey revealed that 29% of those surveyed checked their phone while at a performance, while only 8% viewed such behavior as acceptable; only 4% used social media during a performance. "Theatre Code of Conduct."
40. Hassoun, "Engaging Distractions," 93.
41. As heard by the author when attending an evening performance of *War Paint* on 12 July 2016.
42. The term "silent" here is relative to the activity of holding an oral conversation on the cell phone; depending on how the user sets her/his preferences on a cell phone, texting can involve phone-generated typing sounds or be completely silent.
43. Heim, *Audience as Performer*, 102, 117–118.
44. Sophie Gilbert, "Can Benedict Cumberbatch Save Theater from Cellphones?"

45. Ellipses/pauses in original text. Quoted in Viagas, "Audience Member Tries to Use Stage Outlet to Charge Phone,"
46. Simonson, "In Case You Missed It."
47. Indeed, as alluded to throughout this chapter, a problem with writing about "bad" audience behaviors is the source material available to researchers.
48. Divabehavior, "Patti Lupone stops 'Gypsy' mid-show." The two minute, 43s recording has over a half million views.
49. Itzkoff, "Another Show-Stopping Moment."
50. Itzkoff, "Rose's Turn."
51. Gioia, "AT&T Advertisements, Promoting Phone Use in the Theatre, Continue."
52. Clement, "Are *Avenue Q*'s Bad Idea Bears Behind the Controversial AT&T Ads?"
53. Schechner, *Environmental Theatre*, 40.
54. Schechner, *Environmental Theatre*, 45.
55. "Cell Phones and Theatre Etiquette."
56. Thomas, "Theatre in a Mobile World"; Brantley, "Review: 'Privacy.'"
57. See Swift, "What do Audiences Do? Negotiating the Possible Worlds of Participatory Theatre," *Journal of Contemporary Drama in English*.
58. There are of course many musicals that work to minimize the gaps between song, dance, and narrative. However, as Scott McMillin argues, American musicals as a genre depend on the pleasures found within these gaps and differences. McMillin, *The Musical as Drama*.
59. "Engagement" is defined as "the extent to which one attends to and is immersed in the experience itself": Diehl, Barasch, and Zauberman, "How Taking Photos Increases Enjoyment of Experiences," 120.
60. Diehl, Barasch, and Zauberman, "How Taking Photos Increases Enjoyment of Experiences," 120, emphasis in the original. The study did not address what the impact of taking photos was on those in the vicinity of the amateur photographer, however.

Bibliography

Brantley, Ben. "Review: 'Privacy,' a Play That Urges You to Keep Your Smartphone On." *New York Times* (July 18, 2016), http://www.nytimes.com/2016/07/19/theater/review-privacy-a-play-that-urges-you-to-keep-your-smartphone-on.html.

Burland, Karen, and Stephanie Pitts. "Prelude." In *Coughing and Clapping: Investigating Audience Experience*, edited by Burland and Pitts, 1–6. New York: Routledge, 2014.

Campbell, Scott. "Perceptions of Cell Phone Use in Public: The Roles of Individualism, Collectivism, and the Focus of the Setting." *Communication Reports* 21, no. 2 (2008): 70–81.

Carrillo, Sarah. "Theater Etiquette Pet Peeve?" (July 8, 2015), http://sellingout.com/whats-the-biggest-theater-etiquette-pet-peeve/.

———. "Theater Etiquette Conundrum: Phone Off or On Vibrate?" (July 15, 2015), http://sellingout.com/theater-etiquette-conundrum-phone-off-or-on-vibrate/.

———. "Theater Etiquette Conundrum: Obey House Rules?" (July 29, 2015), http://sellingout.com/theater-etiquette-conundrum-obey-house-rules/.

"Cell Phones and Theatre Etiquette" (September 3, 2015), https://storify.com/howlround/cell-phones-theatre-e.

Clement, Olivia. "Are *Avenue Q*'s Bad Idea Bears Behind the Controversial AT&T Ads?" *Playbill Online* (October 5, 2015), http://www.playbill.com/article/are-avenue-qs-bad-idea-bears-behind-the-controversial-at-t-ads-com-365815.

David Savran, Broadway as Global Brand. Journal of Contemporary Drama in English 5 (1).

de Souza e Silva, Adriana. "Interfaces of Hybrid Spaces." In *The Cell Phone Reader: Essays in Social Transformation*, edited by Anandam P. Kavoori and Noah Arceneaux, 19–44. New York: Peter Lang Publishing, 2006.

Diehl, Kristin, Alixandra Barasch, and Gal Zauberman. "How Taking Photos Increases Enjoyment of Experiences." *Journal of Personality and Social Psychology* 111, no. 2 (2016): 119–40.

Divabehavior, "Patti Lupone stops 'Gypsy' mid-show to yell at a photographer" (October 11, 2009), https://youtu.be/WruzPfJ9Rys.

Forlano, Laura. "Cell Phone Ban." *Gotham Gazette* (February 28, 2003), http://www.gothamgazette.com/index.php/open-government/1733-cell-phone-ban.

Gans, Andrew. "Stanley Stucci Admonishes Audience During Aug. 14 *Frankie and Johnny* Performance" *Playbill Online* (August 15, 2002), http://www.playbill.com/article/stanley-tucci-admonishes-audience-during-aug-14-frankie-johnny-performance-com-107695.

Gilbert, Sophie. "Can Benedict Cumberbatch Save Theater from Cellphones?" *The Atlantic* (August 11, 2015), http://www.theatlantic.com/entertainment/archive/2015/08/can-benedict-cumberbatch-save-theater-from-cellphones/401042/.

Gioia, Michael. "AT&T Advertisements, Promoting Phone Use in the Theatre, Continue; Watch the Video." *Playbill Online* (September 21, 2015), http://www.playbill.com/article/at-t-advertisements-promoting-phone-use-in-the-theatre-continue-watch-the-video-com-363330.

Goldman, John J. "NYC Votes to Curb Annoying Use of Cell Phones." *Los Angeles Times* (February 13, 2003), http://articles.latimes.com/2003/feb/13/nation/na-cellban13.

Hanson, Jarice. *24/7: How Cell Phones and the Internet Change the Way We Live, Work, and Play*. Westport, CT: Praeger, 2007.

Hassoun, Dan. "Engaging Distractions: Regulating Second-Screen Use in the Theatre." *Cinema Journal* 55, no. 2 (2016): 89–111.

Heim, Caroline. *Audience as Performer: The Changing Role of Theatre Audiences in the Twenty-First Century*. New York, Routledge, 2016.

Itzkoff, Dave. "Another Show-Stopping Moment (Not the Good Kind) From Patti LuPone." *New York Times* ArtsBeat online (June 22, 2009), http://artsbeat.blogs.nytimes.com/2009/06/22/another-show-stopping-moment-not-the-good-kind-from-patti-lupone/.

———. "Rose's Turn: Patti LuPone Responds to ArtsBeat." *New York Times* ArtsBeat online (June 23, 2009), http://artsbeat.blogs.nytimes.com/2009/06/23/roses-turn-patti-lupone-responds-to-artsbeat/.

Katz, James, and Jing Wang. "Cell Phone Culture." *MIT Communications Forum* (November 17, 2005), http://web.mit.edu/comm-forum/forums/cell_phone_culture.htm.

Law, Alex, Wallace McNeish, and Linda Gray. "Base Station Fears: The Paradox of Mobile Geography." *Geography* 88, no. 4 (2003): 320–30.

Levine, Lawrence. *Highbrow/Lowbrow: The Emergence of Cultural Hierarchy in America*. Cambridge: Harvard University Press, 1988.

Lewis, Peter H. "Smaller, Lighter, Stronger, Cheaper." *New York Times* online edition (July 21, 1992), http://www.nytimes.com/1992/07/21/science/personal-computers-smaller-lighter-stronger-cheaper.html.

Louie, Elaine. "If the Phone Had a Cord, You Could Strangle the User." *New York Times* (September 30, 1999), http://www.nytimes.com/1999/09/30/garden/design-notebook-if-the-phone-had-a-cord-you-could-strangle-the-user.html.

MacDonald, Laura. "The Sound of Musicals in China," *American Theatre*, (April 25, 2017), http://www.americantheatre.org/2017/04/25/the-sound-of-musicals-in-china/.

MacDonald, Laura and William Everett, ed. The Palgrave Handbook of Musical Theatre Producers. London: Palgrave MacMillan, 2017.

McKinley, Jesse and Nichole M. Christian. "Hark, Hark, That Tweet is No Lark. It's Illegal," *New York Times* (February 13, 2003), http://www.nytimes.com/2003/02/13/nyregion/hark-hark-that-tweet-is-no-lark-it-s-illegal.html.

McMillin, Scott. The Musical as Drama. Princeton: Princeton University Press, 2007.

Middlekauff, Tracey and Josh Brustein. "Issue of the Week: Cell Phones." *Gotham Gazette* (October 21, 2002), http://www.gothamgazette.com/iotw/cellphones/.

"Mobile Technology Fact Sheet." (December 27, 2013; updated, December 2014), http://www.pewinternet.org/fact-sheets/mobile-technology-fact-sheet/.

Myerson, George. *Heidegger, Habermas and the Mobile Phone.* London: Icon Books, 2001.
Neal, Rome. "Cell Phone Battle Turns Bitter" (August 6, 2003), http://www.cbsnews.com/news/cell-phone-battle-turns-bitter/.
Nickerson, Robert C., Henri Isaac, and Brenda Mak. "A multi-national study of attitudes about mobile phone use in social settings." *International Journal of Mobile Communications* 6, no. 5 (2008): 541–63.
Pinchot, Jamie, Karen Paullet, and Daniel Rota. "How Mobile Technology is Changing Our Culture." *Journal of Information Systems Applied Research* 3, no. 1519. (April 2011): 1–10.
Rainie, Lee, and Kathryn Zickurh. "Americans' Views on Cell Phone Etiquette" (August 26, 2015), http://www.pewinternet.org/2015/08/26/chapter-3-when-it-is-acceptable-or-not-to-use-cellphones-in-public-spaces/.
Rebellato, Dan. "Booing," *Contemporary Theatre Review*, 23, no. 1. (February 2013): 10–15.
———. *Theatre and Globalization.* London: Palgrave Macmillan, 2009.
Reeves, Hope. "Despite Cellphone Ban in Theaters, Dialing Continues." *New York Times* (September 13, 2004), http://www.nytimes.com/2004/09/13/nyregion/despite-cellphone-ban-in-theaters-dialing-continues.html.
Samuel, Alicia. "Let it Ring One More Time! Turn off Your Damn Cell Phone" (May 26, 2016), http://broadwayblack.com/turn-off-your-damn-phone/.
Schechner, Richard. *Environmental Theatre.* 2nd ed. New York: Applause Books, 1994.
Schulze, Daniel. "The Passive Gaze and Hyper-Immunized Spectators: The Politics of Theatrical Live Broadcasting" *Journal of Contemporary Drama in English* 3, no. 2 (November 2015): 315–326.
Simonson, Robert. "Things that go Chirp in the Night." *Playbill Online* (February 2, 2007), http://www.playbill.com/article/things-that-go-chirp-in-the-night-com-138150.
———. "In Case You Missed It: Did Something Happen with a Cell Phone?" *Playbill Online* (July 10, 2015), http://www.playbill.com/article/in-case-you-missed-it-did-something-happen-with-a-cell-phone-com-353059.
Swift, Elizabeth. "What do Audiences Do? Negotiating the Possible Worlds of Participatory Theatre," *Journal of Contemporary Drama in English* 4, no. 1. (May 2016): 134–149.
Thomas, Kyle A. "Theatre in a Mobile World: Critiquing Convention and Calling for Innovation" (June 3, 2015), http://howlround.com/theatre-in-a-mobile-world-critiquing-convention-and-calling-for-innovation.
Thomson, Kristin, Kristen Purcell, and Lee Rainie. "Arts Organizations and Digital Technologies" (January 4, 2013), http://www.pewinternet.org/2013/01/04/section-6-overall-impact-of-technology-on-the-arts/.

Viagas, Robert. "Audience Member Tries to Use Stage Outlet to Charge Phone at *Hand to God*." *Playbill Online* (July 6, 2015), http://www.playbill.com/article/audience-member-tries-to-use-stage-outlet-to-charge-phone-at-hand-to-god-com-352658.

Wallis, David. "Noises Off: A Muzzle for Cell Phones." *New York Times* (April 11, 1999), http://www.nytimes.com/1999/04/11/business/business-noises-off-a-muzzle-for-cell-phones.htm.

Wolf, Stacy. "Musical Theatre Studies," *The Journal of American Drama and Theatre* 28, no 1 (Winter 2016): http://jadtjournal.org/2016/03/23/musical-theatre-studies.

———. "Theater Etiquette Conundrum: Are Photos Ok?" (July 23, 2015), https://sellingout.com/theater-etiquette-conundrum-are-photos-ok/.

CHAPTER 6

Digital Fandom: *Hamilton* and the Participatory Spectator

Jessica Hillman-McCord

Michelle Obama called *Hamilton* (Lin-Manuel Miranda's hip hop musical biography of the nation's first treasury secretary, Alexander Hamilton), "the best piece of art in any form that I have ever seen in my life."[1] (Then President-elect Trump, in the exception that proves the rule, called it "overrated"). The initial critical reception was unendingly and unanimously thrilled. "Yes, it really is that good," opened Ben Brantley's *New York Times* review.[2] The show was nominated for a record number of Tony Awards and won eleven. From Beyoncé to Lynne Cheney, Oprah to Eli Manning, Julia Roberts to Eminem, seemingly every major celebrity from politics, Hollywood, and the popular music world attended the show and offered subsequent superlatives on social media. Tickets are still difficult to obtain, and their price breaks records. Productions are set to open across the country, and eventually the world. Upon its release, the companion book, *Hamilton: The Revolution*, hit the *New York Times* Best Seller list and was on back order with most retailers. The Original Cast Recording won a Grammy award

---

J. Hillman-McCord (✉)
Department of Theatre and Dance, State University of New York at Fredonia, Fredonia, NY, USA
e-mail: hillmanm@fredonia.edu

and was the first cast album to ever hit number one on the rap charts. The recorded spin-off into *The Hamilton Mixtape*, with diverse artists from Kelly Clarkson to Busta Rhymes paying tribute to the score, debuted as number one on Billboard's Top 200 albums. Clearly, the unprecedented scale of the *Hamilton* phenomenon has "smash[ed] expectations"[3] artistically and at the box office, forcing the show out of the musical theatre bubble and into mainstream culture. But even for a musical about the founding fathers, *Hamilton*'s digital presence may stand as its most revolutionary element.

There are two audiences for *Hamilton*: those who have managed to score live tickets to the Broadway production,[4] and the much larger fan audience, who get their fix online. For its dedicated fans, *Hamilton*'s digital life offers an integral and inseparable part of the experience. The self-named "Hamiltrash," "Hamilfans," or "Faniltons" express themselves on numerous platforms: Twitter, Tumblr, Genius, Snapchat, YouTube, and more. Some create their own "fan culture," some merely observe. Either way, *Hamilton*'s followers exercise a unique and constantly unfolding relationship with the musical's text, cast, and creative team. Although passionate online fans are not unique to *Hamilton*, several elements of that phenomenon are particularly compelling, and perhaps indicative of the future of Broadway fandom.

In what ways do musical theatre fans differ from much-studied television or media fans? What kinds of responses to their fandom do they share online and why? How do they form digital communities, and how do those communities function? Are fans in control of, or controlled by, the media interests that surround their object of fandom? What better way to address these fascinating and complicated issues than by looking at the most monumentally loved musical sensation to hit Broadway in at least twenty years? The study of *Hamilton* has much to reveal to us in multiple spheres: music, theatre, and American history not least among them, but the show also uniquely demonstrates how musical theatre fandom may function in our digital culture. The Internet's potential for interactivity has not only intensified the kind of personalization process fans have always had with musicals, but has also fundamentally altered that relationship, enabling a new, postmodern presence through interaction and participation in a mediatized community. *Hamilton*'s digital footprint can reveal how and why fans love a particular musical, granting musical theatre new life and leading the form fully into the twenty-first century.

History of Fan Studies

In order to put *Hamilton*'s fan phenomenon into perspective we first need to examine trends in fan studies scholarship. Many early fan studies scholars focused on the fan relationship as a defense against an oppressive culture at large, including implications of fandom as pathology, and fan cultures as "othered," isolated groups. This traditional model implied "weird," over-invested, or obsessive fans. Over the decades that scholars have examined fans, their portrayal has shifted from hysterical, psychologically imbalanced victims of mass culture, to Henry Jenkins' pioneering perspective in the early 1990s of fans as "textual poachers" who subvert larger media forces by claiming and reusing media elements for their own purposes. Jenkins used the example of "Trekkies," who took elements from *Star Trek* and built their own narratives, taking ownership and sometimes even subverting the intent of the original object. Scholars Gray and Sandvoss term this movement, "first stage reclamation," or "fandom is beautiful."[5] In the subsequent social media age where fandom has been mainstreamed, normalized, and embraced by commercial interests, scholars began to reexamine the textual poaching model, pointing out that popular culture acceptance does not necessarily offer uncomplicated emancipation. Recent fandom scholars explore numerous new angles, including the reclamation of celebrity studies, examinations of the silent, non-participatory fan, embrace of psychoanalytical approaches, global versus local fan communities, and the rise of spectacle and performance in fan consumption.

The social media era has changed the traditional distinction between fans and "normal" media consumers. In fact, according to Sandvoss, "the affective attachments of fans reflected in their productivity are at the heart of the digitally driven rise of participatory culture."[6] Scholars are beginning to recognize that fans, rather than being belittled or isolated, are now embraced and courted by media forces. Producers have realized that fan communities are in fact extremely powerful. They therefore have set out to make their products as exciting and palatable to those fans as possible. This is certainly true of musical theatre, where producers now aim to nurture and encourage fans. As Laura MacDonald examines in Chap. 2 of this book, today's theatre producers, worried about the graying of the Broadway audience, are trying to reach the so-called media-active generation. Broadway marketers struggling to reach these young audiences are increasingly turning to new media, particularly the Internet, and are utilizing interactivity to create a new fan relationship. Web interactivity not only alters how producers reach audiences, but also how audiences' interact with live events.

Participatory Fandom

Musical theatre has historically evoked intense fandom. However, musical theatre scholars have only just begun to redress the imbalance in fan studies scholarship. For while cultural studies research regarding television, film, and music continues to proliferate, the field has largely excluded the Broadway musical fan dynamic, an absence that should be redressed.[7] Musicals create obsessive and active fans. Their numbers may be smaller, but their passion burns just as hot as any *Star Trek* or *Twilight* fan. Many of these fans are young, and have grown up with different expectations of what fandom can bring them in the digital world.

Henry Jenkins coined the term "convergence culture," which describes the changing relationship and interdependence between forms of media. This shifting dynamic vastly impacts the fan relationship. As Jenkins states, "rather than talking about media producers and consumers as occupying separate roles, we might now see them as participants who interact with each other according to a new set of rules that none of us fully understands."[8] While the traditional relationship between fan and Broadway musical has always been highly personal, new media complicates the process. D. A. Miller's book, *Place for Us* details the intersection of his obsession with musicals and his gay identity.[9] In a section entitled "In the Basement," he points out that cast albums used to be the central objects offering connection to the ephemeral Broadway experience. Worship of these albums (listening to them repeatedly in your parents' basement, playing all the roles) offered an important ritual of musical fandom. The impulse that created this love of cast albums (and still does) has exploded into diverse outlets for expression in our mediatized culture.

The musical theatre fan now has multiple sources to feed their love and obsession. According to Amy Jensen, interactions between audience and media forms, most specifically the Internet, "place the virtual spectator at the center of the theatrical narrative, which extends beyond the world of the play into the world surrounding the performance."[10] She argues that this new relationship can "alter the dynamic between the audience, the performers, and the text."[11] Now fans can feel part of the process, not just through singing along to cast albums in the basement alone, as Miller describes, but by joining a knowledge-intensive community online. The Internet extends the fan community's reach, both laterally (fans with each other) and vertically (fans with the artists). Through constant media exposure, a modern type of spectator, whom Jensen names the participatory spectator, "has learned to advance theatrical narratives beyond the threshold of the theatre space into their own private space."[12] These interactions occur in myriad, increasingly active, and complicated ways.

Hamilton Phenomenon

In order to examine these new digital relationships, we will turn to the most currently active and intense online musical fandom, for Lin-Manuel Miranda's *Hamilton*. The confluence of new media has allowed *Hamilton* to be a modern kind of smash hit. As David Korins, its set designer points out: "It's the first social media show. It's put theatre at the heart of pop culture conversation and all media conversation. It's already reached a level of fame and recognition that *Rent* took 15 years to reach."[13] Fan scholar Paul Booth argues, "to engage a fannish audience, a text needs to be both familiar and novel at once; it must both surprise and appease."[14] *Hamilton*'s unique blend of hip hop, reenvisioned history, and more traditional musical theatre offers a potent example of this principle.

Hamilton has been a digital phenomenon from the very beginning. An article in *Vogue* points out, "the magical combination of founding fathers and Jay Z references makes *Hamilton* infinitely Internet-y, memeable, and practically unavoidable."[15] The first we heard of *Hamilton* was a viral video of Lin-Manuel Miranda, its creator and star, performing the opening number as part of a celebration of the spoken word at the White House on May 12, 2009. The video, posted six months later on YouTube, has been a viral sensation ever since, with over 4.2 million views as of this writing. As Ron Chernow (who wrote the biography of Alexander Hamilton which inspired Miranda) states in an interview for this chapter, "it's an interesting fact that this show first hit the public … via the Internet before anyone had actually gotten to see it so that people already felt a personal connection to [Miranda] and the material."[16] After various readings, concerts, workshops, and an extended

Off-Broadway run at the Public Theatre increased the hype surrounding the show, *Hamilton* moved to Broadway, opening on August 6, 2015. During the early Broadway run, *Hamilton*'s digital presence continued with #Ham4Ham shows (short snippets of performances from the cast and guests to entertain entrants for the $10 front row seat lottery), with videos widely shared online. After the crowds packing the streets outside the Richard Rodgers Theatre for the live shows became overwhelming and a threat to public safety, Miranda moved the lottery to a digital format, where at first the sheer number of entrants online crashed the server for a day. While security measures were reevaluated, digital #Ham4Ham shows were offered. Eventually the live performances were brought back once a week, which, after Miranda left the show, were briefly hosted by another cast member, Rory O'Malley. While the live shows have ended, occasional digital shows are still offered, including a large-scale concert for the album release of *The Hamilton Mixtape* (which includes covers and tributes to the score by popular artists such as Busta Rhymes, John Legend, and Sia). The #Ham4Ham format proved so revolutionary that the 2016 Tony Awards used the model for its telecast, bringing the casts of the nominated shows outside the Beacon Theatre for brief performances in front of an assembled crowd.

Together with the cast album, *Hamilton*'s massive digital presence extends the reach of what could otherwise be a more localized experience. As Chernow points out: "Broadway by definition is a more local phenomenon because you actually have to be in New York to see it, but I've been struck from the very beginning and I think this is because of Lin and social media, this has been a national and even an international event in a way which is quite incredible."[17] The #Ham4Ham phenomenon is only the tip of the iceberg for *Hamilton*'s online fan experience, which celebrates extensive fan culture contributions and community-forming interactions.

Fan Culture

Jenkins introduces the idea of "transmedia storytelling," where, "to fully experience any fictional world, consumers must assume the role of hunters and gatherers, chasing down bits of the story across media channels."[18] There are numerous sites a *Hamilton* fan must include in their hunting and gathering, including microblogs like Twitter, Tumblr, Instagram, Snapchat, and Facebook, YouTube for video content, and websites like Broadway.com, Playbill.com, or, more unique to this show, Genius.com, a site for hip hop lyric analysis. *Hamilton* fans can find endless means of satisfying their curiosity and devotion online. There they can investigate original fan fiction (including various stories about Alexander Hamilton in modern day high school), animated storyboards illustrating songs from the show, pen and ink drawings of the characters in a boxing ring, even dioramas of key moments in the show made from Legos and Easter eggs. They can purchase merchandise, from bobble heads, to T-shirts, to earrings. They can enjoy video compilations of *Star Wars* or *Batman* intercut with *Hamilton*'s lyrics. They can even find images of founding fathers pouring wax on each other as foreplay or read erotic takes on various character combinations. The digital world is the place for fans who want to create and share these kinds of responses with thousands of other fans, and, if they are lucky enough to break through the noise, with Lin-Manuel Miranda and the rest of the cast and crew.

Jenkins defines "fan culture" as "culture that is produced by fans and other amateurs for circulation through an underground economy and that draws much of its content from the commercial culture."[19] Producing fan culture offers one type of participatory spectatorship. When Jenkins initially investigated these ideas, fan culture primarily existed in this "underground economy" he mentions. The Internet has exploded any notion of "underground." Musical theatre fans increasingly create their own work, and can now, thanks to new technologies, easily share that work publically. The 2005 Pew Internet and American Life Project points out that "more than half of American teens—and 57% of teens who use the Internet—could be considered media creators."[20] These teens, as well as older fans, are being drawn to Internet communities as the best place to get their work in front of audiences. Usually fans' work supports, draws inspiration from, or exists within the parameters of the original object. As Paul Booth states when discussing "media play," "individuals create meaning from activities that articulate a connection between their own creativity and mainstream media, all the while working within the boundaries of the media text."[21] Even work that criticizes the original text tends to exist within these boundaries. Examples of fan culture fall into numerous categories, including fan fiction, fan art, videos, and crossovers. Each of these categories deserves intensive individual future analysis. In the context of this short chapter we will introduce them as part of a larger trend of community creation.

Fanfic

"Fanfic," short for fan fiction, offers a central outlet for media play, and recent examples have crossed over into the mainstream, such as the publishing juggernaut *Fifty Shades of Gray*, which began as *Twilight* fanfic. Before examining *Hamilton* fan fiction in detail, it's worth pointing out an argument made by Aja Romano in *Vox Culture*, in response to criticism about *Hamilton*'s historical accuracy. She comments that, "in essence, *Hamilton* is a postmodern metatextual piece of fanfic, functioning in precisely the way that most fanfics do: It reclaims the canon for the fan."[22] She points out that *Hamilton* utilizes alternate universes (AUs), racebending, and crossover, among other fanfic techniques, to reclaim the canon of American history. We should note that fans are utilizing similar tactics in response to Miranda's text that he himself makes use of in response to the larger historical canon.

The subjects of *Hamilton* fanfic range from Alexander Hamilton in modern high school (often taking part in school governance), other characters' points of view during events of the musical, (for example, Angelica Schuyler's during the Reynolds Pamphlet scandal), other events in Hamilton's life story not portrayed in the musical (for example, his life in the Virgin Islands before his immigration to America), and quite a bit of romantic and/or sexual writing on various pairings of characters, including, most prominently, Hamilton and John Laurens.

This brings us to another element of fandom: "shipping" or "slashing." A popular term emerging from TV scholarship, shipping involves rooting for a romantic and/or sexual relationship between two characters that may not already be paired in the original text. Slashing does the same thing for same sex couples. While this kind of activity could certainly be part of a text's reception before the digital revolution,[23] the Internet facilitates and magnifies this process, forming community through shared interests. John Laurens and Hamilton are the most popular slashed couple in *Hamilton*. Fans also ship actor pairings, and many *Hamilton* fans spend time online slashing Miranda and Jonathan Groff, the actor who originated the role of King George III on Broadway. Despite Miranda's marriage to a woman, the actors implicitly and explicitly encourage this activity; for example, Miranda posted a Vine of him kissing Groff, stating, "the Internet told me to give you this for your birthday."[24] Scholars, including Kristina Busse and Elizabeth Woledge, often credit this devotion to slashing characters as part of the sexual identity formation of the devoted fan.[25] Additional fan scholars often cite slashing as an act of fan resistance, in the mode of Henry Jenkins' textual poachers. In traditional models, slashing same sex couples subverts the heteronormative stance of the text. Interestingly however, due to the embrace of homosexuality in the musical theatre community, and to Miranda's pointed personal acceptance,[26] he affirms fans that slash *Hamilton* characters. For instance, Miranda confirmed to a fan that the line "Laurens I like you a lot,"[27] was a reference to the historical possibility of a Laurens/Hamilton romance. In *Hamilton: The Revolution*, Miranda states, "it is possible that Hamilton and Laurens were lovers at some point—Hamilton's letters to Laurens are every bit as flirtatious as his letters to the opposite sex, if not more so."[28] This historical evidence that there may have been a romantic connection between the two men adds fuel to the slashing fire. As Ron Chernow observed, "that's interesting that Lin would engage in that kind of speculation online with people because usually someone who writes lyrics or poetry [...] they let the lyrics or poems speak for themselves, or let the fans interpret them, but Lin jumps in feet first."[29] Rather than resistance to the fan object, *Hamilton* slashers need not work too hard to subvert their surface text to find the kind of connection they seek.

Fan Art

Hamilton fan art ranges vastly in medium and quality. From professional level pen and ink or charcoal drawings to refrigerator magnets, the range is impressively wide. Professional artists take part, but many are amateur. Images of cast members and characters appear in every medium and are posted on every possible surface, from T-shirts to clay ornaments to digital memes. The art is generally shared online on various social media sites, and often gifted to the cast, either digitally, or through physical delivery to the stage door. Sometimes the artists offer their work as a free gift to the fan community and sometimes they commercialize it, via a site like Etsy. Fans frequently comment on a fan art post, asking where they can acquire or buy a copy of a piece they admire. A large economy of art circulates through this community, seemingly without end.

The ultimate expression of the *Hamilton* fan art community occurred when the artist Arielle Jovellanos brought together forty-five artists to illustrate each of the tracks of the score. She printed limited edition art books of this collection as gifts for the cast/crew. Though numerous fans quickly asked to buy the book, christened the #ham4pamphlet, it was not for sale, although it was widely shared online. Lin-Manuel Miranda tweeted his gratitude in response. Miranda and other cast members regularly acknowledge strong examples of fan art by posting them to their Twitter, Tumblr, or Instagram feeds. Official media sites, like Broadway.com or the *Hamilton* official Twitter and Tumblr pages, highlight their favorite examples by resharing the posts. A fan inscribed all Hamilton's words in the show onto fifteen feet of parchment and Miranda tweeted a picture of himself wearing it as a scarf. A wall backstage at the Richard Rodgers Theatre displays examples and echoes gratitude for fan art,[30] and various cast members thank fan artists on social media and display their work in their dressing rooms. While private accomplishment may be a motivation for creation of fan art, the potential for this kind of reciprocal relationship with the cast and creative team clearly helps to motivate its production, although many fan artists may not reach such heights and hope only for the approbation of other fans. I examine this aspirational attempt to connect to Miranda, the cast, and crew in other work.[31]

Digital Videos

Video responses to *Hamilton* cover the gamut and include animated YouTube video storyboards of individual songs, video compilations of songs with lyrics and images timed to the music, and "nightcoring" videos with the songs sped up and put to techno beats. The videos also include an entire subset of small children of fans (new fans themselves) singing lyrics from the show. Live fan events also produce digital remains. For example, although the #Ham4Ham ticket lottery was at first a weekly live event, its digital presence, shared via social media, extended globally. Additionally, many videos and live digital feeds broadened the reach of the first two BroadwayCon conferences. These fan events incorporate all Broadway shows and encourage attendees to dress up in tribute to their favorite shows (called cosplay).[32] The conferences also offered fans the opportunity to buy souvenirs, get autographs, and meet stars, and held live panels on major shows. In addition to the digital elements incorporated by the conference planners (surveys, opportunities to send questions), fans widely watched videos of the panels on YouTube and Playbill.com, viewing a video of a spontaneous *Hamilton* sing-along before the cast's first live panel over 11,000 times. During the panel, *Hamilton* stars pointed to the immediate power of their online fans, for example when Daveed Diggs told Tumblr fans to quickly research the esoteric facts of his casual mention of Thomas Jefferson's complex feelings towards dogs. Diggs knew that hundreds of fans would quickly jump to satisfy any request, no matter how specific.[33]

Videos of fan experiences at the stage door and breathless reviews of or responses to the show also often appear on YouTube. One series of such responses to the show is from "Jonaalmostfamous," or Jona Bolander, an emerging YouTube personality with over 48,000 followers, who, with her friend Elise, has posted a series of twenty-eight videos (so far) in response to the show. In an interview for this chapter Bolander states:

> The *Hamilton* fandom is very active on social media. I would see fan art on Tumblr and be completely blown away by it. I wanted to contribute to the fandom in a creative way. ... There is so much to explore in this community. The creativity I see from *Hamilton* fans is inspiring and something I hope continues for years to come.[34]

Bolander presents a telling example of the kind of reciprocal relationship fans hope for when they share their art/fiction/video responses: Lin-Manuel Miranda retweeted one of her videos (which climbed to over half a million views in response) and when she and her friend travelled to visit the stage door, Miranda told them he came out that night especially to meet them. This conversation was of course captured and shared in one of Bolander's videos.[35] I explore the two-way relationship with celebrity/fan objects enabled by the Internet in more depth in other work; here we should point out that hope for acknowledgement from the object of fandom is a crucial and integral part of fan exchange.

Crossovers

Paul Booth coined the term "fan pastiche" to describe a subset of fan culture where fans, "amalgamat[e] multiple texts into one."[36] More popularly termed fan "mashups," or "crossovers," they are particularly popular in *Hamilton* fan culture, utilizing a wide range of media texts. *Star Wars: The Force Awakens* was released in 2015, the same year *Hamilton* opened, and the *Star Wars* universe offers a particularly potent source of mashup fan memes and videos. Full Tumblr sites are devoted to memes and GIFs comparing the texts and linking characters, under the hashtag #Force4Ham. Several video mashups of *Hamilton*'s opening number "Alexander Hamilton," have ranged from *Star Wars* ("Luke the Son of Anakin") to other objects of fan culture such as *Batman* ("Batlexander Manilton"). The same song has also served the purpose of political satire of everyone from Germany's Angela Merkel to Donald Trump. *Harry Potter* mashups are also incredibly popular, and a debate on multiple platforms sorting the *Hamilton* characters into one of the four Hogwarts school houses culminated in Emma Watson (who played Hermione in the films) interviewing Miranda online and making the ultimate "Sorting Hat" judgment. Miranda has demonstrated that he follows and delights in these mashups, and started some himself, as when he tweeted a quote from *Hamilton* with a picture of Jon Snow from the television series *Games of Thrones* and asked "#HasThisBeenDone?" He also led fans in cross references that do not mention *Hamilton*, such as a lengthy mashup of hip hop artist Jay Z references mixed with *Les Misérables*, with the attendant hashtag #jaymiz.

Community

Fan culture, in the form of fan art, fanfic, mashups, and the rest of the abovementioned work, is made by a small percentage of fans actively engaged in creating content. It is important to note, however, that this small percentage of users account for over 80% of the content, with a second group only occasionally posting. The large majority of fans silently read or take in fan culture without commenting or making their own content.[37] This creates some debate and discrepancy over what exactly defines a fan. Does "fan" mean someone who actively takes part in contributing to fan culture, or does it include much larger and more silent groups? In our current culture being a fan has been normalized, while certain fan behaviors, like creating fan culture, remain, at least partly, pathologized. The silent, less active majority may not wish to feel negatively categorized, and may not therefore feel fully a part of the community discussed by fan studies scholars.[38]

For those fans who do create, as well as those who may more silently take in others' work, fan culture engenders more than individual satisfaction; it also creates community.[39] Paul Booth states, "fans use digital technology not only to create, to change, to appropriate, to poach, or to write, but also to share, to experience together, to become alive with community."[40] Through creating or viewing fan culture, fans feel like active participants in a community. As Nancy Baym argues, "fandom is generally defined as an intrinsically social phenomenon in which a person becomes a fan, in part, for the social connections or community that fandom entails."[41] Becoming a fan alone does not offer the full range of experiences that a fan community grants. In the case of musical theatre, the Internet offers a virtual community to the isolated fans Miller describes, who used to listen to show tunes alone in the basement. The Internet offers the confirmation that individuals are not alone in their fandom. The cast album still inspires obsessive and repeated listening, but now fans can channel their devotion into a community of like-minded lovers, to satisfy and magnify it there.

Fan communities are not single monolithic entities. Each fan community will have its own set of priorities and skills and also its own set of values and moral judgments. Scholar Cheryl Harris outlines a definition of fandom that highlights the importance of community formation:

> Fandom is reconceptualized as a spectrum of practices engaged in to develop a sense of personal control or influence over the object of fandom (such as a star or text), in which the outcome of one's involvement is not as important as the involvement itself—recognized membership and interaction centering around a common object.[42]

In other words, the community itself may hold more value than the object the community forms around. As Bonanos states in *Vulture*, "social media is great at uniting groups with deep shared enthusiasms who are geographically scattered."[43] This global community together performs the "hunter/gatherer" tasks Jenkins referenced earlier. Although *Hamilton* holds vast power in this moment of intense and widespread acclaim, the community created by its fans may ultimately supplant its power as a text.

Features of Fan Community

Fan communities encompass a whole world of interactions centered on the object of fandom. We can note a few salient features of the *Hamilton* fandom here, in order to serve as an example of the way musical theatre fandom functions in the digital age. The Internet community offers, among other rewards, the pleasure of recognition of one's expertise, or "intensive knowledge," defined by James Gee as "the knowledge each individual brings into an affinity space or knowledge community."[44] Certainly intensive knowledge has been a traditional feature of musical theatre fan culture before the advent of the Internet. Insider information and encyclopedic knowledge of a particular show, including its history, cast members, various recordings, and author biographies, have always been privileged by intensive fans. Online, fans value, display, and most importantly, *perform* this knowledge. Booth describes fan hierarchies, pointing out that those at the top often display intensive knowledge:

> To know the most arcane details from the extant media object … is to be intimately tied with the object of devotion. Fans that can "quote whole sections" of a narrative are thus positioned higher on that hierarchy.[45]

Hamilton fans prize highly specialized information and intensive knowledge of the full world of this particular show: its score, its history, its cast dynamics, and the personal life of its author/star. Fans on multiple online platforms, among them Twitter, Tumblr, Instagram, YouTube, and Snapchat, glory in their privileged knowledge, sharply defining their community by who knows what, and how much they know. For instance, Miranda tweeted a story about a woman who yelled at him on the street on the day of the Off-Broadway opening, "Congratulations on *Hamlet*!" And when he answered that he did not, in fact, write *Hamlet*, she replied, "Yay *Hamlet*!" This has become one of the most popular "inside" jokes for fans of the show: the #yayhamlet hashtag is incredibly popular. As of January 1, 2017 the original tweet has been "liked" 222,225 times and retweeted 61,159 times on Twitter, and limited edition #yayhamlet T-shirts sold out almost immediately when they were introduced into the merchandizing for the show. As Miranda stated in 2015, "it's like an inside joke I have with 78,000 people, it's the weird inside joke for the Hamiltonians who have been sort of following my process through late night writing sessions."[46]

Criticism or debate also makes up a large proportion of online fan interactions. As soap-opera fan scholar Nancy Baym notes, "criticism is usually performed as much as shared."[47] Critique, sometimes brutal, offers a salient feature of musical theatre fans' interactions online, with diva performances, for example, as one particular target. For some time, *Hamilton* fans seemed to be uniquely positive, demonstrating almost universal approval. As Bolander points out:

> The *Hamilton* fandom really took me by surprise because people are so kind and inclusive. … With my videos I have been so lucky to receive an overwhelming amount of positive comments from fellow fans. … It's rare for comments to be mostly positive on the Internet.[48]

Fans leap to the defense of Miranda or the show in response to the very few negative comments that appear. For example, fans react when anyone gives a "thumbs down" to *Hamilton* related YouTube videos. A typical response comes from user Phillip Chen, "to the one guy who disliked this video: you have no soul."[49] In early Spring 2016, a more critical scholarly audience (albeit from largely self-proclaimed lovers of the show itself) began to question some of the politics or representations in *Hamilton*, prompting a quick and angry popular response in addition to a swift rebuttal from other cultural critics. Those who dared to criticize were called "professional Cassandras" or "contesters" in *The Daily Beast*.[50] This leap to Miranda and the show's defense was mirrored in the popular fan responses to criticism. Some cultural critics found middle ground, and as Isaac Butler pointed out in *Slate*, "fans of *Hamilton* often seem motivated by an earnest desire to protect the show. But the show doesn't need protecting. *Hamilton* is now unstoppable."[51]

In fact, in the face of a common "enemy," communities often coalesce more strongly. After the cast read a statement at curtain call to Vice President-elect Mike Pence, who had attended the November 19, 2016 performance, Donald Trump attacked the show, calling it "overrated." In response to Trump, fans continued to passionately defend the show, its cast, and creators. Although there were proclamations from conservatives angry at perceived disrespect to Pence, few to none seemed to come from the fan community. Fans overwhelmingly defended the choice to make the statement, and expressed amusement that those urging #boycottHamilton did not understand the difficult reality of obtaining tickets. Box office for the three productions currently running or about to open (Broadway, Chicago, and San Francisco, as of this writing) was unaffected.

Although the *Hamilton* fandom overall seems to largely get along, scholars of other fan communities often find so-called "fan-tagonism," defined as, "ongoing, competitive struggles between both internal factions and external institutions to discursively codify the fan-text-producer relationship according to their respective interests."[52] In other words, fan competition offers another defining element of fan communities. Although *Hamilton* fans do not yet display large-scale overt fan-tagonism, either spoken or unspoken,[53] fans compete with each other for the most liked or shared tweets, the funniest jokes, or the most responses from Miranda or members of the cast. Official media sanctioned outlets facilitate this competition; there has been a *Buzzfeed* article about funniest *Hamilton* tweets, a *Playbill* article about the best *Hamilton* fan art, and the *Hamilton* official Twitter page has featured the best examples of fan art by retweeting them to a much larger audience. The official *Hamilton* social media pages also called on fans to send in videos of their children singing songs from the show and cut together the best or cutest examples into one officially sanctioned YouTube video per song. Privileged fans also are chosen for special social media honors—for example, certain fans have been allowed to "take over" the official *Hamilton* Snapchat for the day. These are fans who have demonstrated sufficient status and dedication to be chosen above others for this kind of role.

The competition for Miranda's or the other cast/production team members' attention on social media offers perhaps the most intense, though coded, competition. Miranda frequently acknowledges fan tweets, by retweeting or answering them, sometimes by commenting on them as well. In fact, about 65% of his tweets are in response to fans.[54] He acknowledges fan art and fan videos, and grants his typical "BHAHAHAHA" to tweets he finds funny. Miranda grants special attention to fans, like Bolander, who interact with him in more active ways. Those privileged few who have actually interacted with Miranda or the others in the *Hamilton* official sphere are winning a largely unspoken fan competition.

Entwined with fan competition, fans *perform* their fandom. Jenkins argues, "each of us constructs our own personal mythology from bits and fragments of information extracted from the media flow and transformed into resources through which we make sense of our everyday lives."[55] Intensive Broadway fans can make sense of their lives through defining and performing themselves as superfans, an integral part of the excitement engendered by their musical object of adoration. This self-definition also creates or encourages community. Booth concurs, "performance here is key: the fan texts perform a function for fans and fans perform their fandom for each other."[56] For example, a repeated trend online is for those attending the live show to post a requisite photo of the playbill in front of the empty stage before the show starts. Searching the hashtag #yayhamlet or #Hamilton will yield countless examples of this status, a performance of fandom in action. Online comments, whether they be on Miranda's Twitter, Facebook, or Tumblr accounts or text comments left on YouTube videos, also offer a significant outlet for participatory and performative fandom. Scholar Vivian Sobchak argues, "media technologies encourage spectators to see themselves as central figures in mediated narratives and their interactions as performative in some capacity."[57] By commenting online, in any of these numerous outlets, fans may "be a part of the narrative,"[58] as Eliza, Alexander Hamilton's wife sings in the musical. Fans perform their intense love in front of other fans, often in a competitive fashion. Their comments can get "likes" and thereby reach the top of the comments field. If a comment is particularly insightful or funny, fans can receive approbation from the fan community, and if they are lucky, from the objects of fandom themselves, Miranda and the cast. When Miranda replies or retweets a fan, almost inevitably in the comments you will find another fan complimenting the original poster for receiving the star's attention.

Another element of fan competition takes the form of recording and sharing illegal bootlegs of Broadway shows. These fans claim part of the theatrical narrative of a particular production by capturing and sharing it. Such fans portray themselves as knowledgeable, beneficent superfans willing to share their knowledge with others. They perform their ownership of this small piece of the Broadway experience, posting their video to the Internet in order to proclaim that they were in the "room where it happens."[59] While *Hamilton* has been uniquely active and successful at shutting down bootlegs, led by an active campaign by Miranda to explain to fans why they are illegal, they still pop up on YouTube or through Tumblr before being taken down, and the comments generally contain bragging posts from fans who claim to have the entire show as a bootleg. These fans often boast of their willingness to share privately, sometimes for free. Typically, many fans beg for a copy and offer to pay. The owner of the bootleg therefore has power and status within the fan community and can choose either to perform the role of the beneficent gift giver or hardened capitalist.[60] Either way, they have competed and won that status above other fans. Despite this implicit competition, fans generally do not classify it as such. Again, Bolander claims, "*Hamilton* reaches such a wide range of people, and that allows room for learning from each other. It doesn't feel like a competition. We are all just people that love *Hamilton*."[61] Whether this utopic vision is accurate or merely hopeful matters less than the fact that many fans declare, and seem to feel, a sense of camaraderie and equality.

The abovementioned features of fan interaction serve to highlight that a newer, more expansive definition of the Broadway audience must incorporate interactions both inside and outside the theatre. The live experience is greatly affected for many fans by the experiences and associations they carry with them from their interactions online.

Postmodern Presence

The Internet offers more than just the chance for fans to interact with their favorite shows and actors—it also extends the Broadway theatre's reach. Prior to the Internet, the concept of "Broadway" was largely tied to a physical place in midtown Manhattan. Broadway musicals extended their reach only through out-of-town tryouts, tours in selected cities, the occasional television appearance, and physical remnants such as souvenirs and cast albums. But the Internet offers a unique opportunity to expand the "Broadway experience" across the country and the world. Social media multiplies that experience and makes it accessible, so that fans in small towns and in remote areas of the country can also engage with musical theatre on a daily basis. Scholar Chantal Pontbriand defines "postmodern presence" as a condition where "presence is no longer dependent on materiality but instead depends on the artwork's exhibition value, its multiplicity, and its accessibility."[62]

Postmodern presence multiplies fan interaction and extends geographic accessibility. It can also defy the traditional definitions of liveness. For example, *Hamilton* fans could watch Lin-Manuel Miranda's final curtain call live online. The production chose to stream the event live on Facebook and 5.8 thousand fans tuned in at approximately 11 p.m., EST. Although the clip was only about three minutes long, fans could feel part of this live event, sensing presence and global community. Facilitated by the Internet, interactions like these, together with following the cast on social media and making fan culture, create a larger audience that, no matter how distant from New York City, "knows" the performers, has exclusive knowledge of the show, understands the inside jokes, and makes up a community. Fans can celebrate this knowledge online, and eventually (the producers hope), at the box office. Online, a fan can experience the entire world of *Hamilton*, including the history and backstage world of the production, so attending the show becomes only a fraction of the experience of fandom.

Postmodern presence allows what Adorno termed "false unity of identity,"[63] where corporate monopolies can deceive an unwitting populace into sameness. In applying this term to the theatre, Jensen elaborates:

> The false unity of identity tells each audience member that she or he has a special and unique connection to the performance: each has foreknowledge of the plot or perceived intimacy with the performers or special knowledge of the genesis of the work.[64]

According to this argument, the perceived intimacy musicals offer is false. The corporations producing these musicals depend upon individual feelings of connection or specialness, even while encouraging the exact same connection in millions of spectators. Although ideas of false unity of identity have long been examined in media scholarship, Jensen applies this idea to the multiplying Broadway musical spectacles based on films.[65] Indeed, false unity of identity can most easily be associated with the corporate megamusicals "real" musical theatre fans often deride. By certain measures, (originality of form and source material, lack of corporate producers) *Hamilton* seemingly contradicts the conditions leading to false unity of identity. The show has been hailed for the uniqueness of its musical form and its modernization of the treatment of eighteenth-century history. In fact much of the fervor surrounding the fan experience of *Hamilton* depends on understanding the show as something entirely new, different from the tired commercial forms dominating Broadway. The complexities of our mediatized culture, however, do not allow such a simple dichotomy. In fact, despite its originality in some measures, by making a larger audience feel that they somehow, uniquely, *know* the performers or the show, that they understand the inside jokes and are part of the community, *Hamilton*, at least in part, relies on an illusion of perceived intimacy constructed by its online identity.

One may therefore ask: are fans in control of, or controlled by, the Broadway system? Harris argues: "to the media industries, fans have traditionally represented an important constituency to be measured, controlled, co-opted, institutionalized, and appropriated for their value as a ready market for products and as a public relations tool."[66] And although fans might feel they come to their fandom alone and completely of their own volition, Booth argues: "the experience of fandom, of tying one's emotions to media texts, can be actively fostered by the media industries."[67] In fact, scholar Abigail de Kosnick writes that fans' contributions to the Internet should be seen as labor, pointing out that fan contributions offer invaluable marketing value for the objects they adore. She argues that fandom "should be valued as a new form of publicity and advertising, authored by volunteers, that corporations badly need in an era of market fragmentation."[68] Early fan scholars like Jenkins argued that fans were actively offering counter-culture readings and seizing control of their media. But it appears that neither the older model of manipulated fans, nor Jenkins's opposite argument of "textual poachers" can account for the full picture of fan/media producer interactions. As Matt Hills argues, "cult fandom doesn't merely 'escape' or 'resist' the processes of commodification, it also intensifies—and is increasingly caught up in—these same processes."[69]

We might argue that because theatre is a smaller business by numbers, not the conglomerate of television and film fan objects, it may therefore more easily evade the control of corporate or media forces. But the Broadway fan's sense of community and ownership, while feeling intensely personal, cannot escape corporate interests. Jeffrey Seller and a few other individuals produce *Hamilton*, and so we might grant it more artistic individuality and independence than its more corporately driven Broadway neighbors. At least on its surface, the production appears refreshingly unique and "above" toadying to commercial interests. Correspondingly, *Hamilton*'s Internet presence appears to be made up of authentic, engaged people connecting to their fans. But *Hamilton*'s merchandizing, its promotion, and what its actors and production team share or choose not to share online are all shaped, at least in part, by commercial forces. As a result, claims of total autonomy for fan communities are unconvincing.

Laura MacDonald's chapter in this book, on Broadway producers (Chap. 2), explores questions of the Broadway commercial machine in more detail. Thus far, live theatre and Broadway markets have not been fully explored in the context of fan studies, a field in which mass media forces are generally assumed to be at work. As Booth states: "rather than looking at or defining fan/industry relations at all, we can only hope to investigate specific sites and moments of interaction."[70] The *Hamilton* phenomenon can act as one of those sites, and because of its enormous fan following, offers a fascinating test case for future studies of fan interactions within musical theatre.

Conclusion

Where does the mediatized fan relationship leave the live theatre? Hills states that the "cult fan's affective experience is quite literally mapped onto spatial relations. This produces a 'sacred' place which can serve to anchor and legitimate the cult fan's attachments."[71] Elvis fans can travel to Graceland, *Harry Potter* fans can go to Kings Cross Station. In the musical theatre world, the Broadway theatres in Manhattan serve as that sacred space. Before or after fans engage with the Internet presence of a show, they can make a pilgrimage to see the show live. In *Hamilton*'s case, one could pilgrimage to the Richard Rodgers Theatre. The pilgrimage concept offers hope for live theatre. According to Jensen the participatory spectator can serve as "the site of negotiation between the dominant media and theatre. It is in this live body that theatre must compete and collaborate to continue to exist."[72] The primacy of the spectator and their personal negotiation between media and the theatre can encourage new generations to attend live events.

However, the ephemeral nature of theatre changes the rules of the fan relationship. Productions close, cast members change, fans move on to new objects of adoration or persist in loving ones that no longer exist in a sacred space. The Internet allows fan communities of these displaced artifacts to continue to exist despite a hole at the center, the absent live performed production. These realities of theatre change the assumptions of television, music, and film fan scholarship, and theatre scholars must therefore set out to find their own definitions. Broadway producer Kevin McCollum puts it best when he argues that "the more people gravitate toward technology, the more they will hunger for human interaction. Technology is the tool, not the destination, the destination is a live audience."[73] True fans of the live Broadway musical may continue to hope this proves true.

Notes

1. The White House. "The First Lady Delivers Remarks at '*Hamilton* at the White House' Workshop" Filmed [March 14, 2016]. YouTube video, 20:38. Posted [March 2016]. https://www.youtube.com/watch?v=MTrF1MyAjYA.
2. Brantley.
3. Miranda and McCarter, *Hamilton: The Revolution*, 29.
4. As well as the production in Chicago, and the national tour which opened in San Francisco, and as of this writing, an upcoming production in London.
5. Gray, Sandvoss, and Harrington, *Fandom*, 4.
6. Sandvoss and Kearns, "From Interpretive Communities to Interpretative Fairs," 91.
7. Several chapters in this book begin to redress this imbalance. See Sedgman, Bunch, and Clark.
8. Jenkins, *Convergence Culture*, 3.
9. Miller, *Place for Us*.
10. Jensen, *Theatre in a Media Culture*, 176.
11. Ibid.
12. Ibid., 4.
13. "Live Q&A With the *Hamilton* Cast." Facebook Live Video: 30:12. Posted [May 31, 2016]. https://www.facebook.com/HamiltonMusical/videos/1394402060586667/.
14. Booth, *Playing Fans*, 6.
15. Ruiz, "2015 Was the Year of *Hamilton* Obsession."
16. Chernow.
17. Ibid.
18. Jenkins, *Convergence Culture*, 21.
19. Ibid., 285.
20. Jenkins, "Afterword," 360.
21. Booth, *Playing Fans*, 15.
22. Romano, "Hamilton is Fanfic."
23. For example, see Stacy Wolf's examination of lesbian identity formation in response to musical theatre, pre-digital era, in her *A Problem Like Maria: Gender and Sexuality in the American Musical*. Ann Arbor: University of Michigan Press, 2002.
24. Miranda, Lin-Manuel. Vine Post. March 27, 2015.
25. Hellekson and Busse, *Fan Fiction and Fan Communities*.
26. For a more extensive examination of the way Miranda troubles heteronormativity in his role as a "diva" see my upcoming article in a special edition of *Studies in Musical Theatre* devoted to examination of the musical theatre diva.

27. Miranda and McCarter, *Hamilton: The Revolution*, 27.
28. Ibid., 131.
29. Chernow.
30. Evans, "Phillipa Soo: Her Moment."
31. Upcoming in *The Routledge Companion to the Contemporary American Stage Musical*.
32. Another form of cosplay can be seen in the significantly large numbers of *Hamilton* or Lin-Manuel Miranda inspired Halloween costumes shared via social media in October, 2016, on everyone from babies to the elderly.
33. "BroadwayCon 2016—History is Happening In Manhattan: The Hamilton Panel." Filmed [January 22, 2015]. YouTube video, 42:22. Posted [January 23, 2015]. https://www.youtube.com/watch?v=6iyKH1jReCA.
34. Jona Bolander (Vlogger) Email Communication, April 18, 2016.
35. "Meeting Lin Manuel and the *Hamilton* cast! NYC 2016." YouTube video, 24:29. Posted [March 9, 2016]. https://www.youtube.com/watch?v=45fceYg0Je0.
36. Booth, *Playing Fans*, 18.
37. Sandvoss and Kearns, *Ashgate*, 91.
38. Ibid.
39. I examine the fans' vertical and aspirational creation of community with Lin-Manuel Miranda via social media in other work; here we examine bond formation with other like-minded fans.
40. Booth, *Digital Fandom*, 39.
41. Baym, "Talking About Soaps," 112.
42. Harris, *Theorizing Fandom*, 5–6.
43. Bonanos, *Vulture*.
44. Jenkins, *Convergence Culture*, 287.
45. Booth, *Digital Fandom*, 36.
46. "Lin Manuel Miranda in Conversation, Part Three" Filmed [September, 2015]. YouTube Video: 7:58. Posted [October 18, 2015]. https://www.youtube.com/watch?v=UX5Wljhod6o.
47. Baym, "Talking About Soaps," 124.
48. Bolander interview.
49. "Live Ham4Ham 7/6/16, Happy Trails." Filmed [July 6, 2016]. YouTube Video, 8:33. Posted July 6, 2016. https://www.youtube.com/watch?v=P4y3IfHzblI.
50. Mcwhorter, *The Daily Beast*.
51. Butler, *Slate*.
52. Johnson, "Fan-tagonism" 287.

53. The debate between bootleggers and those who side with Miranda is the most fractious fan-tagonism to be found in the *Hamilton* fan community. Those backing Miranda and his personal pleas not to make or watch bootlegs display anger at those who still wish to see them, and who justify watching them due to their inability to either obtain or afford tickets. See also chapters by Bunch, Sedgman, and Clark in this book for further discussions of fan-tagonism.
54. Dale, "Twitter Genius."
55. Jenkins, *Convergence Culture*, 3–4.
56. Booth, *Digital Fandom*, 37.
57. Qtd. in Jensen, *Theatre in a Media Culture*, 168.
58. Miranda and McCarter, *Hamilton*, 110.
59. Ibid., 186.
60. See also Doug Reside's discussion of bootlegs in Chapter 11 of this book.
61. Bolander interview.
62. Pontbriand, "The Eye Finds No Fixed Point on Which to Rest," 155–56.
63. Adorno, *The Dialectic of Enlightenment*.
64. Jensen, *Theatre in a Media Culture*, 14–15.
65. See Chap. 4, by Amy Osatinski, in this book.
66. Harris, *Theorizing Fandom*, 4–5.
67. Booth, *Playing Fans*, 2.
68. de Kosnick, "Fandom as Free Labor," 99.
69. Hills, *Fan Cultures*, 172.
70. Booth, *Playing Fans*, 5.
71. Hills, *Fan Cultures*, 144.
72. Jensen, *Theatre in a Media Culture*, 186.
73. Schmidt, "Broadway Shows Speak to Their Audience."

Bibliography

Adorno, Theodore, and Max Horkheimer. *The Dialectic of Enlightenment*. Translated by John Cumming. New York: Herder and Herder, 1972.

Baym, Nancy K. "Talking About Soaps: Communicative Practices in a Computer-Mediated Fan Culture" in Cheryl Harris and Alison Alexander eds. *Theorizing Fandom: Fans, Subculture and Identity*. Cresskill, NJ: Hampton Press, 1998.

Bonanos, Christopher. "How *Hamilton*'s Free Preshow Performance Became the Best Thing on Broadway." *Vulture*. http://www.vulture.com/2015/12/hamilton-free-show-ham4ham.html.

Booth, Paul. *Playing Fans: Negotiating Fandom and Media in the Digital Age*. Iowa City: The University of Iowa Press, 2015.

———. *Digital Fandom: New Media Studies*. New York: Peter Lang, 2010.

Brantley, Ben. "Review: 'Hamilton,' Young Rebels Changing History and Theatre." *The New York Times*. August 6, 2016. https://www.nytimes.com/2015/08/07/theatre/review-hamilton-young-rebels-changing-history-and-theatre.html?mcubz=1.

Butler, Isaac. "Why Fans of *Hamilton* Should be Delighted It's Finally Stirring Criticism." *Slate*. April 17, 2016. http://www.slate.com/blogs/browbeat/2016/04/17/historians_are_criticizing_hamilton_and_fans_should_be_thrilled.html.

Chernow, Ron. (Author, *Alexander Hamilton*) in discussion with the author, March 7, 2016.

Dale, Michael. "Lin-Manuel Miranda is Broadway's Twitter Genius." *BroadwayWorld*. June 14, 2016. http://www.broadwayworld.com/article/HAMILTONs-Lin-Manuel-Miranda-is-Broadways-Twitter-Genius-20160614.

de Kosnick, Abigail. "Fandom as Free Labor." in *Digital Labor: The Internet as Playground and Factory*. Trebor Scholz, ed. London: Routledge Press, 2013.

Evans, Suzy. "Phillipa Soo: Her Moment." *Broadway Style Guide*. June, 2016. http://broadwaystyleguide.com/2016/06/phillipa-soo-her-moment/?utm_source=twitter&utm_medium=twitterfeed&utm_campaign=PSoo_BSG.

Gray, Jonathan, Cornel Sandvoss, and C. Lee Harrington, eds., *Fandom: Identities and Communities in a Mediated World*. New York: New York University Press, 2007.

Harris, Cheryl. "Introduction: Theorizing Fandom: Fans, Subculture and Identity." in *Theorizing Fandom: Fans, Subculture and Identity*, edited by Cheryl Harris and Alison Alexander. Cresskill, NJ: Hampton Press, 1998.

Hellekson, Karen and Kristina Busse, editors. *Fan Fiction and Fan Communities in the Age of the Internet: New Essays*. Jefferson: McFarland Press, 2006.

Hills, Matt. *Fan Cultures*. London: Routledge, 2002.

Jenkins, Henry. *Convergence Culture: Where Old and New Media Collide*. New York: New York University Press, 2006.

———. "Afterword: The Future of Fandom" in *Fandom: Identities and Communities in a Mediated World*, edited by Jonathan Gray, Cornel Sandvoss, and C. Lee Harrington. New York: New York University Press, 2007.

Jensen, Amy Petersen. *Theatre in a Media Culture: Production, Performance and Perception Since 1970*. London: McFarland & Company, Inc., 2007.

Johnson, Derek. "Fan-tagonism: Factions, Institutions, and Constitutive Hegemonies of Fandom." in *Fandom: Identities and Communities in a Mediated World*, edited by Jonathan Gray, Cornel Sandvoss, and C. Lee Harrington. New York: New York University Press, 2007.

"Lin Manuel Miranda in Conversation, Part 3." September, 2015, published October 18, 2015 7:58. https://www.youtube.com/watch?v=UX5Wljhod6o.

Mcwhorter, John. "The Exhausting and Useless Accusations of Racism Against *Hamilton*." *The Daily Beast*. April 16, 2016. http://www.thedailybeast.com/articles/2016/04/16/the-exhausting-and-useless-accusations-of-racism-againsthamilton.html?via=mobile&source=twitter.

Miller, D.A. *Place for Us [Essay on the Broadway Musical]*. Cambridge: Harvard University Press, 1998.

Miranda, Lin-Manuel and Jeremy McCarter. *Hamilton: The Revolution*. New York: Grand Central Publishing, 2016.

Pontbriand, Chantal. "The Eye Finds No Fixed Point on Which to Rest." Translated by C.R. Parsons. *Modern Drama* 25.1 (March 1982): 154–162.

Romano, Aja. "*Hamilton* is Fanfic, and its Historical Critics are Totally Missing the Point." *Vox Culture*. April 14, 2016. http://www.vox.com/2016/4/14/11418672/hamilton-is-fanfic-not-historically-inaccurate.

Ruiz, Michelle. "2015 Was the Year of *Hamilton* Obsession." *Vogue*. December 27, 2015. http://www.vogue.com/13381337/hamilton-on-broadway-obsession/).

Sandvoss, Cornel and Laura Kearns. "From Interpretive Communities to Interpretative Fairs: Ordinary Fandom, Textual Selection and Digital Media." in *Ashgate Research Companion to Fan Cultures*, edited by Linda Duits, Koos Zwaan and Stijn Reijnders, 91–108. Farnham: Ashgate Publishing Ltd, 2014.

Schmidt, Gregory, "Broadway Shows Speak to Their Audience, and Vice Versa," *The New York Times*, December 25, 2008. http://www.nytimes.com/2008/12/26/business/media/26adco.html?_r=0.

CHAPTER 7

No-Object Fandom: *Smash*-ing Kickstarter and Bringing *Bombshell* to the Stage

Kirsty Sedgman

In the finale song of the musical *Bombshell*, the actor playing Marilyn Monroe pleads with her audience not to forget her. A few years later, audiences are still keeping their promise. This chapter explores the fan communities that have formed around *Bombshell*, a musical created within the imaginary world of *Smash*, a fictional television series about life on Broadway produced by NBC. Here I explain how, in the absence of a real stage production, audiences have brought together an array of digital manifestations in order to keep the show alive.

Drawing on Rebecca Williams' term "post-object fandom"—used to describe the way audiences engage in collective grieving processes when a beloved television series ends—I introduce the idea of "no-object fandom." Investigating digital representations of live performance, I show how audiences develop emotional associations with theoretical texts: ones that they have never seen in full, because these texts do not actually exist outside the fictional world.

K. Sedgman (✉)
University of Bristol, Bristol, UK
e-mail: info@kirstysedgman.com

Fade Out on a Girl

In May 2013, after just two seasons, the television show *Smash* was brought to a sudden end. *Smash* presented a fictional rendering of Big Broadway, with each season broadly structured around the making of a new hit musical. Initially airing on February 6, 2012, the star-studded pilot saw successful writers Tom and Julia (played by Christian Borle and Debra Messing, respectively) team up with producer Eileen Rand (Anjelica Huston) to write a new musical based on the life of Marilyn Monroe. At the same time, the show introduced us to two contending actresses—Karen Cartwright (Katharine McPhee) and Ivy Lynn (Megan Hilty)—whom the media quickly began to call "dueling Marilyns." Over two seasons the role of Marilyn passed back and forth, with the show's characters—and its fans—arguing about who was best suited to the role: Karen, an ambitious ingénue fresh off the bus from Iowa, or Ivy, overlooked veteran of years of Broadway choruses. This narrative thread was laid out for us early on in a particularly stirring sequence, the last scene in the pilot, which showed Karen and Ivy travelling to the audition as they competitively belted out *Bombshell*'s opening number, "Let Me Be Your Star."

As the first season of *Smash* unfolded, in addition to rivaling for the key role the two performers were also seen to vie for the attentions of roguish director/choreographer Derek Wills (Jack Davenport), who started sleeping with Ivy after making an unsuccessful pass at Karen, but who later handed Ivy's role to the doe-eyed newbie, his "muse." In the second and final season, Karen and Derek both ditched *Bombshell* for a new musical, *Hit List*, a modern take on women seeking fame. This season drew its primary tension from the competition between the two shows as awards season rolls around.

Boasting an executive producer credit by Steven Spielberg, it was originally suggested that *Smash*'s musicals would eventually be transferred out of the televised fiction and into a real-life stage production. In the case of *Bombshell* this presented a particular challenge. Much of *Smash*'s narrative centered on the difficulties characters faced trying to bring Marilyn's life to the stage. While the musical's score remained relatively stable and complete throughout the course of the show, the book itself went through a series of modifications. In one especially contentious scene, the show's producer Eileen Rand was forced to choose between two versions: on the one hand, Julia's complex, nuanced script featuring

Marilyn-as-representation, a constructed figure seen through the eyes of the men who made her; on the other, Tom's spectacularized frolic through the glitz and grief of Marilyn's rise to fame. As an early review in the *New York Times* put it,

> I could take issue with the way they talk about Monroe ("There was something about her, how much she wanted to love and be loved"), but that's part of the fun: arguing with the vision of the show as well as the show within the show (and possibly the show outside the show, if Spielberg's plan to do an actual theatre production pans out).[1]

In other words, no single final version of the show existed that could easily be transferred to the stage. Both in reality and also (at least to some extent) in the fictive world of *Smash*, *Bombshell* was always a contested possibility. And as this chapter explains, with no "official" version of *Bombshell* agreed upon, when NBC announced *Smash*'s cancellation it therefore fell to fans to construct an imagined version of how such a musical might actually work on stage.

A Grand and Sweeping Gesture?

Smash was an important venture for its network. Reportedly sucking up "tens of millions of dollars,"[2] the show was NBC's prime candidate for a hit: one that, moreover, was desperately needed. By the end of the 2010–2011 broadcast primetime year, NBC had finished fourth place behind Fox, CBS, and ABC in both the United States' 18–49 ratings and its average viewership figures. Even more damningly, while the three other networks were down between 5.9% (Fox) and 7.9% (CBS) over the previous year, NBC had fallen by 10.1%. As NBC's programming chief Robert Greenblatt explained at the time: "If it doesn't work, we're not going to fall apart. But it's a big hope that it can land and start to turn the tide around for us. It's the biggest, buzziest, loudest, highest-concept thing we have."[3]

Initially the gamble appeared to be paying off. *Smash*'s pilot was, for the most part, ecstatically received. For example, the *Los Angeles Times* review praised the show's creator Theresa Rebeck for managing "to capture the grand and sweeping gesture that is musical theater and inject it with the immediate intimacy of television":

> The exultant anticipatory buzz preceding the premiere of NBC's "Smash" has grown so intense that the conversation is no longer about whether it's any good ("Good? Darling, it's great!") or if it will be a hit for a network that needs one. Instead, everyone's wondering why no one thought of doing this kind of show before.[4]

The pilot was broadcast for US audiences in February 2012 and seemed an immediate success, capturing 11.4 million viewers and a 3.8 rating in the 18–49 demographic range. It is worth noting, however, that the press launch for the pilot had actually taken place a full nine months previously, in May 2011. The show was withheld until mid-season the following year in order to allow the writers to hone *Smash*'s script and songs. This delay, critics have suggested, ultimately "hurt the show. […] [B]ecause the majority of the show was produced in a bubble, the creators had no idea what would click and what wouldn't with the viewers."[5] This led to what many critics considered a wholesale mishandling of the entire enterprise. Particularly worth reading is a scathing analysis written by Kate Aurthur and published on BuzzFeed, which drew its bite from a number of interviews conducted with anonymous insiders:

> [B]y the time the [first season] had its finale in May, it had become an object of ritualistic ridicule: appointment television for hate-watchers, that new American sport created by social media. *Smash*'s unsympathetic lead characters, oddly placed musical sequences, schizophrenic tonal shifts, cartoon-like villains who literally say, "You haven't heard the last of this," and strangely accessorized actors all became fodder for Twitter jokes.[6]

The show's supposed narrative inadequacies, coupled with a downslide in ratings, spelled the end for Rebeck, who was summarily fired at the end of the first season and replaced by Josh Safran. Nonetheless, despite a number of format changes *Smash*'s second season was still largely panned by critics, called "sloppy, over the top in a bad way […] [and] a train wreck you can't look away from"[7] (see Fig. 7.1).

Hobbled further by an injurious schedule change and another nine-month wait between seasons, the show's ratings continued to suffer—until finally on May 10, 2013 NBC announced they were pulling the plug. A couple of weeks later the network aired its two-part finale, which saw *Bombshell* and *Hit List*—along with its respective stars, Ivy and Karen—pitted against each other one last time at the Tony Awards.

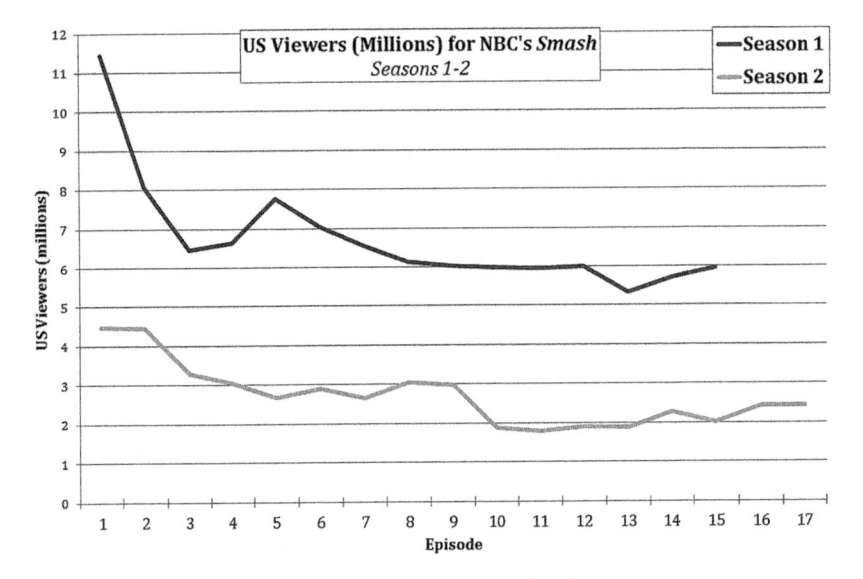

Fig. 7.1 US viewers (millions) for NBC's *Smash*. *Source* Data adapted from Wikipedia, 2015

Hate-Watching and Hope-Watching: "Complicated Smash Feelings"

None of the above is to deny the existence of a sizeable and pervasive *Smash* fan-base. In fact, if Neil Meron, one of the show's producers, is to be believed, since going off air *Smash* "has taken on a cult status."[8] Surveying online discourse posted after NBC's announcement certainly suggests that many audiences were disappointed by the series' cancellation, having been able to find pleasure in watching *Smash* while simultaneously recognizing its flaws. An example of this in action comes from Previously TV's "Rewatch" series, which saw Tara Ariano and Adam Grosswirth conduct an online chat session ("The Talk") while marathon-watching all 32 episodes. In their final recap, Grosswirth opened by explaining that despite having been "fairly critical in this space over the past two months […] I just want to reiterate my sincere love for *Smash*."[9] Both professional contributors balanced the show's problematic elements against its more pleasurable aspects, and considered these in context of the difficulties of making such a big-budget show with an ensemble cast, many of whom had ongoing roles on Broadway at the same time. This section goes on to show that the authors' ambivalence was shared by many of *Smash*'s fans.[10] As one of the post's commentators, Charlie Baker, put it: "Thanks for the rewatch—it definitely took me back to my own *Smash* love and love/hate."[11]

It is worth spending a little time considering that phrase, "love and love/hate," because of what it indicates about audiences' affective engagements with *Smash*. Firstly, though, it is necessary to explain that while many people adored the show, a great many others flat-out hated it. In fact, quite early into its first season *Smash* had already become the nexus for a committed community of "hate-watchers." For example, in a *New Yorker* piece Emily Nussbaum apologizes for her glowing review of the pilot and goes on to explain point by point why "there's so much competition for the worst part of 'Smash.'"[12] This avid detestation shows up in many audience postings, too, through a communal effort to unpick the narrative and uncover every moment in which internal logic falls apart. A thoughtful example of this urge to keep circling around a text's flaws comes from a commentator called queenanne:

> I don't think the show would have made me so mad if they had been honest about what they were doing, but as it plays, it's just a big mess. Why circle the entire pre-show ad campaign around "the competition between Karen and Ivy," when they clearly never intended for there to be any question about who would win? [...] I drove myself crazy for weeks, thinking "Is this because Ivy has just ruined Derek's plans to put a major star in the role because of being so unquestionably IT?" Etc [...] Gah, this show made me want to sling something at the screen![13]

The desire to angrily consume problematic content is an interesting feature of much modern television viewership.[14] As Nussbaum reflects:

> I realize my vehemence is slightly suspect. I mean, why would I go out of my way to watch a show that makes me so mad? On some level, I'm obviously enjoying it. Maybe I secretly love "Smash," at least in that slap-in-the-face "Moonlighting" way.[15]

Sarah Wagenseller Goletz's term "giddyshame" might be helpfully deployed here, used initially to describe the contradictory reactions of "die-hard bookworms" to Stephenie Meyer's *Twilight* series.[16] Goletz explains how these committed readers take overt pleasure in hate-reading Meyer's books, and often form anti-fan communities around shared disdain. Thus, such audiences are able to *take pleasure in displeasure*.

Nonetheless, while there seem to be plenty of people, like Nussbaum, who gained similar kinds of satisfaction from giddyshaming *Smash* during its lifetime, the love/hate divide was for other people less clearly demarcated. This research found that much of the online commentary pointed to a complex interplay between love and loathing, a balancing act that is neatly summarized by Charlie Baker (above) as a "love and love/hate" relationship. Similarly, another commentator, intensebeige, describes this contradiction in terms of "complicated *Smash* feelings":

> While I remember loathing everything to do with Hit List, the songs have grown on me considerably in passing time. So much so that Broadway Here I Come might be my favorite song of the series? I dunno, I have complicated Smash feelings![17]

Rather than hate-watching, these people might more aptly be termed "hope-watchers," as Alan Sepinwall explains:

> Hope-watching [...] isn't the act of enduring a bad show for the sole purpose of mocking it, but rather sticking with it out of of [*sic*] the belief, founded or not, that there is a good show hiding inside the bad one—and that you want to be there at the moment when the good version finds its way out of the bad.[18]

Indeed, the many *Smash* forums are littered with examples of people talking regretfully about how the show's flaws had consistently overshadowed its merits, and eventually dragged it down into oblivion. Here the love/hate balance often meant simultaneously loving *Smash* for what it oh-so-nearly was, and hating it for never quite getting there:

> I wish Smash could have been better, and wish that it had the chance to continue and maybe become so.[19]

> Squandered potential was the downfall of this show. The high points (and there were many) couldn't seem to overcome the low points. [...] I wish it had been good enough to last longer too.[20]

These comments illustrate Sepinwall's own description of hope-watching as akin to a "roller coaster ride." While hate-watching "takes you on one even, surly track," he explains:

> Hope-watchers have great highs and lows, as reasons to believe are swiftly replaced by reasons to doubt, and vice versa. One minute, you're gnashing your teeth and asking, "Why the hell am I still watching this show?" The next, you're fist-pumping and saying, "*That's* why I'm still watching!" The former emotion may be more frequent than the latter, but the latter is so powerful it gives you strength, for a while, to push through the rest.[21]

For many fans, it seems *Smash*'s "great highs" were frequently delivered via its high-octane musical numbers, as the following section explains.

"LET THE MUSIC LIVE"

One of the key reasons for audience pleasure was *Smash*'s repertoire of musical numbers. Some were original compositions, written during the fiction to be part of either the *Bombshell* or *Hit List* score; others were covers of popular chart hits or theatre songs. Some were diegetic—a "term borrowed from film criticism, ... [which] is coming to be used for numbers that are called for by the book"[22]—while others were performed non-diegetically in order to signal something about characters' relationships or inner lives. Even audiences who disliked the series in general often found themselves watching *Smash* for these numbers, which saw pop sensations like Katharine McPhee performing side by side with bona fide Broadway stars such as Megan Hilty, Bernadette Peters, Christian Borle, and Jeremy Jordan:

> It is good to be with my people - no use for Karen, wanted to love the show, ended up loving to loathe it. And yet, I keep a couple of songs (featuring MH, thankyouverymuch) in fairly regular rotation on my iPod.[23]

These songs often leaped to the top of people's playlists, as evidenced by the following exchange:

> I have purchased every single song off of iTunes, and I listen to them regularly. Yeah, I'm THAT person.[24]

> DItto. If you see me belting in my car...9/10 it's Heart Shaped or Let Me Be Your Star. LOL[25]

Particularly revealing were the ways audiences less enamoured with the series overall managed their enthusiasm for the songs, as per this comment by allonsyalice:

> All feelings about Michael Swift aside, I'm 99% sure that Lexington and 52nd Street is my favorite smash song. (He's really good, okay?)[26]

As the above suggests, fans of the musical numbers often worked to put aside their feelings about *Smash*'s narrative and characters in favor of focusing on the function of songs within the in-text musicals. Others consciously separated the characters from the performers who played them, preferring instead to think about Megan Hilty instead of Ivy, for example, as the performer of a particular song, or about Jeremy Jordan rather than his character Jimmy:

> Jimmy KILLS it in Under Pressure. That note is amazing. He is singing his face off and I love it. I hated him for lots of S2 but for some reason that one note redeemed him in my eyes.[27]

> I know what you mean but at those times I just chose to see Jeremy Jordan instead of Jimmy.[28]

> Good point! I do quite like Jeremy Jordan![29]

Exploring these interactions led me to consider the ways audiences negotiated their fandom of *Bombshell* through their engagements—or otherwise—with *Smash*. In order to investigate this further, I performed a small-scale study of online comments posted on YouTube videos of *Smash* performances. On January 4, 2015, I took a sample of the twelve top-viewed videos that presented musical performances of the *Bombshell* score. These videos featured a range of songs and appeared in a variety of formats: some were excerpts from the *Smash* narrative, showing *Bombshell* songs either in rehearsal or performance; others were simply tracks from the official CD cast-recording uploaded to YouTube with an accompanying still frame. These videos were posted by users from all around the world, whose nomenclatures included "Bombshell Smash," "Smash Brasil," "Broadwaycom," and "הערוץ של SmashIsrael." I examined comments from nearly 2000 YouTube posters in total, using a piece of open-source software called Webometric Analyst to download data and assess posters' geographic origins where available. An invaluable description of the software's operation has been produced by its author Mike Thelwall in "Analysing YouTube Audience Reactions and Discussions," so I will not go into the process in detail here. However, it is necessary to echo Thelwall's advice that while—as with any form of online discourse—YouTube comments cannot be understood as an assured marker of wider reactions to cultural texts, this research approach can nonetheless offer a useful way of taking the temperature of public opinion. Here I must also add the proviso that this notional "public" will necessarily be made up of a specific social subset: usually those with strong feelings about the subject, more inclined and able than others to take part in a markedly anglicized form of online discourse.

Indeed, from the 1988 commentators sampled, only a quarter (477) could be traced to a geographic origin, of whom the overwhelming majority—300 users exactly—were situated by their YouTube data within the USA (see Fig. 7.2).

The "Other" category in the graph represents countries with ten or fewer commentators. These 78 people came from more than 50

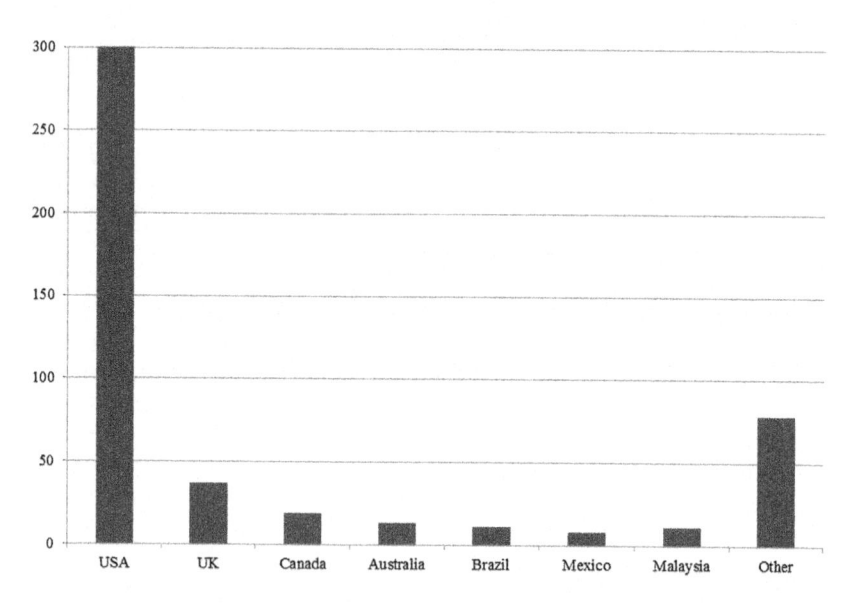

Fig. 7.2 Geographic location of commentators on sampled YouTube videos

locations, ranging from Algeria to Venezuela, and from French Polynesia to the Virgin Islands. This indicates that while *Smash*'s fan-base was especially concentrated within the USA (at least in terms of people most likely to seek out and comment on online videos), the show's popularity has spread much further afield. It is also important to note that while these twelve videos had altogether exceeded five million views, only a tiny handful of the people who watched them chose to leave a comment. Despite these inevitable limitations, online discourse can be a useful window into the orientations of certain viewers, and has allowed me to go some way to addressing the question of what it might mean to watch recorded representations of live performance: a question that Ryan Bunch explores further in the following chapter in this book by considering televised broadcasts of live events. Through my own research I have begun to ask how audiences go about relating mediatized representations of liveness to the *idea* of a real Broadway musical. This chapter might therefore be read as the precursor for further work into how audiences negotiate their fandom outside the online domain.

One revealing finding was how little variation existed in the overall tenor of posts around the world. For many audiences, the primary reason for commenting on these YouTube videos was to publically express their love: whether for the show, its songs, the performers, or for Marilyn Monroe herself. For example, the comments below come from South Africa, the UK, and Belgium (though not necessarily in that order):

> this show mader my life better…im in love with marilyn monroe i names my twins boy and girl marilyn and monroe because im so obbsessed. i have a huuuuge portrait tattooed of her shes my idiol and my hero.[30]

> one of the best songs on the show, i love this the most, plus if they have all the songs that modern in the musical maybe all ppl from all ages can enjoy it, right![31]

> *J'adore cette chanson, elle est trop bien!* <3 (*I love this song, it's too good!* <3)[32]

Another pervasive theme was the debate over which performer was best suited to the role of Marilyn: Broadway superstar Megan Hilty, or pop princess Katharine McPhee, who initially sprang to fame as runner-up on the fifth season of *American Idol*. The press predictably termed this a battle between "Team Ivy" and "Team Karen," and the comments below show how this played out everywhere from Canada to Jamaica to Bulgaria:

> i prefer Katherine cause her voice reminds me of lea michelle but i love Meagan too.[33]

> I agree with you. [...] Karen's songs, while beautiful, makes me want to cry all the time, no matter what she is singing. Ivy's songs fill me with hope and makes me feel like I could take on the world.[34]

> Compleeeeeeeeeeetely agree! I don't hate Karen but I would be _so_ happy if she just gets a record deal at the end and Ivy gets Marilyn.[35]

These debates were frequently shored up by efforts to analyze performers' relative strengths and weaknesses by drawing on specific forms of expertise:

> Perhaps you should check out Katharine (aka Karen) singing Barbra Streisand's Somewhere or Frank Sinatra's I have got you under my skin. Katharine can sing the oldies probably better than most professional crooners today. Believe me, she is not "pop average vocally." She brings the house down with both songs.[36]

> Are you kidding me!!! If you don't study musical theater then you can't judge. [...] Besides you're on here listening to it so something inside of you likes it. Stop hating. They both have beautiful voices Katharine's works better for this part and song. Go Katharine! Amazing!!![37]

As the above suggests, some audiences sought to legitimize their opinions by drawing on systems of criteria provided by "study[ing] musical theater," a tendency that was in turn critiqued by commentators like Countrycowboy08 below:

> I came here to read the comments of Broadway Musical elitist and see how they praise a Broadway actor and mock another one who performed the same song that isn't a stage actor. Didn't fail. You all think that Ivy is better than Karen because she was played by Megan who is a Broadway actress and the latter played by a Reality Show contestant.[38]

For certain disgruntled viewers this perceived "elitism" was the result of friction between Broadway as represented on screen and its real on-stage presence. This tension specifically played out across the line between performer and character, as a later comment by Countrycowboy08 shows:

> Obviously, you're here to praise Megan as herself not as Ivy. I just don't get the ego you "broadway lovers" have. You always think that "Broadway" is a lot higher than those "TV Shows" and stars. You guys criticize Karen because she's played by Katharine who was a contestant of a Reality TV Show. You always think that you are always better and ahead than TV Show lovers. Pathetic.[39]

Meanwhile, others addressed the futility of arguing at all:

> Trying to talk sense into a YouTube comment thread is like…well, I'm not coming up with an appropriate simile but GOOD LUCK WITH THAT.[40]
>
> EVERYONE STOP COMPLAINING AND ENJOY THE FLAPPING MUSIC![41]

Despite these disagreements, audiences still talked about holding out hope that *Smash* would yet be given an afterlife through the continued revival of its songs:

> Speechless. Megan is such an amazing singer. Not losing hope that one day they will bring Bombshell to Broadway.[42]
>
> I really don't understand why it's not coming back for a third season, coz I loved it(!!!), but please please (I beg on my knees) tho it's not coming back, please- PUT "BOMBSHELL" ON BROADWAY!!! X[43]
>
> I'm hoping Katharine McPhee would include this as a track on her upcoming album. or at least, perform this song live pretty please :(If we can't have a season three, at least let the music live![44]

As we now know, fans' pleas to "let the music live" are beginning to be answered. Just after this initial analysis was performed, it was announced that on June 8, 2015 a one-off revival of *Bombshell* would be taking place at the Minskoff Theatre in New York City. This was funded by a highly publicized Kickstarter campaign, which by the time of closure had attracted over 1400 backers and become the largest theatrical crowdsourced event to date. Raising money for The Actors Fund, the

Kickstarter concert earned over $300,000 and presented fans with their first real opportunity to see how the disparate pieces of *Bombshell* might potentially be performed live as a whole. Following the success of the concert, on June 22, 2015 it was finally decided to bring *Bombshell* in its entirety to a real-life Broadway stage. Initially scheduled to launch in summer 2016, despite continued positivity, this plan has not yet come to fruition. The following section examines the unfolding of reactions to the initial news on forums and on the Kickstarter page itself, and demonstrates how the imagined versions of meta-texts produced by anticipatory audiences evolve with each new piece of information.

Broadway Here We Really Come

In her seminal book *Post-Object Fandom*, Rebecca Williams argues that the cancellation of a beloved TV show can produce real, lasting disturbances within the ontological security and self-narratives of fans. These invested audiences use online communities—such as messaging sites, forums, and social networks—as outlets for pleasure and pain. While websites such as YouTube and IMDb (Internet Movie Database) are not "wholly fan-centric, instead offering a more diffuse forum for [...] discussion,"[45] fan forums tend to be populated by concentrated communities of highly committed audiences. These are made up both of amorous viewers and their negative counterparts, "anti-fans," who engage deeply with the texts but whose investments usually take the form of "snarky" critique.[46]

This section draws on a series of conversations posted between October 20, 2013 and June 26, 2015 on a site called Fan Forum (fanforum.com). Under the header of "The BOMBSHELL musical appreciation thread #1," fans of the show have been collectively collating the fragments of *Bombshell* available on the web and constructing an imagined version of how it might work as a real-life Broadway musical. By explicating this process I intend to demonstrate how fans form and maintain connections around non-existent paratexts. Acknowledging the pioneering work of Rebecca Williams, I term this phenomenon *no-object fandom*.

Like many of the YouTube commentators quoted above, the people taking part in this conversation seemed to see the online realm as a space for keeping *Bombshell* alive. According to its creator, Master Fan "airali_glo," the thread was designed to allow audiences to talk about the show "like it was a real musical."[47] By sharing cast lists of the show as it appeared within the fictional universe (where the role of Norma

Jeane Mortenson/Marilyn Monroe was ultimately played by the character Ivy Lynn), along with images and favorite memories, it is therefore possible that audiences are to some extent able to feel as if *Smash* and its paratexts are still out there in the world. However, throughout the thread it is possible to see contributors oscillating between two modes of attention: moving from discussing *Bombshell* as it appeared in the fiction, wherein the part of Monroe was played by a series of fictional characters, to considering how it might actually traverse the boundaries of fiction and appear on a Broadway stage. It was agreed that this would be a challenging process:

> I can see that with songs like they used on the show it would be SO HARD to sing that again and again night after night and after a week your voice would be gone.[48]

[…]

> Yeah, it would be very demanding just like it is right now, like we saw it in the show. …but a stage adaptation would have also another problem: cutting/changing people's favorite parts. They had to change it, but there will always be someone who won't like that they cut a particular song or changed another part. No one would ever be happy.[49]

[…]

> Even if they had to make changes it still keeps the memory alive. I'd take anything happily, but yeah sadly you can never satisfy everyone. The priority would be to make sure it could be doable for one person to play Marilyn.[50]

It was also acknowledged that *Bombshell*'s canon as it appeared on screen was designed to move the narrative of *Smash* forwards, rather than to ensure its stand-alone success as a functional musical:

> Shaiman and Wittman wrote Bombshell for a tv show, not for the stage so obviously we needed to see more Marilyn than others (the story of the show within the show was mainly with Ivy and Karen). We had a Joe Di Maggio solo because it was related to Michael and Julia (same for History Is Made At Night). On a real stage this would be about the real Marilyn, so we'd need to hear also other characters of her life.[51]

In recognizing that *Bombshell* would in reality be an impossible show to produce, fans began to ask: how might it be made possible?

> If you had the chance to add some characters (to give Marilyn some breaks, on stage), who'd you add? More men? Or other women?[52]

> Who would you like to see in a Bombshell musical? If no one from the show's cast was available?[53]

Through ongoing dialogue, contributors began to collectively sort through the partial (often contradictory) pieces of *Bombshell*, and to consider how they might fit together:

> I'd have loved to see all of *Bombshell* produced, if just to see where some of the un-choreographed songs fit into the whole.[54]

I am not the first to notice this phenomenon. Two researchers in particular have begun to pay attention to the attachments fans form with paratextual television shows: those which Paul Booth describes as "doubly fictional," because they are fictional texts constructed within a fictional universe.[55] First, Lincoln Geraghty explained how a real-life fan community of "Questarians" converged around *Galaxy Quest*, a science-fiction television show whose on-screen presence exists only within the eponymous 1999 film.[56] Geraghty describes how fans interpolated an imagined version of the fictive meta-text by conflating the descriptions and snapshots provided within the film with its real-world equivalent, *Star Trek*. Paul Booth later expanded this analysis into considering *SuperWhoLock* and *Inspector Spacetime* fandoms. While the first is an imaginary fan mashup produced by combining CW's *Supernatural* with the two BBC programs *Sherlock* and *Doctor Who*, the latter is a spoof TV show watched by the characters of the real TV show *Community*. Booth describes this audience activity as "emergent playfulness," the texts "at once, both real and unreal": while the shows themselves don't actually exist, fans have nonetheless *made* them real by "collect[ing] what little canon that exists"[57] and "amalgamating multiple texts into one."[58]

However, the fan practices studied within this chapter differ slightly from those described by Geraghty and Booth. Firstly, while *Galaxy Quest* and *Inspector Spacetime*—along with other "famously fictional" texts, such as *Itchy and Scratchy* [*The Simpsons*], *The Alan Brady Show*

[*The Dick Van Dyke Show*], and *The Girly Show* [*30 Rock*]⁵⁹—are all television programs, *Bombshell* and *Hit List* are both represented as live events. This is a significant difference because of the issue of "authenticity" it presents. While this word comes preloaded with conflicting values and cannot therefore be used unproblematically,⁶⁰ what I intend to point towards here is the way that, where television and cinema must constantly negotiate issues of canonicity, *all* scripted live performances contain within them a kind of permanent transience. As Francesca Coppa puts it, for theatre a script or score is merely "a blueprint for a production—a thing used to make another thing."⁶¹ Even when the book and score of a musical remain relatively stable—an assumption that *Smash* itself confronted, by showing tremendous fluctuations in music choices, choreography, and direction throughout the two seasons—their public manifestations will necessarily be different at each new performance. And even in commercial theatre, where "when an actor replaces the original performer of a role he is expected to follow the format of his predecessor,"⁶² it is acknowledged that each iteration will inevitably alter the format of the text. So when Questarians work to produce fan versions of the *Galaxy Quest* television show, or when *Star Trek* fans construct their own web episodes of the missing *New Voyages*, they do so in the knowledge that what they are producing will never be the object itself, as they are highly unlikely to feature the canon's original actors.⁶³ For live performances, though, the question of what constitutes an authentic or "official" version is more heavily contested. For example, fans themselves acknowledged that bringing *Bombshell* to the stage would not necessarily require the input of either Megan Hilty or Katharine McPhee as Marilyn in order to be an authentic iteration: while it was agreed that this would indeed be a boon, musicals are specifically designed to outlive their original casts. This is perhaps one reason why, in imagining how *Bombshell* might actually work on stage, fans were able to balance their dual visions of Marilyn as played by Ivy Lynn/Karen Cartwright with their alternative visions of which real-world musical performers might carry this role.

As Booth explains, it is also the case that the fictive television programs discussed above are all parodies or pastiches.⁶⁴ One of the key pleasures of performing these attachments comes from being *fans of fandom*,⁶⁵ enjoying the self-referential nature of no-object texts. Contrariwise, before *Smash* had even premiered *Bombshell* was already being touted as a genuine possibility, trailing behind it Spielberg's promise that the musical might one day come to fruition. Fans therefore seemed to take seriously the work of sifting through the canon in all its fluctuating forms, and considering how an agreeable production might be constructed from their favorite variants:

> My problem with the Mambo is not the song - I love it and I even dance like an idiot when I listen to it – but the dream sequence of 1x02 that is not the best, imho. It's half dream and half 'audition,' plus the pink light is painful for the eyes and even the Marilyn dress Karen has is not my favorite one. I like MORE the way they staged it in the S1 finale.[66]

While investigating online discourse presents only a partial picture of how diverse audiences respond to cultural events, what it does offer is the chance to watch as debates evolve over time. The *Bombshell* forum presents an emerging picture of how this small group of fans reacted as the Internet drip-fed new canonical additions. This began prior to March 28, 2014 with the announcement that Katharine McPhee and Megan Hilty would be performing a selection of *Smash*'s songs at a forthcoming Gala celebrating the New York Pops orchestra:

> The Bombshell songs were only three: They Just Keep Moving The Line, Don't Forget Me and Let Me Be Your Star.[67]

Contributors used the forum to post pictures of the stars, along with a photo of the show's running order and additional information. This prompted reflection of all the many different ways in which the cast might "keep the Smash/Bombshell (& even Hit List) love alive".[68]

> if they were to do something again with this cast I'll say something musical, it doesn't have to be a musical theater show or movie just having them together as a cast would be great.[69]

> That would be perfect There was talent everywhere! They could also do something for charity, like a recording - not with Smash songs, but others (standards or musical famous classics or original songs, why not). I think I could even buy a Christmas cd, with them. They could also do a play on Broadway – so no singing, just acting.... Maybe this Monday Gala will make them think about some Bombshell stuff.[70]

Following the Gala, which saw *Smash*'s songs performed out of order and out of character, fans agreed: "Now we need a Bombshell only concert, so we can listen live to all songs together."[71] In December that year, their request was answered. Beginning with the phrase "asdfghjkl;"[72] in large black letters, the forum's initiator posted the emotionally-charged announcement that a Kickstarter campaign had been launched for a dedicated *Bombshell* concert. Thus followed three months of excited speculation, as cast members began signing on to the project and the total raised on Kickstarter rose higher and higher:

> I am so happy about this you don't even know how much I wanted something like this to happen in real life and now I get to see it. I know it's for charity but for one night this will be great even though I wanted something of an actual musical but this is still as good as anything I've ever imagined.[73]
>
> Consider that when I opened the page a couple of hours ago it was like 57,000 and now it's already above 100K! Maybe they can use the extra money to record a DVD[74]
>
> I found out today about the Kat and cast thing   It will be an AMAZING SHOW, it seems they'll do also choreographies, right? So also costumes [75]
>
> They've raised $177,111 now[76]
>
> $208.744 now! They couls reach the million dollar this month, it's not that impossible [77]

The decision here to switch away from plain text format and begin representing comments with visual accompaniments has been made to show the significant evolution in the use of emojis. I have written elsewhere about how online viewers use emoticons to describe visceral reactions to live performance recordings, positing that these pictorial inclusions offer a way for audiences to project themselves virtually into the heart of shared experiences.[78] In this forum discussion, what was especially revealing was the sudden shift in mood after the Kickstarter campaign closed, with 1485 backers pledging $318,120 (far exceeding the $50,000 goal). Rewards were priced at a range of levels, with pledges between $10 and $10,000, and all levels were restricted to people living in the United States. The overwhelming majority of backers—1243—chose a level that entitled them to receive advance notification of ticket pre-sale. The problem was that the Minskoff Theatre has a maximum capacity of 1621. Successful backers were allowed to buy two tickets each (quickly reduced from four, after it became apparent how many backers would be clamoring for tickets), which means an approximate maximum of 800 backers successfully purchased tickets. Further adding to the anxiety, when pre-sale opened on April 13 Ticketmaster's system was overwhelmed by the volume of traffic, with hundreds of people simultaneously attempting to enter their access codes. A lot of backers reported that by the time they had managed to get the code working, tickets had already sold out:

> I thought about going but the tickets were so fast gone, it was laughable. […] I just really didnt understand it. I got the pre alert too but they said they would sell the tickets later and then suddenly boom... sold out. guess it all went to those who had an advantage … not fair but oh well[79]
>
> People who had the pre alert were A LOT (someone said they were even more that all the theatre seats!). Too bad😞[80]
>
> That's a shame 😞😢😔 In a way I'm glad it sold out quickly but it is a shame that it was so hard & confusing to get them[81]

Scrolling downwards it is possible to watch the joyful, excited posts turn to dejection and disappointment, compounded by the news that for legal reasons it would not be possible to officially film the concert. Reading the trajectory of these reactions is the online equivalent of watching somebody's face fall. Investigating the Kickstarter comments tells a similar story, with many dissatisfied backers requesting that their pledges be refunded. Phrases like "ripped off" and "terrible fulfillment" were used, with the bitterest disappointment coming from those who were unable to get the website to accept their codes until after tickets had sold out.

A handful of people chimed in to explain that The Actors Fund had not promised tickets to any of their backers—even those who pledged $10,000 were forced to compete using the pre-sale code—and that what people were actually pledging was a charity donation. This led a number of backers to explain that their discontent stemmed not simply from lack of success, but from the feeling that they *hadn't been given a fair shot*. These accounts were often narratively detailed, talking about feeling as if they had no choice but to "blindly" follow the procedure devised by The Actors Fund: a series of updates, an urgent deadline, a code arriving, a chance for a ticket—then cruelly snatched away. Disappointment, frustration, anger, dejection: all could have been avoided not necessarily by providing guaranteed tickets to all backers (people tended to recognize the impossibility of this) but through *transparency and fairness*.

In an article called 'The Value of Being Together?' on Punchdrunk participants, Jan Wozniak argues that when theatre audiences are encouraged to engage in competitive individualistic behavior, this may disrupt their ability to take pleasure in cooperation and shared experience.[82] While Wozniak's article focuses on the ramifications for audiences of taking part in an unstructured immersive event, the Kickstarter comments reveal a similar problem. For these backers, one of the key reasons for investment was the sense that they were collaboratively bringing *Bombshell* to life (albeit in a streamlined form), with people's often lengthy descriptions tracing out the trajectory from collaborative excitement to inequitable disappointment. A couple of people suggested that a more equitable system might have been provided through a lottery, with backers' names drawn on a specific date. What seemed to annoy people was the unjust selection process. The knowledge that they were actively competing with other backers for this one-off event made it difficult to maintain the sense of being in the middle of a productive fan community.

What these comments point towards is a communal desire to play a part in a one-off experience. When their codes failed to work in time, this left many backers on the outside of the event unable to see in. This led backers to plead with The Actors Fund to redress the imbalance by releasing a digital version of the concert. While almost every commentator expressed the hope that they would secure a ticket to the live event, it was generally agreed that digital documentation would be a welcome way of opening up participation to a wider audience. By such means, the sense of a friendly fan community might have been extended and sustained instead of problematically abridged.

It is therefore necessary to reconsider the widespread assertion that live experiences present a privileged site by which audiences may connect with temporary communities. As Philip Auslander reminds us,[83] and as Ryan Bunch points out in the next chapter, the line between liveness and mediatization has become progressively blurred. While this research has found a lingering hunger to take part in co-present events, the digital discourse that surrounds live performances is nonetheless increasingly coopted by audiences to mediate the sensation of taking part in an ongoing, shared experience. This has the potential to offer a more democratic space for participation, with audiences from varying socio-demographic backgrounds coming together from all over the world to inhabit a shared online space.

Conclusion

This chapter has shown how the cancellation of *Smash* left *Bombshell* fans in limbo. Similarly, when the possibility of cancellation was initially raised for British sci-fi TV show *Torchwood* (a spin-off of *Doctor Who*), the initial "lack of certainty surrounding *Torchwood*'s fate place[d] [...] fans in an unusual position: not entirely sure about whether to grieve or mourn the passing of a favorite series or to keep their hope for a return alive."[84] Indeed, the very existence of a specific fan forum thread for *Bombshell*—started in October 2013, seven months after *Smash*'s cancellation—can be read as a hopeful attempt to animate the musical's legacy long enough for it to be officially resuscitated. Through dedicating themselves to such continued activity, fans are increasingly aware of their own power to change the fortunes of beloved texts. While there have always been cases of networks revoking cancellations following disappointed uproar, the recent spate of revivals spearheaded by online streaming services—coupled with the fabled success of the *Veronica Mars* Kickstarter project—has meant it is now more possible than ever that audience demand might inspire discarded programs to be picked up elsewhere. For fans of dying television shows, this suggests, the door *never fully closes*.

This was doubly true for *Smash*'s fans, who remain aware that its musicals may yet have their own afterlife: as live performances independent of the source. Indeed, through continuing to assert their ongoing engagements fans have actually succeeded, step-by-step, in bringing *Bombshell* to the stage. It now remains to be seen whether the musical will ever actually make it to Broadway, and if the show itself will match up to the no-object versions that have emerged in fans' collective imaginations. After all, as Marilyn Monroe herself is supposed to have said: nothing's ever easy as long as you go on living.

Notes

1. Nussbaum, "Had Me At 'Hello!'".
2. Levin, "NBC's Best Friend".
3. Ibid.

4. McNamara, "Television Review".
5. Harnick, "'Smash' Ratings Drop".
6. Aurthur, "Train Wreck".
7. Harnick, "'Smash' Ratings Drop".
8. Paulson, "'Smash' Lives Again".
9. Ariano and Grosswirth, "One More Chance".
10. On request of the publishers, online comments have been presented without disguise. In addition, all audience quotations appear as they are written online, with any spelling or grammatical anomalies retained. This is because I am aware that to snip audiences' posts out of the location in which they were intended to be viewed is to make an ethically-weighted decision, and that changing the format of written material would be to suggest that I have a greater level of expertise than audiences themselves over their intended statements.
11. Ariano and Grosswirth, Below-the-line comments: "One More Chance".
12. Nussbaum, "Hate-Watching".
13. Ariano and Grosswirth, Below-the-line comments: "Workshopping." Note: In order to adhere to necessary space constraints I have cut this online comment down to 111 words from 373. The full rant offers an especially rich example of the extent to which certain audiences "worry away" at a series and its plot-holes.
14. See McCoy and Scarborough for a valuable empirical study that unpicks the "hate-watching" process in detail.
15. Nussbaum, "Hate-Watching".
16. Goletz, "Giddyshame".
17. Ariano and Grosswirth, Below-the-line comments: "Workshopping".
18. Sepinwall, "Hope-Watching".
19. Television Without Pity, "Win and Go Home." Comment by PopCultureBGSU.
20. Ibid. Comment by Molly.
21. Sepinwall, "Hope-Watching".
22. McMillin, *Musical As Drama*, 103.
23. Ariano and Grosswirth, "Norma Jean." Comment by kimberwatch.
24. Ibid. Comment by Kat.
25. Ibid. Comment by swtrgrl.
26. Ariano and Grosswirth, "Workshopping." Comment by allonsyalice.
27. Ariano and Grosswirth, "One More Chance." Comment by Lisin.
28. Ibid. Comment by marceline.
29. Ibid. Comment by Lisin.
30. SmashSongs1, "Don't Forget Me." Comment by EmmaExilexXx.
31. SmashBrasil, "Touch Me." Comment by Shrouq North.
32. Ibid. Comment by Salini Valentine.
33. Selix, "Let Me Be Your Star." Comment by MadamXtinagurl.

34. Ibid. Comment by Ziaheart.
35. Ibid. Comment by selfxmadexstar.
36. Ibid. Comment by Charles Hung.
37. SmashSongs1, "Don't Forget Me." Comment by ImYourVj.
38. Quaseruivo, "Don't Forget Me." Comment by Countrycowboy08.
39. Ibid.
40. Ibid. Comment by Ben Prince.
41. Ibid. Comment by Quinlan Green.
42. Quaseruivo, "Don't Forget Me." Comment by pressedlemon.
43. Ibid. Comment by Tom Idelson.
44. SmashBrasil, "Touch Me." Comment by mne93.
45. Hills, "Making Sense," 113.
46. Williams, *Post-Object*, 10.
47. airali_glo, "BOMBSHELL Musical Appreciation".
48. Ibid. Comment by Ms. Evil RegalQ.
49. Ibid. Comment by airali_glo.
50. Ibid. Comment by speedoflifexx.
51. Ibid. Comment by airali_glo.
52. Ibid.
53. Ibid. Comment by s e r e n i t y.
54. Ibid. Comment by Lutesse.
55. Booth, *Playing Fans*, 54.
56. Geraghty, *Living With Star Trek*.
57. Booth, *Playing Fans*, 57.
58. Ibid., 54.
59. Ibid.
60. Freshwater, "Authenticities".
61. Coppa, Francesca, "Writing Bodies in Space," 237.
62. Beckerman, *Dynamics*, 161.
63. In practice, this is not as simple a distinction as I may have made it seem. As Booth explains, the fan-made *New Voyages* series attracted a sizeable audience and were at least as popular as the official Paramount production (*Playing Fans*, 65), while *Inspector Spacetime*'s generative texts have asserted an actual canonized history (Ibid., 60). Similarly, the spate of new films within franchises such as Star Trek, which recast Zachary Quinto as a young Spock instead of the original actor Leonard Nimoy, have shown how far fans' loyalties to "original" texts can be stretched. And as Booth has recently argued, *SuperWhoLock*'s total fluidity comes from the fact that it *has* no center: there is no originating *SuperWhoLock* text to which fans can return, and so any imaginative expansion is necessarily an act of creation (*Crossing Fandoms*, 5). Nor is this to deny the significance for fans of encountering the 'original' theatrical moment, with

Jessica Hillman-McCord describing in Chap. 6 of this book how audiences work to extend their *Hamilton* experiences through a wide variety of extra-textual engagements. Nonetheless, it is reasonable to suggest that theatre attracts—and even demands—a particular degree of "fluidity in textuality" (*Playing Fans*, 60), as audiences' favorite characters are continuously cast and recast. In fact, "collecting" viewings of multiple actors in a single role is a common practice in musical theatre fandom (see for example Stacy Wolf's "*Wicked* Divas"; Freshwater's "Consuming Authenticities").

64. Booth, *Playing Fans*, 19–20.
65. Ibid., 55.
66. airali_glo, "BOMBSHELL Musical Appreciation." Comment by airali_glo.
67. Ibid.
68. Ibid. Comment by speedoflifexx.
69. Ibid. Comment by Mr♋MrsStinsbatskys.
70. Ibid. Comment by airali_glo.
71. Ibid.
72. Ibid. Note: "asdfghjkl;" is an agreed expression of desperation, frustration, or excitement, used when no actual words will do.
73. Ibid. Comment by Mr♋MrsStinsbatskys.
74. Ibid. Comment by airali_glo.
75. Ibid.
76. Ibid. Comment by speedoflifexx.
77. Ibid. Comment by airali_glo.
78. Sedgman, "Standing Ovation".
79. airali_glo, "BOMBSHELL Musical Appreciation." Comment by Ms. Evil Regal♋.
80. Ibid. Comment by airali_glo.
81. Ibid. Comment by speedoflifexx.
82. Wozniak, "Value".
83. Auslander, *Liveness*.
84. Williams, *Post-Object*, 191.

Bibliography

Actors Fund, The. 2015. "BOMBSHELL from the TV series SMASH - A Broadway Concert," *Kickstarter*. http://www.kickstarter.com/projects/993462222/bombshell-from-the-nbc-series-smash-a-broadway-con/comments. Accessed January 23 2016.

airali_glo. 2013. "The BOMBSHELL musical appreciation thread #1." *Fan Forum*. http://www.fanforum.com/f405/bombshell-musical-appreciation-thread-1-let-me-your-star-63106535. Accessed January 23 2016.

Ariano, Tara and Adam Grosswirth. 2015. "Norma Jean May Be Gone, But We Can't Move On (From *Smash*)." *PreviouslyTV*. http://previously.tv/smash/norma-jean-may-be-gone-but-we-cant-move-on-from-smash. Accessed January 23 2016.

Ariano, Tara and Adam Grosswirth. 2015. "Workshopping And Pill-Popping." *PreviouslyTV*. http://previously.tv/smash/workshopping-and-pill-popping. Accessed January 7 2015.

Ariano, Tara and Adam Grosswirth. 2015. "Why Couldn't NBC Give Smash That One More Chance?" *PreviouslyTV*. http://previously.tv/smash/why-couldnt-nbc-give-smash-that-one-more-chance. Accessed January 23 2016.

Aurthur, Kate. 2013. "How 'Smash' Became TV's Biggest Train Wreck." *Buzzfeed*. http://www.buzzfeed.com/kateaurthur/how-smash-became-tvs-biggest-train-wreck#.caApgwMZpg. Accessed January 4 2016.

Auslander, Philip. 2009. *Liveness: Performance in a Mediatized Culture*. London: Routledge.

Beckerman, Bernard. 1979. *Dynamics of Drama*. New York: Drama Book Specialists.

Booth, Paul. 2015. *Playing Fans: Negotiating Fandom and Media in the Digital Age*. Iowa City: University of Iowa Press.

Booth, Paul. 2016. *Crossing Fandoms: SuperWhoLock and the Contemporary Fan Audience*. London: Springer.

Bore, Inger-Lise Kalviknes. 2011. "Reviewing Romcom: (100) IMDb Users and *(500) Days of Summer*." *Participations* 8:2: 144–164.

Boyle, Karen. 2014. "Gender, comedy and reviewing culture on the Internet Movie Database." *Participations* 11:1: 31–49.

Coppa, Francesca. 2006. "Writing Bodies in Space: Media Fanfiction as Theatrical Performance." K. Hellekson and K. Busse (eds.), *Fan Fiction and Fan Communities in the Age of the Internet: New Essays*, Chicago: McFarland, 225–244.

Freshwater, Helen. 2012. "Consuming Authenticities: *Billy Elliot the Musical* and the Performing Child." *The Lion and the Unicorn* 36: 154–173.

Geraghty, Lincoln. 2007. *Living with Star Trek: American Culture and the Star Trek Universe*. London: IB Tauris.

Goletz, Sarah Wagenseller. 2012. "The Giddyshame Paradox: Why Twilight's Anti-Fans Cannot Stop Reading a Series They (Love to) Hate." In *Genre, Reception, and Adaptation in the "Twilight" Series*, ed. Anne Morey, 147–162. Farnham: Ashgate Publishing.

Harnick, Chris. 2013. "'Smash' Ratings Drop: What Went Wrong With NBC's Musical Drama." *Huffington Post*. http://www.huffingtonpost.com/chris-harnick/smash-ratings-drop-what-went-wrong_b_2821404.html. Accessed January 4 2016.

Hills, Matt. 2010. "Making Sense of M. Night Shyamalan: Signs of a Popular Auteur in the 'Field of Horror.'" In *Critical Approaches to the Films of M. Night Shyamalan*, ed. J.A. Weinstock, 103–118. Basingstoke: Palgrave Macmillan.

Levin, Gary. 2012. "Marilyn, 'Smash' could be NBC's best friend." *USA Today*. http://usatoday30.usatoday.com/life/television/news/story/2012-01-26/Smash-Debra-Messing-Anjelica-Huston/52940518/1. Accessed January 3 2016.

McCoy, Charles Allan & Roscoe C. Scarborough. 2014. "Watching 'Bad' Television: Ironic Consumption, Camp, and Guilty Pleasures," *Poetics* 47: 41–59.

McMillin, Scott. 2014. *The Musical as Drama: A Study of the Principles and Conventions Behind Musical Shows from Kern to Sondheim*. Princeton: Princeton University Press.

McNamara, Mary. 2012. "Television Review: 'Smash' on NBC," *Los Angeles Times*. http://articles.latimes.com/2012/feb/06/entertainment/la-et-smash-review-20120206. Accessed January 4 2016.

Nussbaum, Emily. 2012. "'Smash': It Had Me at 'Hello!'" *The New Yorker*. http://www.newyorker.com/culture/culture-desk/smash-it-had-me-at-hello. Accessed January 3 2016.

Nussbaum, Emily. 2012. "Hate-Watching 'Smash.'" *The New Yorker*. http://www.newyorker.com/culture/culture-desk/smash-it-had-me-at-hello. Accessed January 3 2016.

Paulson, Michael. 2015. "'Smash' Lives Again, in One-Night 'Bombshell' Concert." *New York Times*. http://artsbeat.blogs.nytimes.com/2015/03/11/smash-lives-again-in-one-night-bombshell-concert/?_r=0. Accessed January 23 2016.

Quaseruivo. 2013. "SMASH—Don't Forget Me (Ivy Lynn) #SmashBrasil." https://youtu.be/MfSBl9OT0mw. Accessed January 9 2016.

Selix, Victoria Bryanne. 2012. "'Let Me Be Your Star' by Smash (Lyrics included)." https://youtu.be/huaauJ48JUs. Accessed January 9 2016.

Sedgman, Kirsty. 2016. "What's Bigger than a Standing Ovation?': Intimacy and Spectacle at the Tony Awards", Studies in Musical Theatre 10:1, 37–53.

Sepinwall, Alan. 2015. "Hope-watching vs. hate-watching in TV's new Golden Age." *HITFIX*. http://www.hitfix.com/whats-alan-watching/hope-watching-vs-hate-watching-in-tvs-new-golden-age#Qpv8siyW109IOZwD.99. Accessed January 6 2016.

SmashBrasil. 2012. "SMASH—Touch Me." https://youtu.be/zYmI0KvnHk. Accessed January 9 2016.

SmashSongs1. 2012. "Smash—Don't Forget Me (DOWNLOAD MP3 + Lyrics)." https://youtu.be/2qvwq8ecDwM. Accessed January 9, 2016.

Television Without Pity. 2013. "Smash: Win and Go Home." http://www.televisionwithoutpity.com/show/smash/the-tonys. January 7 2016.

Thelwall, Mike. 2014. "Analysing YouTube Audience Reactions and Discussions: A Network Approach." In *Analyzing Social Media Data and Web Networks*, ed. Marta Cantijoch, Rachel Gibson, and Stephen Ward, 72–97. Basingstoke: Palgrave Macmillan.

Wikipedia. "List of *Smash* Episodes". 2015. https://en.wikipedia.org/wiki/List_of_Smash_episodes. Accessed January 23 2016.

Williams, Rebecca. 2011. "'This Is the Night TV Died': Television Post-Object Fandom and the Demise of *The West Wing*." *Popular Communication* 9:4: 266–279.

Williams, Rebecca. 2015. *Post-Object Fandom: Television, Identity and Self-narrative*. London: Bloomsbury Publishing.

Wolf, Stacy. 2007. "*Wicked* Divas, Musical Theater, and Internet Girl Fans." *Camera Obscura* 22:2:65: 39–71.

Wozniak, Jan. 2015. "The Value of Being Together?" *Participations* 12:1: 318–32.

CHAPTER 8

"You Can't Stop the Tweet": Social Media and Networks of Participation in the Live Television Musical

Ryan Bunch

Recent years have seen the vigorous return of a form of entertainment that has not had much currency for half a century—the live television broadcast of musicals. Inspired by the model of popular musical broadcasts of the 1950s, NBC's *The Sound of Music Live!* (2013), *Peter Pan Live!* (2014), *The Wiz Live!* (2015), and *Hairspray Live!* (2016), and Fox's *Grease Live!* (2016) combine nostalgia for classic musicals and the established medium of television with audience participation through new social interaction technologies. During these broadcasts, viewers use social media platforms like Facebook and Twitter to talk to each other, making these performances notably participatory. The interactions of fans, critics, producers, performers, and others during a live musical involve the dissemination of content across media forms in an example of what Henry Jenkins calls "convergence culture," defined as "the flow of media across multiple platforms, the cooperation between multiple media industries, and the migratory behavior of media audiences who

R. Bunch (✉)
Rutgers University-Camden, Camden, NJ, USA
e-mail: ryan@ryanbunch.com

© The Author(s) 2017
J. Hillman-McCord (ed.), *iBroadway*,
DOI 10.1007/978-3-319-64876-7_8

will go almost anywhere in search of the kinds of entertainment experiences they want."[1]

An aspect of the online conversations during these broadcasts involves negotiations over the meaning of musical theatre and its live performance. Such questions arise out of the converging media interactions themselves, which expose the complications of liveness in mediatized culture, where the conventions of traditional theatre, the televisual, and online interaction meet and compete. In this environment, participants draw upon their preexisting conceptions about musicals and liveness in their assessments of the quality of the productions, communicating these ideas through various participatory practices, including ironic viewing, hate-watching, and critical humor. These conversations are further engaged with the political realities of specific fan communities in particular moments, as in the Black Twitter response to *The Wiz Live!* during the height of the Black Lives Matter movement and in critiques of the gender, race, and sexual representations within the shows. Tweeting on these topics becomes a way of performing identities and political positions in relation to the performances on screen. Although a consensus about the best practices of the live television musical remain elusive, fan and producer interactions have produced ongoing changes in the ways in which it is approached.

Spreading Media and Mediating the Live

The conventions employed in these new live musicals are inspired by live broadcasts of the early years of television and complicated by the differing meanings of the "live" in theatre, on television, and in social media interactions. The most successful of those early broadcasts were NBC's *Peter Pan* (1955) and CBS's *Cinderella* (1957). *Peter Pan*, starring Mary Martin, was a tremendous success in its initial showing, and after audiences sent letters demanding to see it again, NBC videotaped a color performance in 1960, which was broadcast in 1963, 1966, and 1973. Rodgers and Hammerstein's *Cinderella*, starring Julie Andrews on CBS, was similarly later recorded and remade for subsequent airing. The television version of *Peter Pan* was still a nostalgic favorite in 1989 when its release on home video led to a resurgence of its popularity, culminating in a 2000 Broadway revival followed by a touring production with Cathy Rigby, which was also released on DVD.

The new crop of live musicals grew out of both nostalgia for those old broadcasts and the desire to create something new that would attract contemporary audiences to the television networks at a time when on-demand and binge-watching practices had been displacing more traditional appointment viewing. As a television event, the live musical could attract a real-time audience in similar fashion to a sporting event or live talent show such as *American Idol* (2002–2016) or *X-Factor* (2011–2013).[2] Producers Craig Zadan and Neil Meron's idea to revive the live musical tradition from the 1950s was sold to NBC, the same network that had aired the classic *Peter Pan*, in large part to address this need. Their first effort was 2013's *The Sound of Music Live!*, with a cast that included country-pop singer Carrie Underwood as a star attraction, along with Broadway veterans Laura Benanti and Christian Borle, as well as newcomers in the roles of the Von Trapp children. *The Sound of Music Live!* was a ratings success as a television event, attracting 18.62 million viewers and paving the way for annual broadcasts on NBC with *Peter Pan Live!*, *The Wiz Live!*, and *Hairspray Live!*[3]

Promotional materials and press reports for the musicals emphasized the novelty of their liveness. The word *Live!* in the title of each musical invoked an aura of excitement and authenticity, while producers emphasized the logistical challenges and risks for performers in a live broadcast. In a CNN report before *The Sound of Music Live!*, anchor Nischelle Turner observed, "I look at it as kind of like a musical version of Sunday Night Football, because it's three hours of live"—at this point her cohost Brian Stelter, unable to contain his excitement, chimed in—"where *anything* can happen!"[4] Turner further added that the presence of children in the production made the enterprise even more unpredictable. Julie Andrews, wishing Carrie Underwood well in the same report, remarked, "A live broadcast, my God, poor lady!" Turner said she was nervous for Underwood, and Stelter anticipated that the Twitter audience would be there in real time to assess whether things were going well or not. They noted the importance to NBC of getting an audience to tune in live. Each musical was promoted with a "making of" preview airing a few days before the live broadcast in order to take viewers behind the scenes and build excitement for the live event.

As Philip Auslander emphasizes, however, the concept of the "live" in this context is complicated. Liveness is not simply the authentic predecessor and superior of the mediated in a reductive binary, but is only available as a concept in mutual constitution with the concept of mediatization. Further, what perceived distinctions can be made between the live and the mediatized should "derive from careful consideration of how [their] relationship ... is articulated in particular cases."[5] By situating the experience of liveness in relation to the particulars of audience participation through transmedia networks, we might better understand various ways in which liveness is mediated in these musical broadcasts. In this way, the live becomes a relational concept useful for distinguishing a variety of forms and experiences.

The complex relationship between the live and the mediatized has always been a feature of television, which from its earliest days borrowed and adapted its techniques from the theatre and subsequently influenced theatrical practices. Mostly a live medium in its early years, television retains its affect of liveness even when programs are prerecorded (as, for example, in the use of laugh tracks and studio audiences in sitcom tapings). Since, according to Auslander, television is the current culturally dominant medium, suffusing our culture as "the televisual," its representations of liveness have become so influential that, as Lynn Spigel notes, the hyperreal experience of television and its simulation of liveness is even experienced as superior to the traditional live.[6] In response, live theatre, in order to stay current and competitive, has in turn adapted the language and expectations of mediatized entertainment in its aesthetics. Some of these effects, which include amplification and digital imagery, are evident in the live musicals—for example, in the use of light-emitting diode (LED) backgrounds in the sets for *The Wiz Live!* and in the computer-aided imagery (CGI) of Tinkerbell in *Peter Pan Live!*—and contribute to the relational dynamics of the live and the mediated.

A particular manifestation of liveness brought by television, and one which the classic live musicals inspiring Meron and Zadan exploited, is the intimacy of a performance experienced in the home. This idea of home theatre gives its viewers the sense of being close to the events on screen, as though they had front row seats to a private performance. The televisual aesthetic employed in these musical broadcasts thus already carries with it a certain aura of liveness and relationship to live theatre. As we'll see, however, the ideal of intimacy from mid-twentieth century television was at odds with the viewing practices and values of live musical participants in the twenty-first.

Adding musicals into this mix brings in yet another set of values regarding live performance and its perception as such. The kinetic energy of a live performance in the theatre is highly valued by musical theatre fans, who maintain an awareness of performers as themselves in addition to the characters they play. These performers are admired for their singing, dancing, and acting skills, and musical theatre fans' evaluations of performances are based largely on the artistic and technical successes and failures of the actors.[7] Even in film musicals, with their mediated illusions of live performance (or, on the other hand, attempts to make performance seem natural and artless), the embodied talents and personae of singing actors are important to fans. How television musicals handle the presentation of these performances, especially when broadcast live, has important implications for the perceived success or failure of the productions according to audience expectations.

The question of liveness in the musical broadcasts is complicated not only by these already existing notions of the live, but even further by the live participation of users of social media, most notably, perhaps, in the case of live tweeting. The convergence of online media forms with television viewing creates the opportunity for active participation by consumers, as tweets, retweets, and memes allow users to circulate and share ideas. Henry Jenkins, Sam Ford, and Joshua Green refer to this decentered circulation of online content as "spreadable media."[8] Distinct from the use of "sticky media," in which users are drawn to a single destination, such as a website, spreadable media enables a more participatory experience through networked communities. The live musicals rely on both the stickiness of an "old media" live broadcast which draws people to the same "place" at the same time (in front of their TVs on the same channel at the time of broadcast) and the spreadability of online discussion (the tweets, the promotional materials, the trailers, the memes produced by viewers as well as the official ones distributed by NBC and Fox). Audiences, corporations, and industry professionals are able to talk to each other through these networks.

As the concept of liveness has become articulated to new technologies over time, its definition has expanded from the notion of audiences and performers present in the same place at the same time to new ideas such as "live broadcast" and "live recording." The rise of digital culture complicates these notions even further. Nick Couldry, for example, has proposed several new forms of liveness, such as *Internet liveness* (sense of co-presence among users), *social liveness* (sense of connection to others; mobile phones, instant message), *online liveness* (social co-presence on the Internet; from chat rooms to huge international audiences for breaking news on major websites), and *group liveness* (users in continuous contact through mobile phones, calling, texting).[9]

We might, therefore, see the musical broadcasts as combining several different forms of liveness: live television experienced perceptibly in real time; live tweeting and social media participation; and as the live company of co-viewers in homes and at viewing parties. The dislocations of time and space that accompany these experiences further complicate the composition of the live in the experience of television musicals. Live tweeting takes place concurrently with the televised performance but also leaves for the future a record of the liveness as experienced at the time of origin. Tweets provide evidence of who was "there" and what conversations were being had. Differences in time zones complicate the notion of liveness in these broadcasts as well, as viewers in the Mountain and Pacific time zones are exposed to tweets by Eastern and Central audiences while they wait for the musicals to re-air three hours later. Many people, of course, record the broadcasts for later viewing. After each broadcast discussed here, the musical was made available for purchase on DVD and by digital streaming and download in versions that fixed some of the mistakes of the original live performance. Viewers posting on Twitter were aware of these issues:

> About to watch #HairsprayLive ... except it's not live anymore. Does that mean it's like your dad's DVD of the high school musical?[10]

Viewers watched the broadcasts at home and in other physical places such as bars and community centers, where many of them were also tweeting. The convergence of physical and digital space approximated the classic form of liveness—not only were people watching at the same time, but social media interactions reduced separation by space as well. At the same time, social media participants could interact with each other more through Twitter and Facebook than a traditional live audience in the dark and noise-restricted environment of a theatre. In contrast to the use of mobile digital technologies in a traditional theatre space, where cell phones are considered a distraction or sign of disengagement as discussed by Kathryn Edney in Chap. 5 of this book, with the live television musical, digital activity is an essential component of participation with a larger community:

Big cheer in the gay bar for Kurt's high note. #SoundOfMusicLive #TeamElsa[11]

Negotiating Liveness and the Musical

Negotiations of liveness, musical fandom, and the meaning of live television musicals took place within and across a number of different communities involving a variety of differently positioned subjects. Among them were musical theatre fans, theatre and entertainment professionals, critics, scholars, casual viewers, and parents who expressed their views in conversation with each other. Across these communities, some voices were more amplified than others depending on such things as an individual tweeter's social media capital. Media reports on the live tweeting of each musical were stories of their own, allowing media outlets and news organizations to capitalize on the events, further publicizing the shows and NBC, as well as the tweeters, many of whom were probably glad to gain followers. The most widely seen and shared tweets were by celebrities, industry professionals, corporations, and others with large numbers of followers, whose comments were also more likely to be quoted on news media summaries and entertainment sites. For example, screen musicals star Anna Kendrick has been one of the most perennially popular tweeters of the live musicals, and DiGiorno Pizza got in some guerilla adverting by posting humorous tweets during *The Sound of Music Live!*.[12] *The Hollywood Reporter*'s coverage featured the DiGiorno tweets and celebrity reactions from Cameron Diaz, Rosie O'Donnell, and Ronan Farrow.[13] Michael Rothman, for ABC news, compiled celebrity and corporate tweets from DiGiorno, Diaz, Kendrick, Sarah Silverman, and others in "funniest tweets" about *The Sound of Music Live!*.[14] In spite of the democratic potential of spreadable media, then, some have more ability than others to make themselves heard.[15]

Social media participants also took on the role of critics, adding their voices to those of the professionals—in fact, getting their own opinions out before the official reviews by offering their assessments of how things were going in real time. One of the recurring themes during the first two NBC musicals was the complaint that stunt casting of celebrities, instead of experienced musical theatre performers, was having a detrimental effect. A consensus emerged during *The Sound of Music Live!* that Carrie Underwood's singing was good, but her acting left much to be desired. In *Peter Pan Live!*, Allison Williams, star of the television program *Girls* and daughter of news anchor Brian Williams, was considered passable but not strong. Sometimes it was a case of outright miscasting. Although some found ironic charm in Christopher Walken's deadpan performance of Captain Hook, it was mostly panned by those who were familiar with the foppish camp tradition in the portrayal of the character on stage and screen, particularly its embodiment by Cyril Ritchard in the original NBC broadcast. Viewers were also eager to express their opinions on choices made by the producers and creative teams on matters of content and production quality. Many people criticized *Peter Pan*'s extravagant and color-saturated sets, for example, and complained that the rewrites intended to minimize racial and gender stereotypes in the original were insufficient.[16]

As Jessica Hillman-McCord discusses in Chap. 6, online fans "value, display, and most importantly, *perform*" their knowledge of musicals. Tweeting during the live broadcasts offered an opportunity for fans and viewers to demonstrate their expertise. Musical fans who saw themselves as curators of musical theatre's cultural cachet took the opportunity to educate those whose only access to theatre was through the presumably lowbrow medium of television. Some viewers of the live musicals expressed gratitude that musicals were being made for those who would usually not see them, even if they believed that these particular productions were not the best exemplars:

#PeterPanLIVE tonight @ 8 on NBC. shoutout to nbc for continually bringing Musical Theatre into so many homes without it.[17]

Really enjoyed #HairsprayLive So great to see prime time television celebrate musical theater like that! And @KChenoweth, I love you[18]

Producers took on the role of educators as well. Anticipating that many viewers would have expectations based on the film versions with which they might be more familiar, Zadan and Meron emphasized that the broadcasts would be based on the stage shows, and further explained their reasons for choosing to include certain songs from different versions of the show.[19] On Twitter and in website comments during and after the broadcasts, there were discussions, debates, and misunderstandings about the "original" versions of the shows and the assumption of their inherent superiority over the new ones. Internet forums provided musical theatre fans with an opportunity both to demonstrate their own expertise to each other, forging bonds of identification by being in the know, and to educate the less fortunate.[20] As Nancy Baym notes of similar practices in soap opera fandom, "opportunities to voice interpretations and offer information are chances to demonstrate genre competence, creativity, and expertise to others, gaining social status and pleasure from the affirmations that posts receive."[21]

The expectations of live theatre, live television, film musicals, and live tweeting, on which audiences based their evaluations of the live musicals, did not always align with each other, producing dissonant responses. *Peter Pan Live!* and *Grease Live!* both made use of elaborate sets that would not be possible in a traditional live theatre space, the latter with a studio audience as part of the setting, and the reactions were mixed, perhaps because the end result looked neither entirely like live theatre nor entirely filmic. Many viewers felt strongly that the musicals should be performed in front of a live studio audience in order to allow performers to have immediate, encouraging feedback and to fulfill the viewer's expectation that a rousing musical number would be followed by applause. For these viewers, dead air and awkward pauses after the songs robbed them of their impact:

> Seriously, let's do this again, but with a live audience. We are in serious need of applause! #SoundOfMusicLive[22]

Although there are times when we don't expect applause after a musical number, notably in film musicals, these television broadcasts are manifestly not films—they are marked by the televisual aesthetic with its aura of immediacy. The obvious physical effort evident in these performances is associated with in-person liveness, and if there is no audience on screen to applaud after each song, we might feel compelled to do it ourselves, leading to what some experienced self-consciously as applauding to the television for people who can't hear.

> I JUST CLAPPED LIKE I WAS IN THE AUDIENCE!!!!!!! #wizlive[23]

People were also surprised when the cast didn't take bows at the end.

> OH.....I thought they were gonna come out and bow. No? #wizlive[24]

Evidently, in spite of Auslander's skepticism of the mystifying "energy" that exists between performers and spectators in live theatre, these conventions remained powerful and important to audiences' experience of liveness.[25] Kevin Fallon of *The Daily Beast* addressed some of the problems of conflicting expectations in *The Sound of Music Live!*:

> Though it was performed live, it was shot as if it was a movie, on what must be the biggest soundstage of all time—the set was massive. So you never saw a proscenium, stage curtains, or an audience. Laugh lines didn't receive laughter. Vamping for applause after a song never actually had applause to vamp to. The hybrid nature of the project ended up zapping the energy from both worlds—film and live theatre—rather than combining them.[26]

In *Variety*, Brian Lowry raised similar issues.

> The producers still haven't fully overcome the somewhat ironic challenge of how to make these live presentations consistently exhibit sparks of life.... What still hasn't been figured out yet, for this more jaded age, is how to replicate the live experience one enjoys when seeing theater through the distance-creating prism of TV. And while the "live" label should foster a sense of risk, these musicals have been so polished that the prospect of any significant glitches or stumbles appears slim at best.[27]

Lowry's observations about the distancing effect of television seems to contradict theories of television as bringing performances close to the home audience. This only emphasizes the complexity of a situation in which liveness is not a thing to be authentically replicated, but which must be constructed through mismatched media conventions.

The producers themselves had contradictory impulses about the broadcast of live musicals, rooted in a conflict between tradition and novelty. *Peter Pan Live!* had a CGI Tinkerbell, and *The Wiz Live!* had an LED backdrop, yet they insisted on the obvious theatricality of leaving the cables exposed to view in the flying scenes in *Peter Pan Live!* and *The Wiz Live!* They held fast to their practice of not having a studio audience, insisting that the performance was especially for the viewers at home, in spite of the discomfort this caused for home viewers as described above. This commitment was motivated by their desire to recreate the tradition of the live musicals of the 1950s, ignoring viewer suggestions after *The Sound of Music Live!*. Zadan and Meron defended their position, saying:

> We still would like to honor the tradition where this genre was given birth and that's in the '50's. We know that it's taken a while for the audience to get used to it, but in the three years we've been doing it, there's always a cry for live audience but that's not [that] special. What's special is [to] do these on a soundstage and live in the moment without that audience and to allow cameras to come in and get up close and personal and have the audience at home be the live audience.[28]

Nostalgia for an idealized past and the expectations of the present were among the values being negotiated. In this case, the conflict was between the producers' memories of the original musical broadcasts—in which the idea of the home as a private theatre was the ideal—and the expectations of modern audiences, who seemed to be looking for a sense of connection to a larger cohort of live viewers, whether in the form of audible applause or real-time tweets.

Such conversations were multidirectional among viewers, performers, and producers, reflecting the new communicative relations made possible by online social media.[29] Performers thanked the fans for watching, and both fans and fellow professionals congratulated the performers. Carrie Underwood used Twitter to talk back to both professional critics and tweeters who disliked her performance:

> Plain and simple: Mean people need Jesus. They will be in my prayers tonight... 1 Peter 2:1-25[30]

Some people tweeted messages to the performers during the day before the evening broadcast to wish them luck. Tweets could also give producers and media corporations feedback about how many people were engaged with the broadcasts and how well the programs were received. For example, Nielsen's TV Twitter ratings provide a measure of how many times each musical was tweeted or read about on Twitter. Although *The Sound of Music Live!* received 449,000 tweets compared to *The Voice*, which received 1.2 million tweets the same week, *The Sound of Music Live!* topped the Twitter ratings because more unique Twitter users (5.2 million) saw tweets about the musical.[31] In addition, social media monitoring companies like Brandwatch provide the networks with information about the proportions of positive and negative tweets.[32]

Discussions and critiques of the live musicals frequently involved ironic viewing practices, including hate-watching and critical humor. Humorous criticism, expectations of performer failure, and other pleasurable forms of antagonism are a vital part of the negotiations of meaning in live musicals. There were, of course, those who tuned in with the simple intention of criticizing or hate-watching. These included people intent on having a little fun with the musical genre, for example by making comments about the saccharine content of *The Sound of Music* or unfavorably comparing Carrie Underwood to Julie Andrews.

However, much of the impulse to ridicule comes out of musical theatre fan culture and its signature modes of ironic reception, largely rooted in camp. Described as "ambivalent making fun" by Richard Dyer, camp involves simultaneous sending up and devotion to an object of affection.[33] Camp-inflected fandom is also likely to manifest preoccupation with stars and their identities, especially divas, and the desire to see them succeed or fail. Some Tweeters made jokes about Captain von Trapp as a vampire because he was played by Stephen Moyer, who was known for his role in the HBO series *True Blood*, while many remarked on *Peter Pan Live!*'s unconventional sexuality and flamboyant production:

> Tonight they will finally put back the original scene where Von Trapp sucks the blood out of Maria.[34]

> Watching a grown woman play an adolescent boy is perhaps the most sexually confusing moment of my life. #PeterPanLive[35]

> This is what people think will happen if u legalize gay marriage. #walkenhookdancenumber #PeterPanLive[36]

Musical theatre fans' love/hate relationship to musical broadcasts is not at all unique to the live musicals, of course. As Kirsty Sedgman discusses in her chapter in this book, similar practices were held among audiences of *Smash*, who took pleasure in the show's musical numbers while also taking pleasure in pointing out its flaws.[37]

Musicals are also highly quotable and easily referenced through their words, music, images, and bodily affects, which makes them easily translatable into memes employing camp and other affectionate forms of critical humor. For example, a popular meme uses the image of Julie

Andrews spinning on a mountain at the beginning of the classic film version of *The Sound of Music* (1965), with arms outstretched, accompanied by captions such as "This is me not caring about football season" or "Look at all the homework I'm not doing this weekend." After *The Sound of Music*, a meme appeared with the same image proclaiming, "They missed it by that much."[38] The familiarity and recognizability of musicals makes them available for this kind of referential humor, as in the following tweets referencing song lyrics ("the hills are alive"), iconic performers (Julie Andrews), and stars' other well-known performances (Carrie Underwood's hit song "Before He Cheats"):

> The hills need to come alive with the sound of acting lessons. #TheSoundOfMusicLive[39]
>
> I want the fiance lady to start belting "Before He Cheats" during Carrie and the Captain's waltz #soundofmusic[40]
>
> How drunk do you think Julie Andrews is right now? #SoundofMusic[41]
>
> I hope we save Tinker Bell with a hashtag. #PeterPanLive[42]

An added attraction was the possibility of failure in live performance. According to Raymond Knapp and Mitchell Morris, camp's paradoxes rely on the allure of failure, which creates a gap between the desire for a thing and its being sent up.[43] This idea of failure typically involves an ironic or paradoxical mocking of a thing for which the observer has affection, but part of the excitement of these live events was the suspense of not knowing what might happen. Many people made a sport of tuning in to see what would go wrong:

> Can't wait for the next #NBCFail, #PeterPanLive! One can only hope that the wires malfunction…[44]

On some level, the possibility of malfunction is proof of the appealing realness of the live broadcast—the way its errors may break the mediatized perfection to which we are now accustomed.[45] Bert States notes that we see a live actor as both character and performer, and in live performance, we experience sympathy and empathy for a performer, prompted by the fear of an accident that could break the illusion. The live television broadcast retains this relationship between performer and viewer, in contrast to film, in which the relationship between actor and character is somewhat more unified. We bond with the actor, who appears vulnerable, and our applause is not only for a good performance and embodiment of the role, but also in praise for their surviving the performance without mishaps.[46] However, for many musical theatre fans, the performer is just as important as the character, and part of the drama is in the uncertainty of the actor's own performance. Audiences of musicals have kinetic identification with the performances of musical theatre actors, for whom they may root—or whom they may hope to see fail during the uncertainty of live performance.

A number of scholars have commented on the ways in which critical humor and an antagonistic relationship between fans and the objects of their fandom are productive of the dynamics that enable fan participation. Henry Jenkins sees interplay of criticism and creativity as productive in fan cultures. Fans are often frustrated and have feelings of antagonism to the same texts that are the objects of their fandom. Because of their devotion, they must find ways to make popular culture texts work for them when they are less than satisfying as produced.[47] Fandom is made possible by the co-presence of affection and antagonism, which, as Baym notes, allows fans to assert their mastery and stay interested through collaborative involvement with other fans. Humor puts distance between the subject and the text that allows participants to negotiate the meaning of their fandom while encouraging each other to stay involved in spite of a genre's flaws.[48] Derek Johnson goes a step farther, identifying antagonism as the more essential half of the antagonism/affection dynamic. He calls this process "fan-tagonism," describing it thus: "Ongoing struggles for discursive dominance constitute fandom as a hegemonic struggle over interpretation and evaluation through which relationships among fan, text, and producer are continually articulated, disarticulated, and rearticulated."[49] Baym further notes that matters of ownership are central to fans' relationships to the materials as well.[50] Musical theatre fans know the shows and have their own, often closely held, ideas about how they should be executed and who should be cast. As Hillman-McCord notes, criticism and debate are a productive part of online fandom, including those constructed around musical theatre and diva performances.[51]

Criticisms and humorous comments, therefore, were able to coexist easily with genuine feelings of affection, nostalgia, and family as people watched the live musicals:

> I really really want #PeterPanLive to be amazing but if not I'm excited for the hate tweets #PeterPanPlaybill[52]
>
> Set and ready for #PeterPanLive in my Tinkerbell pjs. What you're experiencing right now is jealousy....[53]
>
> Hoping #PeterPanLive opens with "The following program is brought to you in living color on NBC."[54]

The producers seemed to understand this fan-tagonistic dynamic. After some of the success of *The Sound of Music Live!* was attributed to hate-watching, NBC exploited expectations that a similar phenomenon would draw in viewers for their second production. In the lead-up to *Peter Pan Live!*, Allison Williams, who had been cast in the role of Peter Pan, admonished people not to watch cynically, saying:

> If you're going to watch this the same way that you watch a TV show that you hate, but you hate-watch it with all your friends so that you can drink wine and tweet at each other about how it's bad, you need to just go ahead and take those lenses out of your glasses and put in the lenses that you had when you were six.[55]

During the same period of time, however, producer Craig Zadan remarked, "The people with mean things to say, say them. At the end of the day, the mean things and the good things only drive viewership. So what do you want? You want the ratings."[56] A *New York Post* article conveniently provided audiences with information about "Who to Follow on Twitter While (Hate)Watching *Peter Pan Live!*."[57]

THE WIZ LIVE! AND COMMUNAL PERFORMANCE

The most recent musical broadcasts demonstrate ongoing conversations and negotiations among fans, producers, and communities. *The Wiz Live!*, *Hairspray Live!*, and Fox's *Grease Live!* attempted to bring more contemporary fare to the live screen, responding, perhaps, to audience demands for more relatable and relevant shows. *The Wiz Live!*, in particular, resonated with recent events in the African American community, as will be discussed shortly. The networks also tried new approaches in these musicals that were meant to address some of the issues of liveness for which the previous musicals had been criticized. First Fox, and then

NBC, showed an increasing openness to new formats for the presentation of live musicals, incorporating studio audiences and more deliberate engagements with audience participation through social media. Reviews, as well as analysis of positive and negative responses on Twitter by firms such as Brandwatch and Amobee, suggest that these three musicals were more positively received by both professional critics and fans, even while ratings remained modest compared to the initial success of *The Sound of Music Live!*.[58] Perhaps the initial novelty wore off, or perhaps rising quality made them harder to hate-tweet.

After *The Sound of Music Live!* and *Peter Pan Live!*, *The Wiz Live!* signaled an effort to go in a more contemporary direction and appeal to specific segments of the audience for live musicals. One of the criticisms of *Peter Pan* had been that it was an outdated musical that retained racial and sexist stereotypes and with which many younger viewers were not familiar. *The Wiz*, on the other hand, is based on a story most people know (it is the African American version of *The Wizard of Oz*), has a score that still sounds contemporary, celebrates African American culture, and portrays women as powerful and capable. At the same time that a version of *The Wizard of Oz* would naturally attract family audiences generally, *The Wiz* also has devoted followings among specific communities—most importantly, the African American community—where it is a beloved classic and the film adaptation is an important household television viewing tradition. The producers signaled their awareness of this connection, and cast members, including Mary J. Blige, Queen Latifah, and Ne-Yo spoke fondly of their memories of growing up with *The Wiz* and its importance in the black community.[59] There is also intense fandom for *The Wiz* among many people in the LGBT (lesbian, gay, bisexual, and transgender) community, where *The Wizard of Oz* has long been an important subcultural secular religion with Judy Garland as its diva and where *The Wiz* is valued for its emphasis on self-love. Both of these communities have significant overlap with each other and with the musical theatre community, where *The Wiz* is known equally well in the original stage version of 1975 and the film adaptation of 1978. In addition, *The Wiz* is popular with school and community theatres. Each of these fan communities has strong feelings of partial ownership of *The Wiz*.

After the negative response to *Peter Pan Live!*, news that *The Wiz* would be NBC's next live musical was met with a mixture of excitement and apprehension in these communities. On the day *The Wiz Live!* was announced, Twitter users expressed concerns that NBC was tampering with a classic:

> So NBC wants to remake The Wiz. In the words of RuPaul, I only have one thing to say: "Don't F*ck it [up"][60]
>
> [worried emoticon] Don't. Mess. It. Up.[61]
>
> Let's hope it stays black[62]

Whether people were enthusiastic or pessimistic about the *The Wiz Live!*, they were engaged and invested. This level of engagement seemed to receive somewhat more attention from NBC in advance of the broadcast than it did for the previous two musicals. On the official website, one could download and circulate a personalizable meme in which the word *home* in "There's no place like home" was replaced by the name of one's hometown. A Reddi-Whip commercial aired during the broadcast featured students at a school in Hyattsville, Maryland, performing "Brand New Day," promoting the company's support for arts in schools.[63] This commercial likely also reminded viewers of their own participation in community theatre musicals. These official participation prompts paled in comparison, however, to what viewers did with *The Wiz* on their own terms.

In a change of strategy from the celebrity stunt casting that had been criticized in the previous two musicals, newcomer Shanice Williams was chosen through an open casting call to play Dorothy. In the media, Williams was presented as a relatable, ordinary girl getting a big break and having new experiences.[64] Anyone could imagine themselves in this position, especially girls who perform in community or semi-professional musical theatre as Williams had. The same anticipation of vocal or bodily failure in live performance that prompted the desire to see Underwood make mistakes in *The Sound of Music Live!*, motived audiences to pull for Williams in *The Wiz Live!*. Ultimately, audiences were won over by her personality, her strong singing, and her ability to hold her own in a production with bigger stars in spite of a relative lack of experience. The choice of an unknown whom people wanted to see succeed seemed to help with the broadcast's positive reception.

The ratings and reviews for *The Wiz Live!* were strong, perhaps reflecting, in part, the intensity of enthusiasm among core fan groups, especially among African Americans. Positive assessments of the performance were offered by both professional critics and viewers, many of whom felt that NBC had finally got the live musical formula right, and *The Wiz Live!* was the most tweeted live scripted television program ever.[65] It also had the highest social media participation of any live broadcast in the last four years (three times that of *Peter Pan Live!*).[66] No small part of *The Wiz Live!*'s success is attributable to viewership and Twitter activity in the African American community. Average household viewership was highest in urban areas with large African American populations.[67] There may be a connection between this statistic and the high rates of tweeting about the broadcast, since research has shown that African Americans use Twitter at higher rates than any other demographic group. Daniel Fienberg, in a review for the *Hollywood Reporter*, noted that the show had thwarted the new tradition of hate-watching and raised the bar for Fox's upcoming production of *Grease*.[68] Some hapless tweeters agreed:

When it doesn't suck: the live-tweeter's dilemma #TheWizLive[69]

The African American community's reaction to *The Wiz Live!* on Twitter demonstrates not only the ability of these live musicals to bring together communities around the broadcasts themselves, but also that those bonds of community can express important personal and political messages resonating with current events. *The Wiz Live!* was broadcast in the context of the Black Lives Matter movement in December 2015, following several months of especially disheartening instances of institutional and political acts of violence against African Americans.[70] One of this movement's signature methods is hashtag activism, which involves using social media to raise awareness. The series of high-profile acts of violence against black bodies beginning in 2013 roughly coincided with NBC's live musical broadcasts, which began the same year, and *The Wiz Live!* was not the first time the musicals and politics intersected, however briefly. During the *Peter Pan Live!* broadcast in 2014, singer Josh Groban tweeted a picture of the Eric Garner protests in New York City taking place the same night with the comment, "Meanwhile in Alwaysland."[71]

The media tools used by Black Lives Matter, particularly memes and hashtags, brought the movement seamlessly into the online conversations about *The Wiz Live!*. These conversations took place across many online communities, including the one that has come to be known as Black Twitter. Described by the black feminist writer Feminista Jones,

Black Twitter is "a collective of active, primarily African American Twitter users who have created a virtual community."[72] More broadly, Black Twitter is an unofficial online network of people interested in black issues and culture. The Black Lives Matter hashtag (#BlackLivesMatter) had always been closely linked with Black Twitter, so when Black Twitter responded strongly to *The Wiz Live!*, it gave African American viewers an opportunity to express feelings of pride in black excellence while watching, tweeting, and circulating memes. Numerous enthusiastic tweets about *The Wiz Live!* appended the #BlackLivesMatter hashtag or otherwise made reference to recent events:

> Watching the #wizlive I'm so proud to be Black right now!!! My people are doing their thang!![73]
>
> There you have it!!! #wizlive #EaseOnDownTheRoad #BlackLivesMatter [emoticon of raised fists in different skin tones] #WizardofOz #JusticeOrElse[74]
>
> I really needed to have those hours to just enjoy how funny, talented, and creative Black people can be. #TheWizLive[75]
>
> The black and gay beauty on tonight's television screen is making me cry tears of joy #Voguing #TheWizLive[76]
>
> This is so black. I'm in love. #TheWiz[77]
>
> How do we feel about #TheWiz? [accompanied by "Really Proud" gif][78]
>
> Just. Beautiful. Black. Excellence. What a time to be alive [black hands clapping] #TheWiz[79]

In the world, black bodies had been a site of violent struggle, but here the black body in performance was a focal point of empowerment through the magnifying affect of the musical. There was plenty of praise for the veteran performers, but Shanice Williams, in her debut performance for a national audience, became a special point of pride:

> I am so proud of this girl I don't even know. From being a nobody a performance like this must be TERRIFYING and she's killing it #TheWiz[80]
>
> I don't even think NBC realizes the gift it gave our little black girls tonight #TheWizLive[81]

> Just thinking of all the little girls watching #TheWizLive now and seeing a Dorothy that looks just like them, live on NBC. Warms my heart.[82]
>
> YOU NAILED IT SHANICE WE SEE YOU BABY SISSSSSSS #JonesingForTheWiz[83]
>
> All of #BlackTwitter watching the end of #TheWiz right now like: [gif of Taraji P. Henson standing to applaud fellow black actress Viola Davis for her Emmy win][84]

At the end of the broadcast, a fellow cast member posted a video of Williams being cheered by the crew on returning backstage after her widely praised performance of "Home."[85] Simultaneously with these online interactions, people gathered in homes, community centers, and other material spaces for viewing parties. A Cincinnati Black Lives Matter group held a social event to watch the musical, and another group in Seattle used it as a fundraiser for a memorial.[86]

Humorous references to black culture intersected with a camp sensibility in Twitter comments on *The Wiz Live!*. Memes comparing *The Wizard of Oz* to *The Wiz* made analogies to the difference between macaroni and cheese from a box and the authentic dish from an oven, or between raw and fried chicken. Some viewers tweeted about being taken to church by the soulful singing, while others made references to the familiar film version. These tweets relied often on black popular and vernacular references for their expression of identity with the community:[87]

> Lmao the slippers shoulda been bedazzled retro Jordans lmao #TheWiz[88]
>
> If this was BET you wouldn't need to stress abt trying to DVR because it would run like 12 times this weekend. #TheWiz[89]
>
> She went from 0-100 real quick just like a true black momma #TheWizLive[90]
>
> Glinda came outta the sky and she's tew beautiful. Dis tew much. #TheWizLive [accompanied by the popular "Dis Tew Much" meme, featuring a picture of a black gay man in an emotional moment from the MTV series *Catfish*][91]
>
> Who cuttin onions in here?!!!!! [emoticons crying rivers of tears] #TheWizLive[92]

The issues of theatrical and cultural literacy arose again, when some viewers complained that an all-black *Wizard of Oz* was racist. Black Twitter responded swiftly:[93]

> Perfect example of white ignorance. "There would be an uproar if The Wiz had an all white cast." #BlackLivesMatter [black fists] #BlackOnCampus #wtf[94]

> Racist white folk complainin that The Wiz has an all black cast but don't see a problem with the full white cast in Wicked but im [sleeping emoticons] #TheWiz[95]

> We have come full circle with insanity…the all white version of #TheWiz is called #TheWizardOfOz . JUST STOP!!!!!![96]

One humorous tweet, responding to the complaint that the absence of white people in the cast showed a lack of diversity, included a screen shot of a fleeting moment of one inconspicuous white dancer in the chorus, noting that white people were in fact getting the same kind of token representation people of color usually receive.[97]

Perfecting the Live Musical?

Fan and producer interactions have resulted in changes in the live musical over time, but a consensus about what works in these performances remains elusive. *The Wiz Live!*'s production design, as if for a Broadway theatre's proscenium stage, may have contributed to its having a more familiar construction of live performance, which may in turn have contributed to its success relative to the previous musicals. However, there were still complaints that the lack of a studio audience caused the ends of songs to fall flat.[98]

Fox's *Grease Live!* took an entirely different approach. Perhaps unfettered by the nostalgic commitments Meron and Zadan had regarding fidelity to the existing model of live musical broadcasts from the 1950s, it took more extensive advantage of the transmedial and reflexive possibilities of a live performance in the networked age. The producers of *Grease Live!* more actively sought social media participation by viewers and not only included a studio audience, who cheered and applauded vigorously, but used them as extras in crowd scenes, which took place both in a sound studio and on a back lot for outdoor scenes. Fox thus acknowledged audience participation at several levels—within the show, at home, and online. *Grease Live!* further emphasized its meta-theatricality by including Mario Lopez as an emcee who took viewers backstage to see the actors racing from one set to the next at the beginning of each commercial break. When, during the day of the performance, it looked like there would be rain that could affect the outdoor scenes, references to the weather were added to the dialogue.

The issues that had plagued the NBC musicals reappeared in *Grease Live!*, with Fox often taking a different approach and seeming to learn from critiques of the NBC musicals regarding the practices of liveness. The broadcast was praised for its technical superiority to the NBC musicals in television direction, and, like *The Wiz Live!*, it received a positive response on social media.[99] In addition to the studio audience, who, like the viewers at home, were both watching and participating, *Grease Live!* included another theatrical gesture that audiences had missed in the NBC musicals—the performers took bows at the conclusion:

> #GreaseLive was just so damn fun and I love the way they took their bow like in a real Broadway show![100]

Minor technical glitches only added to the aura of the live:

> We're live...sometimes you lose sound! #GreaseLive[101]
>
> OKAY AUDIO WAS OUT FOR A MINUTE I ALMOST CRIED I SWEAT DROPPED SO HARD #GreaseLive[102]

Grease Live! promotions invoked nostalgia just as heavily as the NBC musicals did, referring to the love story as timeless and the musical as a classic.[103] Audiences again sent their best wishes to the performers, and much praise was heaped upon Vanessa Hudgens, who went on with the show after her father had died of cancer the night before.[104] As with *The Sound of Music Live!*, the producers managed expectations ahead of time to circumvent comparisons to the more familiar film version. As before, this did not stop some viewers from complaining that the "original" film was superior and should be left alone, and expert musical theatre fans from coming forward to correct this misconception. One YouTube commenter on a video comparing *Grease Live!* to the movie opined: "Everything that is original will always be the best but the live was good."[105] This message prompted responses from others explaining that the original *was* a live show, and expressing exasperation at having to make such explanations for every live musical broadcast.

In spite of the overwhelmingly positive response, however, there remained mixed reactions to the theatrical and reflexive gestures in *Grease Live!*[106]:

> We said we wanted a live audience. We got intermittent cheering and people staring blankly into the camera. #GreaseLive[107]

Some felt that the on-set audience, emcee commentaries, and backstage glimpses were a distraction from the illusion of live theatre (perhaps commercial breaks are an expected part of televisual "reality" but these elements are not):

> But really this live audience is killing the mood of #GreaseLive......[108]

Whatever reservations there might have been about the Fox approach, NBC evidently was sufficiently impressed to appropriate it for their 2016 musical, *Hairspray Live!*, combining its more exciting elements with some strategies that had worked well with *The Wiz Live!*. Kenny Leon, who had directed *The Wiz Live!* was joined as co-director by Alex Rudzinski, who had worked on Fox's *Grease Live!*. For the first time, NBC moved its operation from New York to Los Angeles, where they imitated Fox's use of a back lot in combination with a soundstage. A live audience was used for the scenes taking place at *The Corny Collins Show* and as bystanders in street scenes. At commercial breaks, there were cutaways to live feeds from major cities, including Baltimore, where the musical is set. It was hosted by Darren Criss, who, like Mario Lopez in *Grease Live!*, took viewers behind the scenes. The role of Tracy Turnblad was cast in an open call, repeating the process followed in *The Wiz Live!*, and giving another newcomer a chance to perform for a mass media audience. Sponsors got directly in on the live performance this time with live commercials from Oreo, Reddi-Whip, and Toyota broadcast right from the *Hairspray Live!* set. This reenactment of live commercials from the early years of television then became part of a new media strategy in which the novelty of the act prompted the tweeting of the brands in connection with the show. *Hairspray Live!* even managed to repeat, in a different way, the political timeliness of *The Wiz Live!*, as its message of racial reconciliation was seen by many as a counterpoint to the election of Donald Trump the previous month.[109] Jennifer Hudson's rendition of "I Know Where I've Been" was especially remarked upon in this context:

> You know that it's not just Motormouth Mabel singing in Hairspray, but its also Jennifer Hudson sending a message in 2016. #HairsprayLive[110]

Reviews were mostly positive, but *Hairspray Live!* attracted about 9 million viewers, a similar number to *Peter Pan Live!*, which must have been disappointing compared to *The Wiz Live!*'s 11.5 million viewers and *Grease Live!*'s 12 million.[111]

The successes of these most recent live musicals are encouraging for the future of the practice, while still leaving many questions about the stakes of liveness and fan participation. While many commentators felt that *The Wiz Live!* was the production that finally "got it right" with its more conventional theatrical style, *Grease Live!*'s approach was sufficiently widely praised that NBC adopted it within the year. In spite of some critics' and fans objections to the meta-theatrical elements such as peeks behind the scenes and some problems with sound, staging, and camerawork, *Hairspray Live!* received mostly warm, if qualified, reviews.[112] NBC has announced that *Bye, Bye, Birdie* will be its live musical for 2017, signaling a continued commitment to youthful, family fare. Fox, after spending two years developing *Grease Live!* in response to NBC's initial success with *The Sound of Music Live!*, has not announced future plans to broadcast live musicals. Their production of *The Rocky Horror Picture Show*, broadcast late in 2016 was not broadcast live, but future plans for the network include live versions of *Rent* and *A Christmas Story*, and ABC has recently announced its plans to get into the game with a live broadcast of *The Little Mermaid*, scheduled for the fall of 2017, that will combine live performances with animation.[113]

Conclusion

In Chap. 6 of this book, Jessica Hillman-McCord invites us to pose new questions about Broadway and its audiences in the digital age. Whereas online fandom for *Hamilton* shows a picture of intense engagement around a single musical theatre text, the social media interactions around live television musicals suggest the formation of temporary communities of viewers out of existing ones. These take place in the moment of performance, but in ways that are not possible in the traditional live theatre environment. Following the logic of Jenkins, we likely do not fully understand the ways in which the roles of musical theatre creators and audiences are changing in the digital environment, nor are they likely to settle into stable and predictable patterns, and the question of whether fans, producers, or corporations are in control of their consumption of the live musical is a complex one, suggested by the multidirectional interactions sampled here.

It is not entirely new for the makers of culture to listen to their audiences. After all, it was the letters from viewers that prompted NBC to remount and tape *Peter Pan* for the 1960s. However, the dialogical nature of the new networks of social media might allow for conversations among the parties that are more immediate, more sustained, and more directly responsive in moments of mediated live performance. In the convergence media environment of these musicals, producers, audiences, actors, professional critics, fans, and others have been able to negotiate over the values of liveness and musical theatre that should inhere in live musical broadcasts. They will no doubt continue to do so as long as the current trend of live musicals endures.

Notes

1. Jenkins, 2.
2. D'Addario.
3. Schwindt.
4. "*Sound of Music* Goes Live on NBC."
5. Auslander, Kindle edition.
6. Spigel, 46–47.
7. For one discussion of these relationships between performers and audiences in musical theater, see Dvoskin, 368.
8. Jenkins, Ford, and Green, 1–5.
9. Auslander, Kindle edition.
10. The Musical Version, Twitter post, December 7, 2016, 11:31 PM, http://twitter.com/musicalversion.
11. Robbie Rozelle, Twitter post, December 5, 2013, http://twitter.com/divarobbie.
12. "Anna Kendrick's 'Peter Pan Live' Tweets Are a Must Read!"
13. "*Sound of Music Live*: The Best Twitter Reactions."
14. Rothman.

15. For more on questions of what viewers and participants are being represented in studies of convergence culture, see Couldry.
16. Gilman.
17. Eric Gelb, Twitter post, December 4, 2014, http://twitter.com/DirectorGelb.
18. Magnus Tonning Riise, Twitter post, December 7, 2016, 11:29 PM, http://twitter.com/MagnusRiise.
19. Ng.
20. Rothman, comments section.
21. Baym, 94; see also Jessica Hillman-McCord's discussion of this practice of fan competition in *Hamilton* in Chap. 6 of this book.
22. Broadway Spotted, Twitter post, December 5, 2013, 8:32 PM, http://twitter.com/BroadwaySpotted.
23. Tiffany Thompson, Twitter post, December 3, 2015, 10:40 PM, http://twitter.com/TiffThomp.
24. Tiffany Thompson, Twitter post, December 3, 2015, 10:44 PM, http://twitter.com/TiffThomp.
25. Auslander, Kindle edition.
26. Fallon.
27. Lowry.
28. Clement.
29. For more on these dynamics, see Chaps. 9 and 10 in this book by Nathan Stith and Emily Clark. Clark's discussion of the relationship among Broadway, reality TV, and the Internet adds yet more fodder to the idea of the musical as crossing genres and media forms.
30. Carrie Underwood, Twitter post, December 6, 2013, 8:06 PM, http://twitter.com/carrieunderwood.
31. Nededog, "NBC's *Sound of Music Live!*"
32. Schwindt.
33. Dyer, 176.
34. Albert Brooks, Twitter post, December 6, 2013, 12:21 AM, http://twitter.com/albertbrooks.
35. Anna Kendrick, Twitter post, December 5, 2014, 12:05 PM, http://twitter.com/AnnaKendrick47.
36. Rory Scovel, Twitter post, December 4, 2014, 11:47, http://twitter.com/roryscovel.
37. For more extensive engagement with this topic, see her chapter in this volume.
38. Tony Cronin, Twitter post, December 6, 2013, 2:03 PM, http://twitter.com/da_buzz.
39. Scott Bishop, Twitter post, December 5, 2013, 9:15 PM, http://twitter.com/thescottbishop.

40. Henry Koperski, Twitter post, December 5, 2013, 9:28 PM, http://twitter.com/HenryKoperski.
41. John Flynn, Twitter post, December 5, 2013, 11:38 PM, http://twitter.com/JFly99.
42. Nerd York City, Twitter post, December 4, 2014, 10:08 PM, http://twitter.com/nerdyorkcity.
43. Knapp and Morris, 146–50.
44. Nathan Labonté, Twitter post, Dec 2014, 6:43 PM, http://twitter.com/labonath151.
45. Goodman.
46. States, 119–20. On the potential for failure in musical theater, see McMillin, 149.
47. Jenkins, 23; Baym, 105–6.
48. Jenkins 24; Baym, 113.
49. Johnson, 286.
50. Baym, 113.
51. See Hillman-McCord in Chap. 6 of this volume.
52. Catherine Elizabeth, Twitter post, December 4, 2014, 6:41 PM, http://twitter.com/kitty_cat234.
53. Carroll Carter, Twitter post, December 4, 2014, 6:38 PM, http://twitter.com/carroll_ann.
54. Harold Itzkowitz, Twitter post, December 4, 2014, 6:41 PM, http://twitter.com/HaroldItz.
55. D'Addario.
56. D'Addario.
57. Morabito.
58. Schwindt; Nededog, "*Hairspray Live!*"
59. Clement.
60. ChefSweetPea, Twitter post, March 30, 2015, 6:58 PM, http://twitter.com/chifkima.
61. e [sic], Twitter post, March 30, 2015, 7:59 PM, http://twitter.com/epiphanE32.
62. Racine, Twitter post, March 30, 2015, 7:18 PM, http://twitter.com/shortiduwop410.
63. Steinberg.
64. "The Moment Shanice Williams Finds Out She is Cast as Dorothy."
65. Maglio.
66. Kissell.
67. Kissell.
68. Fienberg.
69. Glen Weldon, Twitter post, December 3, 2015, 8:19 PM, http://twitter.com/ghweldon.

70. Black Lives Matter is an activist community and movement focused on countering violence against black bodies and systemic racism in policing and the US criminal justice system. Many of its activities focus on instances of police killings of African Americans. In 2013, the hashtag #BlackLivesMatter emerged in response to the acquittal of George Zimmerman in the shooting death of Trayvon Martin. Later Black Lives Matter campaigns involved responses to the shooting of Michael Brown in Ferguson, MO; the choking death of Eric Garner in New York City (#ICantBreathe) in 2014; the death of Freddie Gray after an arrest and possible "rough ride" in Baltimore; the white supremacist mass shooting at Emanuel African Methodist Episcopal Church of Charleston; and the hanging death of Sandra Bland in a jail cell in Waller County, Texas, in 2015.

71. Josh Groban, Twitter post, December 4, 2014, 8:46 PM, http://twitter.com/joshgroban.

72. Jones.

73. Monica Bussey, Twitter post, December 3, 2015, 11:40 PM, http://twitter.com/MoRee0681.

74. Kass, Twitter post, December 5, 2015, 6:57 PM, http://twitter.com/Kottley1.

75. Michael Arceneaux, Twitter post, December 3, 2015, 10:53 PM, http://twitter.com/youngsinick.

76. Ira Madison III, Twitter post, December 3, 2015, 9:23 PM, http://twitter.com/ira.

77. Morgan Jerkins, Twitter post, December 3, 2015, 5:12 PM, http://twitter.com/MorganJerkins.

78. Huffpost BlackVoices, Twitter post, December 3, 2015, 10:11 PM, http://twitter.com/blackvoices.

79. Joseph M. A. Strong, Twitter post, December 3, 2015, 8:27 PM, http://twitter.com/jstrai.

80. Phillip Van De Kamp, Twitter post, December 3, 2015, 8:26 PM, http://twitter.com/MajorPhilebrity.

81. Ira Madison III, Twitter post, December 3, 2015, 10:44 PM, http://twitter.com/ira.

82. Afrobella, Twitter post, December 3, 2015, 8:26 PM, http://twitter.com/afrobella.

83. Feminista Jones, Twitter post, December 3, 2015, 9:08 PM, http://twitter.com/FeministaJones.

84. Coco Bandicoot, Twitter post, December 3, 2015, 10:43 PM, http://twitter.com/ShesSweetVenom.

85. "See Shanice Williams' Standing Ovation from THE WIZ LIVE! Cast & Crew Following the Finale!" *BroadwayWorld*. Accessed December 27,

2016, http://www.broadwayworld.com/article/See-Shanice-Williams-Standing-Ovation-from-THE-WIZ-LIVE-Cast-Crew-Following-the-Finale-20151204.
86. "'The Wiz Live!' Fundraiser (to Support The Black Lives Matter Memorial Garden)," Accessed November 29, 2016, https://www.facebook.com/events/1674116389499012/; "Black Lives Matter Cincinnati Social: The Wiz," Accessed November 29, 2016, http://www.wherevent.com/detail/Black-Lives-Matter-Black-Lives-Matter-Cincinnati-Social-The-Wiz.
87. Gajewski.
88. Yung Metaphysique, Twitter post, December 3, 2015, 5:23 PM, http://twitter.com/SoloExMachina.
89. Attica Scott, Twitter post, December 3, 2015, 6:27 PM, http://twitter.com/atticascott.
90. Becca, Twitter post, December 3, 2015, 6:05 PM, http://twitter.com/MJStarLover.
91. Nessa, Twitter post, December 3, 2015, 7:33 PM, http://twitter.com/curlyheadRED.
92. Gabby SidiBae, Twitter post, December 3, 2015, 9:09 PM, http://twitter.com/GabbySidibe.
93. Shilliday.
94. _Blue.Lux_, Twitter post, December 4, 2015, 6:50 PM, http://twitter.com/_danceFeinTay_.
95. Richie | 876God, Twitter post, December 3, 2015, 9:18 PM, http://twitter.com/RichieMc_.
96. DidSheSayThat, Twitter post, December 3, 2015, 10:00 PM, http://twitter.com/SonnieJohnson.
97. Kass, Twitter post, December 5, 2015, 6:57 PM, http://twitter.com/Kottley1.
98. Lyons.
99. Fienberg.
100. Kevin Dillon, Twitter post, January 31, 2016, 10:02 PM, http://twitter.com/ETKevinsMind.
101. GREASE: LIVE, Twitter post, January 31, 2016, 8:59 PM, http://twitter.com/GoGrease.
102. Vee, Twitter post, 31 Jan 2016, 8.57 PM, http://twitter.com/Vee902.
103. "Grease Live - TV Series News, Show Information - FOX."
104. Roschke.
105. "Grease VS Grease Live," YouTube video, 6:51, posted by Jodie 1995, https://www.youtube.com/watch?v=PMTBD54sqL0.
106. Ryan.
107. Boo-is Frightsman, Twitter post, January 31, 2016, 7:30 PM, http://twitter.com/LouisPeltzman.

108. Brant Sennett, Twitter post, January 31, 2016, 7:33 PM, http://twitter.com/BrantSennett.
109. "I don't think there's a more perfect statement of defiance than #HairsprayLive and it's exactly what we need right now." (David Gordon, Twitter post, December 7, 2016, 10:48 PM, http://twitter.com/MrDavidGordon); "'A Whole Lot of Ugly Coming from a Never Ending Parade of Stupid' - The Donald Trump Story #HairsprayLive." (Jill Biden, Twitter post, December 8, 2016, https://twitter.com/DrBiden).
110. Queen Heffanie, Twitter post, December 7, 2016, 10:22 PM, http://twitter.com/lovelyleiva.
111. Gans; Saraiya.
112. See Siede, for example.
113. Hipes.

Bibliography

"Anna Kendrick's 'Peter Pan Live' Tweets Are a Must Read!" *Just Jared*. Accessed December 24, 2016. http://www.justjared.com/2014/12/05/anna-kendricks-peter-pan-live-tweets-are-a-must-read/.
Auslander, Philip. *Liveness: Performance in a Mediatized Culture*. 2nd edition. New York and London: Routledge, 2008. Kindle edition.
Baym, Nancy K. *Tune In, Log On: Soaps, Fandom, and Online Community*. Thousand Oaks, CA, London, and New Delhi: Sage Publications, 2000.
Clement, Olivia. "*Wiz Live!* Producers Comment on Possibility of Studio Audience and Reveal More About Broadway Transfer." *Playbill*, December 4, 2015, http://www.playbill.com/article/wiz-live-producers-comment-on-possibility-of-studio-audience-and-reveal-more-about-broadway-transfer-com-374307.
Couldry, Nick. "More Sociology, More Culture, More Politics: Or, a Modest Proposal For 'Convergence' Studies." *Cultural Studies* 25, no. 4/5 (July 1, 2011): 487–501.
D'Addario, Daniel. "Live from Neverland: Can *Pater Pan* Help NBC Take Flight?" *Time*, November 20, 204, http://time.com/3596602/peter-pan-allison-williams-christopher-walken.
Dickson, E.J. "The 7 Worst Things about NBC's *Peter Pan Live!*" *Salon*, December 6, 2014, http://www.salon.com/2014/12/06/the_7_worst_things_about_nbcs_peter_pan_live_partner.
Dvoskin, Michelle. "Audiences and Critics." In *The Oxford Handbook of the American Musical*, ed. Raymond Knapp, Mitchell Morris, and Stacy Wolf, 365–77. New York: Oxford University Press, 2011.

Dyer, Richard. *Heavenly Bodies: Film Stars and Society.* London: Routledge, 2004.

Fallon, Kevin. "'Sound of Music Live!' Review: The Hills Are Barely Alive." *The Daily Beast*, December 6, 2013. http://www.thedailybeast.com/articles/2013/12/06/sound-of-music-live-review-the-hills-are-barely-alive.html.

Fienberg, Daniel. "*Grease Live!*: TV Review," *The Hollywood Reporter.* January 31, 2016, http://www.hollywoodreporter.com/review/grease-live-tv-review-860952.

Firestone, Lonnie. "Hairspray Live Is Figuring out How to Perfect the Live Musical." *Vanity Fair*, December 6, 2016. http://www.vanityfair.com/hollywood/2016/12/hairspray-live-nbc-ariana-grande-jennifer-hudson-director-interview.

Gajewski, Ryan. "Where is Toto in *The Wiz Live?*: Twitter Explodes with Reactions." *Us Weekly*, December 3, 2015, http://www.usmagazine.com/entertainment/news/where-is-toto-in-the-wiz-live-twitter-explodes-with-reactions-w158952.

Gans, Andrew. "Hairspray Live! Ratings Down from Last Season's The Wiz." *Playbill*, December 8, 2016. http://www.playbill.com/article/hairspray-live-ratings-down-from-last-seasons-the-wiz.

Gilman, Greg. "*Peter Pan Live!* Gets Roasted by Hollywood on Twitter," *The Wrap*, December 5, 2014, http://www.thewrap.com/peter-pan-live-gets-roasted-by-hollywood-on-twitter.

Goodman, Tim. "*Peter Pan Live!*: TV Review." *The Hollywood Reporter*, December 5, 2014, http://www.hollywoodreporter.com/review/peter-pan-live-tv-review-754093.

"Grease Live - TV Series News, Show Information - FOX." *Grease Live on FOX.* Accessed December 24, 2016. http://www.fox.com/grease-live.

Hipes, Patrick. "ABC Enters Live Musical Game With 'Little Mermaid' Special In October," *Deadline*, May 16, 2017, http://deadline.com/2017/05/the-little-mermaid-live-musical-abc-1202094613/.

Jenkins, Henry. *Convergence culture: Where Old and New Media Collide.* New York: New York University Press, 2006.

Jenkins, Henry, Sam Ford, and Joshua Green. *Spreadable Media: Creating Value and Meaning in a Networked Culture.* New York and London: New York University Press, 2013.

Johnson, Derek. "Fan-tagonism: Factions, Institutions, and Constitutive Hegemonies of Fandom." In *Fandom: Identities and Communities in Mediated Culture*, ed. Jonathan Gray, C. Lee Harrington, and Cornel Sandvoss, 285–300. New York: New York University Press, 2007.

Jones, Feminista. "Is Twitter the Underground Railroad of Activism?" *Salon*, July 17, 2013, http://www.salon.com/2013/07/17/how_twitter_fuels_black_activism.

Katz, Evan Ross. "Twitter Went Ballistic Over *The Wiz Live!*: See the 100 Best Reactions." *Logo*, December 4, 2015, http://www.newnownext.com/twitter-went-ballistic-over-the-wiz-live-see-the-100-best-reactions/12/2015.

Kissell, Rick. "*The Wiz Live!* Ratings Strong: NBC Musical Draws 11.5 Million Viewers." *Variety*, December 4, 2015, http://variety.com/2015/tv/news/the-wiz-live-ratings-nbc-musical-1201653402.

Knapp, Raymond and Mitchell Morris. "Singing." In *The Oxford Handbook of the American Musical*, ed. Raymond Knapp, Mitchell Morris and Stacy Wolf, 320–334. New York: Oxford University Press, 2011.

Lowry, Brian. "TV Review: 'The Wiz Live!'" *Variety*, December 4, 2015. http://variety.com/2015/tv/reviews/the-wiz-live-review-nbc-mary-j-blige-queen-latifah-shanice-williams-1201651164/.

Lyons, Margaret. "The Wiz Needed a Studio Audience." *Vulture*, December 4, 2015. http://www.vulture.com/2015/12/wiz-needed-a-studio-audience.html.

Maglio, Tony. "'The Wiz Live' Is Most-Social Live Special Ever." *TheWrap*, December 4, 2015. http://www.thewrap.com/the-wiz-live-is-most-social-live-special-program-in-nielsen-twitter-tv-history.

McMillin, Scott. *The Musical as Drama*. Princeton, NJ: Princeton University Press, 2006.

McNamara, Mary. "*The Wiz Live!*: Gorgeous, Utterly Sincere and Attitude to Spare." *Los Angeles Times*, December 3, 2015, http://www.latimes.com/entertainment/tv/showtracker/la-et-st-review-the-wiz-live-20151203-story.html.

Morabito, Andrea. "Who to Follow on Twitter While (Hate)Watching *Peter Pan Live! New York Post*, December 4, 2014, http://nypost.com/2014/12/04/who-to-follow-on-twitter-while-hatewatching-peter-pan-live.

Nededog, Jethro. "NBC's 'Sound of Music Live' Tops Nielsen Twitter TV Ratings." *TheWrap*, December 9, 2013. http://www.thewrap.com/nbcs-sound-music-live-tops-nielsen-twitter-tv-ratings.

———. "*Hairspray Live!* Hit a New Ratings Low for NBC's Musicals." *Business Insider*, December 8, 2016. http://www.businessinsider.com/hairspray-live-ratings-social-nbc-musicals-2016-12.

Ng, Philiana. "NBC's 'Sound of Music' Producers on Live Show Fears and Big Expectations (Q&A)." *The Hollywood Reporter*. Accessed December 29, 2016. http://www.hollywoodreporter.com/live-feed/nbcs-sound-music-producers-live-661941.

Roschke, Ryan. "12 Tweets That Perfectly Capture How Brave Vanessa Hudgens Was During *Grease Live*." *Popsugar*, February 1, 2016, http://www.popsugar.com/celebrity/Tweets-About-Vanessa-Hudgens-Performing-Grease-Live-40015707#photo-40015742.

Rothman, Michael. "*The Sound of Music* Live: Funniest Twitter Reactions," *ABC News*, http://abcnews.go.com/blogs/entertainment/2013/12/the-sound-of-music-live-funniest-twitter-reactions/.

Ryan, Maureen. "TV Review: *Grease Live!*" *Variety*, January 31, 2026, http://variety.com/2016/scene/features/grease-live-review-fox-julianne-hough-aaron-tveit-1201693411.

Saraiya, Sonia. "TV Review: 'Hairspray Live!'" *Variety*, December 8, 2016. http://variety.com/2016/tv/reviews/tv-review-hairspray-live-jennifer-hudson-ariana-grande-1201936567/.

Schwindt, Oriana. "NBC's *The Wiz Live!* Dropped a House on Twitter with 1.6 million Tweets During the Show." *International Business Times*, December 5, 2015, http://www.ibtimes.com/nbcs-wiz-live-dropped-house-twitter-16-million-tweets-during-show-2213078.

Siede, Caroline. "A Exuberant *Hairspray Live!* Offers a Light in the Darkness." *A.V. Club*, December 8, 2016, http://www.avclub.com/tvclub/exuberant-hairspray-live-offers-light-darkness-247101.

Shilliday, Beth. "*The Wiz* Racist?: Twitter Explodes in Furious Argument Over Show's All Black Cast." *Hollywood Life*, December 3, 2015, http://hollywoodlife.com/2015/12/03/the-wiz-live-racist-all-black-cast-nbc-twitter.

"*Sound of Music* Goes Live on NBC." YouTube video. 2:34. Posted by CNN, December 5, 2013, https://www.youtube.com/watch?v=8POCwWyvdvw.

"*Sound of Music Live*: The Best Twitter Reactions." *The Hollywood Reporter*, December 5, 2013, http://www.hollywoodreporter.com/news/sound-music-live-best-twitter-663337.

Spigel, Lynn. *Welcome to the Dreamhouse: Popular Media and Postwar Suburbs*. Durham, NC: Duke University Press Books, 2001.

States, Bert O. *Great Reckonings in Little Rooms: On the Phenomenology of Theater*. University of California Press, 1985.

Steinberg, Brian. "Madison Avenue Pushes Back On Price For TV's Live 'Wiz,' 'Grease.'" *Variety*, November 30, 2015. http://variety.com/2015/tv/news/the-wiz-grease-tv-advertising-1201650117/.

Webber, Stephanie. "Peter Pan Live!: Your Funniest Tweets about Allison Williams, Christopher Walken, and More." *Us Magazine*, December 5, 2014, http://www.usmagazine.com/entertainment/news/peter-pan-live-best-tweets-on-allison-williams-christopher-walken-2014512.

"The Moment Shanice Williams Finds Out She is Cast as Dorothy." *Daily Mail*, accessed September 18, 2016, http://www.dailymail.co.uk/video/tvshowbiz/video-1204287/The-moment-Shanice-Williams-finds-cast-Dorothy.html.

Weigle, Lauren. "#TheWiz: *The Wiz Live!* Tweets You Need to Read." *Heavy*, December 3, 2015, http://heavy.com/entertainment/2015/12/the-wiz-live-tweets-twitter-funny-haters-performances.

CHAPTER 9

Digital Technology, Social Media, and Casting for the Musical Theatre Stage

Nathan Stith

In the program for a 1968 exhibition of his work at the Moderna Museet in Stockholm, Sweden, pop culture icon Andy Warhol infamously wrote that "in the future, everyone will be world-famous for fifteen minutes."[1] In 1991, in the early days of the World Wide Web, musician and blogger Momus adjusted Warhol's adage, saying "in the future, we will all be famous to fifteen *people*."[2] The "fifteen people" musical theatre performers in the twenty-first century need to be famous to are the gatekeepers of professional theatre: the casting director. Before an actor can achieve success on the musical theatre stage, a casting director must know the actor, and their work. Nearly every aspect of our lives have undergone significant transformations in the last two decades due almost entirely to our increasing reliance on digital technology and the Internet. The field of casting is no different. Through interviews with New York-based casting directors and actors who are using the Internet and social media in creative and unique ways, this chapter examines the impact digital technology and social media have had on the process of casting and getting cast in the digital age.

N. Stith (✉)
Trinity University, San Antonio, TX, USA
e-mail: nstith@trinity.edu

The tools available via online technology have made getting known by the "right people" fundamentally easier. In her contribution to *A Companion to New Media Dynamics*, author Theresa M. Senft suggests that these online technologies form a kind of stage on which an individual can present herself. Senft says, "related to the belief that the Internet has become a stage is an argument that a successful person doesn't just maintain a place on that stage; she maintains her online self with the sort of care and consistency normally exhibited by those who have historically believed themselves to be their own product: artists and entrepreneurs."[3] Social media platforms such as Facebook, Twitter, Instagram, and YouTube have become vital tools for any actor attempting to gain recognition by the gatekeepers of the professional theatrical world. According to social media experts, the key to creating a successful online identity is credibility. In *Digital Media and Society*, Andrew White suggests that "in order to create a credible persona, a person must not only not be anonymous, but also must convince others that he/she is not impersonating someone else. One of the most effective ways of doing this is by placing oneself within a network of relationships."[4] Social media outlets have made establishing these types of networked relationships far easier. Within moments of joining a social media outlet, a user can virtually connect with hundreds of industry players who can impact his or her career. Further, as Alice Marwick notes in *Status Update*, "strategic online self-presentation plays an enormous role in increasing one's social status, how one is viewed both online and off."[5] The importance of a strong social media presence is vital for any actor attempting to raise their social status within the industry and to get noticed by casting directors. In addition, digital technology and social media have completely transformed almost every aspect of the casting process, from the day-to-day tasks of the casting directors themselves, to the ways casting sessions are organized and run, and most importantly, to the ways casting directors and actors interact.

SUBMISSIONS

When beginning work on a new project, the first job of the casting director is to call for submissions from agents and managers. Casting director Joy Dewing, who began her career with Big League Theatricals over a decade ago, explains the submission process at the beginning of her career:

When I first started as an intern eleven years ago, submissions came in the mail. We would pile and sort them into boxes. During our busy season the floor in our office was just a minefield of submissions, and it would take us days to open and go through them. Then we had to call the agents or actors *on the phone* and schedule appointments. That took another couple of days. Then you had to wait for someone to call you back.[6]

One can only imagine the time it took to schedule appointments for a large-scale musical, not to mention the time-consuming task of opening all of the mail. Casting director Daryl Eisenberg, who has cast many hit Off-Broadway shows, including *Awesome 80s Prom*, notes that during her time as an intern, "my prized possession was my letter opener."[7] Once the appointments were set, the next step was to prep the actors so they knew what to prepare. The process often became a comedy of errors, similar to the childhood game "Telephone." Dewing, who opened her own company, Joy Dewing Casting in 2012 and has cast national tours, including *Annie*, *Mamma Mia*, *Bring it On*, and *Joseph and the Amazing Technicolor Dreamcoat*, among many others, explains: "You'd tell an agent to tell the actor to prep sixteen bars of a 60s folk song and wear a long skirt," says Dewing, "and the actor would show up wearing a Poodle skirt and singing 'It's My Party.'"[8] The process was laborious with ample opportunity for missed communication, confusion, and error.

For the most part, things have changed significantly. Today this entire process is handled online. Dewing says: "Now, all submissions come in electronically and we can click through and schedule them via email, and the whole process takes about one-third of the time it used to … and the prep instructions get copied and pasted, so there's no chance of getting lost in translation."[9] While the relative ease of online submissions has simplified the submission process for agents, actors, and casting directors, it has also decreased the potential for miscommunication and error, allowing the casting director to focus on the most important aspect of their jobs: the process of casting the show.

Casting Process

Digital technology has streamlined so much of our lives that one would think that utilizing tools such as online scheduling for casting calls would be a logical step in the evolution of the casting process. The reality is that online sign-ups for casting calls have only recently found footing in the casting industry. Unlike Equity Principal Auditions and Equity Chorus Calls which are subject to union rules and regulations set forth by Actors' Equity Association, casting directors for non-union productions have had more freedom to explore the use of digital technology in organizing and running these types of auditions. However, the casting directors interviewed for this project have had varying degrees of success with creating online scheduling and sign-up systems for non-union productions. Casting director Michael Cassara is the resident casting director for the New York Musical Theatre Festival and the National Alliance for Musical Theatre, in charge of casting their annual Festival of New Musicals. The logistics of casting multiple shows with multiple creative teams led Cassara to create audition sign-up software (auditionmichaelcassara.net) in 2010, which he has been refining for the past seven years. Actors create an account (with the option to create a link to their Facebook account) and provide pertinent information such as union affiliation, email address, and phone number. Once a particular audition "goes live" actors can sign up for specific time slots on specific dates. Cassara describes his business as a "tech forward office" and although there have been kinks to iron out (including finding a way to allow thousands of actors to sign up at the same time once the audition notice is posted) he sees great opportunities for this type of software, including the ability for actors to submit their headshots and resumes through this system which his office and creative teams could then access on their mobile devices, eliminating the need for actors to bring hard copies to the casting session. Cassara clearly sees the use of digital technology as a logistical tool of the future for open call, non-union casting sessions.[10]

Others, however, are less enthusiastic about the use of online software to handle scheduling and logistics of casting sessions. Casting director Daryl Eisenberg also considers herself to be tech forward in her work. She utilizes digital technology in almost every aspect of the process. During casting sessions she uses chat software to communicate with interns outside of the room, letting them know when she's ready for the next actor to come in. However, she's had little success using online sign-ups for casting sessions; "it was a total failure" she says. The problem, according to Eisenberg, is that actors sign up, but often don't show up. In her first attempt at online sign-up she had a 50% no-show rate. After making some changes to the process she invited 200 actors to an audition via online software and only 13% showed up. "It was embarrassing," she says. "I was sitting by myself."[11] This may sound surprising, given that actors can only obtain employment by actually showing up for auditions. What actors seem to be forgetting is that the act of typing their names and relevant information into the boxes provided by the sign-up software is actually the beginning of the online interaction with the casting director. Marwick advises that "authenticity" is the key to successful online interactions. She says, "authenticity is not an absolute quality ... rather, authenticity is judged over time, in that people's authenticity is determined by comparing their current actions against their past for consistency."[12] By clicking send, the actor is no longer anonymous and in not showing up for the actual audition, the actor risks damaging their authenticity (both online and off) in the eyes of the casting director. Paul Russell's experience with online sign-ups is similar to Eisenberg's. He says: "What shows up is not what's on the list. It's a waste of time, because actors change their minds or don't feel like going out."[13] Joy Dewing has had some degree of success with online sign-ups for auditions, but as she says, "it has its pros and cons." Dewing describes the benefits and drawbacks of online organization of casting sessions:

> It makes for a much saner and more humane experience for the actors, but it adds more work for me and my staff. It allows us to plan ahead better, but leaves us vulnerable to no-shows. Ultimately, it saves my clients money, but it dramatically changes the talent pool in ways one would never expect. It's a work in progress, but I'm glad [Joy Dewing Casting] is one of the pioneers of this new technology.[14]

While handling the logistics of a casting session using online technology is, as Dewing says, a work in progress, it does seem that online management of the audition process will soon become the norm for both union and non-union auditions. In March 2016 Kate Shindle, President of Actors' Equity Association, announced that beginning in the summer of 2016 all Equity Chorus Calls would be handled via online sign-up and in December 2016 Equity Principal Auditions initiated online sign-ups through the union's Member's Only section of its website.[15]

Digital Technology and the Actor

Digital technology continues to transform the way casting directors do their jobs. It has equally altered the way actors interact with casting directors. For the most part, the traditional means for communicating with casting directors and keeping them up to date with an actor's career have gone the way of the messengered casting notices and hand-delivered submission packets. Two decades ago the primary way an actor could interact with a casting director outside of the casting room was by religiously mailing postcards to every casting office in New York. The postcards included the actor's headshot on one side, and a brief summary of the latest reading, workshop, or musical the actor was appearing in along with a hopeful request to be kept in mind for any appropriate projects. Some actors continue to send postcards, and casting directors, like Paul Russell, encourage such time-consuming activities; however, in his book, *Acting: Make it Your Business*, Russell suggests that "to be competitive, the actor must exploit the marketing opportunities of the recent past while continually engaging in new forms of technology of the near tomorrow to sell themselves."[16] In the world of Internet technology, there are three basic ways for actors to become known by casting directors: (a) successfully leveraging social media; (b) online branding; (c) micro-celebrity. What follows is an examination of what these terms mean, how they work, and how successful (or not) they are at gaining the attention and ultimately getting work for an actor in musical theatre.

Social media is a ubiquitous part of most people's lives. What was once used only by tech-savvy millennials is now an integral part of daily life for people of all generations. As more and more people utilize social media sites such as Twitter, Facebook, Instagram, YouTube, and others, the role of these sites in our lives has changed. Individuals are now curating online identities with as much or more care than they take in presenting their offline personas. In her book *Sociology in the Age of the Internet*, Allison Cavanagh theorizes that the Internet is a network which is able to function successfully through the existence of stable identities. She suggests there are two types of what she calls "hyper-identities" on the Internet. The first is reputational, which is related to the commercialization of the self; the second is productive, which allows users to draw the interest of others to themselves.[17] By creating and curating an online identity through social media platforms, professional actors are constructing a kind of stage with which to present themselves to casting directors, producers, directors, and other potential employers. However, as this cultural phenomenon has become more prevalent it is not without its potential pitfalls. Theresa Senft cautions:

> Yet, at the same time that people are beginning to perceive a coherent online presence as a good and useful thing, they are also learning that negative publicity can be quite dangerous to one's employment, relationships, and self-image. This is the source of a growing cultural anxiety regarding 'over-sharing' online, which takes many forms.[18]

There are countless examples of individuals being fired from jobs for making inflammatory online comments, or relationships (personal and professional) ending because of social media postings. The job of the entrepreneurial actor in the digital age is to navigate the murky waters of leveraging social media to create both a "reputational" and "productive" online identity in order to gain the interest and following of casting directors and others without over-sharing or damaging one's professional standing in the industry.

Effectively Using Social Media

In the early days of the Internet the chatroom reigned supreme. Users would virtually "enter" a chatroom of their choosing (often devoted to some type of hobby or interest) where they could interact with like-minded individuals. Anonymity was a significant component of these chatrooms. Users could create an identity for themselves very different from their offline persona, and unless the individuals were to meet IRL (in real life), no one would be the wiser. While such chatrooms and other forums using virtual identities separate from one's offline identity still exist and are widely used, the rise of social media has significantly changed the way people interact and present themselves while online. Instead of creating a new identity, social media platforms ask users to self-consciously create virtual depictions of themselves. However, as mentioned above, in order to be taken seriously by casting directors and others, the online depiction must be credible. Actors attempting to leverage social media to help their careers must create an identity on social media that is an honest depiction of who they "really" are. The difficulty, as Marwick acknowledges, is that "there are fewer identity cues available online than face-to-face," therefore one must be acutely aware in creating and curating a social media-based identity, because "every piece of digital information a person provides, from typing speed to nickname and email address, can and is used to make inferences about them."[19] By filling a Facebook or Instagram homepage with pictures, or posting videos to YouTube, or regularly sending tweets on Twitter, users are creating what Marwick calls "digital tokens [which] become symbolic markers of a personal identity." These markers, says Marwick, "serve a function similar to clothing or bumper stickers: to establish and display one's identity. Just as postmodern identity theorists argue that people construct 'face-to-face' identities through a bricolage of consumer goods, media, fashion, and styles, online profiles allow people to use the language of media to express themselves to others."[20] The opportunities for actors to present themselves (and their work) virtually through social media platforms are limitless. Instead of simply sending a single postcard through the mail and hoping that a casting director actually looks at the headshot and reads the information on the back, actors now have endless possibilities for connecting and interacting with casting directors through social media platforms.

How do actors use social media to interact with casting directors to further their careers? Jonathan Flom, the former head of musical theatre at Shenandoah Conservatory, suggests in his book *Act Like It's Your Business*, that it is relatively easy. Flom says: "Sometimes just 'liking' or commenting on someone's post from time to time is enough to stay in their consciousness, and that can be a big part of the game."[21] Anecdotal evidences suggest this often works. Fred Berman, who is currently playing Timon in Disney's *The Lion King*, says director Joe Calarco, whom he had worked with years ago, was casting the Off-Broadway show *Bury the Dead* produced by the Transport Group. Berman happened to comment on one of the director's social media posts and Calarco called him in for an audition. "He told me later," says Berman, "that seeing me on Facebook reminded him of me."[22] Oftentimes, remaining in the consciousness of a director or casting director is all that is needed to get an audition and potentially secure work.

Another effective social media tool for actors is the uploaded video clip. As Flom notes, "we have made such strides in technology that now virtually everyone has the ability to record their own high-quality video using their phones."[23] A video can be posted to a personal Facebook or Instagram page, or as Flom recommends, actors can create a YouTube channel to display their work. Flom advises, however, that the users "need to be careful to observe copyright laws, but [the clips] can range from cabaret/concert performances to special skills demonstrations … to you in a studio setting performing an original song."[24] Natalie Weiss, who has appeared in national tours of *Les Misérables* and *Wicked* and is widely known from her successful web series *Breaking Down the Riffs*, agrees with Flom. When giving workshops to college students across the country, her biggest piece of advice is, "every performer *needs* to have at least *one* performance video of them online."[25] One never knows when a casting director might want to recommend an actor to a director or creative team. If the casting director can provide evidence of the actor's work with the click of a mouse, the chances of that actor getting called in for an audition (or better yet, getting cast based on the video clip) increase exponentially.

Along with curating an honest, authentic, and credible online identity, successfully interacting with casting directors, and leveraging the potential of social media sites by including video clips to enhance one's career, there is a potential downside to having an active presence on social media platforms. Social media sites lump everyone together. Once individuals connect online, family members, co-workers, colleagues, acquaintances, and potential employers are all grouped together as "friends" or "followers." More importantly, they can *all* see everything that is posted, shared, or commented on. The danger for the actor is, as Marwick notes, that "while in real life it's possible to alter self-presentation depending on whom one is interacting with, in broad social sites one transmits information to many different types of people simultaneously."[26] Recently published books focused on the business of acting, such as Flom's *Act Like It's Your Business* promote the use of social media as an effective marketing tool, but also warn of the dangers of inappropriate posts or over-sharing. Flom writes:

> The first, biggest, and most hard-and-fast rule I must lay down for you is that *nothing* is private. And your reputation is everything. You must remember that mantra every time you go to post something on social media, be it a photo or a 'tweet' or a video. No matter how private your settings are, you should just assume that someone from the industry will see what you have posted, and you *must* ask yourself before pushing 'post' whether it could reflect negatively on you.[27]

This advice is key to actors attempting to successfully leverage social media outlets to benefit their careers. As Jan-Hinrik Schmidt points out in "Practices of Networked Identity," "the notion of online media as a 'virtual reality' that is separate from 'real life' has mostly vanished."[28] Because of this, one's online identity can have an instrumental impact on the perception of one's offline persona. The bottom line is, that not only do actors *need* to use social media to stay in the minds of casting directors, but the material they post online needs to be professional and authentic, *and* the actor must constantly watch what they post and what is posted about them (on their social media pages) to ensure that the identity they are curating via social media platforms is the identity they want casting directors and other industry professionals to see.

All of the casting directors interviewed for this investigation use Facebook, Twitter, and other social media sites as a daily part of their business. They post casting notices, comment on industry news, and interact with actors and other industry professionals. The difficulty for the casting director is often maintaining a professional distance from actors on social media. Each casting director has his or her own approach to social media relationships with actors. Some, like Daryl Eisenberg, only "friend" actors if they know them personally.[29] Joy Dewing also has a separate personal Facebook page, but purposefully makes it difficult to find. As for her business page, she says, "I have strict rules about accepting friend requests. I am very open and vulnerable on Facebook, and I like it that way; so I am careful about my audience on social media." However, she does understand the value of using social media sites to reach a larger audience. "I can reach out to communities of people who don't live in the world of [theatre trade publications, such as] *Backstage* and *Playbill*. I have found opera singers, rappers, gymnasts, cheerleaders, instrumentalists, etc. through social media channels."[30] Casting director Michael Cassara also uses social media to interact with a wide audience. "As a younger casting office in town," says Cassara, "I made a conscious decision to make social media my territory. Early on, I used it as a platform to broadcast projects."[31]

If casting directors are using social media as much as actors, and they understand the value of social media sites as a tool to find and interact with potential talent, how do they wish talent to interact with them? Dewing understands the importance of maintaining an active online social media presence to stay in the consciousness of casting directors and says that it is "just another skill that actors need to have in their toolbox."[32] As evidenced by the numerous workshops, classes, and webinars dedicated to teaching actors how to use this relatively new tool at their disposal, it is important for actors to understand how to effectively leverage social media through online interactions with casting directors. The pitfall that many people fall into when posting on social media sites is examined in Eden Litt and Eszter Hargittai's contribution to *Social Media + Society*, titled "The Imagined Audience on Social Network Sites." Litt and Hargittai assert that users rely on an imagined audience when posting on social network sites. The problem is that, "on the other side of the screen, there are actual people forming impressions—and the imagined audience may not always align with the actual audience."[33] The key to successful online interactions is maintaining a conscious awareness of one's audience and interacting with that audience (both imagined and actual) in an authentic and credible manner.

ONLINE PRESENCE AND CASTING DECISIONS

The factors involved in deciding who gets cast are endless. Certainly talent usually (hopefully?) plays a significant role, but other, less tangible, factors are involved as well. What role, if any, does the relatively new marketing tool of social media play in final casting decisions? For social media sites such as Facebook, it is easy to determine the potential influence an individual has; one only needs to look at the number of "Friends" they have clearly posted on their homepage. As Alice Marwick describes in *Status Update*, Twitter offers several opportunities to determine a user's influence: "Twitter displays one's status in three different ways: follower numbers, re-tweets, and @replies. On Twitter, the number of followers, shown on each individual profile, displays one's "worth" in terms of quantity, while retweets and @replies displays one's worth in terms of the number and (implicit) status of users who publicly acknowledge one's existence."[34] Do casting personnel, creative teams, and producers care about these metrics? Does the number of friends, followers, retweets, and @replies have any influence on casting decisions? In a September 2015 article in *Variety*, author Malina Saval interviewed Mitch Gossett, an agent with Cunningham Escott Slevin Doherty Talent Agency in Los Angeles. According to Gossett, "the casting process has really shifted toward making those social media metrics relevant in casting. If you have two clients up for the same part and one has 6 million followers and one has 27 [followers], they're going to give it to the one with 6 million followers because of the direct access to promotion that will cost them nothing."[35] This may be true for film and television in Los Angeles, but does the number of social media followers have the same impact on casting for the musical theatre stage? Casting directors in New York seem to disagree. Daryl Eisenberg admits: "I have had producers who have asked how many followers an actor has." However, she says "unless they have 13 million Twitter followers, I think that it's kind of irrelevant."[36] Paul Russell acknowledges that "Internet sensations are in our consciousness, but the actor who no one knows, may have a lot of followers, but if you don't have the goods, or the public doesn't know you beyond Twitter, I'm not going to cast you."[37] Joy Dewing disagrees; she says: "It isn't typically the deciding factor and it depends on the project; but yes, I have seen an actor's online presence weigh into the final casting decisions. A producer wants to sell tickets after all. That's their job."[38] Michael Cassara views the issue equally pragmatically. Broadway and regional theatres often cast celebrities in leading roles simply (or primarily) to sell tickets. Cassara suggests that making casting decisions based on social media followers is no different. "It's the same idea," says Cassara, "as having Sally Struthers appear in *The Full Monty* at some regional theatre. Because people know her."[39] Likewise, the actors interviewed for this chapter have differing views on the topic. Actor Colin Hanlon, who has appeared in *Rent* on Broadway as well as the first national tour of *Wicked*, among other credits, points to the reality that "a person can buy followers and know how to get more followers through tagging certain things or using hashtags ... I think talent and talent alone should be the main reason you cast anyone."[40] However, Andrew Keenan-Bolger, whose credits include original Broadway productions of *Mary Poppins*, *Newsies*, and *Tuck Everlasting*, seems to align with Michael Cassara on the topic. He says: "Followers are social currency. They are an insurance policy for producers. It is hard to quantify fan base, but you can look at followers and see real numbers. This many people are interested in what this person is doing or saying. There's something to be said for that."[41] This, according to Marwick is one of the downfalls of social media platforms; "social media has come to promote an individualistic, competitive notion of identity that prioritizes individual status-seeking."[42] In other words, social media sites implicitly conflate large numbers of followers with status. Because status equals power, it follows that high status individuals (those with an abundance of Twitter followers and Facebook friends) would be more desirable to casting decision-makers.[43] Whether or not one agrees with the artistic morality of casting based on social media influence, it does appear to be happening, at least to some degree, in the world of musical theatre. If actors are attempting to leverage social media to become known by casting directors, there's no reason to believe that casting directors and producers aren't also leveraging the social media influence of their actors to sell tickets.

The value of social media platforms for individuals on both sides of the casting table is undeniable. Facebook, Twitter, and other sites allow actors and casting directors to maintain hundreds or even thousands of relationships with the click of a button. Marwick asserts that the true value of social media is that it creates an "ambient awareness" of others in our network. While Twitter feeds and Facebook homepages may often become cluttered with political memes and cat videos, Marwick maintains that what they are also doing is connecting individuals. Social media allows individuals to create "intimate" relationships with acquaintances. Beyond talent, looks, type, and other intangible factors, casting choices also involve the creative team deciding whether or not they want to spend six weeks in a tiny rehearsal studio with this actor. Marwick acknowledges that while many social media sites are "frequently characterized as a chattering stream of irrelevant pieces of information, these pieces of information, gossip, small talk, and trivia serve to create and maintain emotional connections between members of the networked audience."[44] If the actor has a well-curated social media presence, a director or producer can quickly look at an actor's Twitter feed or Facebook page and determine the actor's possible fit with the creative team in a way that is virtually (pun intended) impossible during a three-minute audition or a brief callback.

Online Branding

According to many in both the new media and theatre industries, it is not enough to simply curate a strong online presence through social media platforms in order to be successful. The most effective tool to promote oneself is the latest self-marketing buzzword: self-branding. As Marwick explains, "Self-branding is primarily a series of [corporate] marketing strategies applied to the individual. It is a set of practices and a mindset, a way of thinking about the self as a salable commodity that can tempt a potential employer."[45] Actors like Andrew Keenan-Bolger have embraced the marketing potential of self-branding online. Keenan-Bolger says: "Now more than ever, the entertainment world is a business for every single individual. You have to have a business mind. Your online brand is incredibly important and factors into a lot of decisions that can impact your career."[46] In *Sociology in the Age of the Internet*, Allison Cavanagh describes it thusly:

> In order to gain and keep an audience individuals have in some sense to engage in or orientate to marketing strategies for their own sites ... in order to attract an audience ... the self we present online must be intelligible to this audience, and this requires a certain coherence. In essence, in order to achieve online visibility we must produce ourselves as an easily recognizable "brand" of person.[47]

For the actor, self-branding online involves utilizing every digital tool at one's disposal to create a unified (and accurate) image of who that actor is. Paul Russell describes it this way:

> Your brand defines who you are as an actor. It grows out of your self-awareness and an objective vision of what your talents offer to those who buy—the buyers being both audience and casting decision-makers ... To stand out among the competition you must define who you are and what you can offer. You must define your brand.[48]

Online self-branding for the actor involves creating a coherent, cohesive "package," easily accessible and recognizable. Essentially, the actor must create their own Nike "swoosh." The idea, according to Jonathan Flom, is to "manipulate people's views of our product just like a corporation does." Flom suggests creating a professional website "complete with recognizable images, logos, and catchphrases."[49] The ability for entrepreneurial actors to use the Internet to create, maintain, and market their brand is the most significant new marketing tool of the twenty-first century.[50] "The objective," says Jonathan Flom, "is to have some stellar representation of your talent (and your brand!) searchable on the web."[51] This form of self-marketing simply didn't exist two decades ago.

The old days of sending postcards or a cover letter along with a headshot and resume to casting directors are gone. Self-branding is an integral part of the business of acting in the twenty-first century. Web-savvy musical theatre performers must now devote countless hours beyond maintaining their craft to updating websites, creating professional video clips, tweeting, retweeting, and posting on an ever-growing number of social media websites in order to get noticed by casting personnel and, ultimately, find success on the musical theatre stage.

Micro-Celebrity

The third way in which a musical theatre performer can become known to casting personnel and other industry professionals is the most difficult and often as much the result of good timing and luck as it is talent. A handful of unknown (or relatively unknown) actors have, over the past decade, been able to catapult themselves into the consciousness of casting directors through the creation of viral videos or successful web series. These unknown-performers-turned-Internet-sensations make up a new phenomenon of the twenty-first century: the micro-celebrity.

Theresa Senft defines micro-celebrity as "the commitment to deploying and maintaining one's online identity as if it were a branded good, with the expectation that others do the same."[52] In more succinct terms, Marwick refers to it as "a state of being famous to a niche group of people."[53] Essentially, online content (be it a video, a blog, or some other form of communication) is created by the user and then marketed to the public through sites such as YouTube. What is so unique about content created by micro-celebrities is that the interaction between the user and the public does not end with the content. Traditional celebrities create content (films, television shows, etc.) and then the public consumes it. Generally, that is the end of the interaction between the public and the celebrity. It should be noted, however, that this relationship is changing, especially with regards to Broadway performers who actively interact with their fans online such as Lin-Manuel Miranda,[54] Laura Osnes, and others (for more on the evolving connection between Broadway stars and their fans see Emily Clark's contribution to this volume). Digital micro-celebrities, as Marwick explains, "view their online connections as an audience or fan base, and use communication technologies like Twitter, instant messaging (IM), and e-mail to respond to them." This approach breaks "down the traditional barriers between audience and performer, spectator and spectacle. The micro-celebrity has direct interaction with fans, while traditional celebrities only give the illusion of interaction and access."[55] In addition, as Senft notes, "micro[-]celebrity changes the game of celebrity … [it] blends audiences and communities, two groups traditionally requiring different modes of address. Audiences desire someone to speak *at* them; communities desire someone to speak *with* them."[56] Actors who have successfully leveraged social media to become micro-celebrities have created an atmosphere with their online persona that is approachable and (at least on the surface) appears to desire direct interaction with their fan bases and create communities. Over the past two decades many actors have successfully created online personas or well-known web series which have impacted their careers on stage.

One of the most well-known micro-celebrities is Colleen Ballinger, known to fans around the world as Miranda Sings. It is fascinating to note that new media scholars, such as Marwick, point to "authenticity" as the key component to becoming well known on the Internet.[57] For Ballinger, inauthenticity is what led to her success. Her online persona, Miranda Sings, is a complete fabrication and the polar opposite of the real-life Colleen Ballinger. She presents Miranda Sings in a series of online videos in which the overly-confident Miranda provides misguided voice lessons to aspiring singers, fashion tutorials (including the use of her signature fire engine-red "lisstick"), and general guidance on topics including "how to take a selfie" or "how to sing like Ariana Grande." Ballinger's most recent product, a book titled *Selp-Helf* published by Simon & Schuster's Gallery Books, suggests that the entrepreneurial actor can use her online micro-celebrity to crossover into more traditional forms of media.[58]

Ballinger's micro-celebrity began in the early days of YouTube. She began to notice a number of unknown actors, like herself, posting videos on the new site. She created Miranda in response to what she was seeing online. "YouTube had just become a thing," says Ballinger, "but I didn't understand girls singing to themselves on camera in their rooms. My videos started out as a complete inside joke with friends. Soon, they started going viral. I really wanted the character to be unlikable, so I'd read the comments, and whatever people hated on—Miranda's makeup, stuttering, whatever—I'd do it more."[59] As the videos gained a following, she was quickly embraced by the Broadway community. She was invited to perform at the infamous Jim Caruso's Cast Party at Birdland in New York City, in which she gave an improvised voice lesson to *Jersey Boys* original cast member, Daniel Reichard.[60] Since then she has been asked to appear as Miranda with the cast of *Mamma Mia!* at the annual Broadway Cares/Equity Fights AIDS Easter Bonnet competition and collaborated with *Hamilton*'s Lin-Manuel Miranda on a video.[61] Her online success and Internet micro-celebrity has become a phenomenon; she currently has over seven million subscribers to her YouTube channel.[62] In October 2016, online programming site Netflix premiered an eight-episode scripted sitcom starring Miranda, titled *Haters Back Off* (a reference to her signature response to negative online commenters).[63] While Colleen Ballinger hasn't stopped exploring opportunities on the musical theatre stage, her online micro-celebrity has taken her places she never could have imagined as a recently graduated, struggling non-union performer less than ten years ago.

Another actor who successfully leveraged social media to become a micro-celebrity in the early days of YouTube is Andrew Keenan-Bolger. As a student in the BFA Musical Theatre program at the University of Michigan, Keenan-Bolger was immediately drawn to the potential of YouTube when it launched in 2005. "When YouTube first started," he says, "it was such a millennials game. I started recording videos of friends as a way to share it with friends and family. It ended up being some of the first musical theatre content on the site. So when people typed in 'musical theatre' or 'Broadway' we were what they found."[64] Although the concept of micro-celebrity didn't exist, Keenan-Bolger and his colleagues in the class of 2007 became well known by many in the industry, simply because of the timing. Keenan-Bolger was shocked by the response. "We arrived in New York," he says, "and everyone knew us before we even got here!"[65] Soon after arriving in the city, he was cast in the first national tour of William Finn's *The 25th Annual Putnam County Spelling Bee* where he started creating behind the scenes video blogs showing life on the road. The vlogs (video blogs) garnered a following and as he says, "producers and marketing people started to take note … this was a way to market the tour, and ultimately help my career."[66] In 2010, Keenan-Bolger was cast in a newly revised production of *It's A Bird, It's A Plane, It's Superman* at the Dallas Theatre Center. There, Keenan-Bolger and castmate Kate Wetherhead, whose credits include Broadway productions of *Spelling Bee* and *Legally Blonde*, began toying with the idea of creating a web series. They wanted to create something different, so rather than the usual 3–5 minute long episodes, they began to explore a longer format, something closer to a traditional sitcom. The idea evolved into the highly popular web series, *Submissions Only*, an honest, yet satirical look at the casting process in New York. Soon after, they invited Colin Hanlon to play the leading role of Tim as well as serve as a co-producer. "We had no idea the reach that *Submissions Only* was going to have in our theatre industry," says Hanlon. "It really started as a little pet project for us all ... once we merged with BroadwayWorld.com we were able to track how many views we had and how far around the world people were watching our series. People in Russia, China, Japan, etc., were tuning into our season three premiere." The series is regularly listed as one of the most successful web series on the Internet, but Hanlon realizes that timing played a large role in the series' success as well. He says: "*Submissions Only* was really the first theatrical story-through series. We premiered a year before *Smash* and all of the other series that have popped up over the years."[67] As the series gained "must-see" status within the industry, casting directors took notice, although, as Hanlon notes, "a lot of the assistants and interns in different offices know it because it was, and still is, very popular among the college age kids." The success of the series also helped Hanlon make the transition from successful Broadway actor to television performer. He says the fact that the series was garnering attention in casting offices "allowed me to finally audition for more on-camera projects. People had a reference to see my work." In fact, Hanlon's biggest on-screen success is a direct result of his work with *Submissions Only*. Hanlon currently plays the recurring role of Steven (Mitch and Cam's neighbor) on the hit ABC sitcom *Modern Family*. "The casting director of *Modern Family*, Jeff Greenberg, is a huge *Submissions Only* fan," says Hanlon. "That's how I got called into audition for my role on *Modern Family*."[68]

It's difficult to determine what role *Submissions Only* has had on the careers of Keenan-Bolger, Wetherhead, Hanlon and others (the series regulars include Broadway performers Santino Fontana, Anne Nathan, Max von Essen, and Lindsay Nicole Chambers, among many others), but Andrew Keenan-Bolger does have some advice for aspiring musical theatre performers looking to parlay YouTube web series into success in the industry. He suggests that:

> Attaching a "creator" subtitle to your name puts you in a different box. People want to work with me because they know I'm a creator, not just an interpreter. No one auditions for a new Broadway show. You audition for a reading, which becomes a workshop out of town. The people who get cast in those are people that can advocate for their character. Being a writer and creator makes you a valuable commodity.[69]

Becoming a micro-celebrity can certainly help an actor find success on the musical theatre stage, but as Keenan-Bolger notes, one of the things that really attracts casting directors and producers to performers who have found success online is the inherent creativity they illustrate through the development of original online content.

Actress Natalie Weiss has also achieved micro-celebrity status through her successful web series *Breaking Down the Riffs*. Like Colleen Ballinger, Weiss never set out to garner micro-celebrity status. "My YouTube presence actually happened rather innocently/accidentally," she says. "I was in my senior year at Penn State, performing a song from *Dreamgirls* at the head of my theatre program's house. One of the freshmen happened to film a portion of the performance, put it on a new site called YouTube, and the next day I had a bunch of Facebook friend requests ... Then it just built from there! Eventually I rode the wave and started posting my performance videos ... which led to my own channel [on YouTube]."[70] She has found the most online success with the series *Breaking Down the Riffs*. In the series, Weiss teaches viewers how to break down, analyze, and ultimately sing vocal riffs from well-known pop and musical theatre songs. Her micro-celebrity status grew rather slowly for the Internet. Over the past nine years she's seen her videos go from several hundred views, mostly, according to Weiss, from the younger theatre community, to a collective viewership of over three million fans, students, and teachers around the world. She has performed in concerts and taught master classes around the world, which she says is a direct result of her online presence and Internet fame.[71] New York casting directors have also taken notice. When asked about Natalie Weiss, casting director Michael Cassara stated: "There is no reason I should know who she was when she was a senior in college. But I did."[72]

Although it may be difficult to determine what role the online success of performers like Natalie Weiss and the cast of *Submissions Only* has had on the stage careers of these actors, there are more clear cases of online micro-celebrity leading directly to stage work for an actor. When Joy Dewing was casting the recent non-union tour of *Legally Blonde* she found herself checking her newsfeed on Facebook one afternoon and came across a video a friend had shared on her wall. As she explains:

> The title was "High School Mama Rose." I thought "this ought to be a hoot" and clicked on the video. As I watched this high school senior deliver "Rose's Turn" [from the musical *Gypsy*] *from her guts* I started

thinking, "wait a minute ... this is actually REALLY GOOD!" I decided I needed to meet this girl ... so I stalked her on YouTube, which led me to Facebook, which led me to find the name of her high school in Connecticut. I found her school's website, looked up the name of her choir director, and emailed him ... after speaking with me on the phone and assumedly deciding that I was legit, he connected her to me, and I invited her to come to New York City for a general audition.[73]

The actress was 18-year-old Hannah Rose DeFlumeri and after impressing both Dewing and director Marc Bruni at the audition, she was cast as Vivienne in the tour. The micro-celebrity of DeFlumeri, generated from her viral video, led directly to her professional debut and subsequent success on the musical theatre stage.[74]

What's fascinating about micro-celebrity and the successes of the individuals interviewed above is the importance of timing. Performers like Andrew Keenan-Bolger, Colleen Ballinger, and Natalie Weiss happened to create an online presence at the same time YouTube was introducing itself to the world. One wonders how or if these same artists would find success if they entered the overly saturated world of YouTube today. Examples like DeFlumeri illustrate that it is possible to rise above the clutter of self-produced YouTube videos and parlay micro-celebrity online into success on the musical theatre stage. However, using the Internet to catapult oneself into the consciousness of our culture is no easy task. "In order to differentiate one's personal page from the mass of other personal pages," says Cavanagh, "the author must be prepared to grant the audience more and more intimate perspectives on his or her life and this in turn locks the author into a quasi-pornographic logic of visibility."[75] If one is willing to expose a fully authentic and credible online identity, it can lead to great success. It seems the key is finding the perfect combination of luck, timing, and talent. Interestingly, this is not so different from finding success the old-fashioned way.

Conclusion

Digital technology has transformed nearly every aspect of our lives. Casting for the musical theatre stage is no exception. Online technology has changed the way casting directors do their job. The rise of social media has made it easier (for better or worse) for actors to interact with casting directors. Online self-branding has created new tools for actors to market themselves. Micro-celebrity has produced entirely new opportunities for actors to achieve success both online and on the stage. The Internet has made some aspects of the process easier. Digital technology has made the submission process faster, the logistics of running a casting session more streamlined, and allowed actors and casting directors to interact with greater ease and less effort. However, this new technology also forces actors to navigate a sometimes tricky balance between presenting an authentic version of themselves online without over-sharing. As Theresa Senft theorizes, the Internet has created a community of actors and industry players who are "individuals bound in strange familiarity; the familiarity that arises from exchanging private information with people from whom we are otherwise remote."[76] This strange familiarity can be detrimental to actors who are not carefully curating their online brand, but it can also lead to tremendous opportunity and unexplored avenues for success for an actor savvy enough to leverage this new technology to their advantage. The truth is, however, that we are likely only seeing the beginnings of the impact digital technology and social media will have on musical theatre as a whole and casting in particular. The technological advances and changes have come quickly, and one can only imagine what the future holds for casting in the digital age.

Notes

1. Bockris, *The Life and Death of Andy Warhol*, 219.
2. Senft, "Microcelebrity and the Branded Self," 350, original emphasis.
3. Ibid., 347.
4. White, *Digital Media and Society*, 34.
5. Marwick, *Status Update*, 5.
6. Joy Dewing, interview with author, November 6, 2013.
7. Daryl Eisenberg, interview with author, November 4, 2015.
8. Dewing, interview.
9. Ibid.
10. Michael Cassara, interview with author, October 15, 2015.
11. Eisenberg, interview.
12. Marwick, *Status Update*, 120.
13. Paul Russell, interview with author, November 3, 2015.
14. Dewing, interview.
15. Shindle, Kate, "Evolution," last modified March 22, 2016, https://members.actorsequity.org/equitynews/archive/2016/03/.
16. Russell, *Acting: Make It Your Business*, 106–107.

17. Cavanagh, *Sociology in the Age of the Internet*, 121–125.
18. Senft, "Microcelebrity," 347.
19. Marwick, "Online Identity," 355.
20. Ibid.
21. Flom, *Act Like It's Your Business*, 119–120.
22. Fred Berman, interview with author, October 28, 2015.
23. Flom, *Act Like It's Your Business*, 170.
24. Ibid., 120.
25. Natalie Weiss, interview with author, November 3, 2015.
26. Marwick, "Online Identity," 360.
27. Flom, *Act Like It's Your Business*, 25.
28. Schmidt, "Practices of Networked Identity," 369.
29. Eisenberg, interview.
30. Dewing, interview.
31. Cassara, interview.
32. Dewing, interview.
33. Litt and Hargittai, "The Imagined Audience on Social Network Sites."
34. Marwick, *Status Update*, 95.
35. Saval, "Digital Revolution Pushes Youth Talent Agents to Change Their Game."
36. Eisenberg, interview.
37. Russell, interview.
38. Dewing, interview.
39. Cassara, interview.
40. Colin Hanlon, interview with author, October 30, 2015.
41. Andrew Keenan-Bolger, interview with author, October 30, 2015.
42. Marwick, *Status Update*, 17.
43. See Emily Clark's discussion in this volume on the impact reality television star's celebrity status has had on Broadway casting.
44. Ibid., 216.
45. Ibid., 166.
46. Keenan-Bolger, interview.
47. Cavanagh, *Sociology in the Age of the Internet*, 123.
48. Russell, *Acting*, 103.
49. Flom, *Act Like It's Your Business*, 11.
50. As Kathryn Edney notes in her chapter "Cell Phone Technology and Audience Behaviors," included in this volume, this type of marketing and self-promotion is an encouraged use of the cell phone, as long as it's outside of the performance space.
51. Ibid., 120.
52. Senft, "Microcelebrity," 346.
53. Marwick, *Status Update*, 113.

54. See Chap. 6 in this volume.
55. Marwick, *Statue Update*, 118.
56. Senft, "Microcelebrity," 350.
57. Marwick, *Status Update*, 114.
58. Elinzano, "The 8 Most Popular You Tube Personalities."
59. Tyler, "Miranda Sings Santa Barbara."
60. Egger, "She'd Like to Teach the World To Sing."
61. Sims, "Colleen Ballinger Talks YouTube Character Miranda Sings."
62. YouTube. "Miranda Sings." Accessed October 18, 2016, https://www.youtube.com/user/mirandasings08.
63. Spangler. "Miranda Sings Announces 'Haters Back Off' Netflix Premiere Date."
64. Keenan-Bolger, interview.
65. Ibid.
66. Ibid. See also Chap. 2 in this book.
67. Hanlon, interview.
68. Ibid.
69. Keenan-Bolger, interview.
70. Weiss, interview.
71. Ibid.
72. Cassara, interview.
73. Dewing, interview.
74. DeFlumeri appeared in the national tour of *Bullets Over Broadway*, which ended its run in July 2016.
75. Cavanagh, *Sociology in the Age of the Internet*, 124.
76. Senft, "Microcelebrity," 352.

REFERENCES

Berman, Fred (Actor), interview with author, October 28, 2015.
Bockris, Victor. *The Life and Death of Andy Warhol*. New York: Bantam Books, 1989.
Cassara, Michael (Casting Director), interview with author, October 15, 2015.
Cavanagh, Allison. *Sociology in the Age of the Internet*. Maidenhead, England: Open University Press, 2007.
Dewing, Joy (Casting Director), interview with author, November 6, 2013.
Egger, Robin. "She'd Like to Teach the World To Sing." *The Times*, May 2, 2010, accessed January 4, 2016, http://infoweb.newsbank.com/resources/doc/nb/news/12F76AE6F4E371A8?p=UKNB.
Eisenberg, Daryl (Casting Director), interview with author, November 4, 2015.

Elinzano, Maureen. "The 8 Most Popular You Tube Personalities." *Desert News*, January 22, accessed January 4, 2016, http://www.deseretnews.com/article/865620046/The-8-most-popular-YouTube-personalities.html?pg=all.

Flom, Jonathan. *Act Like It's Your Business*. London: The Scarecrow Press, Inc., 2013.

Hanlon, Colin (Actor), interview with author, October 30, 2015.

Keenan-Bolger, Andrew (Actor), interview with author, October 30, 2015.

Litt, Eden and Eszter Hargittai. "The Imagined Audience on Social Network Sites," *Social Media + Society*, January–March 2016, accessed February 16, 2016, doi: 2056305116633482.

Marwick, Alice E. "Online Identity," in *A Companion to New Media Dynamics*, ed. John Hartley et al. Oxford: Blackwell Publishing, Ltd., 2013.

———. *Status Update: Celebrity, Publicity, & Branding in the Social Media Age*. New Haven: Yale University Press, 2013.

"Miranda Sings." *YouTube*. Accessed October 18, 2016, https://www.youtube.com/user/mirandasings08.

Russell, Paul. *Acting: Make It Your Business*. New York: Backstage Books, 2008.

———. (Casting Director). Interview with author, November 3, 2015.

Saval, Malina. "Digital Revolution Pushes Youth Talent Agents to Change Their Game," *Variety*, September 1, 2015, accessed October 23, 2015, http://variety.com/2015/tv/spotlight/digital-revolution-pushes-youth-talent-agents-to-change-their-game-1201582677/.

Schmidt, Jan-Hinrik. "Practices of Networked Identity," in *A Companion to New Media Dynamics*, ed. John Hartley et al. Oxford: Blackwell Publishing, Ltd., 2013.

Senft, Theresa M. "Microcelebrity and the Branded Self," in *A Companion to New Media Dynamics*, ed. John Hartley et al. Oxford: Blackwell Publishing, Ltd., 2013.

Shindle, Kate. "Evolution." *Actorsequity.org*. Last modified March 22, 2016, https://members.actorsequity.org/equitynews/archive/2016/03/.

Sims, James. "Colleen Ballinger Talks YouTube Character Miranda Sings." *BroadwayWorld*, August 27, 2010, accessed January 4, 2016, http://www.broadwayworld.com/article/Colleen-Ballinger-Talks-YouTube-Character-Miranda-Sings-20100827.

Spangler, Todd. "Miranda Sings Announces 'Haters Back Off' Netflix Premiere Date." *Variety*. June 24, 2016, accessed October 18, 2016, http://variety.com/2016/digital/news/miranda-sings-haters-back-off-netflix-1201803320/.

Tyler, Hayden. "Miranda Sings Santa Barbara." *Santa Barbara Independent.* March 4, 2014, accessed January 4, 2016, http://www.independent.com/news/2014/mar/04/miranda-sings-santa-barbara/.
Weiss, Natalie (Actor), interview with author, November 3, 2015.
White, Andrew. *Digital Media and Society: Transforming Economics, Politics and Social Practices.* New York: Palgrave Macmillan, 2014.

CHAPTER 10

Keeping the Celebrity Flame Flickering: Reality Television Celebrities on Broadway and Fan Interaction Through Digital Media

Emily Clark

Daniel Boorstin famously wrote that a celebrity is "a person who is known for his [*sic*] well-knownness."[1] With hit reality television programs like *American Idol* (2002–2016) democratically creating new celebrities out of ordinary people,[2] while also permitting direct participation between viewers and contestants, America's celebrity frenzy has increased at a rapid pace, and the theatre is following suit. Broadway is a different place than it was even twenty years ago.[3] P. David Marshall, in "New Media—New Self: The Changing Power of Celebrity," states: "The symbiotic relationship between media and celebrity has been ruptured somewhat in the last decade through the development of new media ... [which is] changing the relationships and mediations between user and public personality."[4] With the abundance of celebrity journalism and increase in nearly twenty-four hour media celebrity coverage via the ubiquity of the Internet and social media, the terrain of the arts and entertainment industries has been altered. Producers believe

E. Clark (✉)
Graduate Center, City University of New York, New York City, NY, USA
e-mail: eclark@gradcenter.cuny.edu

© The Author(s) 2017
J. Hillman-McCord (ed.), *iBroadway*,
DOI 10.1007/978-3-319-64876-7_10

233

audiences crave star power, and while not a new casting strategy, the idea that a "name" is necessary has led to celebrity names appearing on Broadway marquees with increased intensity. Celebrities who are cast in Broadway productions interact with audiences in ways never seen before and mediated access between fan and celebrity is nearly limitless. Chris Rojek writes that the Internet "gives stargazers unprecedented opportunities to participate, in conjunction with stars, in building celebrity brands and, through the laptop, the iPad and the mobile phone, increases the saturation of celebrity culture to round the clock status."[5] This chapter investigates the tenuous merger of Broadway culture, reality television, and the Internet, as exemplified in the careers of Laura Osnes and Bailey Hanks.

Due to the accessibility the Internet provides, "celebrities are being reworked and reformed in terms of their value and utility by audiences and users,"[6] providing a specialized lens into their lives. Celebrities themselves and their handlers are often behind this digital reworking. Osnes' rise to celebrity on the Broadway stage was through a vehicle created in order to actively engage home viewers: reality television. Familiar with these tools of engagement from her television origins, she continues to engage with fans, both old and new, through her savvy social media accounts. Marshall describes: "For some, the website actually reconstructs 'home' into a virtual space that is both public and private, where the web is a place of performance and staging of the self."[7] Through her Internet presence, she provides enough access to titillate and engage with fans, but not enough to encourage invasion into her life, as other celebrities beyond the theatre encounter. In essence, her social media presence offers an extension of her performances, her "extratextual dimension."[8]

Osnes' seemingly overnight Broadway fame began after winning NBC's *Grease: You're The One That I Want!* (2007), awarding her the starring role of Sandy in the revival of *Grease* (2007–2009). Due to her participation in a competitive talent-based reality television series, at-home viewers not only watched and engaged with her personality on television, but also specifically voted her to championship. These audience members had a part in her success and celebrity and contributed to her being cast on Broadway. For many, Osnes and performers with similar television backgrounds are "friends" of knowing audience members, more so than celebrities from any other media, due to the familiarity established between performer and audience in the comfort of their living rooms, as described by Marshall in *Celebrity and Power: Fame in Contemporary Culture*. These fans therefore choose to support them in their Broadway endeavors. Bailey Hanks came to Broadway from a similar background, as winner of MTV's *Legally Blonde:* The Search for Elle Woods (2008). She subsequently was the last to play the leading role in *Legally Blonde* (2007–2008) before it closed on Broadway. The series utilized a similar format to other reality television shows, forging connections between the contestants and viewers through personal interviews, revealing more intimate details with behind-the-scenes exclusives online. It did not, however, allow the viewing audience to interact with the television show and contestants through voting. I argue that by presenting the show in this documentary format as opposed to a more interactive one, the show failed to draw viewers to the theatre to see the result of their participation in democratic celebrity formation. I further argue that although both Osnes and Hanks emerged from similar reality television origins, only one of the two performers has transcended the negative connotations of the reality television image, through a combination of talent, technique, and Internet savvy.

A "star" is one who is recognized in his or her field, upheld above the masses, yet it would be inaccurate to use the term "celebrity" synonymously. Graeme Turner clarifies that "the precise moment a public figure becomes a celebrity ... occurs at the point at which media interest in their activities is transferred from reporting on their public role ... to investigating the details of their private lives."[9] Once interest in an actor's private affairs becomes more important than their performance, they are no longer merely a star, but a celebrity. By this definition, celebrities are not common in the theatre, but as this chapter demonstrates, digital presence can cause this to change. Probing and reporting on the private lives of celebrities provides the opportunity for a more personal connection between fan/audience and the celebrated individual, and typically the more the audience can self-identify with the celebrity, the longer their celebrity status lasts. The ability to see oneself as living "just like" the celebrity is crucial to prolonging celebrity status.

In an effort to expand their brands, astute Broadway performers are utilizing the Internet and social media to increase their accessibility to those not physically in the audience, enabling them to witness aspects of their lives through the Internet. Rojek describes the Internet as "the domestic system of fame ... a do it yourself approach to fame acquisition,"[10] which has outlets such as vlogs, YouTube, Facebook, Instagram, and Twitter providing a wide-reaching audience a more intimate connection with the theatre performer. For example, on Facebook, one can "be friends" with the performers themselves (although generally only on a specially constructed public profile) and can be much more aware of the intimate details of that performer's life. Osnes has become a Broadway star, bypassing the primarily pejorative patina of reality television celebrity. However, her clever use of social media allows her to remain on a bridge connecting theatrical stardom and celebrity, a place where few Broadway stars find themselves, (although, as previously mentioned, this is changing in today's increasingly digital world). Many to most Broadway performers now utilize the digital landscape through social media accounts to post video clips and interact with fans.[11] By forging far reaching connections with individuals, expanding their fan bases, and engaging with potential audiences across the globe, performers' accessibility may encourage the formation of theatrical celebrities. This could potentially replace the financial pressure for non-theatrical celebrities to grace the Broadway stage. By examining Osnes' initial reception on Broadway and her ability to "crossover" as a "legitimate" theatrical presence, we can see the crossroads of Broadway's possibilities. Her talent earned her a place in the television competition, her ability to connect with at-home viewers allowed her to win her Broadway debut, and her talent, in combination with her celebrity status, has led to her play five leading roles on Broadway in six years, two of them Tony nominated. Osnes' vlog "The Princess Diary: Backstage at *Cinderella* with Laura Osnes" allowed backstage and dressing room access while she was starring in *Cinderella* (2013), in addition to a glimpse into her personal life. Having transitioned from a democratic celebrity to a Broadway star, she understands the importance and necessity for performing aspects of her daily life in order to remain in the celebrity sphere, as that perceived accessibility is responsible for her initial fame.

The Aura of Celebrity

In Benjamin's essay "The Work of Art in the Age of Mechanical Reproduction," he asserts that art contained an "aura," inherent in its ephemerality; art's "unique existence" is the "eliminated element" in modern times, where art can be mass-produced and marketed. Benjamin writes:

[A]ura is tied to [the actor's] presence; there can be no replica of it. The aura which, on the stage, emanates from Macbeth, cannot be separated for the spectators from that of the actor. However, the singularity of the shot in the studio is that the camera is substituted for the public. Consequently, the aura that envelops the actor vanishes, and with it the aura of the figure he portrays. ... While facing the camera [the actor] knows that ultimately he will face the public, the consumers who constitute the market. This market, where he offers not only his labor but also his whole self, his heart and soul, is beyond his reach.[12]

But that market is in reach when the star appears in the theatre. Suddenly, a live audience, absent for much of the star's work, is sitting a few feet away. Benjamin continues: "The cult of the movie star, fostered by the money of the film industry, preserves not the unique aura of the person but the 'spell of personality,' the phony spell of a commodity,"[13] but when a star performs live on stage, an aura, according to Benjamin, exists. Additionally, while performing in a Broadway musical, the "tricks" only available to film actors created by "special camera angles, close-ups, etc.,"[14] are no longer present and the actor no longer "lacks the opportunity of the stage actor to adjust to the audience during his performance."[15]

According to Benjamin, while watching film or television, the celebrity's aura disappears through the camera and screen. However, when seeing larger-than-life celebrities from film or viewing "friends" from television performing on stage, their aura pervades due to the liveness and ephemerality of their performance in a shared space. For viewers who enjoy watching reality television and are enthralled by these personalities, a relationship is not created with a character, but with the individuals themselves and their celebrity. Rojek, heavily criticizing the current celebrity climate, writes: "Today ... the public has a keen, apparently inexhaustible, and in the view of many social commentators, seriously unbalanced interest, in the toings and froings of celebrity culture."[16] This obsession, with nearly round the clock media coverage into the lives of celebrities, is what Sean Redmond refers to as "fame culture." Redmond argues that "*fame culture* offers 'ordinary' and 'extraordinary' people the chance of a heightened level of intimacy."[17] For the majority of reality television programs, no merit is necessary for the individuals to achieve celebrity status; they simply need to be of interest to targeted audiences. The "heightened level of intimacy" that "electrifies one's experience of the world"[18] of which Redmond speaks, can, by extension, be experienced when viewers at home are directly invited to participate in the making of reality television stars on talent-based programs, such as *American Idol* and *So You Think You Can Dance*. As opposed to other competitive programs like *Survivor* and *The Bachelor*, the sense of audience/contestant relationship is heightened because talent-based programs allow direct participation, where the at-home viewer is provided with the option of taking part in the voting process, democratically participating in choosing the show's winner.

STARS, CELEBRITIES, AND REALITY TELEVISION

The direct nexus between the participating voter and contestant creates agency for the viewer and "[t]he immediacy of interaction produces social intimacy"[19] between performer and audience. Here consumption is active; therefore, audiences can see themselves directly responsible for the celebrity of the individual. If the performer is cast on Broadway, audiences are by extension responsible. Mark Andrejevic, in *Reality TV: The Work of Being Watched*, writes that the promise of reality television is that "spectators shall become participants. The many shall take on the role previously monopolized by the privileged few: power will be shared with the people."[20] While he continues by acknowledging that this is not what necessarily comes to fruition in "reality," in the case of Broadway casting, a focal point of commercial popular culture, the participatory nature of reality television has shifted the industry. Where audiences once had no input in the construction of a Broadway musical, today, thanks to the proliferation of the platform and democratic celebrities who come from it, reality television has given audiences more of a voice in deciding who they see on stage.[21] Through consumption, audiences have fashioned celebrities out of everyday people who get the extraordinary experience of performing on Broadway. However, reality television celebrities battle harsh critique and skepticism from the Broadway community, critics, and fans, and as this chapter will show, do not always succeed unscathed.

When watching celebrities perform in Broadway musicals, fans who have been drawn to the theatre are watching individuals with whom they have created some form of para-social relationship, a relationship "which occur[s] across a significant social distance—with people 'we don't know.'"[22] In other words, fans have become so familiar with the personal lives of celebrities that they believe they are actually acquainted with the famous figures themselves. Adrienne Lai points out, "in order for celebrity para-social relations to be perpetuated, the individual must be able to believe that the celebrities are not so distant from those in their social circles."[23] The media, with increasing intensity, shows a consuming public that celebrities are "just like" them by reporting on their private everyday pursuits. Because of this, the boundary between celebrity and fan is being broken, and "[a] sense of closeness to these celebrities is developed."[24] Whether due to charisma, the "it" factor, talent, evanescence,[25] or the belief that these celebrated individuals are friends, when audiences come to the theatre to see their beloved movie star, television personality, music idol, and/or reality show figure, their celebrity status creates a sense of intimacy. Marvin Carlson, in *The Haunted Stage: The Theatre as Memory Machine*, refers to the haunted body as, "the recycled body and persona of the actor ... and its effect upon reception."[26] He writes: "It is difficult, perhaps impossible, once [an actor's] career is under way, for them to avoid a certain aura of expectations based on past roles. The actor's new roles become, in a very real sense, ghosted by previous ones."[27] Carlson's work specifically discusses the characters that each actor plays throughout their career haunting their body from performance to performance, but it is by extension clear that celebrities are also haunted by their private lives when performing on stage. By taking his theory one step further, using audience reactions via social media, blogs, and chatrooms where individuals share their personal experiences, I argue that when these well-known figures, celebrities, appear on the Broadway stage, they create a unique aura, one that differs from Benjamin's use of the term when discussing liveness and ephemerality in theatrical performance. This theatrical aura is a different one than Benjamin describes, one combined with the familiarity of false intimacy created by celebrity status and media coverage. The specific type of aura itself is dependent upon the genre that celebrity emanates from. Because of the different type of relationship created between the celebrity and the public in each field outside of the theatre, a corresponding new relationship is created between the two inside a theatrical space.

In *American Idolatry: Celebrity*, Commodity and *Reality Television*, Christopher E. Bell focuses on competitive talent-based reality shows and acknowledges that there is something different about shows like *American Idol* or *The Voice* as opposed to the various *Real Housewives* series or latest Kardashian television endeavor. It would be difficult to argue that the personalities who are featured on the latter examples have "talent;" they are not actors, singers, dancers, or writers. They are filmed and viewed "being themselves" on television. The former at least present their contestants with the semblance of merit in combination with the package of media creation. Regardless of worthiness or category, according to Bell, for many, their appearance on any reality television show has given them a veneer; they are already some form of a proven commodity, which, in the world of Broadway, is a marketable catch.

Bell continues, "By virtue of winning *American Idol* (or placing highly in the competition), the contestant is more favorably positioned to enter the marketplace with a higher degree of desirability and a greater chance at success,"[28] even if that success is in a field that *American Idol* disparaged throughout the series: musical theatre on Broadway. Numerous high placing contestants and winners of *American Idol* have gone on to perform on the Broadway stage.[29] Here, the advantage of having participated in a pop music competition, receiving a modicum of exposure, has given these individuals an advantage in terms of casting. Their exposure on television sets across the country (and beyond) has given them some form of symbolic capital that translates into recognizability, a key factor in the current Broadway climate. Like those trying to find their place in the music industry without the brand of a reality television series affixed to their names, finding oneself cast as a lead in a Broadway musical is becoming increasingly more difficult sans some form of celebrity patina.[30] It is extremely common to see these roles go to a "name," or celebrity with recognition beyond the theatre, some of whom have not worked towards a career in the art of theatre. For producers who cast talent-based competitive reality television stars, there is the additional bonus of the audience having participated in these performers' celebrity, having voted for them over the course of their tenure on *American Idol*, or other shows of its variety. There is a stronger relationship between the celebrity and viewer than one created through a passive audience:

> For television audiences, participation [by voting, playing the online games, and commenting on social media and message boards] may instill a feeling of belonging in a show's audience, fostering a community and enhancing the relationship between a viewer and an entertainment production.[31]

That connection is often taken a step further. By supporting and voting for their favorite contestants/performers, the audience may feel a direct connection with their "friend" with whom they've formed a para-social relationship through the television set, and their success can be seen as a direct connection with the home viewer. Casting directors, directors, and producers perform the traditional casting process. In this new model, as opposed to being entirely removed from the process and purchasing tickets to attend, the audience arguably has some agency. Reality television celebrities are primarily cast due to an already established connection made with American, and in some cases, global audiences. When audience members in turn go to see a reality television contestant perform on Broadway, they are actually in the room with a "friend." Here the new aura is most potent—the "friend" whose celebrity has been encouraged through watching the television show in the comfort of the fan's home, is performing live on stage for a fleeting time. Not only are they playing a role, but they are individuals who have accrued a celebrity status and all that comes with it, including intrusive public knowledge of private information. Most importantly, the fans know they are in a way responsible for the celebrity's performance. This is certainly the case regarding competitors on talent-based reality television programs where Broadway is the prize. The argument can additionally be extended to *American Idol* contestants who have gained celebrity due to television viewers and fans, and go on to perform on Broadway in part because of their name recognition.

THE ORIGINS OF REALITY TELEVISION

The first interactive competitive series, *The Original Amateur Hour*, aired in 1948. In the show, "viewers voted for their favorite acts by calling the show or sending postcards."[32] Richard M. Huff points out that, "for the most part, those appearing on the show never made it big in the entertainment world."[33] In the 1980s *Star Search* became "a platform for future stars" as contestants competed for their shot at fame, but there was not yet a proliferation of shows with this format. Su Holmes and Deborah Jermyn note that at the end of the twentieth century, "global 'event' formats of Reality TV (such as *Big Brother*, *Popstars*, and *Survivor* etcetera)"[34] began to rise in popularity, expanding the presence of reality television across the globe. *American Idol* premiered on the Fox network in June 2002.[35] Its premise was "a nationwide talent show in which viewers would select the next big new singer."[36] The increased presence of reality television in the media not only led to a further proliferation of shows of this genre built on the model provided by *American Idol* and with similar goals, such as *America's Got Talent* and *The X Factor*,[37] but the permeation of stars generated from the form in other areas of popular culture, including Broadway musicals.

Amber Watts, in "Melancholy, Merit, and Merchandise: The Postwar Audience Participation Show," describes the ubiquity of talk show programs and quiz show formats that were created in the 1950s, "featur[ing] individuals disclosing real-life troubles on-air in hope of receiving some reward in return ... offering cash and prizes as the solution to personal tragedy ... [which] promised to transform the lives of participants in significant ways."[38] Similarly, the competitive talent reality television shows also tap into this structure, as participants' life stories are foregrounded in order to make them appear more worthy of the home viewers' sympathy and vote. Watts continues by pointing out that on these early shows in the genre, "the interview served as an entry point for audiences to understand and root for contestants, and a ... participant's tragic backstory would almost certainly enhance a viewer's emotional investment in her overall success in the game."[39] Interviews continue to be a primary focus of reality television today. The same can certainly be said of the competitive talent genre of reality television, where it is important for the contestant to present an attention grabbing backstory,[40] "for viewers at home, particularly those with backgrounds similar to those of the contestants, there was likely a multi-tiered feeling of achievement that came from identifying with them,"[41] and, by extension, voting for them. For shows like *American Idol* and *So You Think You Can Dance*, where the winner's primary reward includes a record contract for the individual or a tour with the group, this model works well, but for NBC's 2007 experiment *Grease: You're The One That I Want!*, where the reward was, "the most unique prize in television history,"[42] leading an ensemble of actors in a Broadway musical, talent was of utmost importance. Bell claims: "In participatory competitive reality television, it is not the talent of the contestant we are rewarding, but the way in which the transformation of this ordinary citizen speaks to our own potential triumphs."[43] If this is true, what happens when talent is not the primary criterion for winning a talent competition? Knowing that the model lends itself towards sympathetic identification and reward votes, as "reality television producers and viewers still love the nobody from nowhere who wins it all,"[44] the judges of *Grease*, including director/choreographer Kathleen Marshall, had a "tricky balancing act"[45] to play.

Voting for Sandy and Danny

Grease: You're The One That I Want! was a competitive talent reality show that asked American television viewers to select the two individuals who were to play the characters Danny Zuko and Sandy Dumbrowski in the 2007 Broadway revival of the musical *Grease*. The eventual winners were Max Crumm and Laura Osnes. *Grease: You're The One That I Want!* ran weekly on NBC,[46] premiering on Sunday, January 7, 2007 with the finale airing on Sunday, March 25, 2007.

Once contestants had been narrowed down, their relationships were established with the studio audience, but more importantly, the voting audiences at home, through a brief biography, providing the imperative backstory. These biographical packages helped to create a level of intimacy with the viewing audience at home, with the contestant introducing that audience to family members, letting them into their own home, and telling personal details about their lives. At the conclusion of each video interview, they each were given a moniker, differentiating each Sandy or Danny from each other, and assigning them a role type, e.g., "Spiritual Sandy," or "Boy Band Danny." Eventual series winner Osnes' backstory was engaging, and that, in addition to the archetypal role that emphasized how "ordinary" she was, became a powerful combination that was a significant factor, in conjunction with her talent, in securing the role of Sandy.

Osnes' entire interview was extremely important in establishing her "type." Osnes was introduced in this episode as "a small town girl." Her backstory began in a dressing room, with Osnes describing how she left Minnesota where she was playing the role of Sandy at Chanhassen Dinner Theatre for this competition. She described how she had just become engaged to her fiancé and took the camera crew shopping for wedding dresses with her. The interview continued with Osnes stating, "Everybody thinks I'm a very sweet Sandy. I don't drink, I don't swear, I don't rat my hair, and I would get ill from one cigarette," interrupted by a clip of Olivia Newton-John from the film *Grease*. Osnes continued: "But I can be sexy too, if I need to be." Her description of herself, combined with the inclusion of the film clip, is extremely important.

Thus far, she presented the audience glimpses of Laura Osnes; this moment presented Sandy. She told the voters that she *really* was the character of Sandy, sweet and innocent but able to be who she needed to be for the man she loves. Finally, Osnes was dubbed "Small Town Sandy."[47]

As "Small Town Sandy," Osnes was made to seem more "ordinary" to connect more closely to at-home viewers.[48] Each factor of how Osnes presented herself or, perhaps more accurately how the television producers presented her, will continue to "haunt" her, in the Marvin Carlson sense, throughout her career. According to Amanda Scheiner McClain, the interview itself "allows the audience intimate and banal knowledge of the contestant, fully removing any distance-created aura. This intimate type of fame is hinged upon the idea that the person on reality TV is interchangeable with the audience member."[49] By being established as a small town approachable friend, Osnes began to establish elements of the new aura she will eventually exude on the Broadway stage.

The second Broadway revival of *Grease* began its run at the Brooks Atkinson Theatre on July 24, 2007 and opened on August 29, 2007. This production of *Grease* was not a successful critical venture. Michael Riedel, theatre columnist for the *New York Post*, wrote "the Broadway community despised *You're The One That I Want*,"[50] and that "Broadway was put off by the cheesy production values, poorly staged musical numbers and cookie-cutter nobodies who auditioned to play Danny and Sandy,"[51] adding that "everybody ... [was] so disgusted, [they were] going to be gunning for the production."[52] The producers opened the door for these types of critiques by relying upon the ghosts created through the reality television series to fill seats and sell tickets. With Casper-like ghosts come the ghouls.

Although the television series that spawned the Broadway production failed to do well in the ratings, "an average of 7.5 million viewers per episode is a massive increase in the number of folks normally exposed to direct Broadway marketing."[53] Due to this exposure, the revival's "advance ticket sales had reached $17 million."[54] This is despite the gossip reported by Riedel, who professed one week following the finale of the television series that "the phones at Ticketmaster were, I'm told, ringing off the hook because a lot of viewers who bought tickets to *Grease* weren't happy with the actors chosen to play Danny and Sandy."[55] According to one of Riedel's sources: "There was a bit of a frenzy ... They wanted their money back."[56] Despite the gossip, which was never confirmed by the producers or Ticketmaster, *Grease* performed well at the box office, only seeing a significant dive in attendance capacity more than a year after opening.[57]

As the producers intended, fans of the series attended *Grease* on Broadway. According to Crumm, they "had between 100 and 200 people waiting at the stage door after every performance."[58] He described the stage door fan experience as "both fun and crazy" and "taxing," and recalls that "at first there weren't even … barricades set up outside after the show to control the mobs waiting to meet the cast."[59] Crumm continued:

> Eventually they realized we needed them and they also had to provide us with a car to take us home after the shows. … You see, people were following us and it became really weird. I guess some guys are better at dealing with that sort of thing but I soon came to the realization that I really enjoy doing the show for the people in the audience but after the performance I like to retreat off. I'm friendly but not as friendly as some people would want me to be at the stage door.[60]

Here Crumm described his distaste for the para-social relationship that fans formed with him through their television sets, by watching and voting. For film, television, and reality television celebrities, encounters with fans are primarily left to chance. But as a performer in a Broadway musical, fans knew exactly where Crumm would be eight times a week.

Having performed the roles of Danny and Sandy for one year, both Osnes and Crumm left the production. Osnes soon joined the Broadway revival of *South Pacific* (2009) and Crumm retreated from the celebrity life and left New York for more than two years because he "wanted to lay low for a bit."[61] While talk of continuing the model of the television series to "recast *Grease* every year"[62] did not come to fruition, the production continued to utilize reality television celebrity replacement casting, including additional *Grease: You're The One That I Want!* contestants and *American Idol* alum Ace Young, for example. Despite doing relatively well at the box office and recouping its investment in its fifty-second week,[63] *Grease* closed on January 4, 2009, following 554 performances.

MTV's Broadway Casting Endeavor

Having learned from the harsh criticism of the Broadway community for allowing America to cast leading roles on Broadway through reality television, MTV opted to produce and air a different casting show of its own. Instead of allowing viewer participation in the voting process, *Legally Blonde: The Search for Elle Woods* chronicled the casting process for the replacement of the leading role in the musical. Those involved in the show were primarily professionals responsible for casting in the theatrical world itself, the director/choreographer, Jerry Mitchell, and a casting director, Bernard Telsey. This series claimed to show a behind-the-scenes look into what it takes to be cast in a Broadway musical, albeit with quirky reality television caveats. In the end, the series was more of a glitzy audition, failing to create the more intimate connection between viewer and personality that voting shows permit.

The first of the brief series aired on June 2, 2008, and it immediately became clear that this was slightly different than its predecessors. It quickly eliminated contestants, acquainting the audience with only a handful of performers. Eventually the judges selected the next Elle Woods, Bailey Hanks. One necessary aspect of the reality television format was there, the presentation of the contestants outside of the audition room, familiarizing them with the viewers. However, it was clear from the beginning of the series that the show was framed around one specific competitor, one presented with an amateurish persona, the eventual winner. In the initial episode, Hanks was portrayed distinctly differently. With her South Carolina-accented Southern charm, she stated: "I'm from a small town, I've never been to New York ... I've never even been on a plane. It's just so much bigger than life, than my small town."[64] She was clearly juxtaposed with other contestants on the series who had more experience and a New York sensibility. It is important to acknowledge that the series was aired after the casting decisions had already been made; the winner had already been chosen. Therefore, the editing of the series was done with the knowledge of that winner in mind. This foregrounding was quite purposeful with the hope that this empathetic relationship would translate into Broadway ticket sales.

Hanks began performances as Elle Woods in *Legally Blonde* on July 23, 2008, two days after the series finale. According to the data collected by The Broadway League, her first eight weeks in the production showed an increase gross of only approximately $7000; seating declined.

After thirteen weeks, *Legally Blonde* closed. There are important factors regarding the musical's closure following Hanks' casting. The musical had already been open on Broadway for over a year and Hanks was a replacement lead. A total of 12.5 million viewers had already seen *Legally Blonde* in the comfort of their homes, and without the Broadway ticket price, when MTV aired the production with its original cast the previous year.[65] Additionally, with the finale airing only two days prior to Hanks' replacement casting, that left little time for fans to travel to New York and attend the show to see a contestant they had favored. Importantly, while the series tried to draw connections between viewers and the contestants, the thrill of voting each week for the woman viewers really wanted to see as Elle Woods was not a part of this series. While a direct correlation cannot be drawn, audience agency was missing and the television series was not a successful draw to Broadway, as planned.

The Ghosts of Reality Television

Carlson describes not only the inevitability of the existence of an actor's ghosts but the purposeful acknowledgement of this phenomenon in American commercial theatre through the program biography. When Osnes was starring alongside her co-victor in *Grease*, these associations were quite obviously purposeful; the objective of *Grease: You're The One That I Want!* was to create a built-in audience for the Broadway musical, therefore the featuring of their images and associations with the television program were key to the marketing of the show. Additionally, this performance certainly featured heavily in their *Playbill* biographies. For example: "LAURA OSNES (Sandy) is honored to be making her Broadway debut at age 21, having recently won the role of Sandy on the NBC talent competition series '*Grease: You're The One That I Want*.'"[66] The remainder of Osnes' biography continues to paint her as the girl-next-door type established on the television series, ascribing her with the ghost the producers constructed, "Small Town Sandy," who the viewers/voters came to know and love. However, as Osnes amassed Broadway credits, and her caliber grew, her biography, and the ghosts haunting her, shifted.

Following her performance in *Grease*, Osnes starred in five other Broadway productions: *South Pacific* (2009–2010), *Anything Goes* (2011), *Bonnie and Clyde* (2011), *Rodgers and Hammerstein*'s Cinderella (2013–2014) and *Bandstand* (2017). The first three *Playbill* biographies name not only her Broadway debut in the revival of *Grease*, but that this was a result of having won NBC's *Grease: You're The One That I Want!*. Neither her biography for *Rodgers and Hammerstein's Cinderella* nor *Bandstand* make mention of her participation in a competitive reality television series. Why would Osnes no longer mention the competition that led to a leading role on Broadway in her list of previous credits, as she had done before? Following her subsequent leading lady roles on Broadway, culminating in a Tony nomination for the role of Bonnie Parker two years prior, Osnes was embraced by the theatrical community as a Broadway star, and her casting no longer necessitated the lingering celebrity glamor of a reality television series. She attempted to deliberately exorcise the ghost of reality television, perhaps hoping it would only be called upon to haunt her body in performance, by those who had knowledge of her previous body of work. Many fans have commented on her initial *Grease: You're The One That I Want!* audition clip posted on YouTube, calling her, "a Broadway star" and "legend,"[67] identifying with her differently than simply as contestant. As more people are introduced to Osnes' work, a simple search can unite the new fan with the performer. For even though new fans may not have watched the series when it originally aired, they have the ability to view and experience her entry into celebrity, going back in time to be there "from the beginning." Despite having removed the credit from her *Playbill* biography, Osnes ultimately acknowledges that the television show was a significant moment in her life: "It was absolutely life-changing. It was the opening of a door and the golden ticket to my dream come true."[68] The television series provided Osnes with an opportunity that she may not have ever had. It launched her from a performer presented as comfortable with her place as an actor in regional theatre, to a Broadway leading lady.

Osnes Backstage and Online

While performing in *Cinderella*, Osnes created a vlog series for Broadway.com entitled "The Princess Diaries: Backstage at *Cinderella* with Laura Osnes."[69] This two-season, sixteen-episode series (with views ranging from approximately 70,000 to 370,000), provided fans with behind-the-scenes access and information, not only about the musical, but Osnes herself. Each episode was primarily filmed by Osnes, using a personal handheld camcorder. She began the first episode, "A Royal

Costume Fitting," which aired on February 28, 2013, by introducing herself and letting her viewers know that they are "about to start a very exciting journey together."[70] In each video, Osnes provided fans with tidbits of information about the show, for example, going to costume fittings, backstage footage from the wings, and recording sessions for the cast album. But more importantly for her personal celebrity, she divulged private information about herself, including what she liked to eat, and welcomed fans inside her apartment. Over the course of the series viewers were introduced to her parents, brought into her dressing room repeatedly, watched her attending sleepovers with friends, witnessed her reaction to being nominated for a Tony Award, and more. She repeatedly showed the "shenanigans" that she and others in the cast involved themselves in, so that viewers were in on the backstage jokes and games. This successful venture has continued during her most recent production, *Bandstand* (2016), in "With the Band: Backstage at *Bandstand* with Laura Osnes" for Broadway.com.

Osnes has had a public Twitter presence since 2012, @LauraOsnes, and currently boasts approximately 69.9 thousand followers. While extremely small in comparison to non-theatrical personalities (Kim Kardashian West has more than 55.6 million followers, for example) she regularly utilizes her Twitter account, providing fans around the world access to what Marshall terms the "extraordinary everyday."[71] Marshall writes: "Not only are individuals revealing a great deal about their innermost thoughts and feelings … they are designing those renditions for others to read *and* respond to."[72] Osnes' posts are primarily related to her career, but there are also strategic glimpses into her personal life, including photographs of her husband and dog, and events with her friends, many of whom are former co-stars from various projects. Her posts elicit comments and retweets, with fans hoping to engage with her in this "personal" space, "Laura, you are sooo talented and such an inspiration!"[73] Some wished her well on her wedding anniversary, "OMG CONGRATS!!!!!!"[74] and "YOU GUYS ARE SO CUTE."[75] As long as individuals are following an account, they can receive notifications any time that person tweets.

It is important to note that there are several Twitter handles dedicated to Osnes put together as a space for fandom, @OsnesFans or @LauraOsnesFan, for example. Additionally, a locked account, @LauraAnnOsnes, may be her personal account unavailable to those personally unknown by her. Many celebrities own such accounts. Her public account is geared towards fans and often the photographs and comments are clearly designed for that particular audience. Rarely does Osnes engage with followers beyond initial tweets, which are clearly attuned to her fan audience. Yet the fans often engage with each other. Twitter permits individuals to link their digital acquaintances, immediately calling more attention to the posts.

Fans Strike Back

As this chapter has discussed, celebrity culture and the Internet have the ability to forge para-social relationships between fans and celebrities, and "friends" don't always get along.[76] Rojek describes the "automatic, weightless communication available at the flick of a switch"[77] that the Internet brings. This immediacy allows posts to celebrity social media accounts that may have seemed innocuous, to have the ability to knock a celebrity from their pedestal. In 2012, four years after *Legally Blonde* closed on Broadway, Bailey Hanks posted an image on Instagram and Facebook of her meal at the fast-food chain Chick-fil-A, simply reading: "It's a feast!!! #chickfila #1 w/a large sweet tea and a fudge brownie!"[78] The response from fans and members of the Broadway community to this post was swift and angry. Chick-fil-A is known as a company that makes financial contributions to anti-LGTBQ (lesbian, gay, transgender, bisexual, queer) organizations, and Hanks was called out on social media for the perceived hypocrisy of her actions. In a letter addressed to Hanks and published in *The Advocate* and *The Huffington Post*, actor John Carroll wrote:

> I would like to hold you accountable for your stance on the whole fried chicken thing ... Just a reminder—you were plucked out of obscurity by a team of gay men, gay men who not only believed in you and gave you the chance of a lifetime, but who treated you with loving kindness and respect. These are the same gay men you discriminated against by publicly supporting Chick-fil-A.[79]

Hanks responded by blocking her Twitter access to the public and deleting the Facebook post in question, and she is no longer publicly present on any social media platform. This serves as an example of a celebrity's digital presence exposing too much and working against the implicit goal of brand enhancement.

The Internet and Broadway Celebrity

Broadway celebrity is, according to celebrity theorists, a misnomer, regardless of what theatre fans believe. According to this argument, the term "Broadway celebrity" is a contradiction in terms because public interest in the private lives of Broadway performers has not yet eclipsed their talent as Broadway stars. Celebrity status in the theatre is difficult to achieve. Being a Broadway performer requires tremendous skill, which is often at odds with empty celebrity values, particularly celebrity created through reality television. Daniel Herwitz notes that "television, tabloid, talk radio … are the pure form of commodity value, the system that sets the value [of] celebrity,"[80] and while theatrical stars do appear on television and radio talk shows to promote their latest productions, they have rarely, until recently, discussed their lives beyond their work. While the glimpses into the private lives of Broadway musical theatre performers have been of primary interest to those fans already within the theatrical domain, rarely is this seen on a global or even national scale,[81] although this is changing. Because of the relatively inconsequential demand for a deeper look into those performers' lives, media outlets rarely, if ever, report on them. However, as this chapter has discussed, a shift is occurring in the ways the theatrical community and media interact, setting the stage for the emergence of Broadway celebrities. Osnes, for example, finds the balance between the girl-next-door democratic celebrity and Broadway star, using digital media to do so. Other Broadway performers in the twenty-first century, such as Audra McDonald and Laura Benanti, and most particularly Lin-Manuel Miranda,[82] are also increasingly exploiting this new digital arena.

One popular way for Broadway actors to interact and work with young fans and aspiring performers is by participating as instructors in a variety of masterclasses run by several companies. There are in-person workshops, school groups visiting New York can sign up for a dance class with cast members of Broadway shows, or one can sign up for summer programs, such as Camp Broadway, Broadway Artists Alliance, and Broadway Fantasy Camp, where workshops are taught by several Broadway veterans. In an effort to reach not only the country, but the world, Broadway Masters, an online masterclass program, was established in the fall of 2016. The classes feature a variety of Broadway performers, including Osnes, as one of the vocal instructors. From the comfort of their own home, participants can purchase month or year-long packages, which include courses, concerts, and other special events. While this is a new program whose effects cannot yet be quantified, Osnes' participation furthers audience access to her as artist and individual.

Conclusion

Following the third season of the series, *American Idol* judge Paula Abdul made note of the influence the reality talent contest has on the entertainment industry and young individuals vying for exposure and a chance in the field. She stated, "Now it's like, 'How am I ever going to make it unless I'm on a show like *American Idol*. I'll never make it.' Whoever would have thought that that's what people would be saying?"[83] These shows have affected the Broadway landscape in significant ways, involving casting, expectations of performers, and the sound itself. Ben Brantley wrote in 2005: "When it's time for a big ballad on Broadway these days, theatergoers can pretend they are still in their living rooms, basking in the synthetic adrenaline glow of their favorite TV show,"[84] and many expect that same connection to the performers created in their homes, when they attend the live theatre. They want to see the people that they voted for on television, on stage. Fans want to experience that semblance, even if the reality television stars are playing characters that are completely different from their popstar image.

In his review for *The New York Times* of *Grease* in 2008, Brantley wrote; "The message of this latest *Grease* is that anyone, famous or not, can star in a Broadway musical, a natural enough conclusion in the era of YouTube and *American Idol*, when the right to be a celebrity is perceived as constitutional."[85] He continued; "But for this sensibility to work, a theatergoer has to be personally invested in its stars' doing well. Those who religiously watched *You're The One That I Want* may cheer Mr. Crumm and Ms. Osnes the way high school students might root for their chums in the class play."[86] This is the exact connection *Grease*'s creative team, and other musicals that cast contestants from reality television, hope for. Producers bank on para-social relationships that are forged in the living room, and bolstered and solidified through voting and participation on social media and Internet platforms. In other words, audiences will pay to come to see their "friends" perform on Broadway. Both Osnes and Hanks have similar backstories: they are plucky young women, raised outside of the New York theatre world, who won a competitive reality television series which led to their debut as leading ladies in Broadway musicals. While Hanks has essentially been removed from the realm of celebrity pop culture,[87] perhaps a comment on her lack of digital presence, Osnes remains. She established herself as a fixture in the Broadway community, engaging in the world of social media that accounts for her celebrity. Today, her Instagram homepage reflects upon the "small town" ghosts that launched her success on reality television. For despite her transformation into a musical theatre star, Osnes will always be just a "Minnesota girl living her broadway [*sic*] dreams."[88]

Notes

1. Boorstin, 57.
2. *American Idol* followed in the footsteps of its British predecessor *Pop Idol*, which ran in the United Kingdom from 2001 to 2003.
3. This phenomenon also can be seen in productions on the West End which merits further exploration and analysis, but is beyond the realm of this chapter.
4. Marshall, 634.
5. Rojek, 12.
6. Marshall, 644.
7. Ibid., 638.
8. Ibid., 635.
9. Turner, 8.
10. Rojek, 10–11.
11. See Chap. 9 by Nathan Stith in this volume.
12. Benjamin, 27.
13. Ibid.
14. Ibid., 25.
15. Ibid.
16. Rojek, 4.
17. Redmond, 27.
18. Ibid.
19. McClain, 182.
20. Andrejevic, 3.
21. See Chap. 9 by Nathan Stith in this volume.
22. Ibid., 7.
23. Lai, 227.
24. Ibid., 227.
25. Terms in reference to the awe of celebrity by Max Weber, Joseph Roach, Elizabeth Currid-Halkett, and Chris Rojek, respectively.
26. Carlson, 53.

27. Ibid., 67. See also Osatinski's discussion of Carlson's "ghosting" in Chap. 4.
28. Bell, 194.
29. The growing list of *American Idol* alumni on Broadway includes Clay Aiken, Frenchie Davis, Diana DeGarmo, Constantine Maroulis, Ace Young, Fantasia Barrino, Jennifer Hudson, Justin Guarini, Tamyra Gray, Taylor Hicks, and Jordin Sparks, among others.
30. See Chap. 9 by Nathan Stith in this volume.
31. McClain, 183.
32. Ibid., 121.
33. Ibid., 122.
34. Holmes and Jermyn, 3.
35. Huff, 122–3.
36. Bell, 40.
37. Ibid., 126.
38. Watts, 302.
39. Ibid., 305.
40. See McClain, 39–52.
41. Watts, 310.
42. "Grease: You're the One That I Want (Episode 4)."
43. Bell, 68.
44. Robertson.
45. Ibid.
46. There was no episode on Sunday, February 4, 2007, as it coincided with Superbowl XLI.
47. "Grease: You're the One That I Want (Episode 4)."
48. Additional monikers were "Ballerina," "Baby," "Spiritual," "Serious," "Rock Chick," and "Emotional" Sandy.
49. McClain, 24.
50. Riedel.
51. Ibid.
52. Ibid.
53. Rooney.
54. BWW News Desk.
55. Riedel.
56. Ibid.
57. The week ending September 7, 2008 only seated 55% capacity and only 45% of its Gross Potential, earning almost $200,000 less than the previous week, according to the statistical data provided by The Broadway League. Yet only one other week in the entire run sold in that range. See "Grease."
58. Panarrello.
59. Ibid.

60. Ibid.
61. Ibid.
62. Robertson.
63. BWW News Desk.
64. "Legally Blonde: The Search for Elle Woods, Episode 1."
65. Hetrick.
66. "Laura Osnes." *Playbill*.
67. "Laura Osnes' Audition for Grease."
68. Knight.
69. All episodes can be accessed on Broadway.com.
70. "The Princess Diaries: Backstage at *Cinderella* with Laura Osnes."
71. Marshall, 635.
72. Ibid., 638.
73. Marklin, Marika. 2017. Twitter Post. January 4, 1:22 PM, https://twitter.com/marika_marklin/status/816756784983605248.
74. Danielle. 2016. Twitter Post. December 24, 4:43 AM, https://twitter.com/ghostgirl42601/status/812639834367991808.
75. Belle. 2016. Twitter Post. December 24, 4:21 AM, https://twitter.com/comewhatcriss/status/812634234426978304.
76. See discussions of "fan-tagonism" in a different context in Chaps. 6 and 8 of this volume.
77. Rojek, 11.
78. McGonnigal.
79. Carroll.
80. Herwitz, 18.
81. See Jessica Hillman-McCord's Chap. 6 in this volume.
82. See Chap. 6.
83. *American Idol*: The Search for a Superstar.
84. Brantley, "How Broadway Lost Its Voice to *American Idol*."
85. Brantley, "As Seen on TV! Danny and Sandy 4-Ever and Ever."
86. Ibid.
87. Hanks' last known performance was in *9 to 5: The Musical* in Tennessee in 2012.
88. "lauraosnes." Instagram. Accessed July 17, 2016.

References

American Idol: The Search for a Superstar. Directed by Ken Warwick, and Nigel Lythgoe. Houston: R2 Entertainment. DVD, 2002.

Andrejevic, Mark. *Reality TV: The Work of Being Watched*. Lanham, MD: Rowman & Littlefield Publishers, Inc., 2004.

Bell, Christopher E. *American Idolatry: Celebrity, Commodity and Reality Television*. Jefferson, NC: McFarland, 2010.
Benjamin, Walter. "The Work of Art in the Age of Mechanical Reproduction." In *Stardom and Celebrity: A Reader*, eds. Sean Redmond and Su Holmes, 23–33. London: Sage Publications Ltd, 2007.
Boorstin, Daniel. *The Image: A Guide to Pseudo-Events in America*. New York: Vintage Books, 1992.
Brantley, Ben. "How Broadway Lost Its Voice to *American Idol*." *The New York Times*, March 27, 2005. Accessed July 10, 2016.
———. "As Seen on TV! Danny and Sandy 4-Ever and Ever." *The New York Times*, August 20, 2007. Accessed July 6, 2016.
BWW News Desk. "GREASE to Close on Broadway January 4, 2009." *BroadwayWorld*. December 3, 2008. Accessed July 16, 2016.
Carlson, Marvin. *The Haunted Stage: The Theatre as Memory Machine*. Ann Arbor: University of Michigan Press, 2001.
Carroll, John. "Gays Giveth and Gays Taketh Away: An Open Letter to Bailey Hanks." *Advocate*, August 10, 2012. Accessed October 12, 2016.
"Grease." *International Broadway Database*. Accessed July 2, 2016.
"Grease: You're the One That I Want (Episode 4)." *YouTube* video, 1:23:21. December 5, 2013. Accessed July 17, 2016.
Herwitz, Daniel. *The Star as Icon: Celebrity in the Age of Mass Consumption*. New York: Columbia University Press, 2008.
Hetrick, Adam. "Legally Blonde MTV Broadcast Reaches Millions." *Playbill*, October 17, 2007. Accessed January 22, 2017.
Holmes, Su and Deborah Jermyn, eds. *Understanding Reality Television*. New York: Routledge, 2004.
Huff, Richard M. *Reality Television*. Westport, CT: Praeger, 2006.
Knight, James. "*Disaster* Max Crumb [*sic*] and Laura Osnes Talks [*sic*] *You're the One That I Want* Before *Grease Live*." *Classicalite*, January 27, 2016. Accessed July 10, 2016.
Lai, Adrienne. "Glitter and Grain: Aura and Authenticity in the Celebrity Photographs of Juergen Teller." In *Framing Celebrity: New Directions in Celebrity Culture*, eds. Su Holmes and Sean Redmond, 215–229. New York: Routledge, 2006.
"Laura Osnes." *Playbill*. Accessed July 6, 2016.
"Laura Osnes' Audition for Grease." *YouTube* video, 0:33. August 22, 2007. Accessed July 16, 2016.
"Legally Blonde: The Search for Elle Woods, Episode 1." *YouTube* video, 42:12. May 28, 2015. Accessed July 16, 2016.
Marshall, P. David. *Celebrity and Power: Fame in Contemporary Culture*. Minneapolis: University of Minnesota Press, 1997.

———. "New Media—New Self: The Changing Power of Celebrity." In *The Celebrity Culture Reader*, ed. P. David Marshall, 634–644. New York: Routledge, 2006.

McClain, Amanda Scheiner. *American Ideal: How American Idol Constructs Celebrity, Collective Identity, and American Discourses.* Lanham, MD: Lexington Books, 2011.

McGonnigal, Jamie. "What Happens When a Broadway Star Supports Chick-Fil-A?" *Huffington Post*, August 9, 2012. Accessed October 9, 2016.

Panarrello, Joseph. "BWW Interview: Max Crumm is the One That You Want in *The Fantasticks*." *Broadwayworld*, September 19, 2014. Accessed October 12, 2016.

Redmond, Sean. "Intimate Fame Everywhere." In *Framing Celebrity: New Directions in Celebrity Culture*, eds. Su Holmes and Sean Redmond, 27–43. New York: Routeledge, 2006.

Riedel, Michael. "*Grease* and Desist." *New York Post*, April 4, 2007. Accessed July 3, 2016.

Robertson, Campbell. "For This Broadway Musical, the Casting Agents are TV Viewers." *New York Times*, January 6, 2007. Accessed July 6, 2016.

Rojek, Chris. *Fame Attack: The Inflation of Celebrity and Its Consequences.* London and New York: Bloomsbury Academic, 2012.

Rooney, David. "Review: *Grease*." *Variety*, August 19, 2007. Accessed July 6, 2016.

"The Princess Diaries: Backstage at *Cinderella* with Laura Osnes." *Broadway*. Accessed July 17, 2016.

Turner, Graeme. *Understanding Celebrity.* London: Sage Publications Ltd, 2004.

Watts, Amber. "Melancholy, Merit, and Merchandise: The Postwar Audience Participation Show." In *Reality TV: Remaking Television Culture*, eds. Susan Murray and Laurie Ouellette, 301–320. New York: New York University Press, 2009.

"With the Band: Backstage at *Bandstand* with Laura Osnes." *Broadway*. Accessed May 2, 2017.

PART III

Digital Dramaturgy, Scholarship and Criticism

CHAPTER 11

The Advantages of Floating in the Middle of the Sea: Digital Musical Theatre Research

Doug Reside

At the top of the second act of the musical adaptation of the comic strip, *Li'l Abner*, Doctor Rasmussen T. Finsdale sings of his vision of a utopian future in which "scientists control the human race."[1] The song is one of the least subtle articulations of the anti-technology politics of a musical that portrays a world in which the elite's fascination with scientific progress can lead to a disregard for, and even the elimination of, humanity. The anxiety persists throughout many of the musicals of the mid-to-late twentieth century. Don Quixote, the *Man of La Mancha*, battles windmills and, ultimately, the rationalist, Dr. Carrasco. *Sweeney Todd* becomes a mass murderer when he joins his right arm to the technology of the razor and begins to plan "like a perfect machine."[2] These kinds of stories are not unique to musical theatre, of course, but, regardless of form, they generally express an anxiety that is commonly felt when an older technology is replaced with a new one that radically alters the human experience.

This anxiety seems especially acutely felt when it comes to technologies of preservation. In the well-known passage in Plato's *Phaedrus* in which Socrates expresses suspicion of the technology of writing he argues that written speeches "have no parent to protect them" and are "are

D. Reside (✉)
New York Public Library for the Performing Arts, New York, USA
e-mail: dougreside@gmail.com

© The Author(s) 2017
J. Hillman-McCord (ed.), *iBroadway*,
DOI 10.1007/978-3-319-64876-7_11

tumbled about anywhere among those who may or may not understand them."[3] Socrates complains that paintings, speeches, and writings all "maintain a solemn silence" when questioned, and so leave interpretation (and the possibility for misinterpretation) up to the receiver.

In 1889, when Sir Arthur Sullivan encountered Edison's phonograph for the first time and was asked to record his reactions on one of the cylinders he remarked:

> For myself I can only say that I am astonished and somewhat terrified at the result of this evening's experiment. Astonished at the wonderful form you have developed, and terrified at the thought that so much hideous and bad music will be put on record forever.[4]

Despite the obligatory well wishes to the inventor, it is clear Sullivan felt a real sense of anxiety at the thought of the possibilities for preservation that the technology permitted. The machine threatens the human ability to decide to forget.

There has been much anxiety over the last decade, some of it expressed, admittedly, by this author, about the effect the increasing dependence on digital tools in all art forms will have on the historical memory of this present moment. The typescripts, film negatives, and telegrams that tell the story of the theatre of a generation or two ago have been replaced by Google Docs, JPEGs, and posts on Facebook walls. The archives of twentieth-century theatre consisting of crumbling scrapbooks, fading mimeographs, tightly bound typescripts on onionskin, and vinegar-syndrome prone acetate negatives were anything but durable, but they at least had a materiality and legibility that could be comprehended by a researcher in the archives. Today, much of the history of Broadway is stored on a variety of digital storage devices, some owned by corporations with little incentive to invest in long-term preservation. Data is often encoded in file formats readable only by very niche software maintained by small companies whose entire existence may well be shorter lived than the Broadway run of *The Phantom of the Opera* (1988-current). Archivists, though largely aware of the urgency and magnitude of the problem, must struggle, often with annually diminishing resources, to adapt an infrastructure designed for the preservation of physical artifacts to the needs of new kinds of collections (all while continuing to care for the mountains of paper documentation produced in previous decades).

Often, when this issue arises at academic conferences, the message is received like a performance of *Les Misérables* (1987). The audience listens, shakes their heads at the tragedy, stands to applaud the call to "join in our crusade," and then goes off for drinks thinking, if they recall the story at all after the exit music plays, that there is little they themselves can do. However, most do not fully recognize the remarkable research opportunity afforded by so-called "born-digital" archives if they are properly preserved. The abstract risk of loss is not coupled with the concrete value of preservation. The urgent need to adapt archival practices and priorities is real, but to repeat this refrain too often obscures the good news that these archives provide better tools for studying the history of theatre than ever before existed.

Libraries and archives must figure out how to preserve this content, but researchers must also figure out how to use it. Born-digital archives are as varied as their traditional analog counterparts, and it's possible that the most exciting collections have not yet come into public archives and their uses have not yet been imagined. Even today, though, it is clear that these collections provide new and more complete ways of understanding the individual's creative process, reconstructing productions, discovering hidden social networks, and comparing interpretations of texts in performance.

Understanding the Creative Process

Archives have regularly collected the process work of artists. The New York Public Library holds lyric sketches by Oscar Hammerstein II, drafts of music by Richard Rodgers, and early scripts for major works of theatre. Many of these documents represent versions of works that were completely rewritten over the long development process even the most gifted artists undertake to get their work on the Broadway stage. Serviceable rhymes or lines that almost work are replaced with more natural or elegant ones with a scratch of the pencil and a marginal annotation.

Paper collections documenting this kind of development tend to be analogous to a set of "first day of school" pictures. They contain important drafts representing significant milestones in the development of the work. Digital collections, on the other hand, can be more akin to a time-lapse video of a plant growing from a seed in which each frame represents a photograph taken every day over a series of weeks. I've written elsewhere about the way in which Jonathan Larson's floppy disks at the Library of Congress allow this kind of moment-by-moment tracking of the history of the writing of the musical *RENT* (1996), but any digital archive with enough backups can provide this kind of information.[5]

In the case of *RENT*, Jonathan Larson used a version of Microsoft Word (5.1) that saved small changes to the bottom of the file with code that instructed the software how to integrate the revisions into the base text of the file. As a result, the textual scholar can uncover the incremental changes that Larson introduced each time he hit the save button. Moreover, Larson saved dozens of iterations of the text on different floppies, and each file is time-stamped by his Macintosh operating system with the precise millisecond at which the file was created and last modified. The result is an incredibly detailed textual history of the musical.

Although today most writers do not use floppy disks, cloud storage services like Dropbox and Google Drive offer similar features. Some maintain such a detailed revision history that a keystroke-by-keystroke history of a text could be studied. These features of digital drafts allow scholars to understand the genesis of the text at a level of detail no collection of paper typescripts could ever provide.

Further, digital collections now contain much more than text files. Researchers of scenic and costume design can now study the development of work created in graphic design software (e.g. Photoshop or Illustrator). Like modern versions of Word, these programs maintain extensive revision histories. Moreover, programs like Photoshop encourage designers to create their work by designing a series of "layers"—graphical elements and filters that can be stacked together. By manipulating these layers, researchers can deconstruct a design to better understand how it was put together.

For instance, in the Derek McLane files at New York Public Library, there are a series of digital production photos that exist both as standard, "flat" JPEG files and also as "layered" Photoshop (PSD) files. When the PSD files are opened in Photoshop, it is possible to view a stack of layers, which are placed over the original photo to suggest possible changes. In files for the 2015 revival of *Gigi*, McLane has a layered PSD file that depicts one of his set models (see Figs. 11.1 and 11.2).

The top layer is a copy of the arches at the top of the model with a slightly darker gold color. When the top layer is turned off in Photoshop, the arches are seen in a much lighter gold. The layer with the darker

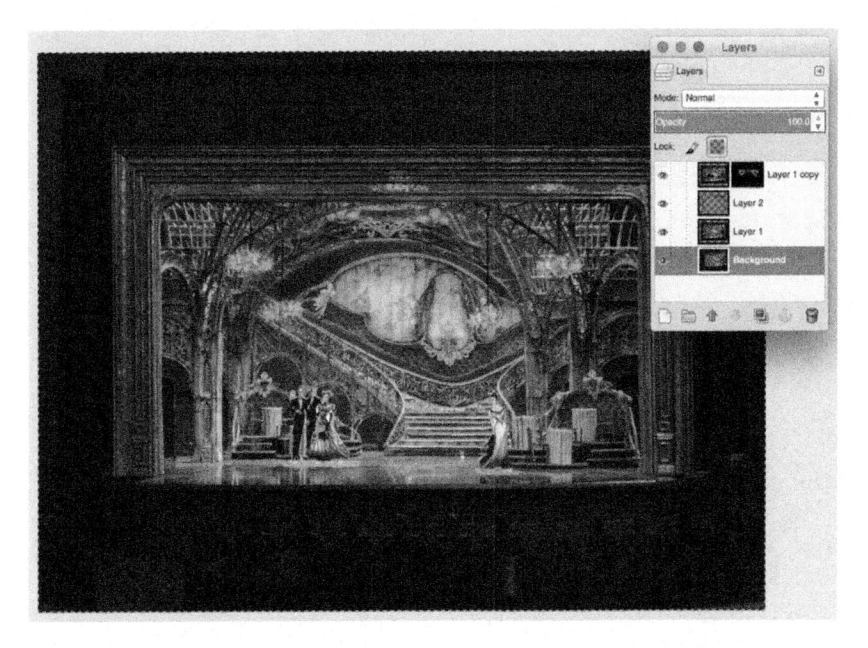

Fig. 11.1 McLane layered PSD file, *Gigi*

arches themselves can be studied alone by turning off the background layers.

Although the use of multi-spectral imaging technologies have recently allowed scholars to begin to perform a similar kind of analysis on physical art (and sometimes discover hidden drafts of other paintings),[6] this kind of work has historically been too destructive for scholars to perform on original works of art. Digital files, though, allow researchers to freely dissect an exact copy of an artist's work while an untouched copy remains safely preserved in a digital repository.

Recreating Productions

Scholars and archivists often use software "emulators" to simulate older computing environments. The Internet Archive has created the "Internet Arcade," a webpage on which visitors can play 1980s video games (*PacMan*, *Space Invaders*, *Defender*, etc.) designed to be played on large consoles in a public space.[7] Obviously, some of the experience is

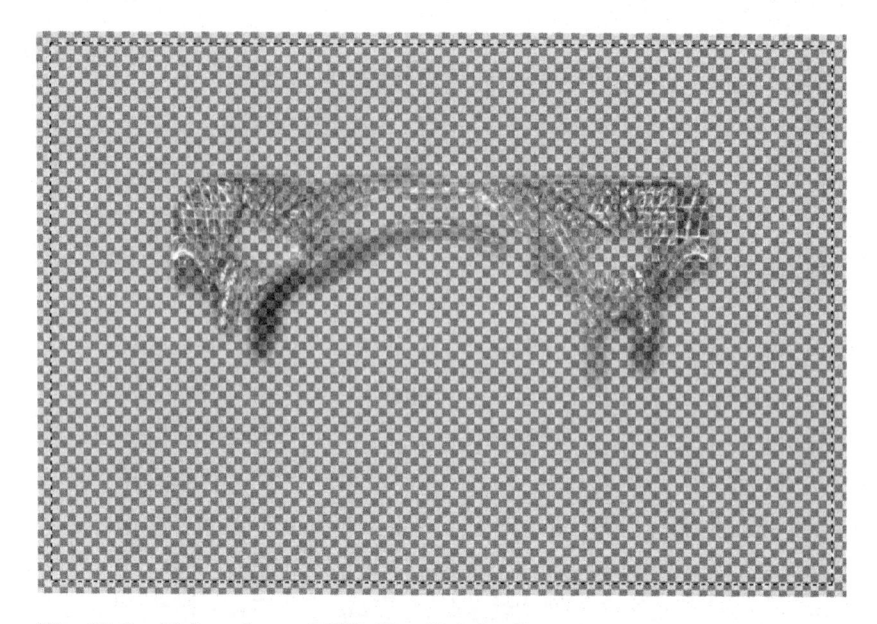

Fig. 11.2 McLane layered PSD file, *Gigi*, detail

lost in this recreation. Most laptops and tablets don't have the joysticks or trackballs that were built into the original console and so players use the keyboard to navigate the game instead. Players sit in front of a small screen instead of standing before the console. The social environment, the smell of pizza and beer that pervaded 1980s video arcades, and the noise of nearby games are all absent on the Internet Arcade website. Still, the software on the Internet Arcade webpage executes exactly the same computer code used by the original game consoles. As an increasing number of theatrical designs are controlled by software (e.g. remotely controlled moving sets, digital lighting and sound boards), it may be possible to create emulators to execute the original code that ran a production's lighting, sound, and mechanical cues in a digitally-simulated 3D environment.

The first step for such an emulator would necessarily be a recreation of the theatre auditoriums (or at least the stage areas) themselves. To continue the analogy of video game emulators, the auditorium and stage are the "screen" which presents the game. There have been a few attempts to use 3D digital technology to recreate theatre buildings. In 2001, Christa Williford surveyed 3D digital reconstructions of French theatre buildings[8] created at a time before 3D models could be easily displayed on the web. Hugh Denard of King's College has recently finished construction of a recreation of Dublin's Abbey Theatre in the gaming platform, Unity.[9] In the brief, mad moment in which half of the digital humanities community was obsessed with Second Life, several recreations of the Globe and other historical theatres were constructed within the virtual world. Some of these Second Life theatres occasionally served as venues for a kind of digital puppet theatre in which digital avatars would perform roles before an audience of other avatars in the digital space. The Second Life Shakespeare Company, for instance, constructed a replica of Shakespeare's Globe Theatre and staged virtual productions of Shakespeare within it.[10]

Even outside of Second Life, there have been projects that have attempted to stage performances in digital 3D theatres. One of the oldest web-based projects, David Saltz's 2004 Virtual Vaudeville project, included an impressive 3D model of a Vaudeville Theatre presented in Shockwave Director. An animated recreation of several Vaudeville acts was "staged" in the space and lit using digital approximations of period lighting.[11] Lighting Designer Beverly Emmons has created a web-based archive of lighting designs that preserves lighting documents for thirteen shows and includes a simulation of the design for the 2006 Broadway revival of *A Chorus Line*.[12] This author, with Hamilton College researcher and game designer Greg Lord, is currently working on a project funded by the National Endowment for the Humanities to create a more generalized platform for emulating theatrical designs in Unity (the platform used by Hugh Denard for his Abbey Theatre recreation). The plan is to create a set of 3D auditoriums based on Broadway and Off-Broadway houses and a tool for ingesting digital information created for a production so that shows that have long since closed can be simulated using the code that actually was used during the original run. Using a Swedish software program called Capture, Michigan State University lighting designer and project team member Shannon Schweitzer has already emulated the first scene of *Sunday in the Park with George* based on the original lighting and stage designs (see Fig. 11.3).

Fig. 11.3 *Sunday in the Park with George* emulation by Shannon Schweitzer

Revealing Hidden Information

Sometimes, as one studies these digital files, whether to examine the creative process or recreate a production, one finds information that may not have even been known to the person who created it. Both individual computer programs and contemporary operating systems embed in the files they create a great deal of information about the circumstances under which a file was created or last modified (including the name of the user who performed the action). Consider, for instance, the scenic design in Fig. 11.3, rendered in a drafting program called VectorWorks by scenic designer Mikiko Suzuki MacAdams.[13] The design includes the insignia of the scenic designers' union, Local 829, in the lower right-hand corner. MacAdams likely pasted this insignia into the design from a file on her hard drive (see Figs. 11.4 and 11.5).

The design (and the insignia) can be examined by opening the file in VectorWorks, but additional information can be discovered by using a text editor instead (like Notepad ++ or TextWrangler). A good text editor can be used to open any file and reveal any textual content within it. As a result, you can sometimes find bits of text in files that are not immediately visible when the file is opened in the program that created it.

Opening MacAdams' VectorWorks file reveals a string of text in the section that defines the union logo:

%%Creator: CorelDRAW 10

%%Title: USA-829-Double-Logo.eps

%%CreationDate: Wed May 15 16:07:19 2002

%%For: Carl A. Baldasso

This hidden information reveals that the logo was created by a man named "Carl A. Baldasso" (whose LinkedIn page suggests is still working as a scenic designer and member of the 829 union) on May 15, 2002 at 4:07 in the afternoon using CorelDraw 10. By itself, this is likely a relatively inconsequential bit of information, although, like much of the information preserved in our archives, it is impossible to predict when someone (perhaps a scholar interested in the history of theatrical unions) will one day find it a key piece of evidence in an argument not yet conceived.

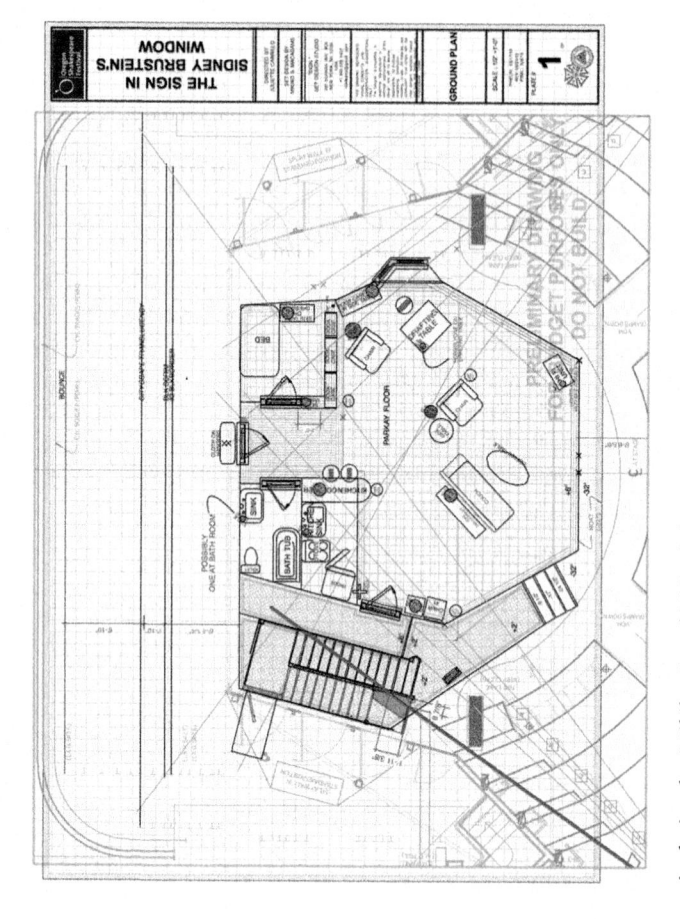

Fig. 11.4 A scenic design by Mikiko Suzuki MacAdams

Fig. 11.5 A scenic design by Mikiko Suzuki MacAdams, detail

Exposing Theatre Networks

The information about Mr. Baldasso and his logo, though, is perhaps most likely to be useful as a contribution to the aggregate data about the network of individuals who are responsible for creating theatre on Broadway. If enough such data was gathered, it would be possible to bring to light subtle details in the narrative of commercial theatre history. At the moment, though, there is already on various Broadway websites (BroadwayWorld, PlaybillVault, and the Internet Broadway Database [IBDB]) enough data to begin to usefully study Broadway's professional networks. Consider for example, the graph in Fig. 11.6 (constructed from a subset of online data about those employed by Broadway musicals that ran longer than 1000 performances). The blue circles represent people and the red circles, musicals. In the center of Fig. 11.7 is a blue dot for Michael Keller who has served as the "musical coordinator" for many of the biggest hits on Broadway.

272   D. RESIDE

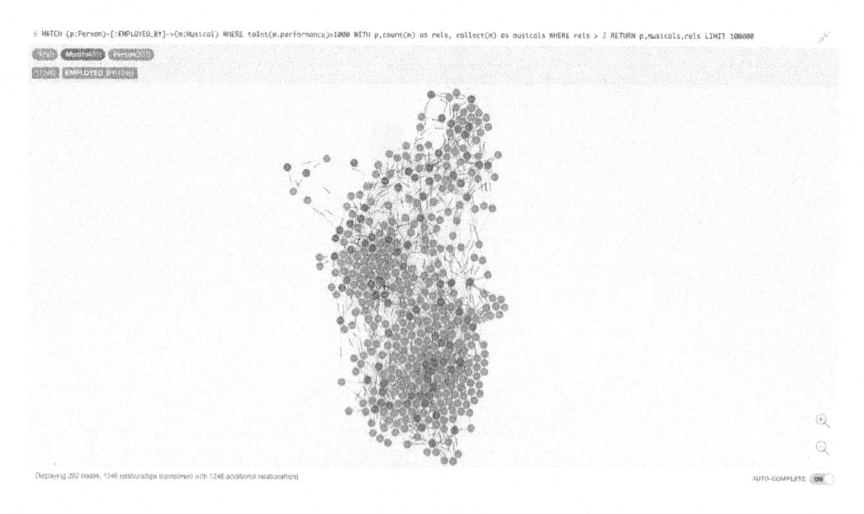

Fig. 11.6   Graph of Broadway's professional networks

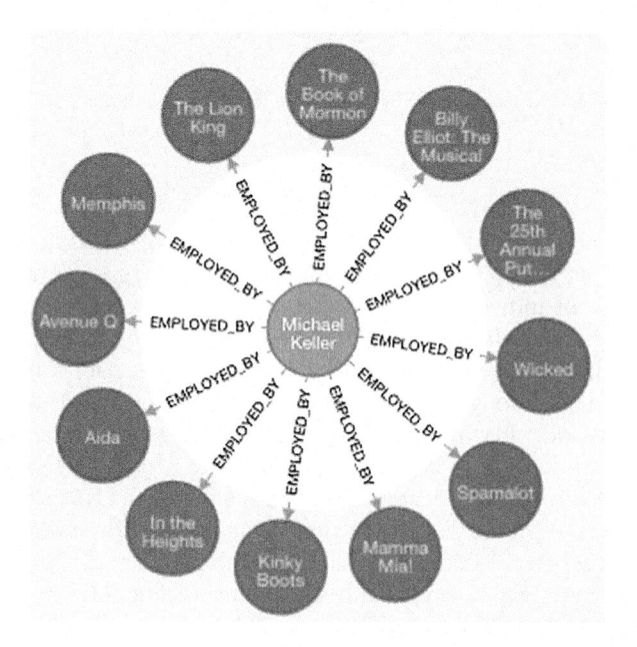

Fig. 11.7   Graph of long-running Broadway shows for Michael Keller, detail

Few others working on Broadway today have worked on so many long-running shows. It might be tempting, then, to try to predict the success of a Broadway musical based on the presence of Mr. Keller on the payroll, but a quick look at his IBDB page also reveals he has worked on many less commercially successful shows as well (including *Amazing Grace*, *Honeymoon in Vegas*, and *Glory Days*).[14] Still, if one was interested in the history of the position of musical coordinator, the graph suggests that a conversation with Mr. Keller might be beneficial.

Gaining a meaningful understanding of the social networks of Broadway probably requires better datasets than are currently available, though. It may be possible to acquire additional data by engaging fans to transcribe digitized copies of programs. The New York Public Library project, Ensemble, on which this author was a participant, invited members of the public to join an effort to transcribe performing arts programs to create a large, open dataset of performing arts information not currently available online.[15] This project has been picked up by Yale University, and researchers at the Beinecke are now working to build a version of Ensemble that can be "franchised" to other archives. This data could be made open for public use and structured in a way that it could be connected (or linked) to other open, structured datasets. Once done, the result would be what is now commonly referred to as structured, linked, open data (see Fig. 11.8).

Scanning programs for this kind of transcription can be expensive though; developers on Ensemble are still working to create an interface capable of engaging a large number of transcribers and directing them to provide the kind of data needed. In the meantime, born-digital archives are, naturally, more immediately accessible to the processing power of computers. Software developers and data scientists can parse these archives to extract names of people (like logo designer Carl A. Baldasso) and begin to reveal their stories.

Perhaps some of the richest sets of data about theatre past and present, though, will come from born-digital and digitized archives of theatrical photographs. For most of the twenty-first century, theatre photographs have largely been taken with digital cameras. Theatre archives around the world have also dedicated significant resources to digitizing photographic negatives. Using face recognition software (such as the algorithm used by Facebook to suggest the name of a friend you might want to "tag" in a photo), it may soon be possible to identify faces across large collections of digitized historical theatrical photos and reveal

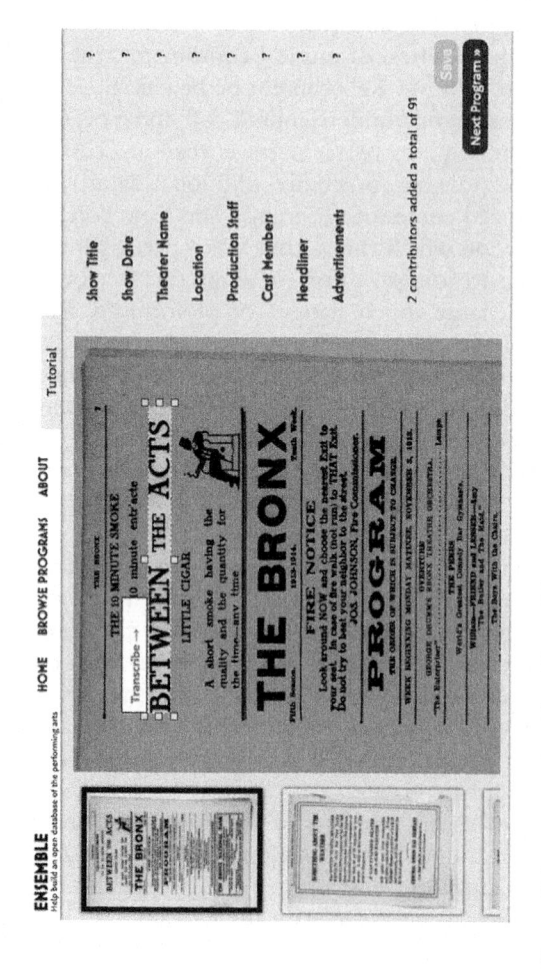

Fig. 11.8 Transcribing programs using Ensemble

previously forgotten identities of, for instance, chorus and ensemble members whose names were not included in the official captions.

Perhaps the most useful tool for tracking theatrical networks, though, will be the email boxes and social network interactions of those in the industry. By studying who was Facebook friends with whom, and who "liked" what tweets, marketers are already able to identify a good deal about the purchasing behavior of individuals. Scholars might one day use the same data to better understand the theatrical culture of the twenty-first century. Such prosopographic studies have been used to reveal the networks of the ancient world, but gathering the data has, historically, been extremely difficult and time consuming. However, as archives begin to acquire the Gmail boxes and, perhaps, Facebook accounts of theatrical personalities, it will be much easier to write algorithms to quickly construct network graphs of the social systems that create theatre.

Preserving this data while it still exists will be a significant challenge. In the first decade or two of the popular use of email, (c.1990–2010), messages were usually downloaded to personal computers, and all but the most important emails were often deleted after being read. In this way, email closely resembled paper correspondence files of previous generations. If the authors kept the electronic media (e.g. floppy and hard disks) to which their important emails were saved, they may be preserved by digital archivists. The Michael John LaChiusa papers at New York Public Library, for instance, include a few floppy disks of emails LaChiusa had saved, and which library staff migrated to the digital repository.[16] Most email services today, though, store email "in the cloud," on machines that are never seen by users. Although some, including Gmail, allow users to export their email to downloadable files, relatively few know about this feature or think to use it. Further, email is now only one, and often not the preferred method, of digital interaction. Just as telegrams once provided a means for sending fast, short notes to colleagues and friends, the Broadway community of today often sends short, informal notes via cell phone text messages or via instant messages sent through services like Google or Facebook. Many of these messaging tools allow users to export their messages in the same way as their email, and archives will need to encourage donors to regularly export all of this content and send it to institutions that can preserve them (even if under tight restrictions that prevent access for a lengthy embargo period).

More public messages (e.g. notes of well wishes or congratulations for an opening night) may be posted via social media. Unfortunately, it can be relatively difficult for archives to preserve this data. Often, platforms disappear without much notice—Friendster closed down quickly and digital archivists like Jason Scott's Archive Team rushed to preserve what they could before the pages disappeared.[17] The Library of Congress has been archiving public twitter feeds since the early days of the service, but more interesting data for future researchers may be found on the semi-private social networks of artists on platforms like Facebook. The legal permissibility of crawling private Facebook networks is not entirely settled, and the technology to store and recreate these networks in an archival environment is still developing. In the meantime, archives should encourage donors and potential donors to regularly export what they can from their social networks and deposit it into digital repositories, and archives must continue to develop legal and technical mechanisms for collecting, preserving, and providing useful access to this data.

Comparing Multiple Performance in Private Archives

Perhaps even more complicated from a legal and ethical perspective are the huge archives of unauthorized digital video recordings of theatre available online. Over the past decade, it has become increasingly easy for individual audience members to record videos of performances with easily concealed digital video cameras, and to share these widely via platforms such as YouTube and Vimeo and in digital media "lockers" like Mega.com and Google Drive. The result is that live theatre is now much more fully documented and accessible on video than ever before, albeit through ethically and legally dubious means.

Bootleg documentation of theatre is not unique to the digital era, of course. In the time between the original production of *Hamlet* and the authorized publication of the folio seven years after Shakespeare's death, at least two editions of the play had been published without the author's permission. In an introduction to the first edition of the folio, two of Shakespeare's colleagues write to potential audiences who may leaf through the pages in the bookseller's stall:

> Where before you were abused with diverse stolen, and surreptitious copies, maimed, and deformed by the frauds and stealthes of injurious imposters that exposed them [the texts in the folio are] offered to your view

cured and perfect in their limbs … It is now public and now you will stand for your privileges we know to read and censure. Do so, but buy it first.[18]

The editor's plea is remarkably similar to that of Lin-Manuel Miranda, who, in the months before the official cast recording was released, responded to a fan request for an audio bootleg of his musical *Hamilton* on Tumblr:

> We're going to make a really good recording of the show this summer and I want you to hear that. I'm thrilled you haven't heard a shitty, half-iphone recorded version yet, because I spent 6 years writing this and when you hear it, I want you to hear what I intended. I'm sorry theater only exists in one place at a time but that is also its magic. A bootleg cannot capture it. I'm grateful and glad you want to hear it, and I want you to hear it RIGHT. I ask your patience.[19]

Both Miranda and the editors of the folio argue against the illicit copies not only because they potentially deprive the rights holder of financial reward, but also because they feel the unauthorized versions present an inferior product that could damage the reputation of the work.

These concerns are not entirely unwarranted. Certainly, early quartos of *Hamlet* present a text that is generally agreed to be inferior to the one in the folio (the first edition is even called, the "Bad quarto" by Shakespeare scholars). For instance, Hamlet's famous existential meditations in the "To be or not to be" soliloquy are represented in the "Bad quarto" as simply: "To be, or not to be, I here's the point, To Die, to sleep, is that all? I all: No to sleep, to dreame, I mary there it goes."[20] Likewise, contemporary theatre bootlegs are usually recorded on small and relatively inexpensive equipment concealed from house managers in ways that often degrade the quality of the video and audio. They also represent a particular production which, due to the nature of live theatre, may include mistakes or less than ideal performances.

However, it should be noted that while the first folio and the *Hamilton* cast recording may present a version of their respective works that most closely resembles the creators' ideal representation of the piece— it may be a version that was never seen by any audience on stage. Authorized versions often erase the very liveness that Miranda gestures positively towards in his Tumblr post. The first quarto of *Hamlet* may not represent *Hamlet* as Shakespeare wrote it, but the folio likely fails to accurately present the play as the original audiences saw it.

It does not follow, of course, that anyone has the moral right to insist on preserving and owning any version of a text not approved by the creator. Like Eliza Hamilton in Lin-Manuel Miranda's musical, one might make the claim that the "world has no right" to know anything about those writings or performances the creators have not chosen to make public. Eliza burns Hamilton's letters to her; Miranda has the legal right to issue takedown notices or sue anyone who posts an unauthorized recording of his musical.

However, it is useful to consider what these recordings represent. When Miranda posted his response on Tumblr, there was no legal recording of *Hamilton*. Fans in love with the work simply couldn't wait, and a market developed for less than perfect versions. It's by now such a familiar story that it hardly bears repeating. In the early days of the commercial Internet, record labels, movie studios, and publishers moved slowly to adapt to exploiting the affordances of rapid, low-cost duplication and distribution the technology made possible, and, in the absence of authorized digital editions or any adequate way to prevent the distribution of illegal ones, piracy flourished. Today both law enforcement and legal options have improved. Many now legally purchase music, movies, and books in digital form and receive, in exchange for payment, not a physical object but a stream of electronic pulses that are eventually converted to something meaningful by software on our phones, tablets, and laptops.

The performing arts, however, have been especially slow to embrace these new avenues of distribution. A distrust of mass media has long pervaded the live performing arts industry which, by nature, exists in contradistinction to mediated performance. Although some enterprising innovators such as the Metropolitan Opera, Broadway HD, Digital Theatre, and Britain's National Theatre have experimented with providing commercial access to digital video of recorded performances, in most cases authorized video recordings of the performing arts do not exist. When they do, they typically capture only one performance by a single cast. There is generally no authorized way for members of the audience for a Broadway show to obtain a video recording of the exact performance they saw. As a result, bootlegs flourish.

Video bootlegging predates the Internet, of course, but the ease with which digital bootlegs are created and copied gives them greater potential influence than those created and stored on analog media. Digital bootlegs, especially when posted to easily searchable sites like

Vimeo, Tumblr, or YouTube have the potential to create new audiences for live shows from geographical regions very far from New York City. The musical *Wicked* has been one of the most bootlegged shows since it opened in October 2003 (roughly eighteen months before the public launch of YouTube). In its first nine months on Broadway, *Wicked* did very well (rarely dipping below 80% of its gross potential), but it was not a mega-hit. It received a mixed review in the *Times* and had to compete with the still very successful runs of *Hairspray* and *Mamma Mia!* and a very popular return engagement of Nathan Lane and Matthew Broderick in *The Producers* during the winter and spring. Although it was selling out by the early spring, it did not regularly reach 100% of its gross potential until after the Tony awards in June 2004 (after losing the best musical award to *Avenue Q* but broadcasting an exciting performance of "Defying Gravity" to potential tourists from across the world). Throughout the 2004–2005 season, the show regularly sold at between 100 and 110% of its gross potential. Then, in the 2005–2006 season it managed to increase its revenue to over 110% of its gross. The original cast had left the show by then, perhaps decreasing the operating costs of the production, but the musical demonstrated it could run without major stars in the leading roles.[21]

Around this time, videos of *Wicked* began to proliferate on YouTube. While it is not absolutely clear that the mass bootlegging of *Wicked* contributed to its ascent from a successful production to a mega-hit, the activity certainly has not hurt it. The show is so widely bootlegged that many bootlegging sites that break their titles into alphabetically ordered blocks (e.g. "Videos N-R") have a separate page just for various videos of *Wicked*, yet the show continues to sell at or near its gross potential even now, over ten years into its run. Fans began to compare their favorite Elphabas and express their love for the show in YouTube comments. As Stacy Wolf has noted, fan communities of teen and tween girls began to develop around the show and they used digital platforms to find each other and share their excitement. In *Changed for Good: A Feminist History of the Broadway Musical*, Wolf notes: "As active, perceptive spectators, they [*Wicked* fans] debate interpretations of moments in the show and analyze performances of different actors in minute (admittedly sometimes excruciating) detail."[22] Of course, analyzing and comparing different versions of the same work in "minute (admittedly sometimes excruciating) detail" has been the province of textual scholars for centuries. Fans may be outpacing scholarship in developing a practice of close reading different video recordings of the same show to better understand the work and its interpretations. There is an enormous opportunity for theatre scholars to develop theoretical and ethical frameworks for "reading" the enormous and invaluable corpus of digital bootleg videos.

Conclusion

Born-digital archives open endlessly fruitful avenues of research, but much of their potential cannot yet be realized, as public access to the digital archives of Broadway theatre is still very limited. Most of the major institutional repositories (e.g. New York Public Library, the Library of Congress, the Harvard Theatre Collection, the Harry K. Ransom Center) are still developing the infrastructure and expertise to care for and provide access to these kinds of collections. Preserving digital data is difficult. Developing secure and reliable digital storage expansive enough to preserve the massive amount of digital data created by the theatre industry, creating and maintaining software that can provide access to files created with long obsolete software, and negotiating tricky legal and ethical issues require a level of financial support and staff expertise that few archives have available. This is, again, the sad refrain of so much discussion of this moment in archival history. Loss is imminent unless immediate care is taken. Perhaps, as the research community understands the potential value at risk, the shared sense of urgency will lead to greater investment. The rewards are enormous.

Notes

1. *Li'l Abner: Original Broadway Cast Recording.*
2. *Sweeney Todd: The Demon Barber of Fleet Street: Original Broadway Cast Recording.*
3. "Plato, from The Phaedrus."
4. Sullivan, Arthur.
5. Reside.
6. "Hidden Figure in Leonardo Da Vinci Notebook Revealed—Collection Care Blog."
7. Internet Arcade.
8. "17th Century French Playhouses: An Online Learning Resource."
9. "Abbey Theatre, 1904."

10. "The SL Shakespeare Company: Homepage."
11. "Virtual Vaudeville—A Live Performance Simulation System."
12. "The Lighting Archive."
13. MacAdams, Mikiko Suzuki.
14. "Michael Keller—Broadway Cast and Staff—IBDB."
15. "Ensemble: Help Build an Open Database of the Performing Arts."
16. "Michael John LaChiusa Papers."
17. "With Friends Like These: Archive Team Saves Friendster."
18. "William Shakespeare's First Folio."
19. Gioia, Michael. For further explanation of bootlegs and fan videos specific to *Hamilton* see Chap. 6.
20. "The Shakespeare Quartos Archive."
21. "Broadway Grosses."
22. Wolf, Stacy Ellen.

References

"17th Century French Playhouses: An Online Learning Resource." Accessed November 11, 2016. http://people.brynmawr.edu/cwillifo/ParisPlayhouses/.
"Abbey Theatre, 1904." Accessed November 11, 2016. http://blog.oldabbeytheatre.net/.
"Broadway Grosses, Broadway Box Office Grosses—2016-11-06." Accessed November 12, 2016. http://www.broadwayworld.com/grosses.cfm.
De Paul, Gene, Norman Panama, Melvin Frank, Al Capp, Johnny Mercer, Edie Adams, Peter Palmer, et al. *Li'l Abner: Original Broadway Cast Recording*. Sound recording. New York, NY: Columbia Broadway Masterworks, 2002.
"Ensemble: Help Build an Open Database of the Performing Arts." Accessed November 11, 2016. http://ensemble.nypl.org/.
Gioia, Michael. "Throw Down! Lin-Manuel Miranda Responds to Tumblr Post Seeking Illegal Hamilton Bootleg." *Playbill*. March 27, 2015. http://www.playbill.com/article/throw-down-lin-manuel-miranda-responds-to-tumblr-post-seeking-illegal-hamilton-bootleg-com-345407.
"Hidden Figure in Leonardo Da Vinci Notebook Revealed—Collection Care Blog." Accessed November 11, 2016. http://blogs.bl.uk/collectioncare/2016/01/fugitive-figure-in-leonardo-da-vinci-notebook-revealed.html.
Internet Arcade. Accessed November 11, 2016. http://archive.org/details/arcade_mpatrol.
"The Lighting Archive." Accessed November 11, 2016. http://thelightingarchive.org/.
MacAdams, Mikiko Suzuki. Design for Oregon Shakespeare Festival Production of The Sign in Sidney Brustein's Window. Private archive.

"Michael John LaChiusa Papers." Accessed November 11, 2016. http://archives.nypl.org/the/23071.

"Michael Keller—Broadway Cast & Staff| IBDB." Accessed November 12, 2016. https://www.ibdb.com/broadway-cast-staff/michael-keller-12666.

"Plato, from The Phaedrus." Accessed November 10, 2016. http://www.units.miamioh.edu/technologyandhumanities/plato.htm.

Reside, Doug. "'Last Modified January 1996': The Digital History of RENT." *Theatre Survey* 52.2 (2011): 335–40. ProQuest. Web. 10 Nov. 2016.

"The Shakespeare Quartos Archive| Home." *University of Maryland, College Park*. Accessed November 12, 2016. http://quartos.org/.

"The SL Shakespeare Company: Homepage." Accessed November 11, 2016. http://slshakespeare.com/.

Sondheim, Stephen, Hugh Wheeler, Angela Lansbury, Len Cariou, Paul Gemignani, and C. G. Bond. *Sweeney Todd: The Demon Barber of Fleet Street: Original Broadway Cast Recording.* Sound recording. New York, NY: Masterworks Broadway : Distributed in the USA by Sony BMG Music Entertainment, 2007.

Sullivan, Arthur. "*After Dinner Toast at Little Menio.*" Accessed September 19, 2017. https://www.nps.gov/edis/learn/photosmultimedia/upload/EDISSRP-0155-14.mp3.

"Virtual Vaudeville—A Live Performance Simulation System." Accessed November 11, 2016. http://vvaudeville.drama.uga.edu/.

"William Shakespeare's First Folio: The Preface to the First Folio." Accessed November 12, http://www.shakespeare-online.com/biography/firstfolio.html.

"With Friends Like These: Archive Team Saves Friendster." ASCII by Jason Scott, August 23, 2011. http://ascii.textfiles.com/archives/3233.

Wolf, Stacy Ellen. *Changed for Good: A Feminist History of the Broadway Musical.* New York: Oxford University Press, 2011.

CHAPTER 12

Recanonizing "American" Sound and Reinventing the Broadway Song Machine: Digital Musicology Futures of Broadway Musicals

Sissi Liu

Two decades ago, on November 11, 1997, a *New York Times* article entitled, "Undiscovered Bach? No, a Computer Wrote It," reported a human-machine contest in the field of music composition—the first such case the world had ever witnessed. A music theory professor at the University of Oregon, Dr. Steve Larson, competed with a computer to compose music in the style of Johann Sebastian Bach, and, startlingly at the time, lost the contest to the computer. All the listeners decided that the piece composed by the computer named "EMI" (Experiments in Musical Intelligence, pronounced "Emmy") was genuine Bach. The man behind EMI, computer scientist and composer David Cope, was able to use 1990s technology to have a computer analyze samples, use pattern-matching algorithms to compile a "dictionary" of the musical "words" Bach liked to use (characteristic chords, melodies, and rhythms, along with rules of syntax) and then cherry-pick the pieces he decided

S. Liu (✉)
The Graduate Center, City University of New York, New York City, NY, USA
e-mail: muse.du.theatre@gmail.com

that sounded the most like Bach.[1] Now, twenty years later, could the same thing happen to Broadway musicals? Could a well-designed computer program that knows all the quirks and tricks of writing a popular Broadway number beat a flesh-and-blood composer in creating genuine-sounding hit Broadway songs? The answer seems to be a predictable yes. In the past two decades, digital musicology, music information retrieval (MIR), and machine learning have developed to such an extent that music pattern recognition is now a recognized field of study in computer science. A large enough grant that puts together a team of top computer programmers and musicologists can make wonders happen. In fact, such an endeavor, supported by major grants, has already come to fruition. In February 2016, London's West End premiered the world's first computer-generated musical, *Beyond the Fence*.

In this chapter, starting with *Beyond the Fence*, I introduce the technology behind the world's first computer-generated musical and the current advancement of digital musicology, which make possible what I call the Broadway Song Machine, or a comprehensive set of secret formulas detected in hit tunes of Broadway musical canons. I argue that the Broadway Song Machine is not a rigid and unalterable set of formulas. It is contingent upon what constitutes Broadway musical canons, which constantly evolve and change—particularly so in the face of new technology and methodology in the digital age. I argue that the canonization and recanonization processes of Broadway musicals are crucial to the making of "American" sound in the past and present, and the prediction of what it would be in the future. I thereafter critically explore the recanonization processes of Broadway musicals in the digital age and suggest ways that "American" sound should be recanonized, and the canons diversified.

Technology Behind the World's First Computer-Generated Musical

Commissioned by the art-oriented television channel Sky Arts, *Beyond the Fence* began at Cambridge University, where researchers from the Machine Learning Group analyzed thousands of musicals to determine what makes a hit or a flop. They decided that the following elements make a hit musical: romance or death (or both), a female lead, a story set in Europe, and a happy ending. The project was then transferred to Goldsmiths at the University of London, where researchers used the "What-If Machine," a three-year project that received funding from the European Union and involved teams at five institutions, to generate central premises. The aim of the "What-If Machine" was to build a software system that is able to "invent, evaluate and present fictional ideas with real cultural value," and take on creative responsibility in arts and science projects.[2] After discarding many what-if style ideas built on combining topics in surprising ways, the "What-If Machine" derived the central premise for the musical: "What if there was a wounded soldier who had to learn how to understand a child in order to find true love?" From there the project moved to the Complutense University of Madrid, where a computer system called PropperWryter, developed by Professor Pablo Gervás, took over the task of building a core narrative arc. Set in UK in 1982, *Beyond the Fence*, a new musical about "hope, defiance, unity and love," tells the story of a mother (Mary) and her mute daughter (George) who protest in a peace camp against the arrival of US cruise missiles. When Mary is about to lose George to the authorities, she finds an unlikely ally in a US airman (Jim Meadows). Mary is thus faced with choosing between doing what is best for George and staying true to her own ideals.[3]

After the computer decided the setting, the plot, and the narrative arc, human writer/composer duo Benjamin Till and his husband Nathan Taylor, best known in the UK for broadcasting their wedding as a musical, called *Our Gay Wedding: The Musical*, wrote most of the book and lyrics. Till and Taylor conscientiously chose a historical background pertinent to the world affairs today. Greenham Common Women's Peace Camp (1981–2000) was first established to protest against the placing of nuclear weapons as well as the arrival and siting of cruise missiles at Royal Air Force Greenham Common in Berkshire, England. Tens and hundreds of women protesters entered, disruptively and subversively, what had been usually considered "masculine" spaces. Many of these women were mothers who stood up for the safety, peace, and human rights of their children and future generations, resembling the Women's March in January 2017. While protesting, these women cut down parts of the circumferential fence of the Greenham Common, and attempted to seal off the base. In the musical, the "fence" is that between the protesters and the army, and as the story evolves, the audience is able to see the action from both sides. An *Independent* review calls the Greenham setting "the thing that makes it zing."[4] Apart from Mary, George, and Jim, other key characters include Margie, who mothers the camp; Helen, a girl with a weight problem who has trouble finding her feet and her confidence; and Ceridwen, a heterosexual woman who finds the "No Men" policy at the camp to be very difficult. Act I builds up to a high-energy song and dance, "At Our Feet," when the Berkshire Truancy Officer threatens to take George away. Act II closes with a reenactment of the historical event in December 1983 when 50,000 women circled the base and protested.

The music was mostly composed by Android Lloyd Webber and the FlowComposer system. Android Lloyd Webber is a computer composition system created by Dr. Nick Collins from Durham University, based on a machine-listening analysis of musical theatre music. The FlowComposer system is a research project funded by the European Research Council (ERC) and coordinated by François Pachet, the Director of the Sony Computer Science Laboratory in Paris.[5] The algorithmic compositions that Android Lloyd Webber and FlowComposer generated were then curated and arranged by Till and Taylor into 16 musical numbers. Producer Christian Gale declared to *The Guardian* that the project "is not about taking humans out of the creative process at all."[6] It is true that while computer programming started the project, human beings were the ones who put it together. A talented ensemble of live actors performed the show.

The reviews for the show were generally positive. A *Telegraph* review on February 27, 2016 called *Beyond the Fence* "no mean feat … in a world where flops are the norm."[7] An *Independent* review claimed: "Despite my reservations I was won over."[8] Reviewers mostly found the music enjoyable and fun, making references to previously hit musicals. A review in *Londonist* remarked: "It's quite fun to try and spot stuff the tech has re-purposed: a bit of *Chicago* here, a bit of *The Lion King* there."[9]

Despite many reports and reviews on the world's first computer-generated musical, there was little coverage on the technology behind the computer composition system, how the system detected formulas of hit songs, what tools were used, and which songs were analyzed. This leads to a series of questions this chapter explores: What are the state-of-the-art digital approaches to analyzing music that enable modeling after hit musicals? What is the status quo of digital musicology today? How can these advanced technological inventions be applied to Broadway musicals?

Digital Musicology Status Quo

Digital musicology is the study of music—both music per se and music-related information—using applied computational and informatics methods. To obtain music-related information, researchers consult collections of bibliographic data, socio-historical and biographic information, and performance ephemera, much of which are in the process of being digitized with inventories or finding aids accessible to the general public. For instance, the New York Philharmonic Digital Archives, funded by the Leon Levy Foundation, has digitized printed performance programs, business records, and photos, in addition to marked music scores and marked orchestral parts.[10] In order to "mak[e] its own contribution to the Open Data movement," New York Philharmonic makes its data "available for study, analysis, and reuse."[11] It offers open-source performance history metadata—the information about performance history data, such as program ID, full orchestra name, season number, location, venue, date, and length of concert. Metadata, here available in XML and JSON, provides shortcuts to finding and working with particular instances of data.[12]

In terms of music per se, the crux of digital musicology, two main approaches guide the research: analysis of scores and analysis of audio files. Large collections of scores already exist, for instance, OCVE (Online Chopin Variorum Edition), funded by Andrew W. Mellon Foundation, provides a large amount of digital images of manuscripts and first editions of selected works by Chopin. The Juilliard Manuscript Collection offers 140 items of priceless autograph and working manuscripts, sketches, and first editions, which are of great interest to performers and scholars.[13] Stanford University's Center for Computer Assisted Research in the Humanities offers Digital Resources for Musicology (DRM), a website that links to substantial open-access projects and repertories, some of which provide audio collections under "Historical Audio and Video."[14] Harvard University offers a complementary mix of projects at Online Resources for Music Scholars (ORMS).[15] Not surprisingly, the existent well-funded digital databases tend to house Western music, especially European classical music. Up till now, there is no open-access digital archive that offers digitized music scores of Broadway musical theatre. Building such an archive would be crucial in applying digital musicology to the analysis of Broadway musicals. Since selected vocal scores—scores that consist of only two parts, voice and piano—of most hit Broadway musicals are in print, it should be undemanding to create a preliminary archive that contains images of Broadway musical theatre vocal scores, given copyright clearance.

Copyright is an unavoidable issue for digitization of Broadway musical theatre scores. According to US Copyright Act, the copyright terms of works first published in the USA are categorized according to the date of publication and in the sentence end conditions. It is worth noting that there have been explicit exemptions for libraries and archives found in the Copyright Act. The fair-use exemption is one of the most important principles in copyright law.[16] With copyright expired or fair use allowed, the musical scores are digitized into portable document format (PDF) files. Thereafter, music optical character recognition (OCR) or optical music recognition (OMR) technologies in software such as SmartScore are able to transform PDF files into computer analyzable musical instrument digital interface (MIDI) files with limited inaccuracy.[17]

In the age of big data, digital tools such as Humdrum and music21 offer human researchers unprecedented assistance in analyzing large corpora of musical scores within short periods of time. In the 1980s David Huron started creating Humdrum Toolkit, a set of software tools to assist music research.[18] All Humdrum file formats are ASCII (American Standard Code for Information Interchange) text.[19] Since its release in 1993, it has remained one of the most widely used toolkits in digital musicology. A library of virtual musical scores (108,703 files) in the Humdrum **kern data format is held at DRM, Stanford University.[20] Humdrum Toolkit is able to detect and analyze chord-voicing patterns, dissonance patterns, rhythmic patterns, and handle more subtle issues such as the doubling of the leading tone in certain harmonic contexts. In 2006, Michael Cuthbert and Christopher Ariza started developing music21 at MIT, a python-based tool that builds on Humdrum and existing encoding frameworks such as MusicXML and MEI (music encoding initiative), tools designed for sharing sheet music files between applications and for archiving sheet music files in a machine-readable format. Advertising itself as "extremely easy" to use, music21 enables its user to use one single line of music21 code to display a short melody in musical notation. It also supports conversion of files from Humdrum's **kern data format to MusicXML for editing in music notation and composition software such as Finale or Sibelius. Supported by grants from Digging Into Data Consortium, music21 now has grown to be one of the most popular tools in digital musicology.

In addition to tools built for analyzing musical scores, great technical progress has also been made in audio analysis, especially in MIR, an interdisciplinary research endeavor that started to mature in the late 1990s, supported by developments in information retrieval, audio engineering, digital sound processing, musicology and music theory, cognitive science, computer science, and machine learning. The retrieval subjects of MIR are the seven aspects of music, or "seven facets of music information" proposed by J. Stephen Downie in 2003, which are "the pitch, temporal, harmonic, timbral, editorial, textual and bibliographic facets."[21] The pitch is represented by the vertical position of a note on the staff, or the highness/lowness of a note. The temporal facet illuminates the information regarding the duration of musical events. The harmonic facet concerns harmonic progressions, or simply harmonic events, such as chords, which are created by pitches aligning vertically. The timbral facet comprises all aspects of tone color. Performance instructions, such as fingering, ornamentation, dynamic instructions, bowing, articulations, accents, slurs, make up the editorial facet. The textual facet covers the lyrics of songs, arias, chorales, and so on. The bibliographic facet considers a work's title, composer, arranger, lyric author, publisher, edition, publication date, discography, performer(s), and so on.

The first five facets are all audial elements of music, and are therefore particularly relevant to audio signal processing. Audio signals, which are electronic representations of sound waves, may be represented either in digital or analog format, and the signal processing may take place in either medium. State-of-the-art audio signal processing tools such as Matlab toolboxes (MIR Toolbox and Timbre Toolbox), Aubio, PsySound3, sMIRk, SuperCollider SCMIR toolkit, and libraries like Essentia (an open-source C ++ library for audio analysis and audio-based MIR) have facilitated progress in areas such as tonality and rhythm feature extraction, timbre recognition, song structural segmentation, key (or key signature) estimation, chord recognition, genre recognition, music emotion recognition, and auto-tagging.[22] However, one prevailing problem with audio signal processing is the unavoidable inaccuracy of the processed result. For instance, despite recent developments, automatic disambiguation of melody (telling the main melodic line apart from the lines that harmonically support the melody) from polyphonic sources—for instance, instrumental passages in Broadway musicals, or a sung trio, quartet, or a chorus—has remained a challenge.[23] Considering the rate of inevitable errors in audio signal analysis due to today's technological limitation, the more effective way to achieve accuracy in digital musicology is through analyzing scores in lieu of audio files.

Broadway Song Machine

How can the digital tools for analyzing music and detecting patterns be applied to Broadway musical theatre? Do Broadway hit numbers have a distinct sound like Bach does? As the most distinctive and the most beloved form of US theatre, Broadway musicals are known for producing an "American" sound, especially for international practitioners and scholars. Here I provide an ad hoc definition of "Broadway musicals" as original musicals composed by US artists (native or immigrant) for the US stage that are performed in Broadway theatres in the theatre district in Manhattan, New York. Under this definition, musicals that originated from the West End such as *The Phantom of the Opera* and *Cats*, despite their contribution to the Broadway sound, are excluded from the list of Broadway musicals.[24] *The Lion King*, however, in spite of its international creative team, is based on a US film, produced by Disney Theatrical Productions, and premiered in the USA. It should therefore fall under this definition of Broadway musicals.

In traditional musicology, researchers tend to study the history of musical styles and song forms and types, and to use a Schenkerian approach to analyze individual songs within their social, cultural, and performance contexts.[25] Composer and scholar Lehman Engel, in his 1975 book *The American Musical Theater*, and musicologist Paul Laird, in his chapter "Musical Styles and Song Conventions" in *The Oxford Handbook of The American Musical*, both provide a useful typology for songs in musicals. They include song types such as the "I want" song, "eleven-o-clock number," "charm song," "rhythm song," and "ballad;" song styles like "12-bar blues influenced style," "jazz-influenced style," "Tin Pan Alley style," "Latin dance style," Rock and Motown style; and song forms such as ABBA, ABAB, ABAC.[26] For instance, if a traditional musicologist analyzes the opening number "All That Jazz" in the longest-running Broadway musical, *Chicago*, she will quickly conclude the following after studying the score: the song type of "All That Jazz" falls under "charm song" (usually not plot or character driven, and used to charm the audience); its song style is jazz-influenced; the song form is AABA in the keys of C, D flat, D (elevating a half step each time), and back to C; the chord progression can be condensed as I-V-I

(Tonic-Dominant-Tonic). Beyond those basic conclusions, the musicologist may explore the song in further detail, exploring the use of augmented chords, jazzy sixth and ninth chords, melodic and harmonic structure and so on, in the context of Broadway musical in the 1970s and John Kander's compositional styles.

Digital musicology also explores style or genre detection and song form recognition, derived from melodic, harmonic, temporal, and rhythmic patterns; but more importantly, it looks for musical patterns within a great amount of music data. A well-trained musicologist can quickly figure out the style or form of one song by looking at the score, but one million different songs would most definitely burn her out. A computer handles big music data with ease, once the music data is encoded into machine-analyzable language. Digital musicology is able to detect, with the help of the human musicologist, patterns of highly formulaic Broadway hit songs and solve questions like these: What are the ten most common chord progressions in the verse part of a song? How many—and roughly what percentage of—Broadway hit songs end with a perfect authentic cadence (progression from V to I)? How many use the most common I-IV-V-I (or Tonic-Subdominant-Dominant-Tonic), or I-V-I, or jazz-influenced II-V-I structure? How often are 9th, 11th, 13th chords, French augmented 6th chord, or Neapolitan 6th chord used? How often does pan-diatonicism appear in Sondheim's musicals? Do the hit songs from the same decades have similar structures? These are the exact issues that will lead to the unearthing of the Broadway Song Machine.

The Broadway Song Machine is not a fixed set of secret formulas detected in hit tunes of Broadway musical canons. It is contingent upon what constitutes Broadway musical canons, which evolve and alter throughout time. Some musicals that made the canon list in 1970 may not make it in 2017. What are the Broadway musical canons at present? How does one generate the most up-to-date list of Broadway musical canons? Which musicals best represent "American" sound? The answer to these questions lies in the canonizing process of Broadway musicals. It is the canons that determine the shape of the Broadway Song Machine and formulate "American" sound. The canonizing process is therefore crucial to the making of "American" sound in the past and present, and the prediction of what it would be in the future.

Canonizing Broadway Musicals in the Digital Age

Before the advent of electronics, operas and ballets were canonized through the repertory system. The more frequently a work was performed, the higher it was elevated on the scale of canonization. Frequency of performance was also key to the canonization process of Broadway musicals, especially before the digital age. Digital technology has not only made accessible—to the general public—information such as the exact number of performances each musical has had on Broadway and the number of revivals and adaptations a musical has received, but also has, as my colleagues Doug Reside, Bryan Vandevender, and Bud Coleman have pointed out in this section of the book, fundamentally challenged the traditional processes of archiving, dramaturgy, and criticism of Broadway musicals. Digital approaches have introduced new benchmarks that add to, challenge, and disrupt the traditional means through which we measure the canonization of Broadway musicals. Observing the accessibility and impact of digital technology and approaches, I propose six methods of evaluation, or metrics, which determine the canonization of Broadway musicals.

Metric One: Length of Run, or the Number of Performances of a Musical

As the most traditional means to measure the success of a Broadway musical, length of run indicates the popularity of a show. Ticket sales in Broadway theatres that house over 500 people straightforwardly determine the number of performances and the number of audience members in direct contact with a live production. Playbill On-Line (playbill.com), the oldest and most widely used website providing news and featured articles about the theatre industry, offers an up-to-date list of all Broadway shows that have run more than 800 performances and the exact number of performances each one has received.[27] According to the list, the longest-running ten US Broadway musicals as of June 2017 are:

Top 1. *Chicago* (1996 Revival)
Top 2. *The Lion King*
Top 3. *A Chorus Line*
Top 4. *Wicked*

Top 5. *Beauty and the Beast*
Top 6. *Rent*
Top 7. *Jersey Boys*
Top 8. *42nd Street*
Top 9. *Grease*
Top 10. *Fiddler on the Roof*

Metric Two: Award-Winning Status of a Musical

The Antoinette Perry Award for Excellence in Theatre, or the Tony Award, which recognizes achievement in live Broadway theatre annually, is the highest award for a Broadway musical. For musicals, the Tonys consist of four awards in performance categories and ten awards in production and technical categories, including the four most coveted: Best Musical, Best Revival of a Musical, Best Book of a Musical, and Best Original Score. Official approval by the American Theatre Wing and The Broadway League puts a musical on a critically sanctioned pedestal, thus narrowing the gap between popular and scholarly appreciation. Historically, the Tony Award for Best Musical or Best Revival of a Musical tends to dramatically lengthen the run of the winning musical.

The annual Pulitzer Prize for Drama recognizes a theatrical work staged in the USA in the previous calendar year. Inaugurated in 1918, it is one of the oldest and most distinguished awards for theatrical works. Only six musicals in history have won both the Tony for Best Musical and the Pulitzer Prize for Drama: *South Pacific* (1950), *Fiorello* (1960), *How to Succeed in Business Without Really Trying* (1962), *A Chorus Line* (1976), *Rent* (1996), and *Hamilton* (2016). Inevitably, most of these tend to rank high on the Broadway musical canon list.

Metric Three: The Number of Revivals and Adaptations of a Musical

The global circulation of Broadway musicals also offers significant reference to evaluating levels of canonization. The touring information of all the Broadway musicals within the USA is readily available on the Internet Broadway Database (ibdb.com), owned by The Broadway League. Revivals and adaptations in and outside of the USA can also be found on Wikipedia pages of individual musicals; however, the anonymity and unpredictable credibility of Wikipedia entries pose potential threats of error. The Broadway League offers "Current and Upcoming

International Broadway Shows" on their official website, but the countries are limited to only the United Kingdom, Australia, France, Germany, Japan, New Zealand, and Spain.[28] Further efforts will be needed for a complete list of exported musicals in countries like Korea, China, Singapore, Mexico, Brazil, South Africa, and the Netherlands. The more revivals and adaptations a musical has had, the higher it gets on the canonization scale.

Metric Four: The Number of Notable Studies on a Musical

Since the legitimization of musical theatre studies as a discipline in the 1990s, an increasing number of books and articles on Broadway musicals have come to the fore. The most common way of evaluating the impact of an academic study in the field is to quantitatively measure the times it has been cited by other studies. In terms of journal articles, Web of Science, Scopus, and Google Scholar provide both journal-level and article-level metrics. Journal Citation Reports (JCR) on the Web of Science platform include Impact Factor—the number of citations in a given year, 5-year Impact Factors, and Eigenfactor Score—which is calculated with a more complex algorithm. Journal Analyzer of Scopus offers h5-index, or how many of the articles in a journal have been cited h times or more, over a 5-year period. On the article level, the user of Web of Science, for instance, can search for articles under "Topic," and then sort relevant articles by citation numbers from high to low. However, this process requires hand selection of articles, as search phrases for topics such as "Broadway musical theatre" or "Broadway musicals" understandably do not generate all of the studies on individual Broadway musicals.

As for citation numbers for books on Broadway musicals, Google Scholar is the go-to resource. To evaluate the impact of the book and the musicals in it, one would first rank the studies by citation numbers using python or any other programming language, and then count the times each musical is studied. However, one problem with this method is that some of the most important and well-cited musical theatre books, such as Gerald Mast's *Can't Help Singin': The American Musical on Stage and Screen* (cited 158 times according to Google Scholar as of June 2017), are survey books that do not offer chapter-length studies on individual musicals. Mast's book, for instance, is mostly organized around musical theatre masters such as Jerome Kern, the Gershwins, Rodgers and Hart, Cole Porter, and Rodgers and

Hammerstein, and touches upon a large number of musicals in each chapter. The solution to this problem is, again, to handpick books that devote chapters to individual musicals, as well as articles whose subjects are individual musicals.

Another issue in digitally extracting the number of notable studies on a musical is the correlation between citation number and publication date. If a book published in 1951 shares the same citation number as a book published in 2015, the newer book should probably be ranked higher. In fact, Stacy Wolf's *Changed for Good: A Feminist History of the Broadway Musical* (2011) and Ethan Mordden's *Coming up Roses: The Broadway Musical in the 1950s* (1999) have both been cited 66 times as of June 2017, according to Google Scholar. In order to more fairly rank them, it might be useful to modify the citation number in accordance to its publication date, to divide the citation number by the number of years the book or article is published. Here the variable of modified citation number for *Changed for Good* would be $66/6 = 11$, higher than that for *Coming up Roses*, $66/18 = 3.667$.

The use of research metrics in academia has been under debate, and measuring the impact of a study quantitatively leaves space for inaccuracy. The number of significant studies on a musical should be the result of both digital calculation and analog selection. After ranking the studies in the category of books and articles, it would be up to the researcher to decide where to make the cut (at the modified citation number of 2, or 1, or 0.5) for the "notable" studies on a musical. The combination of both digital and analog means in research on humanities subjects tends to generate results of the highest accuracy and reliability.

Metric Five: Traditionally Highly Regarded Musicals in the Field

The first three metrics for Broadway musical canonization are all based on historical facts available digitally. The fourth metric is based on digital calculation plus minimal human selection of chapter- or article-length studies of musicals and the degree of "notable studies." Metric Five here adds a dash more of human touch: a list of musicals that are traditionally taught and studied in higher education. This list might vary from one musical theatre expert to another, but is unlikely to be very dissimilar. A feasible way to verify the similarity is to collaborate with initiatives such as the Open Syllabus Project (opensyllabusproject.org) and build a large online syllabi bank that reflects which musicals are most taught in musical theatre history classes in higher education around the USA.

Considering the above five metrics, I put together a tentative and debatable list of Broadway musical canons, from 1920s to 2000s divided by decade, as follows:

2000s: *Wicked*
1990s: *Chicago* (Revival), *Rent*
1980s: *La Cage aux Folles, 42nd Street*
1970s: *A Chorus Line, Company*
1960s: *Fiddler on the Roof, Cabaret, Hello Dolly!*
1950s: *The King and I, My Fair Lady, West Side Story*
1940s: *Oklahoma!, South Pacific, Kiss me Kate*
1930s: *Porgy and Bess, Anything Goes*
1920s: *Show Boat*

Recanonizing Broadway Musicals and Reinventing Broadway Song Machine

The "canonizing" of Broadway musicals is an ongoing process that is constantly shifting and evolving. Canonizing always happens in the present, looking back at history and assessing the past. The five metrics I have proposed determine the canonizing process. There is one more metric, vital in the digital age, which I'd like to propose. This sixth metric evaluates and determines the present and the future—and constitutes what I call the "recanonizing" process. Recanonizing is a critical process of reevaluating the past and making changes for the future. Whereas the traditional canonizing process has less to do with individual human intervention than with hard collective facts, the recanonizing process is all about individual human agency. In the digital age, recanonizing may primarily take two forms. One form is direct digital presence. This can be realized through social media activities such as tweeting and blogging about a musical. The other form is the production and circulation of knowledge and information via traditional media (in the configuration of a stage production, a TV interview, a journal article publication, and so on) that leads to digital presence.

Metric Six: Personal Canonization of Musicals

Personal canonization of musicals is an endeavor that only comes forth in the digital age. "Personal" indicates individual (re)production and/or dissemination of information online; "personal canonization" designates individual effort in influencing the collective evaluation of the merit of musicals. In the digital age, our daily individual tweeting, retweeting, link sharing, event sharing, and blogging are starting to collectively make a tremendous impact on the canonization of musicals. In our current society, futurist Rolf Jensen argues, "people's trust in government, major businesses, organized religion, and other traditional institutions is at a historic low, but there is a silver lining: We are placing more trust in each other. An unprecedented age of individual initiative will soon be fully upon us."[29] The democratization of information gathering, though a likely threat to traditional politics, is a boon for recanonizing musical theatre. Individual opinions and concerns, when transmitted online, could have the efficacy of communally playing a major part in public discourse, not only influencing fan culture and ticket sales, but inspiring producers and musical theatre makers in critically and creatively shaping the future trends of Broadway musical theatre. As Luke Tredinnick points out, "media content no longer radiates out from the epicenter of its production, but filters through society and culture by transmission between individuals within a social network. [...] Individuals intervene in content, reshaping, recontextualizing and reconstructing its meaning."[30]

The canonization of Broadway musicals is increasingly influenced by the growing digital impact on what we think about musical theatre as ordinary audience members, write about as fans and scholars, teach about as educators, and advocate about as critical thinkers and activists in everyday life. Citation database Scopus has already detected the individual influence on social media, as it has launched the "Altmetric" (altmetric.com), where altmetrics—alternative ways of assessing the impact of authors and publications by including mentions in sources such as social media—are measured and become an indispensable part of research metrics. Altmetric monitors the following sources for mentions of research outputs:

1. Public policy documents and their references to published research
2. Over 2000 mainstream media outlets around the world
3. Online reference managers such as Mendeley.com

4. Post-publication peer-review platforms such as Pubpeer.com and Publons.com
5. The English language version of Wikipedia, where new mentions or edits are identified automatically
6. The Open Syllabus Project (opensyllabusproject.org) where book titles appear in the course syllabi of over 4000 institutions around the world
7. A manually curated list of over 9000 academic and non-academic blogs
8. Scopus citation information for items that have also received attention from other sources
9. Recommendations of individual research outputs from F1000 (f1000.com), an open science publishing platform for life scientists that offer immediate publication and transparent peer review
10. Social Media mentions, including Facebook (mentions on public pages only), Twitter, Google+, LinkedIn, SinaWeibo and Pinterest
11. Multimedia and other online platforms such as YouTube, Reddit, Q&A (stack overflow)[31]

Of the eleven sources listed on the Altmetric official site, five sources (5, 6, 7, 10, 11) are ones to which every individual can make a direct contribution, through creating and editing Wikipedia pages, uploading course syllabi, writing blogs, making mentions on social media, and posting videos on YouTube. Three sources (3, 4, 9) enable researchers to contribute by participating in academic reference managers and providing and tracking peer reviews. These sources greatly enable the individual to play an indispensable role in shaping where the field is going, and such a role will become increasingly impactful as digital social networks continue to grow. The recanonizing of Broadway musicals begins with individual efforts to make changes happen.

Diversifying the Canon

Why are changes to the canon necessary? A significant problem posed by the tentative 1920s'–2000s' Broadway musical canons list above is a sore lack of diversity in musical theatre makers. Whereas only roughly 20% of the roles on Broadway go to actors of color, according to surveys by AAPAC (Asian American Performers Action Coalition), there are practically no creators of color in the tentative canons list.[32] All the creators (composers, librettists, book writers) of the musicals listed are uniformly Caucasian male. There is a wide range of musical styles and ethnic music influences Broadway musical canons represent, (Latin American, Asian, African, Oceanic) but not a single creator of color in sight. Nor is there a female creator. This situation has only started to change in the 2010s, when *Hamilton* (2015), created by a Latino composer/writer/actor, became the hottest musical of the decade; and *Fun Home* (2015), one of the most epoch-making musicals of the decade (with a lesbian protagonist for the first time in Broadway history) was created by a three-person female team, composer Jeanine Tesori and lyricist/book writer Lisa Kron working with cartoonist Alison Bechdel (whose graphic memoir the musical is based on). In 2016, *Shuffle Along, or, the Making of the Musical Sensation of 1921 and All That Followed* emerged as a recanonizing effort of the 1921 Broadway musical revue created by an all-African American team. The reworked piece still retained an all-African American creative team, with George C. Wolfe writing the new book, based on the original book by F. E. Miller and Aubrey Lyles, and original music and libretto by Eubie Blake and Noble Sissle.

The revival/reworking of *Shuffle Along* is a compelling example of recanonizing Broadway musicals via traditional media—the staging of a show—leading to increasing digital presence. Having been on his mind for decades, this project was deeply personal for 61-year-old George C. Wolfe.[33] "I found this pictorial history of Broadway that had about 15 pages on 1921," he said. "Now 'Shuffle Along' was the biggest hit, but all they had was a paragraph at the end. How could it be a footnote to 1921 when it was the biggest show in 1921? How does something that matters so much end up not mattering at all?"[34] The show had an epic run of 474 performances in 1921. Wolfe also pointed out that *Shuffle Along* was "the first musical of the Jazz Age" that introduced African American idioms to Broadway, as Blake's jazz songs and fast syncopation "altered the form" of the early American musical and geared Broadway toward an entirely new direction. It was the first Broadway musical that featured a love scene between two black characters. It was also the first to have a chorus of female dancers. It greatly accelerated the production of shows about African Americans. The original musical has been revived on Broadway twice, in 1933 and 1952, neither time successfully. Wolfe suggested that the beginning of the Depression and the start of the Eisenhower years were not auspicious times for revivals.[35] The musical's fading into oblivion, suspects Wolfe, was caused by "a cultural tendency to undervalue pioneering contributions by black artists."[36]

It had to take a famous artistic director like Wolfe himself to successfully recanonize and restage a historically important hit Broadway show created by African Americans that has declined into obscurity. Because of his significant position as an award-winning theatre director and his decades of experience working with top theatre artists on and off Broadway, Wolfe was able to invite on board six-time Tony-winner Audra McDonald, two other Tony-winning performers Brian Stokes Mitchell and Billy Porter, as well as Tony-winning choreographer Savion Glover. The star-studded team of Tony winners earned the 2016 production 10 Tony nominations, including the Best Musical. There could not be a greater success in restaging one's personal canon—an important but long forgotten piece that deserves to be revived and restaged.

Recanonizing endeavors such as George C. Wolfe's *Shuffle Along* (2016) mark the beginning of a potentially more diversified Broadway musical canon. Apart from unearthing and reworking lesser-known Broadway musicals of cultural significance, it is also crucial for young musical theatre makers and producers to be aware of the diversifying demands of the US culture while creating future canons-to-be. According to the US Census, demographically, the white majority in the USA will be gone by the year 2043, and the USA will then become a majority-minority nation with no ethnic group making up a majority. All the minorities, now 37% of the US population, are projected to make up 57% of the population in 2060.[37] As the USA turns into a majority "people of color" nation, the "American" sound will accordingly change, adapting to the demands of a more diversified and inclusive audience with more racial, ethnic, and cultural awareness. The recanonizing process of Broadway musicals is crucial to reevaluating what "American" sound has been, should be, and will turn out to be. It is not just rethinking the past, but also making changes happen for the varigated futures. Changes have indeed been seen on Broadway in 2016, a year of unprecedented diversity, with Latin American creators of *On Your Feet*, Asian American creators of *Allegiance*, and African American songwriters of *The Color Purple* revival.

Conclusion

The digital musicology futures of Broadway musicals are varied. Digital musicology offers tools to rethink and reassess the past. Dissecting the Broadway musical canons of each decade generates an understanding of how "American" sound has evolved over time, and in which enduring deep structures have remained throughout history. Digital musicology could be used to detect the many African, Latin American, Caribbean, Asian, and Pacific Islander music influences in the canons, and trigger the creation of digital databases of non-white music. It could also be used, with the last metric in mind, to inspire studies of past lesser-known but culturally significant canons-to-be. The patterns it detects in the past canons are to be broken and surpassed, and new and more diverse "American" sounds are to be created and the Broadway Song Machine reinvented.

Digital musicology provides a splendid pedagogical tool for future composers and students of musical theatre who are interested in song forms, recognizable chord voicing, and rhythm patterns—or the making of the Broadway Song Machine. There has been an increasing number of composers on Broadway who have never received conservatory musical training, such as Lin-Manuel Miranda (creator of *Hamilton*)—a theatre major in college, or Jay Kuo (creator of *Allegiance*), who was trained as a lawyer. Broadway welcomes self-taught musicians who know how to write good songs, and digital musicology of Broadway musicals provides a shortcut for these aspiring composers. Pedagogically, digital musicology also helps students understand the history of Broadway songwriting and the making of "American" sound. Similar to other digital humanities subjects, digital musicology should be studied together with textual and archival material regarding socio-economic context and the cultural history of musical theatre.

Last but not least, digital musicology challenges human musical theatre composers to be more creative and less predictable. EMI, the computer that defeated the music professor in the Bach case at the beginning of this chapter, was invented by David Cope out of frustration, to help with his composer's block. Despite its stunning performance, EMI was criticized for "fall[ing] far short of capturing the full essence of a composer's work [because] it has no passions, no memories and knows nothing about life, [and] it was cut off from the messiness of the real world," and that "pseudo-compositions work better 'locally' than 'globally'—while EMI is dutifully imitating patterns involving small clusters of notes, it is missing out on longer-ranging orders."[38] Similar doubt was cast on *Beyond the Fence*, the world's first computer-generated musical that ran at the Arts Theatre in London for less than two weeks, from February 22 to March 5, 2016. *The Telegraph* commented: "What we have here is a bizarre synergy, almost a Faustian pact, in which soulfulness just about survives."[39] *Engadget* similarly echoed: "Computers can help write a musical, it seems, but they can't yet write a good one."[40] *New Scientist* concluded: "As the curtain falls on *Beyond the Fence*, it's clear that the UK's musical theatre talents can sleep peacefully at night with little to fear from Android Lloyd Webber and his crowd of cybernetic pretenders."[41] Digital technology only works with historical materials and past hits; living human composers with an eye for the future are able to create new sensations that fall under no existent and predictable formula.

In the age of computer-generated drawings, songs, orchestral works, poems, and even films, the futures of Broadway musical theatre still lie in flesh-and-blood human beings with real live human experience, love and hope, pain and struggle, and an indissoluble longing for a better tomorrow. So we come back to the question at the beginning of the chapter: "Could a well-designed computer program that knows all the quirks and tricks of writing a popular Broadway number beat a flesh-and-blood composer in composing genuine-sounding hit Broadway songs?" In the short term, the answer is yes, the computer may write a few better songs. As the technology advances, the computer may even make greater wonders than what human beings have imagined today. In the long run, however, the answer is a definite no. The existence of digital musicology and computational music is to assist human beings in becoming better musical theatre scholars, musicologists, and composers. Because of the available state-of-the-art digital technologies, the always developing "American" sound might evolve even faster. At the careful hands of critically thinking, culturally aware, socially conscious, and artistically visionary living human musical theatre makers and producers, the new and more diverse "American" sound of the future might just be around the corner.

Notes

1. Johnson, "Undiscovered Bach? No, a Computer Wrote It."
2. See http://www.whim-project.eu.

3. "Beyond the Fence Tickets," London Theatre Direct.
4. Williams, "Beyond the Fence, Arts Theatre, Review."
5. Colton, "Beyond the Fence: The first West End Musical Conceived and Crafted by Computer."
6. Brown, "World's First Computer-Generated Musical to Debut in London."
7. Cavendish, "Beyond the Fence, Arts Theatre, Review: 'Computer Says So-so'."
8. Williams, "Beyond the Fence, Arts Theatre, Review."
9. Black, "Computer-Penned Musical Beyond the Fence Reviewed."
10. See http://archives.nyphil.org/index.php.
11. New York Philharmonic Github, https://github.com/nyphilarchive/PerformanceHistory/. Github is an online repository hosting service that offers a version control system used for software development and source code management. The service was founded in 2008.
12. XML (Extensible Markup Language) is a markup language that encodes documents in a format that is both human readable and machine readable. JSON (JavaScript Object Notation) is a data-interchange format that is language independent and uses conventions familiar to programmers of the C-family languages, such as C, C ++, Java, JavaScript, Perl, Python, and so on.
13. See http://juilliardmanuscriptcollection.org.
14. See http://drm.ccarh.org.
15. See http://hcl.harvard.edu/research/guides/onmusic/.
16. The Copyright Act lists four factors to be considered when determining whether a particular use is fair: 1) The purpose and character of the use, including whether such use is of a commercial nature or is for non-profit educational purposes; 2) The nature of the copyrighted work; 3) The amount and substantiality of the portion used in relation to the copyrighted work as a whole; and 4) The effect of the use upon the potential market for, or value of, the copyrighted work. Other factors might also be taken into consideration.
17. See http://www.musitek.com. OMR technology is still in the process of development. At present, SmartScore still requires human proofreading.
18. The Toolkit is a syntax within which representations can be defined, and runs on PERL, Ruby, and Python. Syntax in programming language is a set of grammatical rules and structural patterns governing the use of words and symbols for issuing commands, writing code, and so on. PERL, Ruby and Python are all general-purpose programming languages. PERL is the oldest of the three, in use since 1987. Ruby and Python are among the most popular programming languages. Ruby is

used by companies such as GitHub, Twitter, and Hulu. Python is used by Google, Yahoo Maps, Dropbox, YouTube, Venmo, and so on.
19. Huron, "Music Information Processing Using the Humdrum Toolkit," 11.
20. **kern scheme allows the encoding of pitch and duration, as well as accidentals, articulation, ornamentation, ties, slurs, phrasing, glissandi, barlines, stem-direction, and beaming, according to Humdrum.org.
21. Downie, "Music Information Retrieval," 297.
22. See Proceedings of the 17th International Society for Music Information Retrieval Conference, 2016.
23. Byrd and Crawford, "Problems of Music Information Retrieval in the Real World." See also Creager et al., "Nonnegative Tensor Factorization with Frequency Modulation Cues for Blind Audio Source Separation," 211–217.
24. The British invasion musicals are largely considered Broadway musicals in the USA, as they have influenced the current expectation of the Broadway sound. However, to be more focused in the study of "American" sound, this article limits "Broadway musicals" to only "US Broadway musicals."
25. Schenkerian analysis is an approach of music analysis of tonal music based on writings of music theorist Heinrich Schenker (1868–1935). A Schenkerian analysis of a passage of music shows the underlying structure of that passage.
26. Engel, *The American Musical Theater*, 77–131, and Laird, "Musical Styles and Song Conventions," 33–44.
27. See Viagas, http://www.playbill.com/article/long-runs-on-broadway-com-109864.
28. See https://www.broadway.org/broadway-shows-international.
29. Jensen, "The New Renaissance is in Our Hands," 51.
30. Tredinnick, *Digital Information Culture*, 106.
31. See "Sources of Attention," Altmetric, altmetric.com/about-our-data/our-sources.
32. See "Stats Report," Asian American Performers Action Coalition, http://www.aapacnyc.org/stats-2014-2015.html.
33. Marks, "George C. Wolfe: A Theater Man on a Mission to Do a Forgotten Show Justice."
34. McNulty, "How 'Shuffle Along' Director George C. Wolfe Brought Back the 1921 Show that Changed Broadway Forever."
35. Feldberg, "Famed director George C. Wolfe betting on his hybrid production of 'Shuffle Along'."
36. Marks, "George C. Wolfe: A Theater Man on a Mission to Do a Forgotten Show Justice."
37. See 'US Census Bureau Projections Show a Slower Growing, Older, More Diverse Nation a Half Century from Now,' United States Census Bureau.

https://www.census.gov/newsroom/releases/archives/population/cb12-243.html.
38. Johnson, "Undiscovered Bach? No, a Computer Wrote It."
39. Cavendish, "Computer Says So-so."
40. Souppouris, "The First 'Computer-Generated' Musical Isn't Very Good."
41. Pringle, "Beyond The Fence: How Computers Spawned a Musical."

Bibliography

Asian American Performers Action Coalition. 2016. Stats Report, 2014–15. http://www.aapacnyc.org/stats-2014-2015.html. Accessed September 18, 2016.

Beyond the Fence Tickets. 2016. London Theatre Direct. https://www.londontheatredirect.com/musical/2212/beyond-the-fence-tickets.aspx. Accessed October 21, 2016.

Black, Stuart. 2016. "Computer-Penned Musical Beyond the Fence Reviewed." http://londonist.com/2016/02/computer-penned-musical-beyond-the-fence-reviewed. February 29. Accessed September 16, 2016.

Brown, Mark. 2015. "World's First Computer-Generated Musical to Debut in London." *The Guardian*, December 1. https://www.theguardian.com/stage/2015/dec/01/beyond-the-fence-computer-generated-musical-greenham-common. Accessed September 21, 2016.

Byrd, D., & Crawford, T. 2002. "Problems of Music Information Retrieval in the Real World." *Information Processing & Management*, 38, 249–272.

Cavendish, Dominic. 2016. "Beyond the Fence, Arts Theatre, Review: 'Computer Says So-so'." *The Telegraph*, February 27. http://www.telegraph.co.uk/theatre/what-to-see/beyond-the-fence-arts-theatre-review-computer-says-so-so/. Accessed August 14, 2016.

Colton, Simon. 2016. "Beyond the Fence: The First West End Musical Conceived and Crafted by Computer." *MetaMakers Institute*, February 22. http://metamakersinstitute.com/2016/02/22/beyond-the-fence/. Accessed August 12, 2016.

Downie, J. Stephen. 2003. Music Information Retrieval. *Annual Review of Information Science and Technology* 37. Edited by Blaise Cronin, 295-340. Medford, NJ: Information Today.

Engel, Lehmann. 1975. *American Musical Theater*. New York: Macmillan.

Feldberg, Robert. 2016. Famed director George C. Wolfe betting on his hybrid production of "Shuffle Along." *North Jersey*, March 20. http://www.northjersey.com/arts-and-entertainment/theater/imagining-a-landmark-s-origins-1.1530610. Accessed September 14, 2016.

Hirtle, Peter B., Emily Hudson, and Andrew T. Kenyon. 2009. *Copyright and Cultural Institutions: Guidelines for Digitization for US Libraries, Archives, and Museums*. Ithaca, NY: Cornell University Library.

Huron, David. 2002. Music Information Processing Using the Humdrum Toolkit: Concepts, Examples, and Lessons. *Computer Music Journal* (26) no. 2, 11–26.

Jensen, Rolf. 2013. The New Renaissance is in Our Hands. *The Futurist*, September-October 2013, 51–55.

Johnson, George. 1997. Undiscovered Bach? No, a Computer Wrote it. *New York Times*, November 11.

Laird, Paul. 2011. Musical Styles and Song Conventions. In *The Oxford Handbook of the American Musical*, eds. Raymond Knapp, Mitchell Morris, and Stacy Wolf, 33–44. New York: Oxford University Press.

Marks, Peter. 2016. George C. Wolfe: A Theater Man on a Mission to Do a Forgotten Show Justice. *The Washington Post*, April 15. https://www.washingtonpost.com/entertainment/theater_dance/george-c-wolfe-a-theater-man-on-a-mission-to-do-a-forgotten-show-justice/2016/04/13/d8d02804-00ce-11e6-9203-7b8670959b88_story.html. Accessed September 12, 2016.

McNulty, Charles. 2016. How "Shuffle Along" Director George C. Wolfe Brought Back the 1921 Show that Changed Broadway Forever. *Los Angeles Times*, April 25. http://www.latimes.com/entertainment/arts/theater/la-et-cm-george-wolfe-20160425-column.html. Accessed September 12, 2016.

Pringle, Stewart. 2016. Beyond The Fence: How Computers Spawned a Musical. *New Scientist*, March 3. https://www.newscientist.com/article/2079483-beyond-the-fence-how-computers-spawned-a-musical/. Accessed August 14, 2016.

Proceedings of the 17th International Society for Music Information Retrieval Conference, 2016.http://dblp.uni-trier.de/db/conf/ismir/ismir2016.html. Accessed August 8, 2016.

Seymour, Lee. 2016. Why Broadway Is So White, Part 2 - A Change Is Gonna Come (Maybe). *Forbes*, April 20. http://www.forbes.com/sites/leeseymour/2016/04/20/why-broadway-is-so-white-part-2-a-change-is-gonna-come-maybe/#45c5208068a1. Accessed August 25, 2016.

Souppouris, Aaron. 2016. The First "Computer-Generated" Musical Isn't Very Good. *Engadget*, March 2. https://www.engadget.com/2016/03/02/beyond-the-fence-computer-generated-musical/. Accessed Sep 12, 2016.

Tredinnick, Luke. 2008. *Digital Information Culture*. Oxford, UK: Chandos Publishing.

US Census Bureau. 2012. Projections Show a Slower Growing, Older, More Diverse Nation a Half Century from Now. https://www.census.gov/newsroom/releases/archives/population/cb12-243.html. Accessed February 10, 2013.

Viagas, Robert. 2016. Long Runs on Broadway. Playbill Online. http://www.playbill.com/article/long-runs-on-broadway-com-109864. Accessed September 16, 2016.

Williams, Holly. 2016. "Beyond the Fence, Arts Theatre, Review: Despite my reservations I was won over." *Independent*, February 27. http://www.independent.co.uk/arts-entertainment/theatre-dance/reviews/beyond-the-fence-arts-theatre-review-despite-my-reservations-i-was-won-over-a6900836.html. Accessed September 16, 2016.

Databases and Online Gateways

The "What-If Machine": whim-project.eu
New York Philharmonic Digital Archive: archives.nyphil.org/index.php
New York Philharmonic Github: github.com/nyphilarchive/PerformanceHistory
Online Chopin Variorum Edition: chopinonline.ac.uk/ocve
The Juilliard Manuscript Collection: juilliardmanuscriptcollection.org
Online Resources for Music Scholars: hcl.harvard.edu/research/guides/onmusic
Digital Resources for Musicology: drm.ccarh.org
Humdrum Toolkit: humdrum.org
music21 Toolkit: web.mit.edu/music21/
Music Imaging Technologies: musitek.com
Essentia: essentia.upf.edu
Playbill Online: playbill.com
Internet Broadway Database: ibdb.com
Web of Science: apps.webofknowledge.com
Scopus: scopus.com
Broadway League: broadway.org
Altmetric: altmetric.com
Mendeley: mendeley.com
Pubpeer: pubpeer.com
Publons: publons.com
The Open Syllabus Project: opensyllabusproject.org

CHAPTER 13

Rise Again Digitally: Musical Revivals and Digital Dramaturgy on Broadway

Bryan M. Vandevender

Since the early 1990s, musical revivals have been one of the most popular and pervasive theatrical entertainments on the Great White Way. Broadway producers, in an attempt to draw audiences through appeals to nostalgia and the promise of time-tested fare, routinely mount new productions of previously successful musicals. In doing so, they provide theatregoers with the opportunity to encounter (or perhaps reencounter) some of the most celebrated works of the musical theatre canon. Larry Stempel, author of *Showtime: A History of the Broadway Musical Theater*, contends that prevalence of revivals on Broadway evinces the significance of certain musical properties. As he states, "the current trend goes beyond the perennial exercises in caution of audiences choosing a show on name recognition, or producers investing in a safe bet. It rests also on the cultural capital that has accrued to a certain repertoire of musicals in the recent past."[1] The repertoire to which Stempel refers—that collection of musicals that have enjoyed a healthy afterlife on Broadway—is composed chiefly of landmark properties from the Golden Age of Musical Theatre whose value presumably correlates to the manner

---

B.M. Vandevender (✉)
Department of Theatre and Dance, Bucknell University,
Lewisburg, PA, USA
e-mail: bryan.vandevender@bucknell.edu

© The Author(s) 2017
J. Hillman-McCord (ed.), *iBroadway*,
DOI 10.1007/978-3-319-64876-7_13

in which the musicals first penetrated and remained within the American cultural zeitgeist. Such estimable works as *Oklahoma!* (1943), *Carousel* (1945), *Guys and Dolls* (1950), *West Side Story* (1957), *Gypsy* (1959), *Fiddler on the Roof* (1964), and *Man of La Mancha* (1965) became emblems of their era and garnered widespread attention for their libretti, scores, stars, and authors. As musicals have become less culturally pervasive in the post-Golden Age era, the cultural capital ascribed to these same works today appears to be located in both their earlier acclaim and their capacity for endurance. A given musical's ability to retain its relevance and audience appeal despite age and the continuous passage of time assumedly increases its suitability for revival—a presumption that might explain why certain canonized properties (such as those mentioned above) routinely receive new Broadway productions.

While certain musicals have demonstrated an abiding mettle or vitality over the course of decades, they are also products of the historical moment that first produced them. Musicals are aesthetic artifacts that reflect the prevailing musical idioms, choreographic modes, and dramaturgical methods of their original era. They are social documents that depict the dominant discourses and reigning values of the cultural moment from which they first emerged. Consequently, all musicals—no matter how abiding—are bound to their past in some manner. As time passes, the divide that separates a musical's original era and the present grows increasingly larger. This temporal chasm might prove inconsequential to audience members with prior knowledge of a given work or a highly developed historical imagination; however, it threatens to prevent less informed spectators from fully appreciating or engaging with the revived musical. To this end, musicologist Bruce Kirle contends the reception of a musical in later years necessarily rests on an understanding of the material conditions that informed its creation due to the fact that "historical context not only influenced the texts of these musicals, but also helped shape the way these productions were performed and received by their audiences."[2] Herein lies a paradox that underpins the project of revival. Musicals chosen for revival because of their alleged endurance will always bear ties to the past that carry the potential to erode a property's cultural intelligibility in the present.

The task of orienting spectators to the world of a play or musical often falls under the purview of theatre critics (as Bud Coleman discusses in the next chapter of this book) and production dramaturgs. Following a model outlined in the eighteenth century by Gotthold Ephraim Lessing, the widely acknowledged progenitor of professional dramaturgy, dramaturgs frequently function as educators for the theatergoing public and provide information that will familiarize patrons with both the historical moment that a given play depicts and the historical moment from which it first emerged—outlining the assumptions, anxieties, social mores, codes of conduct, vernacular, and major events that characterized the eras in question.[3] Dramaturgs also customarily offer an assessment of the play's aesthetic merits, a summary of its production history and extant criticism, biographies of its primary authors, and any other knowledge that might help to increase a viewer's ability to comprehend the intricacies of a production. The methods used to disseminate this information vary widely and range from the creation of lobby displays, program notes, and study guides, to the organization of audience forums and community outreach events. Patrons who consume dramaturgical content (regardless of the specific form it takes) become better acquainted with a play and its era, and theoretically, better prepared to regard the play in performance. Consequently, the instructive function of dramaturgy carries the potential to aid the overall project of revival. In educating theatregoers, works of the past become more comprehensible, and thereby more viable in the current day.

While the presentation of dramaturgical research is often a rarity on the Great White Way, two producers of Broadway revivals have demonstrated a longstanding commitment to education by sharing their dramaturgy and instructional content through many of the means outlined above. In recent years, however, these companies have expanded their methods of audience engagement in a concerted effort to fully participate in our rapidly expanding digital culture. As a result, their dramaturgical content is also made available to audiences by way of the Internet. Roundabout Theatre Company (RTC) and Lincoln Center Theater (LCT) maintain online blogs that allow potential patrons to learn about the plays that they produce and the research that informs their productions. During the 2014–2015 Broadway season, both organizations produced revivals of notable musicals and presented dramaturgical content in relation to the musicals on these websites. The works in question provided Broadway audiences with two distinctly different experiences of revival. RTC's chosen musical—Cy Coleman, Betty Comden, Adolph Green's *On the Twentieth Century* (1978)—presented the organization with the opportunity to reintroduce theatregoers to an award-winning musical that had not received a full Broadway production since its premiere over three decades earlier. Conversely, LCT's revival of *The King and I* (1951) served to broaden audience knowledge of a much-celebrated Rodgers and Hammerstein classic. The blogs curated for these revivals offer insight into how theatre companies engage with audiences in the digital age and the manner in which they prepare spectators to regard past musicals in the present day. They also demonstrate remarkable new opportunities for teaching and learning that previous methods of dramaturgical display had not been able to afford. In utilizing web-based platforms to present dramaturgical content, RTC and LCT have arguably revolutionized the project of revival by demonstrating that musicals of the past need not languish in the past. Educating spectators by way of the Internet allows these erstwhile works to rise again digitally.

The role of the dramaturg and the function of dramaturgy in contemporary theatre practice are multifaceted and necessarily change given the idiosyncrasies of a particular play. Even so, Michael Mark Chemers, author of *Ghost Light: An Introductory Handbook for Dramaturgy*, cites the collection and application of knowledge that will allow theatre artists to transform a play into a performance "that makes sense to a living audience at this time in this place" as fundamental to all dramaturgical enterprise.[4] Dramaturgs might assist the play's authors (playwright, composer, or lyricist) as they craft a script or score. They might also serve the director, designers, and actors as they prepare the play for production. This chapter focuses expressly on dramaturgy as it educates audiences and aids in their reception of a play. Moreover, the term digital dramaturgy, as it appears throughout this chapter, refers to information or educational content that theatre companies curate and make available to patrons through online platforms. It is worth noting that some of the individuals interviewed for this chapter are not trained or self-identified dramaturgs. However, the educative function of their work fits within the model of dramaturgy outlined by Lessing and Chemers.

Roundabout Theatre Company and *On the Twentieth Century*[5]

From its founding in 1965, the not-for-profit RTC has maintained a mission to restage classic plays and musicals for contemporary audiences. The company's operation of five theatre spaces, its presentation of seven to ten productions each season, and its subscriber base of

46,000 members make RTC one of the leading producers of revivals on Broadway. Artistic Director and CEO Todd Haimes claims that the company regularly revives works that would not normally receive a commercial production on Broadway due to their age or lack of name recognition.[6] Consequently, the company holds the distinction of mounting the first Broadway revivals of such musicals as *She Loves Me* (1993), *Company* (1995), *1776* (1997), *Follies* (2001), *The Boys from Syracuse* (2002), *Nine* (2003), *Pacific Overtures* (2004), *The Apple Tree* (2006), *110 in the Shade* (2007), *Sunday in the Park with George* (2008), and *The Mystery of Edwin Drood* (2012). While perennial favorites such as *The Pajama Game* (2005), *Pal Joey* (2008), *Bye Bye Birdie* (2009), and *Anything Goes* (2011) are occasionally included in a season's offerings, the company remains committed to restaging properties that exist outside Broadway's usual revival repertoire.

According to Ted Sod, the company's Education Dramaturg, a significant percentage of RTC subscribers represent baby boomers and several of the company's efforts to familiarize theatregoers with a play or musical's historical context cater to this population's desire for embodied exchange that occurs in real time.[7] To this end, RTC's Education Department installs dramaturgical displays in the lobby of each theatre for patrons to peruse prior to a performance. The department also hosts a series of audience outreach events as part of its Theatre Plus program, a company initiative since the 1990s that invites subscribers to interface with RTC company members and teaching artists, as well as distinguished theatre scholars, cultural historians, musicologists, and critics. Offering attendees an opportunity to broaden their knowledge about a given play (its authors, historical setting, production history, and major themes) or to learn more about the process of staging a revival, Theatre Plus functions regularly take the form of dramaturgical presentations, panel discussions, lectures, interviews, and post-performance forums. Additionally, RTC's Education and Artistic Departments publish dramaturgical content for every RTC production in its *Upstage Guide*. A key component of the company's many education programs, the publication is prepared for audience members of all ages, including high school students who attend RTC revivals. Each guide contains short articles related to the company's dramaturgical research, as well as a glossary of terms and concepts, a production history for the revived play, artist statements from the production's designers, lesson plans for teachers, and a complete bibliography.

Much of the dramaturgical content published in *Upstage Guide* and displayed in the lobby of RTC theatres is also featured on the company's online blog. Launched in 2008 as an extension of RTC's official website, the blog was first utilized as an instrument for online marketing. Its content generally consisted of casting announcements, production photos, critics' reviews, notices of upcoming special events, and statements from the company's Artistic Director and CEO, Todd Haimes. In the years that immediately followed, the blog became a platform for displaying artifacts from RTC's growing archive, such as costumes, masks, scenic renderings, prompt books, and posters. It also provided the Education Department with the opportunity to publish select *Upstage Guide* articles on the web. Sod claims that the company's choice to publish dramaturgical content online was originally rooted in an attempt to diversify their subscriber base and present educational materials related to RTC productions in a manner that might reach millennials. The expanding literature on adolescents in the digital age suggests that this web-based appeal to young theatregoers was shrewd due to their reliance on the Internet as a primary (and often only) source for obtaining information. Scholars John Palfrey and Urs Gasser refer to millennials as "digital natives"—a term that describes their immersion in digital technologies since birth—and contend that this generational cohort turns to digital platforms before consulting any other informational source. In *Born Digital: Understanding the First Generation of Digital Natives*, they contrast millennial approaches to information gathering with those utilized by previous generations: "Research once meant a trip to a library to paw through a musty card catalog and puzzle over the Dewey Decimal System to find a book to pull off the shelves. Now, research means a Google search—and, for most, a visit to Wikipedia before diving deeper into a topic. They simply open a browser, punch in a search term, and dive away until they find what they want—or what they thought they wanted."[8] RTC's continued use of the web then reflects the company's intention not only to include millennials in their audience engagement efforts, but also to commit to instructing theatregoers regardless of their generational affiliation. As Sod states: "We try to educate our audiences no matter what age they are and we try to offer information in a variety of mediums so that [patrons] can choose what is right for them. Millennials tend to gravitate to the Internet when they are looking for information about a production. If we're doing our job right, then our blog is one of the first sites they will find."[9] Because RTC's repertoire routinely includes works that might be unknown to younger audiences, the company's blog represents more than an instrument for cultivating a web-savvy millennial audience. It functions as a compelling tool that is uniquely suited for educating a new generation of theatregoers.

The most recurrent information that RTC prepares for its audience guide and online blog concerns genre. The company's repertory represents a wide array of periods and styles including, but not limited to Restoration comedy, kitchen sink realism, Modernist drama, Absurdism, and the Golden Age Musical. Because the conventions of these genres might appear foreign to some spectators, members of the Education and Artistic Departments compose short articles that describe the disposition of a given performance mode and explicate the defining characteristics for which it is known. These essays tend to be brief, illustrative, and composed in a vernacular appropriate for high school readers. As *On the Twentieth Century* represents the melding of two distinctly different genres, the Education and Artistic Departments prepared articles on both of the musical's stylistic influences: American operetta and screwball comedy. These articles would presumably play a decisive role in younger theatregoers' reception of the musical, as both performance traditions have been relatively absent from American popular culture for decades. In order to familiarize readers with *On the Twentieth Century*'s stylistic singularity, the entries outlined the genesis and forebears of both genres, enumerated their major tenets, and remarked on their major works. The article addressing American operetta worked to situate Cy Coleman's score to *On the Twentieth Century* within a tradition of such early American operettas as Rudolf Friml's *Rose-Marie* (1924) and Sigmund Romberg's *The Desert Song* (1926). Similarly, the major conventions of screwball comedy—physical comedy and slapstick, mistaken identity, improbable plot twists, mockery of religious fanaticism, class conflict, sexual innuendo, and a war of the sexes waged between a mismatched couple—were elucidated through a discussion of the Hays Code and the films that helped to satiate Depression era audience's thirst for humor, including Frank Capra's *It Happened One Night* (1934), Howard Hawks' *Bringing Up Baby* (1938), and Preston Sturges' *The Lady Eve* (1941).

While these articles aim to illuminate the complexities of two distinct genres concisely and descriptively, their efficacy in print is arguably limited due to the fact that operetta and screwball comedy are modes of performance best discerned through spectatorship. The essays as published for RTC's online blog, however, prove to be remarkably dynamic as they provide opportunities for uninformed readers to observe exemplars of both genres in performance. Each blog entry contains embedded audio and video files that allow users to stream clips of the representative works mentioned above. Consequently, visitors to the site are able to supplement their reading by listening to Jeanette MacDonald sing "Indian Love Call" from the 1936 film adaptation of *Rose-Marie* and observing the comic timing utilized by the preeminent stars of screwball comedy: Cary Grant, Katharine Hepburn, Clark Gable, Claudette Colbert, Henry Fonda, and Barbara Stanwyck. In addition to streaming media, the web edition of these articles include links to the Internet Movie Database and Encyclopedia Britannica Online that supply users with additional information about the actors, directors, composers, titles, events, and terminology mentioned in the essays.

Hyperlinks are a prominent feature of RTC's blog and used to similar effect in most all of the entries relating to *On the Twentieth Century*. Embedded within an article's text, these links direct readers to a wide array of secondary websites—sites external to RTC's official domain—and grant immediate access to supplementary information on a given topic, thereby expanding a user's knowledge of the subject almost instantly. As a single blog entry can contain anywhere from ten to fifty hyperlinks, each article then functions as a discrete wellspring of concentrated knowledge. An article on the cultural prominence of train travel in the 1920s and 1930s, for example, presents a brief history of the Twentieth Century Limited, the luxury steam locomotive which serves as the primary setting for *On the Twentieth Century*'s main action, while a smattering of strategically placed hyperlinks provide readers with access to websites addressing the history of New York City's Grand Central Station and the advent of the Pullman car. Other links lead users to biographical profiles for some of the train's most famous passengers (Marshall Fields, Walter Chrysler, and William Wrigley Jr.) as well as websites that display primary resources and archival documents, such as original reviews of the Twentieth Century Limited published by *The New York Times*, *New York Herald Tribune*, and *Time* in 1938.

The presence of these hyperlinks allows readers to engage in a continuous and immediate process of discovery not afforded by more traditional forms of dramaturgical display. Because of the web's expansive and expeditious nature, users who visit the connected websites extend their learning in a manner that is faster and more immersive than reading program notes or perusing lobby installations. The inclusion of hyperlinks within blog entries, however, does not ensure that readers will search for information beyond the confines of RTC's official website. Visitors to the blog can elect to merely scan a given article's text, and in so doing, replicate the experience of perusing a print copy of *Upstage Guide*. Nevertheless, hyperlinks present readers with the option to continue their acquisition of knowledge, thereby empowering them to design their own highly individualized process of information gathering. The agency afforded by hyperlinks not only aligns with the ethos of digital natives, but also fulfills one of their foremost desires. In *Grown Up Digital: How the Net Generation Is Changing Your World*, Don Tapscott suggests that millennials value choice above all else and frequently view the Internet as an instrument uniquely designed for the purpose of exercising their presumed freedom.[10] Furthermore, Douglas J. Loveless and Bryant Griffith argue that hyperlinks do not merely endow readers with choice, but rather prompt a more thoughtful engagement with written materials, encourage synthesis, and arouse discernment: "Readers of hypertext do not read passively; instead they actively search information, make connections between various forms of text, and develop understandings across an array of sources … this empowerment comes from the capability of readers to follow multiple hyperlinks to multiple texts based on readers' interests and needs."[11] The appreciable benefits of hyperlinks—speed, absorption, freedom, and the simulation of higher order thinking—certifies that readers of RTC's online blog who travel across the web by way of hyperlinks actively participate in a process of discovery that passive blog readers and devotees of traditional dramaturgical consumption do not.

In addition to articles addressing questions of genre and historical context, the RTC blog regularly publishes profiles of the artists associated with a revived play or musical's creation. In the case of musical revivals, Ted Sod customarily interviews any living members of the property's authorial cohort. The transcripts of these conversations appear in both *Upstage Guide* and on the RTC blog. Consequently, readers of the dramaturgical content prepared for RTC's productions of *Cabaret*, *The Mystery of Edwin Drood*, *Bye Bye Birdie*, and *110 in the Shade* have received insights into the conception and development of the musicals from the likes of John Kander, Joe Masteroff, Rupert Holmes, Charles Strouse, Lee Adams, and Tom Jones. A different approach to addressing authorship, however, was utilized for the content relating to *On the Twentieth Century*. The Education and Artistic Departments composed an article on the music and career of the musical's composer, Cy Coleman. As published on the RTC blog, the essay includes hyperlinks to Playbill's online archive, *Playbill Vault*, that provide readers with access to cast information, songs, videos, and production photos for several of Coleman's other Broadway musicals, including *Wildcat* (1960), *Little Me* (1962), *Sweet Charity* (1966), *Seesaw* (1973), *I Love My Wife* (1977), *Barnum* (1980), *City of Angels* (1990), *The Will Rogers Follies* (1991), and *The Life* (1997). Users who were previously unacquainted with Coleman's oeuvre are able to learn more about his musicals in performance and discover his melodic sensibility through representative samples of his songs. Attending to the musical's librettist and lyricist team, Betty Comden and Adolph Green, Sod published an interview with Amanda Green, daughter of Adolph Green and the lyricist for such Broadway musicals as *High Fidelity* (2006), *Bring It On* (2012), and *Hands on a Hardbody* (2013). In her conversation with Sod, Green specifically addressed the legacy of her father's partnership with Comden, her recollections of their writing process, her memories of the original Broadway production of *On the Twentieth Century*, and her participation in the RTC revival, which involved the penning of new lyrics for the musical's eleven o'clock number, "Because of Her."

Along with his interview of Green, Sod published the transcripts of his discussions with three other figures associated with the revival—director Scott Ellis and headlining stars Kristin Chenoweth and Peter Gallagher. Sod's interviews with RTC artists are a hallmark of both *Upstage Guide* and the RTC blog. Because the transcripts are reproduced for a predominantly teenaged readership, Sod tends to pose questions pertaining to the subjects of education and creative process. As a result, interview participants often recount their training, the early years of their careers, the manner in which they approach their work, and some of the specific artistic choices they made for the RTC revival on which they have collaborated. In the interviews pertaining to *On the Twentieth Century*, Chenoweth, Gallagher, and Green offered their personal analyses of the musical's central conflict and relationships, as well as advice to young musical theatre enthusiasts who are considering a career in the professional theatre.

While many of the entries published on the RTC blog encourages users to deepen their knowledge of a given play using the Internet, another featured article entreats them to pursue a more immersive experience away from the web. A recurring series entitled "Read/Watch/

Do" presents readers with an extensive list of print reading materials and educational media that they might consult for additional information about a given production's historical setting, subject matter, or principal themes. Compiled by one of the company's Artistic Associates, the lists frequently contain links to retail websites where users can purchase books and documentary films. For *On the Twentieth Century*, former Artistic Associate Olivia O'Connor directed readers to Amazon.com and encouraged them to obtain a print copy of Ben Hecht and Charles MacArthur's *Twentieth Century*, the 1932 play that served as the inspiration for *On the Twentieth Century*, as well as such reference texts as Ethan Mordden's *The Hollywood Studios*, Thomas Schatz's *The Genius of the System: Hollywood Filmmaking in the Studio Era*, and Peter T. Maiken's *Night Trains: The Pullman System in the Golden Years of American Rail Travel*. The list also included links to Turner Classic Movies Online and The Criterion Collection Online where users can peruse and procure assorted screwball comedies of the 1930s for home viewing. The most novel feature of "Read/Watch/Do" blog posts, however, is a catalogue of suggestions for live endeavors and embodied educational encounters that require users to step away from the web and disconnect from digital platforms. These lists enumerate a play's cultural references and include hyperlinks to information about novels, songs, public figures, landmarks, recipes, and colloquialisms mentioned in the text. These hyperlinks invite readers to enter the world of the play's action and create a corporeal experience that might have been shared by its characters. In reading period literature, learning and singing songs of the day, preparing and consuming the era's popular dishes, and giving voice to its vernacular, users resurrect some of the material trappings of a revived play's zeitgeist and enhance their knowledge of the past through experiential learning. Readers can experiment with most of the aforementioned activities in the privacy of their homes, but the blog posts also entreat them to consider the educational opportunities that exist throughout Manhattan and the outer boroughs of New York City. Readers of the article for *On the Twentieth Century* are directed to the official websites of New York City's Transit Museum and the Classic Film Tour hosted by Turner Classic Movies. The first of these attractions invites participants to investigate the Golden Age of train travel by surveying related artifacts and archival material, while the second transports them to an array of Manhattan locations famously represented in films from the 1930s to the present. For a more consuming experience, O'Connor published a link to Pullman Rail Journeys, a transportation service that provides passengers with the opportunity to travel from New York City's Penn Station to such destinations as Chicago, New Orleans, and Albuquerque in carefully restored mid-century Pullman cars, reminiscent of those utilized by the Twentieth Century Limited. The embodied nature of these learning experiences may not reflect the values or predilections of digital natives; however, the encounters themselves presumably aid in the expansion of a participant's historical imagination. These individuals, having been acquainted with the materiality of past eras, are presumably better prepared to appreciate the historicity of a revived property than the casual blog reader.

In the case of all of the dramaturgical articles published on RTC's blog, the Internet functions as more than a platform for displaying content. The articles' recurrent use of hyperlinks and embedded media suggests that the Internet is always an instrument for further research and discovery. As hosted by RTC's official website, the blog then functions as an informational hub that introduces readers to a given musical—its historical context, genre, and authors—and then provides them with the guidance and tools needed for locating additional information and resources. As a result, the process of familiarizing audiences with the past—work that is vitally important to the project of revival—is presumably made faster, more productive, more extensive, and more compelling to digital age audiences.

LINCOLN CENTER THEATER AND *THE KING AND I*[12]

LCT, established in 1985, produces dozens of plays and musicals each season in its three performance spaces located within Manhattan's Lincoln Center for the Performing Arts. While the company does not necessarily preserve a mission to produce revivals, LCT frequently stages notable works of the past in productions helmed by some of the most distinguished artists working in the professional theatre. The company's repertory includes the plays of William Shakespeare, Richard Brinsley Sheridan, Anton Chekhov, Lillian Hellman, Eugene O'Neill, Clifford Odets, Thornton Wilder, Arthur Miller, and Edward Albee. Revivals of musicals have been less of a fixture in LCT's production history as the organization has spent considerable time developing and producing new works of musical theatre. Since its founding, LCT has presented over twenty original musicals including *Sarafina!* (1988), *My*

Favorite Year (1992), *Hello Again* (1993), *A New Brain* (1998), *It Ain't Nothin' But the Blues* (1999), *Parade* (1999), *Contact* (1999), *The Light in the Piazza* (2005), and *Women on the Verge of a Nervous Breakdown* (2011). The illustrious cohort of composers and lyricists whose work has premiered on LCT stages includes Stephen Flaherty and Lynn Ahrens, Michael John LaChiusa, William Finn, Jason Robert Brown, Adam Guettel, Scott Frankel and Michael Korie, David Yazbek, and Harry Connick Jr. Despite this concentration on new works, LCT has staged notable revivals of *Anything Goes* (1987) and *The Most Happy Fella* (1992). The organization has also maintained a productive partnership with Rodgers and Hammerstein: An Imagem Company (formerly the Rodgers and Hammerstein Organization) that resulted in highly acclaimed revivals of *Carousel* (1994) and *South Pacific* (2008) staged in the company's Broadway house, the Vivian Beaumont Theater.

According to Anne Cattaneo, LCT's Resident Dramaturg, the dramaturgical research collected for LCT productions is intended to serve artists through the rehearsal process and is not customarily shared with audiences. As she states: "The best dramaturgy is invisible. You should be able to detect the research in the production itself."[13] Even so, the organization has employed a variety of strategies to educate their patrons over the years. All of these methods are aimed at providing contextual information about a given production and represent an attempt to exploit the appeal of numerous media. Telecasts, print publications, and audio recordings allow the organization to reach not only its 30,000 members, but also theatregoers across the nation. A teacher resource manual is prepared for the organization's Open Stages Program, an educational initiative that brings over 3500 New York City high school students to LCT productions each season. This guide includes short essays addressing the play's historical and geographic settings, cultural zeitgeist, authors, and genre, as well as suggestions for classroom activities and an extensive bibliography of books, films, and websites. A second publication titled *Lincoln Center Theater Review* (*LCT Review*) is intended for a more mature readership and resembles a literary journal in that the collected articles aim to situate a given play within the context of recurring cultural dialogues or a protracted historical narrative. Contributors include cultural historians, anthropologists, literary critics, novelists, poets, playwrights, journalists, and other public intellectuals. Founded in 1987 by playwright John Guare, the publication maintains a mission to serve select LCT productions by printing content that supports and subtly expands a director's interpretation of the play, provides historical context, and indicates avenues for discussion.[14] Consequently, the magazine features essays, interviews, memoirs, and poems that mediate on a play's principal themes, the historical events it depicts, the era in which it was written, its authorship, its production history, and its relevance in the present day. Guare also contends that the magazine "should function as an ideal [theatergoing] companion. It should give you things that you can talk about at dinner after seeing the show, as well as articles and visual material that you'll want to go back to days later."[15] As of this writing, *LCT Review* is edited by Alexis Gargagliano with Guare and Cattaneo serving as Co-Executive Editors. Of the sixty-seven issues published to date, the magazine has featured the words and thoughts of such notable luminaries as Margaret Atwood, W. H. Auden, Mikhail Barysnikov, Eric Bentley, Robert Brustein, Gwendolyn Brooks, Harold Clurman, Emily Dickinson, Dave Eggers, Henry Louis Gates Jr., Charlotte Perkins Gilman, Elia Kazan, Steve Martin, Toni Morrison, Sarah Ruhl, Stephen Sondheim, Paula Vogel, Alice Walker, Wendy Wasserstein, and E. B. White. While *LCT Review* is prepared as a print publication and made available to LCT patrons before the start of a performance, visitors to the company's official website can access the magazine prior to their arrival at the theatre. The current issue, along with the publication's entire back catalogue, appear on the website as portable document format (PDF) files that users can download. These digital editions of *LCT Review* are identical to the print copies found in the lobby of LCT theatres.

The edition of *LCT Review* dedicated to *The King and I* featured a wealth of contextual information including an analysis of geopolitical relations and social dictates associated with King Mongkut's rule of Siam in the late nineteenth century, an assessment of Oscar Hammerstein II's adaptation of *Anna and the King of Siam*, an interview with the revival's creative team, and essays addressing the history of female expatriates in Asia and the choreographic processes that Jerome Robbins used to stage "The Small House of Uncle Thomas." The issue also included excerpts from such primary sources as King Mongkut's personal correspondences and Anna Leonowens' memoir, *The English Governess at the Siamese Court*. Moreover, the magazine served to highlight a key aspect of director Bartlett Sher's vision for *The King and I* by addressing global responses to the education of women in the developing world. In his analysis of the musical's libretto, Sher identified Tuptim as an important agent of change and viewed Anna's promise to provide her with an English language edition of *Uncle Tom's Cabin* as a significant gesture that awakens Tuptim's ability to challenge authority and demonstrates the transformative power of learning.[16] *LCT Review* reinforced this evaluation by publishing Pakistani activist Malala Yousafzai's 2014 Nobel Lecture, which passionately advocates for the education of women and girls. Excerpts from *Uncle Tom's Cabin* and assessments of the novel's cultural legacy penned by playwrights Branden Jacobs-Jenkins and Katori Hall also appeared in the publication.

In addition to its use of print materials, LCT employs its online blog as a tool for educating theatregoers. The site was launched in 2006 and intended as an audience resource for LCT's production of Tom Stoppard's *The Coast of Utopia*—a three play cycle depicting thirty years of philosophical debate in nineteenth-century Russia. Linda Mason Ross, Director of Marketing for LCT, reports that the vast scope of the play's action, combined with its reliance on philosophical discourse, warranted the creation of a new mechanism for sharing information with LCT patrons.[17] The popularity of the web content curated for *The Coast of Utopia* motivated the organization to utilize the blog again for its forthcoming revival of *South Pacific* and to keep the site live indefinitely. In its current state, the site features such promotional content as production photos and streaming videos that display performance highlights, rehearsal footage, testimonials from LCT artists, and post-performance audience reactions. It also serves as a host for an ongoing series of essays penned by Brendan Lemon, a critic whose coverage of arts and culture events has appeared in *Financial Times* and *The New Yorker*. Lemon composes articles relative to all current LCT productions on an almost weekly basis. The essays are generally brief, written in a fast-paced journalistic parlance, and routinely chronicle the process of preparing a new production for the LCT stage and the period of its subsequent run.

The critic generally begins a new collection of articles with an examination of a play's authorship and an explanation of LCT's early preparations for the production. As a result, Lemon's coverage of *The King and I* began in October of 2014, six months prior to the revival's official opening and three months in advance of its first rehearsal. His first post included excerpts from Lemon's 2008 interview with the late Mary Rodgers and offered commentary pertaining to the popularity and endurance of Rodgers and Hammerstein properties, while later entries addressed the strategies employed in restoring the score to *The King and*

I, the inspiration for and creation of James McMullan's poster design, and the challenges of orchestration as described by the revival's Music Director, Ted Sperling. Lemon's continuous attention to process granted his readers rare insight into the practices and procedures used by LCT to produce a musical revival. From the first company meeting and read-through to the first preview performance, the critic charted a narrative path toward opening night (and later the Tony Awards) that observed the creation of costumes, the teaching of choreography, the construction of scenery, and the filming of a television commercial. In the months that followed the revival's opening, Lemon continued to compose blog entries on *The King and I* that addressed backstage rituals, the departure and arrival of principal actors, student matinees, understudies, production merchandise, the company's preparations for the annual Gypsy of the Year competition hosted by Broadway Cares/Equity Fights AIDS, and the revival's eventual closing in June 2016.

Lemon asserts that the content of his blog entries changes with each production and is dependent upon two chief factors: whether the play in question is a premiere or a revival, and the degree of access he is granted to a production's rehearsals. With regard to the former, the critic charges that his coverage of a new work generally observes the development of a script while his essays addressing a revival treat a play as a fixed work and instead examine its place within an author's oeuvre, reveal its cultural significance and legacy, and describe the methods that LCT artists are employing to prepare the piece for contemporary audiences. The latter determinant plays a significant role in Lemon's reporting, as one of the blog's chief goals is to document the evolution of a production. LCT directors frequently invite Lemon into their rehearsal rooms and allow the critic to take inspiration for new blog entries from what he observes there. Conversations with directors, actors, and designers addressing the virtues and challenges of a given project also provide fodder for additional articles. As a result, the subjects addressed in the essays vary widely and are often uniquely tied to a given production.[18]

According to Lemon, the rise and proliferation of social media platforms has greatly changed the function of his essays for the LCT blog. In earlier years, the critic's documentation of process was relatively uncommon, as the work conducted in a rehearsal hall or a theatre's backstage was not intended for public consumption. This privacy has waned in more recent years due to the fact that theatre artists frequently share moments of process by way of Twitter, Instagram, Facebook, YouTube, and other digital applications. As Lemon states: "The rehearsal room was once a semi-private space. The backstage of a theatre was once a semi-private space. With the assistance of social media, performers and directors have transformed both of these locations into semi-public spaces."[19] Lemon argues that artists' continued use of social media has only served to excite theatre enthusiasts' and increase their desire for process stories. While digital platforms may have stripped the critic's essays of their original novelty, they have yet to provide their users with the same focus and depth of commentary found in his entries for the LCT blog. In his estimation, interest in behind-the-scenes labor combined with the limitations of certain social media applications made his reporting more vital: "Social media tends to provide short responses or captures of what's going on backstage or in the process of mounting a production, and what it is not very good at is giving context or documenting process in a slightly more nuanced way ... because of its depth, the blog is as valuable as ever."[20] LCT's continuous support of the blog for over a decade suggests that the organization also views the site and its content as beneficial. To that end, LCT advertises the publication of new blog entries via Facebook and Twitter. Internet users who follow LCT on these platforms are able to offer comment on Lemon's articles or share them with a wider audience.

While not trained as a dramaturg, Lemon does aim to educate his readers and periodically composes articles that provide historical context, such as a biographical profile of the real Anna Leonowens that not only outlines how she differed from her stage counterpart, but also identifies a range of novels, films, and works of dramatic literature depicting her life in Siam. Another essay describes the contents of a Playbill for the original Broadway production of *The King and I* and placed its various advertisements within the context of American life in the early 1950s. Anne Cattaneo's dramaturgical research is also periodically referenced in essays that recount the critic's one-on-one discussions with various members of a production's creative team. An article outlining Lemon's conversation with director Bartlett Sher reveals the wealth of the contextual information that informed his interpretive treatment of *The King and I*, including the nature of Thailand's tributary relationships and the history of Western imperialism.

An additional feature of the LCT blog is its growing collection of Platform Podcasts. During the course of a given season, LCT hosts a series of panel discussions with LCT playwrights, directors, actors, and designers titled Platform Talks. These events, held on the Lincoln Center campus, are free and open to the general public; however, limited seating prohibits the organization from admitting all interested attendees. In order to make these conversations available to a wider audience, LCT records each Platform Talk and offers a digital document of the event to blog readers as a streaming podcast. By way of the podcast, listeners learn more about a given production's evolution—the manner in which the assembled artists collaborated, the rationale for their artistic choices, and the research that supported those choices. The Platform Talk organized for *The King and I* featured a conversation with director Bartlett Sher and choreographer Christopher Gattelli, and was moderated by LCT's Associate Producer of Musical Theatre, Ira Weitzman. In response to questions of process, Gattelli recounted his efforts to replicate Jerome Robbins' choreography for "The Small House of Uncle Thomas," and then adapting it for the Vivian Beaumont Theater's thrust stage, while Sher revealed the slight amendments made to the libretto used for the revival (informed by different iterations of the text) and explained his restoration of the frequently-cut second act song, "Western People Funny." He also offered his own appraisal of King Mongkut's behavior by explaining the monarch's fear of impending Western conquest (such as France's colonization of Cambodia) and his motivations for polygamous marriage.

LCT's blog is markedly more self-contained than RTC's blog. The absence of hyperlinks to auxiliary websites indicates that LCT utilizes the Internet as a means of displaying information rather than a springboard for further discovery. Additionally, the content published on LCT's blog differs from the material prepared by RTC in that it tends to privilege the illumination of process rather than the analysis and examination of product. Even so, the site is remarkable in terms of the volume of content it offers readers with each passing week. Lemon's regular essays and the Platform Podcast make the often-invisible work of production development visible—investing blog readers in a performance by revealing the means by which it is made. Furthermore, these forms of media do contain traces of dramaturgical research. Regular readers of the blog receive small doses of contextual information that will inform and ready their reception of an LCT production.

Conclusion

In her article "Digital Dramaturgy and Digital Dramaturgs," LaRonika Thomas charges that the ongoing development of a digital social world will require dramaturgs—the most frequent intermediary between artists and audiences and the theatrical work itself—to employ virtual tools and to work within virtual spaces in order to interest and engage twenty-first-century theatregoers.[21] As digital platforms continue to swell and information continues to materialize in a variety of virtual settings, the methods that theatre companies use to engage and educate audiences will similarly evolve. The gradual expansion of online archives that Doug Reside discusses in Chap. 11 could introduce patrons to primary documents and ephemera—or at least digital proxies—related to a given production at such institutions as the New York Public Library and the Library of Congress. Likewise, the growing abundance of streaming media services could provide audiences with access to research materials that are more performative in nature: recorded theatrical performances, documentary films, sound recordings, and the like. Digital archives and streaming media represent only two dramaturgical tools that theatres might utilize in the digital age. More online instruments will surely surface. While digital dramaturgy efforts in the United States have become increasingly common within the regional theatre landscape, they are still relatively scarce on Broadway where production websites generally serve as a platform for displaying promotional media and selling tickets. The Internet, however, has become a vitally important tool in Broadway publicity and commerce. As other chapters in this volume note, fan communities organize in online spaces and producers routinely turn to web platforms and social media to generate interest in productions. The ubiquity of digital technology within the current Broadway landscape suggests that contemporary theatregoers are uniquely suited to consume dramaturgical content through digital means. The online blogs maintained by RTC and LCT provide readers with immediate access to a diverse array of dramaturgical resources, thereby allowing them to learn more about a play or musical regardless of their proximity to Broadway. With regard to the organizations' musical revivals, the blogs perform the decisive task of familiarizing readers with the revived property. Musical theatre enthusiasts from around the world who frequent these websites are treated to a bounty of information about past works and their present day revivals. Consequently, the organizations and their online blogs provide a model for preserving and, to borrow language from Sissi Liu's chapter on digital musicology, recanonizing musicals of bygone eras. Reviving these musicals on the stage and the web gives the properties a contemporary relevance that make them well suited for stewards of the digital age.

Notes

1. Stempel, *Showtime*, 647.
2. Kirle, *Unfinished Show Business*, xviii.
3. Schechter, "In the Beginning There Was Lessing ... Then Brecht, Müller and Other Dramaturgs," 18.
4. Chemers, *Ghost Light*, 3.
5. A plot synopsis and complete song list for *On The Twentieth Century* can be accessed at http://www.guidetomusicaltheatre.com/shows_o/on_the_twentieth_century.htm.
6. American Theatre Wing, "Downstage Center: Todd Haimes."
7. Ted Sod in conversation with the author, August 2015.
8. Palfrey and Gasser, *Born Digital*, 6.
9. Sod.
10. Tapscott, *Grown Up Digital*, 34.
11. Loveless and Griffith, *Critical Pedagogy for a Polymodal World*, 110.
12. A plot synopsis and complete song list for *The King and I* can be accessed at http://www.guidetomusicaltheatre.com/shows_k/king_and_i.htm.
13. Anne Cattaneo, in conversation with the author, July 2016.
14. Ibid.
15. Quoted in Lemon, "*Lincoln Center Theater Review*: A Celebration."
16. Cattaneo.
17. Linda Mason Ross, in conversation with the author, September 2016.
18. Brendan Lemon, in conversation with the author, September 2016.
19. Ibid.
20. Ibid.
21. Thomas, "Digital Dramaturgy and Digital Dramaturgs," 506.

Bibliography

American Theatre Wing. "Downstage Center: Todd Haimes." Podcast audio. *American Theatre Wing Website*. MP3. Accessed December 22, 2014. http://americantheatrewing.org/downstagecenter/detail/todd_haimes.

Chemers, Michael Mark. *Ghost Light: An Introductory Handbook for Dramaturgy*. Carbondale, IL: Southern Illinois University Press, 2010.

Kirle, Bruce. *Unfinished Show Business: Broadway Musicals as Works-in-Process.* Carbondale, IL: Southern Illinois University Press, 2005.

Lemon, Brendan. *"Lincoln Center Theater Review:* A Celebration." *Lincoln Center Theater Website.* January 6, 2016. http://www.lct.org/explore/blog/lincoln-center-theater-review-celebration/.

Loveless, Douglas J. and Bryant Griffith. *Critical Pedagogy for a Polymodal World.* Rotterdam, NLD: Sense Publishers, 2014.

Palfrey, John and Urs Gasser. *Born Digital: Understanding the First Generation of Digital Natives.* New York: Basic Books, 2008.

Schechter, Joel. "In the Beginning There Was Lessing ... Then Brecht, Müller and Other Dramaturgs," in *Dramaturgy in American Theater: A Source Book*, edited by Susan Jonas, Geoffrey S. Proehl, and Michael Lupu, 16–24. Fort Worth: Harcourt Brace & Company, 1997.

Stempel, Larry. *Showtime: A History of the Broadway Musical Theater.* New York: W.W. Norton and Company, 2008.

Tapscott, Don. *Grown Up Digital: How the Net Generation Is Changing Your World.* New York: McGraw Hill, 2009.

Thomas, LaRonika. "Digital Dramaturgy and Digital Dramaturgs," in *The Routledge Companion to Dramaturgy*, edited by Magda Romanska, 506–511. New York: Routledge, 2015.

CHAPTER 14

The Ever-Evolving World of Twenty-First Century Musical Theatre Criticism

Bud Coleman

"I believe the trade of critic, in literature, music, and drama, is the most degraded of all trades, and has no real value," Mark Twain wrote in an autobiography that was published a century after his death. "However, let it go. It is the will of God that we must have critics and missionaries and Congressmen and humorists. We must bear the burden."[1]

I don't share Mark Twain's disdain of critics as necessary evils. Theatre critics provide a public record of performances, champion artists, and celebrate the art of live performance whether their work appears in print or digitally. Their purpose is to inform theatre lovers, to provoke thought and discussion, and to offer an autonomous assessment of an evanescent experience, for posterity. As noted film critic Pauline Kael reminded readers: "In the arts, the critic is the only independent source of information. The rest is advertising."[2]

B. Coleman (✉)
University of Colorado Boulder, Boulder, CO, USA
e-mail: Bud.Coleman@colorado.edu

© The Author(s) 2017
J. Hillman-McCord (ed.), *iBroadway*,
DOI 10.1007/978-3-319-64876-7_14

Decline of Print Newspapers

As newspapers shrink the size of their newsrooms in the twenty-first century, many professional theatre critics found themselves without a job. For the ten years between 2004 and 2014, newspapers lost $30 billion in advertising revenue. During that same time, online advertisements brought in only $2 billion in revenue, so with a $28 billon shortfall in the industry, staff reductions were unavoidable. The entire workforce of newspapers in the USA has shrunk 39% in the last 20 years.

The portion of US adults who get their news from print newspapers (20%) is less than those who listen to the radio (25%), those who use news websites and apps (28%), and all forms of television (78%). Until circa 2006, however, newspapers outranked radio and the Internet as the public's main source of news.[3] As theatre and/or dance performances are almost never reviewed on the radio or television, arts lovers (and artists) depend on newspapers, magazines, journals, and blogs for news and critiques of the arts. In the UK, *The Independent on Sunday* laid off seven of their arts critics in one go in 2013. The largest monthly dance publication, *Dance Magazine*, put its reviews online before doing away with them entirely in 2013. By 2015, there were only two full-time dance critics left in the USA: Alastair Macaulay of *The New York Times* and Sarah Kaufman of *The Washington Post*. In 2016, *The New York Times* announced it would no longer be covering the art scene outside of its metropolitan area, and *The Boston Globe* gutted its arts section as well. When there is an arts review, it is generally shorter than they used to be: in 2014, *The New York Times* reduced their reviews' length by 20%; they now average 400 words. *The Atlantic*'s Madison Mainwaring estimates that freelance dance critic Joan Acocella "devotes as many words to dance annually as [Arlene] Croce used to on a monthly basis."[4] Deborah Jowitt wrote approximately 1600 words a week in her column in *The Village Voice* (c. 1970–2007). (Depending on font size and formatting, a typed page averages 200 words, so Jowitt was writing the equivalent of eight typed pages a week.) Olaf Jubin's analysis of reviews published in newspapers between 1957 and 2002 confirmed that London reviews became increasingly shorter during this time period.[5]

Just as live theatre, that "Fabulous Invalid," always seems to be on the brink of extinction, so too has theatre criticism been seen as imminently vulnerable. "Criticism is passing, as many of us know, through a difficult phase," S. L. L. Littlewood, president of *The Critics' Circular*, wrote in 1923.

"Its field is becoming more and more restricted. There are fewer papers than there were before the war and less space even in these."[6] If Littlewood thought the situation was dire in 1923, what would he think of the state of affairs in the twenty-first century?

Littlewood would be horrified to learn that in just one year (2007–2008), 25% of American journalists covering the arts were fired.[7] And he certainly would be alarmed to know that the Newspaper Association of America changed its name in 2016 to the News Media Alliance. The fact that the trade organization that has represented newspapers since 1887 decided to remove the name of the media which defined it seems depressingly ironic. While the number of newspapers has shrunk from 2700 in 2008 to roughly 2000 in 2016, Littlewood would be relieved to learn that newspapers are "reaching more people than ever" due to their online platforms.[8]

Much blame is aimed at the Internet for the demise of newspapers. In point of fact, the pressure on newspapers started with the rise of television. With network television, we no longer had to pay for the news we consume. As we became disinclined to pay for our news in print, it became a simple economic reality that print news organizations had to cut staff. And by "paying" I don't just mean buying a subscription for a hard copy or online publication, I also mean theatre companies buying advertising in these platforms. How many arts organizations are you familiar with who complain year after year that they never get any newspaper coverage of their work, yet they never spent a dime on advertising in those publications?

Writing for *The Atlantic*, Madison Mainwaring contends that the decline in the number of professional arts critics is also due to a cultural shift: "Pop culture has superseded high culture as the locus of the critical discussion."[9] Whereas twentieth-century arts editors steered their reviewers to "high art" events, the democratization of the web reveals that more people are interested in food, film, video games, and other forms of pop culture. Pop consumers did not wait for mainline critics and arts editors to change their focus; instead, they started writing their own reviews and tributes on personal blogs and social media.[10]

Former president of the German Society for Theatre Research, Christopher Balme agrees that arts editors and professional critics sowed the seeds of their own demise:

> If theatre criticism's central function is simply recommendation: to see or not to see, or in Peter Brook's phrase, "hounding out incompetence,"

then the arts pages, the feuilleton, oscillate between tipster and professional grump, neither of which resonate much beyond the specialist circle. It is my contention that the theatrical public sphere has become a largely autonomous, even hermetic domain, largely aloof from the public sphere of the wider community and that theatre criticism is complicit in this process of self-isolation.[11]

While there are multiple factors that got us to where we are, locating cause (or blame) does nothing to help restore employment to those who had been full-time arts critics, nor will it improve the quality of reviews.

Responding to the decline of employment by their members, the American Theatre Critics Association, Inc. (ATCA) in 2010 redefined what it meant to be a "professional" theatre critic:

> Membership is open to all who review theatre professionally, regularly and with substance for print, electronic or digital media. ATCA understands "professional" normally to mean you are paid for your reviews and there is some editorial or other supervision of your criticism—e.g., it is not disseminated only on a personal, unsupervised website. But even such websites may qualify you for membership upon further review by the membership committee, considering such measures as substance, reputation and track record. Normally, any applicant must have been a published critic for at least a year.[12]

Faced with hemorrhaging membership, the organization wanted to cling to criteria (being paid and being supervised by an editor) that most published critics in the USA could not meet. Recognizing the tide was against them, ATCA opened the door that membership may be awarded to those non-paid, non-refereed authors. No doubt acknowledging the inevitable elimination of the traditional full-time critic employed by a news organization, Brad Hathaway, Vice-Chair of the ATCA Executive Committee, asked the question in 2015: "Could we be at the end of an era of theatre criticism as a profession?"[13]

The New Yorker's Nathan Heller posed an even broader question in 2016: "What's the point of a reviewer in an age when everyone reviews?"[14] Heller immediately debunks the stance that "critics have essential skills that Blogging Bob does not." But Heller is not willing to turn to Yelp when he wants thoughtful analysis of a film, a book, or the performing arts. Rather he looks for voices who "contribute to a climate in which creative work is taken seriously, and thus dignified as a pursuit."[15] (We'll return to this notion of tone later in this chapter.) Agreeing with film critic A. O. Scott (and others) that "criticism is an art in its own right,"[16] Heller goes on to posit: "What criticism shares with art, in other words, is a particular kind of magic: an exchange through which we transfer our attention and our trust to a different imagination, hoping that [...] another person may begin to speak our minds."[17]

While it is a fact that the number of newspapers and the number of arts reporters shrank in the early twenty-first century, many mourners of this shrinkage never entertain the question: Was theatre criticism—and specifically musical theatre criticism—published prior to the recent economic downturn (c. 2008) of a standard that we would consider "good?" A fascinating study by Olaf Jubin in 2010 contains a content analysis of 1824 reviews published between 1957 and 2002 in the United States, Germany, Austria, and the United Kingdom, concerning the works of Stephen Sondheim and Andrew Lloyd Webber. Jubin's findings were a revelation. Whether we look to reviews to provide a public record and/or to guide theatre lovers to buy a ticket or not, Jubin found that of the American reviews of the works of Webber and Sondheim published between 1957 and 2002, 12.7% contained factual errors. British reviews fared better (11.5%) while German-language publications in Germany and Austria contained a factual error rate of 23.8%. Clearly, with this amount of misinformation, neither the consumer nor the historian was well served by musical theatre criticism in print journalism.

Jubin's analysis revealed other weaknesses in reviews of works by Lloyd Webber and Sondheim. Writing about musical theatre is more complicated than writing about non-musical works as the number of elements (and contributing artists) is larger than is typical to construct non-musical plays. Nevertheless, Jubin found that "most reviewers" "tend to focus in their articles on the composer and his/her music," ignoring the contributions of the lyricist, librettist, and choreographer, authors of the other "texts" of a musical. For example, "the press in German-speaking countries has an alarming inclination to reduce the show's creative team of authors to its composer. This can be observed in more than half of the articles (52.8%) and relates to a below-average interest in the lyricist, whose name—in the 1990s—is not even mentioned in 45.1% of the articles." Designers are equally ignored, as most reviewers focus only on the acting when they turn their attention to the production elements.

Reviewing musicals is a tall order. How does one process—in one viewing—all the various elements that go into a production: book, lyrics, music, direction, choreography, costumes, scenery, lighting, props, acting, dancing, singing, orchestrations, musical direction, sound design, projections, and so on? And how can you satisfactorily cover all of these elements in less than 400 words? Of course, reviewers are going to be drawn to those elements they know and understand best, and can therefore speak confidently about. That said, Jubin found that "neither the English-nor the German-speaking critics ever inform their readers about their personal or artistic beliefs" or "why they employ the criteria they use."[18] Therefore, since "the critics' knowledge and their capacity for understanding seem to be boundless, the reviewer who openly admits that he or she is baffled or out of his or her depth when dealing with a particular production is a rare exception indeed," occurring less than 3% of the time. Given these facts and the modest number of column inches available to each review in print journalism, it is small wonder that Jubin posits that "musicals are at present being reviewed by the wrong critics."

One laudable upside to the decline in the number of full-time, professional critics is that the Internet landscape is more open to authors from different backgrounds and experiences. An appallingly small number of white men yielded a huge amount of power as theatre critics in this country in the twentieth century, power we conferred upon them as we used their reviews for our own purposes. So even in the "Golden Age" of theatrical criticism (if it ever existed), those in the critic's chair were not representative, or necessarily knowledgeable, of the range of theatre produced in this country. For every Brooks Atkinson (1894–1984), drama critic for *The New York Times* for 31 years, who championed Eugene O'Neill and the Off-Broadway movement, there are those critics (John Simon, Clive Barnes, Dorothy Parker) who thought little about attacking those artists whose work (or even appearance) they did not like.

While reviews posted online may not benefit from an editorial process prior to publication, readers are often able to respond, question, or even contradict an opinion posted online. This conversation, this community building, is far richer than anything that was realized in the "Letters to the Editor" format for print publications. Indeed, the twenty-first century might be seen as a "Golden Age" of theatrical criticism as the field has changed from a handful of "experts" to a vital, virtual dialogue between writers and those who love the art form. Jarkko Jokelainen suggests that moment might already be here as "there is arguably more arts and culture journalism than ever"[19] thanks to numerous digital outlets.

Andrew Haydon points to a specific incident in 2007 which demonstrated that the "second wave of writing about theatre online seemed to enjoy a cultural energy and momentum quite beyond anything that had greeted the first gradual and tentative wave of theatre websites" (c. 1997–2006).[20] In that year, an interview with the playwright Edward Albee was published in *LA Weekly*:

> The big problem is the assumption that writing a play is a collaborative act. It isn't. It's a creative act, and then other people come in. The interpretation should be for the accuracy of what the playwright wrote. Playwrights are expected to have their text changed by actors they never wanted. Directors seem to feel they are as creative as the playwright.[21]

The story was picked up by UK's *The Guardian*, and would have ended there in a pre-Internet world. But online, conversations and debates began to form around what Albee meant by this pronouncement. Haydon feels that the ongoing discussion was "an education":

> Here was the very stuff that was missing from newspaper criticism and "features" about theatre. Here were some of the brightest minds making and/or writing about theatre offering new, live debate on a subject that they chose and cared about. [...] The "blogsphere" was making something valuable that had been lacking in mainstream theatre coverage. It was making it possible for new voices and schools of thought to be widely read, where before a process of gate-keepers ensured that more-or-less a single vision of what theatre was had prevailed since about 1956.[22]

Haydon points to 2012 as a turning point in the status of online blogs and critiques, highlighting those posted about a play which opened in London that year. *Three Kingdoms*, written by British playwright Simon Stephens, featured actors from the Estonian Teater NO99, three British actors, and performers from the Munich Kammerspiele ensemble. The production had received rave reviews in Munich and Tallinn, but the British mainstream press was mixed, with some very negative assessments. Poor ticket sales seemed to doom the production until positive reviews began to appear online. Ticket sales picked up and the end of the run sold out. Haydon sees this as a milestone, as "online criticism now had an infrastructure, a readership and reach. It could sell-out performances of a show that had been panned by the mainstream. The voices of those who disagreed with the mainstream assessment were now part of the ecology." Fans of a cult hit musical like *Parade* (1998) can wonder if the production had opened when the Internet was more robust, would the online community have been able to create enough buzz to extend its run past the 84 performances it achieved when it opened on Broadway?

Indeed, the rise of commentary and discussions about musical theatre on the Internet might have occurred even without the diminished presence of theatre criticism in print publications, as the Internet can provide features not possible in print publications: multiple authors reviewing the same work, no gatekeepers keeping contributors out, no length restrictions, and the opportunity for endless responses.

Who Needs Theatre Criticism?

West End theatre owner and producer Nica Burns criticized the UK national newspapers in 2016 for cutting back on their arts coverage, claiming that "proper, erudite" reviews are "critical" for performers and writers.[23] But this statement, echoed by many in the USA and Europe, begs the question: *who* is served by "proper, erudite" reviews? As playwright critic Jonathan Mandell reminds us, theatre criticism does "not exist to inspire and enrage theatemakers [*sic*]. Their purpose is to guide theatre audiences, to provoke thought and discussion, and to offer an independent assessment of an evanescent experience."[24]

That said, in terms of practice there are five main beneficiaries of theatre criticism today. First, in our capitalistic theatre market, certainly performers, writers, and producers benefit from encouraging reviews, as they generally have a positive impact on box office sales. Second, the public benefits by learning what art is happening in their locale, and well-written arts criticism can give the public information to make an informed decision as to whether or not to attend (which might include buying a ticket to) an event. Third, positive reviews are often used by writers and producers to apply for grants in order to help fund their next project. Fourth, those artists who have an appointment in academia benefit from complimentary reviews in terms of gaining a job, then keeping that job with promotion and tenure. Fifth, historians look for reviews as a record of not only how the play or musical was staged, but also what might have been the audience reaction to a performance, that most ephemeral of experiences. If there is any part of this discussion where there is agreement, it is the perceived loss to theatre history if no one is writing a record of what is being performed. David Cote, the theatre editor of *Time Out: New York* and contributing critic on NY1's *On Stage* argued:

> The decline of journalistic reviewing, the decline of general reader reviewing that's intelligent, informed and not just a consumer report, that is a little more in depth but is not quite a piece of academic criticism ... [is] sad. You can document things on video or, of course, publish plays. You can put things online. You can put things in archives. But I think a really apt and vivid piece of writing about a live event is crucial to its memory.[25]

Christopher Balme echoed this sentiment in 2015: "Indeed, the critic is the crucial link between the performance event and the wider theatrical public sphere of readers and potential audiences, reporting on the performance not only in terms of its value but also, occasionally, in its actual eventness, when the critic becomes a reporter of things witnessed, an ethnographer of the performance."[26] Without reviews, future theatre historians will be at a loss to create a narrative of a time and place without written accounts by aesthetic judges, ethnographers, and reporters of the theatrical event.

Cote appears to be just as hierarchical as Burns' call for "proper, erudite" reviews, as, for Cote, "academic criticism" doesn't appear to make the cut. At the same time, Cote, Balme, and Burns seem to have little interest in the volume of writing that is available digitally. For the historian genuinely interested in locating a context for a performance, why not look into tweets, Facebook postings, blogs, Yelp reviews, and academic criticism?[27] If we agree that Blogging Bobbie is not inherently inferior to a full-time professional critic at *The New York Times*, then digital content should be evaluated on its own merits, and not automatically dismissed due to how it is distributed.

The aggressive democratization of public commentary available on the Internet is a far cry from the five to fifteen reviews for a Broadway show that might be written by full-time New York City critics working for established newspapers and magazines. Recall that Heller desired a "climate" where "creative work is taken seriously," whereby the critic has "dignified" their work and identity. Burns ("proper") and Cote ("intellectual") also plead for a particular tone in reviews, without explicitly defining their evaluative yardstick. Alison Croggon reminds us that the "crassness and illiteracy" of the content on the web "can surpass belief. ... And yet, the Internet is where I can find some of the most dynamic and intelligent commentary on art and society."[28] What clearly bothers many traditionalists is that there is no Internet Editorial Staff separating trash from treasure. However, what some see as a liability others applaud as a way for new voices to join in the conversation.

While most twenty-first-century critics seem to be very pessimistic about the future of their professional and arts criticism, Sarah Kaufman of *The Washington Post* remains upbeat: "We have to be flexible with the times. I don't know what the future of journalism will look like, but I feel very bullish on arts journalism in general. There will always be an audience for it because it draws passionate people."[29]

Alternative Models

Contemporary innovators are not waiting for someone else to write the future; they have already created their own contributions to this new world of theatre criticism in the twenty-first century. Recognizing that younger theatre enthusiasts look for news and information differently than their parents, interesting alternative models seem to be popping up all the time.

The UK theatre organization, A Younger Theatre in London, started as a blog in 2009, has since "grown to become a publication, production company and resource for emerging creatives."[30] As a service to the industry, they have posted on their website:

> "Want us to review your show?"
>
> If you have a show you would like one of our reviewers to attend please send a press release, or details with at least two weeks notice. Please note: you will only receive an email from the reviews@ account upon requesting of tickets. If we do not contact you we have not been able to allocate a reviewer for your show. Please contact Sam on: reviews [at] ayoungertheatre.com.[31]

They post these reviews on their own website. While A Younger Theatre is "committed to supporting and nurturing emerging creative talent in theatre and the arts,"[32] they appear to review almost anything. One sign of the status of A Younger Theatre's reviews is the fact that two of their regular contributors, Kate Wyver and Fergus Morgan, have been nominated to *The Stage*'s 2016 Critic Search from more than 280 entries.

In Los Angeles, the theatre website, *Bitter Lemons*, has offered a similar service starting in 2015, but they charge $150 for a review ($125 goes to the critic). Called the Bitter Lemon Imperative, this arrangement was immediately denounced by the American Theatre Critics Association:

> While it does not guarantee a favorable review or allow theater companies to choose the reviewer, this pay-for-play arrangement creates a clear appearance of conflict of interest. That appearance, even if spurious, undermines the crucial credibility of not only the *Bitter Lemons* critics, but all critics. Our profession has fought for decades to preserve the image of independence. When our work is put out for sale to those we cover, we are concerned not just for criticism itself, but for the bypassing of editorial judgment in deciding what to cover and what not to cover.[33]

The ATCA is clinging to the importance of a high art/low art hierarchy as they suggest that only editors have the insight/taste/intelligence to decide "what to cover and what not to cover." This mindset of telling the audience what they should care about is part of the reason why alternative digital forums have evolved: people want to talk to other people who care about what they like; they don't want to be told that something they care about doesn't deserve to be reviewed.

The website *Bitter Lemons*, prior to this experiment, did not publish their own reviews, rather they scanned reviews by other entities in order to come up with their own rating (the LEMONMETER), from 100% "sweet" to 100% "bitter." Fueled by theatre companies' desire to be seen and written about, the paid review scheme is working. Nevertheless, *Bitter Lemons*' credibility was challenged in summer 2016 when the Hollywood Fringe Festival issued a press release that they would no longer advertise with *Bitter Lemons* (as they had done since their debut in 2010), due to *Bitter Lemons*' Editor in Chief and Founder, Colin Mitchell's stance on long-time actor abuse at Chicago's Profiles Theatre. Mitchell's June 9, 2016 article states that he is not "blaming the victim," but rather advocating for "taking responsibility for your own career, your own body and your own dignity."[34] Nevertheless, public reaction was swift and negative, with seventy comments in the first week the article was posted online.

The day after Mitchell's article was posted, the Hollywood Fringe Festival—which produces musicals and operas, along with other genres—announced they would no longer work with *Bitter Lemons*:

> Providing a safe space is essential to our job. We do not condone abuse. We believe that abuse is given an extended life when victims are told they are to blame. In solidarity with all individuals who have been victims of abuse, the Hollywood Fringe Festival will no longer work with or endorse *Bitter Lemons*.[35]

The day after the Hollywood Fringe Festival press release, *Bitter Lemons* announced that Colin Mitchell had been removed as Editor in Chief, as his recent article about "the Chicago theatrical community crossed from controversial into unacceptable."[36] It is too early to know the full impact of Mitchell's removal from *Bitter Lemons* and/or the lack of financial support from the Hollywood Fringe Festival.

Recognizing that new theatre bloggers do not have an established reputation, and therefore have difficulty attracting readers, Mark Shenton and Terri Paddock created MyTheatreMates.com as a platform for bloggers. By aggregating the work of many writers in one place, the hope is that all—readers and bloggers—will benefit from this "shopping mall" of bloggers. As of this writing, eighteen writers are listed as "Syndicate Mates," with a solicitation for others to apply for this status. Admission criteria includes:

- You have your own personal website
- You post original theatre-related content on your personal website at least once a fortnight
- You can provide three professional arts references (e.g. artists you have interviewed or, if you review, producers or publicists who already regularly provide you with complimentary press tickets to shows)
- You are active on Twitter[37]

While there is no editor telling the bloggers at MyTheatreMates.com what to review, nor is there someone editing their work, there is clearly a selection process in play by Shenton and Paddock to decide which writers will appear under this masthead.

A handful of respected arts critics like Deborah Jowitt, Jill Dolan, and Michael Feingold have moved to publishing their own work online.

A hopeful sign of a positive change in this new world is that Jill Dolan and Michael Feingold became the first online critics to win the George Jean Nathan Award for Dramatic Criticism (2010 and 2015, respectively). But would these widely respected authors have a readership and win awards if they had not already established themselves in print? (Jowitt wrote for *The Village Voice* for 40 years, Feingold for 30+, and Dolan has published six books, in addition to her blog). How will the next generation of writers find or create venues for their opinions that can ultimately attract an audience for their digital work?

Finding readers is one challenge facing neophyte writers, paying their bills is another. Fast on the heels of Canadian Prime Minister Justin Trudeau's 2016 announcement that the government would be investing CAD 1.9 billion in the country's arts and culture over the next five years, the Canadian Theatre Critics Association called for the creation of the Canadian Council for Critics. Given that the Canadian Council for the Arts' budget will double under this new scheme, the theatre critics association proposed that 1% of the budget for the Canadian Council for the Arts be used to distribute micro-grants of $10K to $17K to bloggers who write about Canadian publicly funded art.[38] Former theatre critic for the *Calgary Herald*, Stephen Hunt reasoned that since Canada had decided that it is "in the public interest to create publicly funded Canadian art," then "it's in the public interest to create a framework, at a modest cost, that allows them to do that."[39] As of this writing, the proposed Canadian Council for Critics has not been funded.

Fans—and detractors—have long posted their opinions about productions on their own personal social media sites. Yet when Yelp and TripAdvisor began collecting ratings, comments, and photos from the public, live theatre became another commodity like a restaurant meal, a hotel room, or a cruise ship, that consumers can review and rate on a five-star scale. Others can comment on these postings, and report a review that they feel is inaccurate. As musicals are attended by more people (and run longer) than non-musicals, they inspire more posts on Yelp and TripAdvisor. For example, there were two posted reviews of the 2017 revival of *The Little Foxes* (starring Laura Linney and Cynthia Nixon) on Yelp, compared to 103 reviews for *Hamilton* and 630 for *Wicked*. Indeed, *Wicked* defied more than gravity when it opened on Broadway in 2003. Many mainstream critics trounced the musical: "overproduced, overblown, confusingly dark and laboriously ambitious jumble" (*Newsday*); "The show's twenty-two songs were written by Stephen Schwartz, and not one of them is memorable" (*The New Yorker*); Ben Brantley only liked the performances of Idina Menzel and Kristin Chenoweth, finding the rest of the musical to be a "bloated production that might otherwise spend close to three hours flapping its oversized wings without taking off" (*The New York Times*).[40] Nevertheless, fans flocked to the musical, making it a franchise unto itself: as of 2015, companies around the world had grossed $3.1 billion and the show had been seen by 38 million people in nine different languages. The Broadway and London stagings are still running (2017) and the musical stands as the eleventh longest-running musical in Broadway history.

While the consumer watchdog approach on sites like Yelp and TripAdvisor typically attract only those who loved or hated something, other fans eschew giving a rating to their favorite musical, and instead are inspired to create their own art, which usually takes the form of a YouTube video. Some postings are in the aesthetic of Aristophanes' *The Frogs*, where the new creation is its own production, while at the same time is a critique of a play, musical, film, and so on. Other fan creations include lip sync by new characters ("Drag Queen Performs *Frozen*"), musical mash-ups ("'I Dreamed a Dream' from *Glee*"), documentaries about inaccuracies in the musical ("Top 10 Things *Hamilton* Got Wrong!"), and so on.[41]

One of the more unusual examples of performed criticism was inspired by the reaction to playwright Neil LaBute's new adaptation of Shakespeare's *The Taming of the Shrew*, first produced by the Chicago Shakespeare Theatre in 2010. Writing for *Time Out Chicago*, theatre critic Caitlin Montanye Parrish praised parts of the production, but was unimpressed by LaBute's additions to the text. According to Oona Hatton:

> Within hours, a writer identifying her/himself as LaBute left a scathing response in the comments section of the online review. Calling Parrish's piece a "sorry excuse for theatrical criticism," "neil labute" launched into a spirited exchange that grew to include over fifty comments from an estimated twenty-five participants.[42]

Dismissing theatre critics as "freeloaders," "neil labute" goes on to note that, "critics are the one element that is of little or no use to the creative process." S/he celebrates the creative element that the audience brings to the performance, while denouncing that the identity of "the critic will always be reactive and parasitic."[43] Fascinated by the phenomenon of crowdsourcing theatre criticism, Hatton took the 50+ posts and turned them into an online radio play, *The Time Out/Neil LaBute Radio Play*, performed by Chicago actors. Hatton argues that "this 'performance of criticism' offers a viable, even superior alternative to the traditional theatre review." By "interrogating assumptions [...] about who is eligible to participate in theatre criticism; it is also an inquiry into the form that criticism might take."[44] While Hatton prefers to look on the positive side of crowdsourcing theatre criticism, she marvels at the virtual space that allows anyone with an Internet connection the ability to espouse opinions, ask questions, and dialogue at a pace and scale that would have been unheard of just twenty years ago. But Hatton acknowledges that this democratic space is a masquerade ball: the reader has no assurance who is actually speaking. Did the real Neil LaBute post all sixteen entries addressed to Parrish, or did multiple people sign on as "neil labute?" Do the postings by "William Shakespeare," "Frank Oz," "Will Smith," and/or "Aaron Eckhart" mean more or less than those presumably posted by a "real" person?

As the actors recorded their parts individually, they had not heard the complete play until Hatton posted it online; most were surprised at the difference in reading the transcript and hearing it performed. After the play had been played online 172 times, Hatton asked her actors why no comments had been posted. Actor "Donna" suggested: "I think it's because the piece amplifies the weirdness and ridiculousness of online commenting."[45] It is somewhat ironic that a play that sought to celebrate the crowdsourcing of theatre criticism ended up stopping the conversation.

What's Next?

In the state of Colorado, the last full-time theatre critic was let go by *The Denver Post* newspaper in 2014. The biggest regional theatre in the state, Denver Center Theatre, promptly hired Moore as its own in-house content creator. John Moore is no longer a critic; rather he creates subject matter more in line with what Gotthold Lessing did in Germany with the Hamburg Dramaturgy: provide context for a production and advocate for the role of live theatre in our culture.

Romanian theatre critic Cristina Modreanu, having weathered the fall of Communism, and also the end of state support of the arts, posits that the only way for theatre criticism to survive in Romania is for critics to have a day job: teaching, writing articles for magazines, translation, freelancing for theatres, and so on. Responding to Jake Orr, who posits that theatre criticism is destined to be a "niche art-form" written by hobbyists, Modreanu instead sees a future for criticism written by "informed consultants" who are "active in the editorial field connected to [the] arts—as authors, translators, editors of specialized books—academic or not—which can bring the arts closer to more people."[46]

In this vein, college professor and blogger Karen Fricker celebrates a long list of critics and bloggers who also teach at universities (including herself), calling this role of academia in theatre criticism to be a "critical" part of the infrastructure. In 2014, Fricker posted an article, "The crisis in theatre criticism is critics saying there's a crisis."[47] Responding to Mark Shenton, Chair of the Drama section of the London (UK) Critics' Circle, who wrote that people writing for free were contributing to the demise of "quality journalism," Fricker rejected this stance by arguing that the digital realm is more about opportunities than it is a threat.

While certainly not everyone agrees with Alison Croggon that "the digital media have ushered in a golden age of criticism and commentary for the arts,"[48] most might celebrate the multiplicity of voices which are now filling the Internet conversations. At their best, these postings reflect a "gregarious public intellectuality," but often they are mean-spirited, crass, uncivil comments, more intent on silencing the conversation than building it. But, as Croggon reminds us, the word "amateur" derives from the Latin verb for love. And, if these lovers of theatre follow Harold Clurman's advice to "err more on the side of generosity rather than the opposite zeal" and "enlighten rather than carp or puff," we indeed would be primed for a "golden age of criticism and commentary for the arts."[49]

In the pre-Internet era, reviews did not linger forever online, but genuinely became almost completely inaccessible 24 hours after they appeared in print. One thing that few seem to be concerned with today is that reviews on the web—the well-written and the borderline libelous—can haunt an artist, a musical, a theatre company forever. But just as no one knows the various directions the genre of musical theatre will expand into as the twenty-first century marches on, so too will the worlds of theatre criticism continue to morph. As there will always be prospective audience members who want to read about a production—whether or not they are able to attend—and those who want to share their opinion about a work of art, theatre criticism in some form will continue, even as the platforms it appears in continue to change.

Notes

1. Qtd. in Mandell.
2. Qtd. in Hemley.
3. Barthel.
4. Qtd. in Mainwaring.
5. Jubin.
6. Qtd. in Jokelainen.
7. Mainwaring.
8. Rutenberg.
9. Mainwaring.
10. See Chap. 6: *Hamilton* and the Participatory Spectator.
11. Balme.
12. American Theatre Critics Association website.
13. Hathaway.
14. Heller.
15. Ibid.
16. Qtd. in Heller.
17. Heller.
18. Jubin.
19. Jokelainen.
20. Haydon.
21. Qtd. in Haydon.
22. Haydon.
23. Qtd. in Hemley.
24. Mandell.
25. Qtd. in Purcell.
26. Balme.
27. See chapters by Reside and Liu in this volume for discussions on how to incorporate these digital sources.
28. Croggon.
29. Qtd. in Mainwaring.
30. A Younger Theatre. http://www.ayoungertheatre.com.
31. Ibid.
32. Ibid.
33. Qtd. in Purcell.
34. Mitchell.
35. Hollywood Fringe Festival.
36. Box.

37. http://mytheatremates.com/about-us/join/
38. Hunt.
39. Hunt.
40. Qtd. in Fallon.
41. See Chap. 6 on *Hamilton* fan culture for a discussion of these kinds of fan/critical responses to musicals.
42. Qtd. in Hatton, 103.
43. Qtd. in Hatton, 103.
44. Hatton, 103, 104.
45. Qtd. in Hatton, 111.
46. Modreanu.
47. Karen Flicker, "The crisis in theatre criticism is critics saying there's a crisis," (posted 11 September 2014) on "The Mental Swoon" (https://karenfricker.wordpress.com), accessed 17 September 2017.
48. Croggon.
49. Qtd. in "The Complete Critic's Qualifications."

Bibliography

A Younger Theatre. http://www.ayoungertheatre.com.
American Theatre Critics Association web site. Accessed 1 August 2016. http://americantheatrecritics.org/apply-for-membership/.
Balme, Christopher. "In Extremis: Theatre Criticism, Ethics and the Public Sphere." *Critical Stages/Scènes Critiques* (December 2015). Accessed 15 July 2016.
Barthel, Michael. "Newspapers: Fact Sheet." Pew Research Center website (15 June 2016). Accessed December 28, 2016. http://www.journalism.org/2016/06/15/newspapers-fact-sheet/.
Birchall, Paul. "Pay Your Money, Take Your Chances: Is This Any Way to Run a Theatre Review Website?" *American Theatre* (22 June 2015). Accessed 15 July 2015.
Box, Enci. "*Bitter Lemons* removes Colin Mitchell as Editor in Chief." *Bitter Lemons* (11 June 2016). Accessed 24 November 2016. http://socal.bitter-lemons.com/learn/article/3456.
Brown, Mark. "Between Journalism and Art: The Location of Criticism in the Twenty-first-Century." Ed. Duska Radosavijevic. *Theatre Criticism: Changing Landscapes*. London: Bloomsbury Methuen Drama, 2016.
Croggon, Alison. "The return of the amateur critic." *Australian Broadcasting Company News* (28 September 2010). Accessed 24 November 2016. http://www.abc.net.au/news/2010-09-14/29938?pfmredir=sm.
Delin, Kevin. "Updated: Hollywood Fringe Ends Relationship with *Bitter Lemons*." *Footlights* (10 June 2016). Accessed 24 November 2016. http://

footlights.click/2016/06/10/hollywood-fringe-ends-relationship-bitter-lemons/.

Fallon, Kevin. "A 'Wicked' Decade: How a Critically Trashed Musical Became a Long-Running Smash." *The Daily Beast*. (30 October 2015). Accessed 1 May 2017. http://www.thedailybeast.com/a-wicked-decade-how-a-critically-trashed-musical-became-a-long-running-smash.

Fricker, Karen. "The crisis in theatre criticism is critics saying there's a crisis." *The Mental Swoon* (11 September 2014). Accessed 28 December 2016. https://karenfricker.wordpress.com/2014/09/11/the-crisis-in-theatre-criticism-is-critics-saying-theres-a-crisis/.

Gerard, Jeremy. "Revamping New York Times Regional Theatre, Restaurant & Arts Coverage," *Deadline* (31 August 2016). Accessed 5 May 2017. http://deadline.com/2016/08/new-york-times-culture-restaurant-coverage-1201811588/.

Hathaway, Brad. "Who Speaks for Theatre in the Digital Age? (We Should!)." *Critical Stages/Scènes Critiques*, no. 12 (September 2015). Accessed 15 July 2016.

Hatton, Oona. "'Hey, asshole: you had your say': The Performance of Theatre Criticism." *Theatre Topics* 24: 2 (June 2014): 103–124.

Haydon, Andrew. "A Brief History of Online Theatre Criticism in England." Ed. Duska Radosavijevic. *Theatre Criticism: Changing Landscapes*. London: Bloomsbury Methuen Drama, 2016.

Heller, Nathan. "Says You: How to be a critic in an age of opinion." *The New Yorker* (7 March 2016): 62–66.

Hemley, Matthew. "Nica Burns: 'Proper, erudite' reviews critical to Theatre Community." *The Stage* (8 August 2016). Accessed 1 August 2016. https://www.thestage.co.uk/news/2016/nica-burns-proper-erudite-reviews-critical-to-theatre-community/.

Hollywood Fringe Festival. "Fringe Statement on *Bitter Lemons* Article," (10 June 2016). Accessed 24 November 2016. http://www.hollywoodfringe.org/learn/article/3454.

Hunt, Stephen. "On the disappearing art of Theatre Criticism." *The Globe and Mail* (October 14, 2016). Reprinted in *Capital Critics' Circle* [Canada] (14 December 2016). Accessed 26 December 2016. www.capitalcriticscircle.com/on-the-disappearing-art-of-theatre-criticism/.

Jokelainen, Jarkko. "Anyone Can Be a Critic: Is There Still a Need for Professional Arts and Culture Journalism in the Digital Age?" 2014. Reuters Institute for the Study of Journalism. The Helsingin Sanomat Foundation. Web. 10 July 2016.

Jubin, Olaf. "Experts Without Expertise? Findings of a comparative study of American, British, and German-language reviews of musicals by Stephen

Sondheim and Andrew Lloyd Webber." *Studies in Musical Theatre* 4:2 (2010): 185–197. Web. 28 April 2017.

Mainwaring, Madison. "The Death of the American Dance Critic." *The Atlantic* (5 August 2015). Accessed 11 July 2016.

Mandell, Jonathan. "Are Theatre Critics Critical? An Update." *HowlRound* (1 April 2015). Accessed 5 July 2016.

Mitchell, Colin. "Regarding the Chicago Profiles Theatre Abuse Story: Where is the Personal Responsibility?" *Bitter Lemons* (9 June 2016). Accessed 28 December 2016. http://socal.bitter-lemons.com/learn/article/3449.

Modreanu, Cristina. "Reinventing Theater Criticism: An Intensification of the Possibility of Truth." *Critical Stages/Scènes Critiques*, no. 10 (October 2014). Accessed 15 July 2016.

Purcell, Carey. "Is Paying for Reviews the New Journalism? *Time Out*'s David Cote Weighs In." *Playbill* (17 June 2015). Accessed 24 November 2016.

Rutenberg, Jim. "Pursuit of the News Can Live On As the Newspaper Fades Away." *The New York Times* (5 September 2016): B1, B4.

"The Complete Critic's Qualifications." 14 February 2011. ATCA (American Theatre Critics Association) website. Accessed 24 December 2016. http://americantheatrecritics.org/position-papers/2011/2/22/the-complete-critics-qualifications.html.

CHAPTER 15

Looking Backward, Looking Forward: An Afterword

Elizabeth L. Wollman

Major advances in technology have long fueled anxiety and mistrust among a populace that nevertheless simultaneously, often even eagerly, embraces each new development. A case in point: as I write this, millions of Americans, reeling from an exceptionally angry and deeply contentious presidential race that has culminated dramatically and most unexpectedly, are locked in myriad heated debates over whether and how media saturation borne of the Internet age has worked to polarize, dupe, outsmart, betray, fail, and possibly destroy us. Many of these debates are, of course, taking place in person and in real time: in classrooms and teach-ins, at organizational rallies and community meetings, in neighborhood watering holes and around dinner tables. But just as many—perhaps even more—are taking place online, in the very social media sites that we collectively worry have plunged us into this new, uncertain world to begin with. Has digital technology led to our undoing and if so what can we do, we ask one another over and over again via digital technology.

E.L. Wollman (✉)
Baruch College, New York City, NY, USA
e-mail: Elizabeth.Wollman@baruch.cuny.edu

© The Author(s) 2017
J. Hillman-McCord (ed.), *iBroadway*,
DOI 10.1007/978-3-319-64876-7_15

Uncertainty and anxiety about what technology has wrought and how we might tame it are especially intense at the moment. But as medieval woodcuts depicting ghoulish devils smirking while working at printing presses imply, the fretful and highly uncertain embrace of technological advances can be traced back for centuries. In a *New Yorker* piece about the conspiracy theorist and fake news purveyor Alex Jones, the journalist Andrew Marantz points out that while we now "think of the printing press as a boon for science and reason," it initially aroused enormous suspicion in part because it was embraced "by hacks and crazies" who used it to publish highly specious material "in vernacular languages while reputable scientists" continued to write in Latin, and that sorting out the ensuing confusion and misinformation "took about two hundred years."[1]

The printing press, of course, eventually won the world's embrace, but deep concern about technology hasn't ceased. Long before the Internet came along to lay waste to our minds—even, as some headlines we're not sure we believe insist, to actually "rewire our brains" in the process—video games were of greatest concern, especially the sex-, gore-, and violence-filled ones. Before that, television was most at fault for rotting our brains, gobbling up our industriousness, and thoroughly destroying the futures of our children. And of course, Americans complained mightily about such gadgets even as we gave into them, tsking in long holiday checkout lines where we waited to purchase top-of-the-line color televisions, the newest in game cartridges, the hottest and most sophisticated game consoles on which to play.

Film and radio, too, were once far more responsible for civilization's imminent decline than they seem to be at present, now that we're all so busy being concerned about the Internet. Erotic prints, dime novels, and comic books, too, aroused enormous suspicion when technology first advanced far enough to unleash them on the pure, unwitting masses. Let's not even start with recorded sound, which has long been proof of the Devil at work. The Dark One has, through history, apparently had full access to a remarkably long list of dangerously ruinous, brain-warpingly evil music genres: hot jazz, rhythm and blues, rock and roll, heavy metal, punk, hip hop.

In short, advances in technology have long been and will probably always be, at least upon introduction, scary to a lot of people. This is because technology entices us, makes us want more of it, makes itself endlessly useful, even as we are collectively unsure about what, precisely, each new advance will do to our minds, our lives, our worlds.

None of the articles in this fine collection is specifically about technology-related cultural anxieties and the contradictions therein. But then, just about every one of them does touch, even if only tangentially, on the ways Broadway simultaneously resists and embraces important technological advances, whether on stage, behind the scenes, as an industry, or as a locus for scholarly study. As an institution, Broadway, like the culture it endlessly processes and reflects, has from inception been as dependent on technological advances as it has been wary and resentful of them.

Can you blame it for its careful distance, really? As a mirror of the culture, place, and time its entertainment product operates in, Broadway often projects not only our collective joys, ideals, mores and ethics, but also our sorrows, worries, and darkest concerns. As an institution, Broadway has pretty good reason to reflect a fear and loathing of technological advances. After all, live theatre has been threatened by—and in some way or another forced to adapt to—just about every technological advance we've seen in the American entertainment world since the turn of the century.

With the exception of the sheet music industry, which in consolidation as Tin Pan Alley was as enormously beneficial to the commercial theatre industry as the commercial theatre industry was to it, the advent of entertainment technology has put Broadway regularly on the defensive through most of the twentieth and well into the twenty-first century. If one considers the fact that the contemporary Broadway musical—the kind with a cohesive plot, and songs and dances that make sense within the plot's framework—didn't really come to fruition until the late 1920s at earliest, one could make the argument that Broadway musicals have basically been fighting to remain fresh, appealing, and relevant in an increasingly technological world since before they were even born. Since musicals are Broadway's biggest cash cow, the commercial theatre industry has certainly had good reason to adapt to the newest technological advances and to fret mightily about doing so in the process.

When it came to the first mass-mediated threat live entertainment faced, various segments of the commercial theatre industry were not only tolerant, but perfectly happy to exploit it for financial benefit. In the early twentieth century, silent films were regularly shown in vaudeville houses, not only in the newly minted Times Square (before 1904, a desolate locus for the city's carriage industry, most famous for its prostitutes and stench of horse manure), but all over the country. Showing short films—of people kissing or dancing, of water being poured, of trains pulling into stations—not only allowed vaudeville audiences to marvel over the newest technological innovations, but perhaps more importantly allowed vaudeville's incredibly hard-working performers to take more frequent breaks during the course of their marathon show days.

Yet as film grew more sophisticated, simple adaptation developed into increasingly unfairly weighted competition: Hollywood became enormous and moneyed, and its movies more technologically sophisticated and easy to transport nationwide (and eventually worldwide). This was especially the case once "talkies" were introduced in 1927, a mere two years before the Great Depression made movies the easiest and cheapest go-to for Americans seeking escapism, while simultaneously forcing Broadway to limit its offerings and cut back on the excess, frivolity, and spectacle that had helped define American commercial theatre entertainment through the 1920s in the first place.

Smaller in scale than it was during its commercial heyday in the 1920s—when it wasn't atypical for well over a hundred shows to run in a single season on Broadway—commercial stage musicals cut back sharply, managing in the process to remain not only viable but newly sophisticated, challenging, and innovative through the so-called Golden Age that took root between the Great Depression and World War II. Unable to compete, Broadway toned down and embraced the enemy, if sometimes grudgingly, whenever it could. Composers, lyricists, directors, and choreographers regularly went west for work in Hollywood, returning east to focus with new intensity on fewer productions that had to matter more, whenever there were budgets to stage them at all. No longer as vital to national entertainment as it was in decades prior, a slighter, leaner Broadway not only kept itself alive but, at least aesthetically, managed to grow, mature, and innovate.

Meanwhile, even as it lured theatre audiences away, Hollywood paid the commercial theatre industry a backhanded favor by depicting, in countless movie musicals, the magic of Broadway: the thrill of sitting in its plush seats, of taking in its dazzling nightlife, of marveling at its bright lights, of making it big as a performer and getting to tread the boards in a big, glitzy Broadway show.

As a number of contributions to this volume make clear, the relationship between film and Broadway continues at present to be, if often mutually beneficial, simultaneously fraught. Almost a century since the advent of the talking picture, Broadway continues to walk a very fine line when it comes to film, which it now emulates both aesthetically and behind the scenes while simultaneously clinging to its own history, traditions, and aesthetics.

Broadway is no longer just walking such a tightrope when it comes to film. As the twentieth century progressed, the commercial theatre industry also needed to strike increasingly careful balances with any number of other entertainment-related technological advances: television, contemporary popular music, gaming, the Internet. It has, perhaps understandably, revealed itself to be ever wary, even as it has devised out ways to adapt itself to the modern world. The "Fabulous Invalid" may have been notoriously slow to figure out how to mutually benefit from the advent of television, how to embrace rock music (and, later, hip hop), and how to utilize the Internet, but that's because each advance in technology can work as easily to disrupt the communality of the theatrical space as to enhance it.

Think, for example, of the many contradictions so neatly pointed out in these very pages. Broadway audiences—most of whom have, at this point, thought nothing of purchasing their tickets online after perusing any number of websites devoted to available shows—arrive at a Broadway theatre eager for an evening of live entertainment. Once in their seats, they are treated to a performance by actual human beings who nevertheless often offer interpretations of characters made world-famous via the mass media. Their voices are almost always enhanced—if also disembodied—by means of increasingly sophisticated digital sound design employed by most every production, though apparently still denigrated enough to call into question its Tony-worthiness. Actors often appear before sets designed to be increasingly cinematic, performing numbers that are either entirely original or previously made famous on film, television, or via the newest streaming sites.

As they watch, some audience members benefit enormously from the use of infrared hearing devices, which help them understand words and lyrics they might otherwise be unable to catch. Still other audience members need to be reminded regularly not only to turn off their phones, but also to stop constantly looking at them—or at their increasingly teeny tablets, or at their newly tricked-out watches—during the performance.

Meanwhile, behind the scenes, members of the theatre industry bemoan how cinema-sized and derivative Broadway has become, even as they seal production deals with members of Disney Theatricals, check in with members of the marketing department who deal in social media, design a costume that will make an actor look like an animated rabbit or fairy or ogre or frog, or set a light cue instantly with the click of a mouse. And fans, some of whom know every word to a show they have not yet seen, thanks to pirated versions uploaded on YouTube, wait eagerly at the stage door after a performance to see their favorite performers live and in the flesh—so they can preserve the moment by taking a selfie.

Musical theatre scholars and arts journalists, too, alternately weigh in on news of yet another jukebox musical or film adaptation, consider (as I once, admittedly foolishly, did) boycotting all stage musicals that came from movies or television shows, scoff at audience members who behave in the theatre as if they were in their living room or a local multiplex, and herald the death of Broadway as a site for artistic independence and creative innovation, before eating our words in the face of *Fun Home* (2015) or *Hamilton* (2015) or—dare I say—*The Lion King* (1997). Then we run off to the New York Public Library at Lincoln Center to watch any one of thousands of musicals that have been digitally recorded. Or we choose, instead, to remain in the comfort of our offices or homes, streaming beautifully filmed clips on YouTube or sharing in the joy of countless musical theatre fans by checking out the latest bootlegs. For clarification about what we're watching, we can just as quickly download books and articles that in recent memory we needed to locate in dusty stacks, check out at the front desk, and copy or take reams of notes about.

All of Broadway and its many devotees, then, will continue to embrace and to resist technology by equal measures, because that is what the culture Broadway was bred from does, and probably always will do.

A few weeks ago, I went, Internet-purchased and pre-printed ticket in hand, to the Music Box Theatre on Broadway to catch a matinee. Irving Berlin and the producer Sam Harris had the Music Box built in 1921 to house Berlin's annual music revues; the building, frequently celebrated as beautiful enough to earn its name, was probably also state-of-the-art for its time. The Music Box is currently host to Benj Pasek and Justin Paul's *Dear Evan Hansen*, which transferred from Off-Broadway's Second Stage Theatre after a sold-out run there in spring 2016. Ensconced at the Music Box, *Dear Evan Hansen* is currently one of the biggest hits of the 2016–2017 Broadway season, as well as what seems to be the first Broadway musical to focus on the myriad ways digital technology can simultaneously unite and distance, help and harm, comfort and disrupt.

The technology that has been applied to the production jibes well with its contemporary themes: *Dear Evan Hansen* is sleek and beautiful look at and listen to. It features excellent sound design: its on-stage rock band and the voices of its performers have been carefully mixed and lovingly balanced. The show's set, all shiny panels and gliding set pieces, reflect the inviting, liquid glass surfaces of laptops, tablets, and phones. The look of the production benefits enormously from the work of Peter Nigrini, described on the musical's website as a "pioneer in the integration of digital projection technology and live theatre" and someone who, I suspect, will breed countless imitators (and competitors) in the next decade or so.[2] Nigrini's many projections are stage-sized reproductions of the kinds of things most Americans see all day, every day, on our myriad screens: text messages, photographs, the banners and logos of social media sites, lengthy lists of comments filled with hashtags and @ signs.

One of the most powerful moments I've recently experienced in a theatre took place during the performance of *Dear Evan Hansen*. Early in the second act, Evan—charged with giving a speech at a school assembly about Connor, a classmate who committed suicide and who much of Evan's school community erroneously believes was Evan's close friend—stumbles over his notecards. Overcome with the weight of the many small lies he's told or untruths he's perpetuated, which have built into something he can no longer control, Evan becomes consumed with stage fright. He stammers at first, and then he simply stares, awkward and gaping, into the theatre for an uncomfortably long stretch of time.

In response to this long, quiet moment depicting a deeply uncomfortable deer-in-headlights reaction, the audience sat in breathless silence; you could've heard a pin drop or, perhaps more fittingly, an incoming message on an unsilenced cell phone go *peep*. But no one moved, no pin dropped, no cell phone pinged. While I could not see the entire theatre from where I sat, I like to think that no one thought, even for a moment, to check their phones or futz with their Apple watches as Ben Platt, the actor playing Evan, stared, terror-stricken and desperate, into the dark, tense house. The production's gliding set pieces, silky sound mix, and perfectly lit projections helped make the show as enjoyable as it was, but it was this agonizingly long moment of collective silence—for the discomfort, ultimately a silent celebration of theatre's utterly electrifying humanness, emotionalism, *liveness*—that will, I am certain, remain with me longest.

For all its embrace of digital technology, after all, liveness is the one weapon the stage musical can still lord over every mass-mediated entertainment form that has come down the pike. As many of the essays in *iBroadway* conclude, Broadway will survive so long as it continues to honor its liveness, even as it adapts technologically. Without the excitement that is generated when people gather together in the dark to watch other people sing, dance, emote, and even occasionally freeze in terror, what's the point of theatre? We might occasionally leave a venue humming the scenery, but that's never what it's all about. Theatre—memorable theatre, anyway—is ultimately about moments of human connection, however small and fleeting. Despite what the most recent fake news claims, my guess is that no cinema-sized advance in technology—no matter how thrilling, innovative, or desirable—will ever manage to rewire our brains enough to steal the power of liveness away from Broadway.

Notes

1. "Dept. of Joneses: News Blues." *The New Yorker*, December 19 and 26, 2016: 4–46.
2. http://dearevanhansen.com/cast-and-creative/ Accessed 16 December 2016.

Index

A

Act Like It's Your Business, 214, 215, 228
Actors, 2, 9, 10, 21, 36, 65, 66, 79, 83, 95–97, 101, 105, 110, 126, 136, 138, 148, 161, 169, 177, 186, 194, 197, 207–214, 216–222, 225–227, 237, 240, 242, 244, 251, 279, 286, 298, 312, 316, 324, 325, 337, 345, 355
  casting of, 2, 207, 209
  ghosts of previous roles, 78, 247
  online branding of, 212
  program bios of, 247
Actors Equity Association, 210, 211
Actors Fund, The, 157, 164, 165
Agents, 19, 32, 208, 209, 228
Agony and Ecstasy of Steve Jobs the Musical, The, 59
Altmetric, 297, 298, 304
American Idol, 155, 175, 233, 238–242, 245, 252–255
American Theatre Critics Association, 334, 341, 347
Archives, 2, 262, 263, 269, 273, 275, 276, 280, 287, 288, 327, 339
  born digital, 314
  New York Philharmonic Digital, 287
Atlantic, The, 28, 105, 332, 333
Audience, 4–7, 18–20, 22, 25, 28–31, 37, 51–52, 58–60, 76, 77, 79, 80, 82, 84–86, 97, 99–113, 122–123, 133, 134, 137, 142, 150, 154, 167, 168, 191, 217, 219–220, 226, 228, 244–245, 250, 252, 263, 267, 285, 290, 297, 300, 310–315, 325–326, 338, 340, 341, 343–344, 346, 355, 357
  behavior research, 4, 8, 95–97, 99–100, 102–107, 130, 165, 173, 275, 326
  etiquette, 95, 102–104, 106–109
  participatory spectator, 45, 123
Auslander, Philip, 44, 75, 165, 175
AVByte, 6, 63–67, 69

B

Baldasso, Carl A., 269, 273
Ballinger, Colleen, 222–223, 225–226, 229

Bareilles, Sara, 34, 39
Beyond the Fence, 11, 284–286, 302–303, 305
Black Lives Matter Movement, 174, 190
Black Twitter, 174, 190–191, 193
Bolander, Jona, 129, 141
Bolger, Andrew Keenan, 33, 218–219, 223–224, 226, 228
Bombshell, 8, 145–148, 152–153, 157–163, 165–166, 168–169
Book of Mormon, The, 31, 39, 76
Booth, Paul, 123, 125, 129–130, 160
Bootlegs, 135, 142, 277–279, 356
Branding, 6, 31, 35, 212, 219–220, 226
Breaking Down The Riffs, 215, 225
Broadway, 2, 5–6, 9–10, 17–24, 26–33, 35–39, 46–56, 59–63, 66, 68–70, 73, 76–77, 80–81, 83, 88–89, 96–97, 102, 110, 120–122, 124–126, 128, 132–139, 142, 145–146, 150–152, 155–159, 162, 166, 174–175, 193, 194–196, 198, 209, 214, 218, 221–224, 228–229, 233–255, 262–263, 267, 271–273, 275, 278–281, 284, 286–302, 304, 309–311, 313, 318, 321, 324–325, 327, 336, 338–339, 343–344, 353–356, 358
  community, 20, 23, 24, 27, 33, 37, 49, 120, 124, 126–127, 132–135, 137–138, 222, 238, 244, 246, 248, 250–251, 253, 275, 280, 338
  great white way, 22, 47, 61, 74, 97, 309, 311
  league, 20, 49, 102, 246, 293
  marketing of, 17, 33, 247
  revivals, 46, 76, 292–294, 299, 309, 311–313, 317, 320–321, 327
  ticket lotteries, 17, 23, 26
  ticket distribution, 4, 6, 17–20, 23–27, 29–34, 36–37, 84, 87, 120, 128, 133, 163–165, 218–219, 244, 246, 248, 278, 292, 297, 327, 338, 355, 356
BroadwayWorld.com, 56, 60–61, 224

C
Canadian Council for the Arts, 343
Canonizing, 291–292, 296
Carlson, Marvin, 7, 18, 46, 74, 76, 77, 79, 239, 244
Cassara, Michael, 210, 216, 218, 225, 227
Casting, 2, 9–10, 179, 189, 207–221, 223–228, 234, 238, 240–241, 245–248, 252, 314
  agencies, 25
  directors, 2, 9–10, 207–210, 212–221, 224–227, 241
  reality television influences of, 2, 10
Celebrity, 9–10, 49, 119, 121, 129, 179, 189, 212, 221–223, 225–228, 233–241, 245, 248–253
  aura of, 236, 239
  culture, 49, 120–121, 226, 234–235, 237, 238, 250, 253
  digital presence of, 9, 120, 236, 250
  in casting, 224
  micro, 212, 221–223, 225–227
  private lives of, 235, 251
  relationship with media, 2, 8, 21, 48, 50, 54–55, 67, 80, 83, 96, 120–123, 126, 128–129, 134, 139, 151–152, 176, 184–186, 208, 213, 216, 219, 221, 233, 237–241, 243, 245–246, 250, 252, 318, 325, 354
  status, 49, 224–225, 234–237, 239, 241, 251

Cell phone, 7, 8, 95–112, 228, 275, 357
  ban, 102, 103
  etiquette, 95, 98, 102, 104, 106–107
Chernow, Ron, 123, 127, 140
Choreographers, 61, 354
Commercialism, 6
Convergence Culture, 7, 9, 122, 140–142, 173, 198
Copyright Act, 288, 303
Criticism, 2, 10, 11, 126, 132, 133, 152, 184, 186, 246, 292, 311, 332–341, 343–346

D

Dear Evan Hansen, 6, 51–52, 356, 357
Death Of A Salesman, 99–100
DeFlumeri, Hannah Rose, 226
Dennehy, Brian, 99, 106
Dewing, Joy, 208–209, 211, 216, 218, 225, 227
Digital, 1–13, 17, 27, 29, 33, 35, 36, 39, 43–70, 73–88, 100, 111, 120, 122–128, 130, 132, 140–142, 145, 165, 176–178, 196–197, 207–210, 212–214, 220–221, 226–228, 234–236, 250–251, 253, 262–268, 273, 275–276, 278–280, 284, 286–292, 295–299, 301–302, 304, 311–312, 314, 317, 319, 320, 322, 325–328, 334, 336, 339, 341, 343, 346–347, 351, 355–358
  age, 2–5, 7, 10, 29, 43–50, 52–68, 84, 88, 132, 196, 207, 213, 227–229, 284, 288, 292, 296, 297, 299, 302, 312, 314, 319–320, 327–328, 336, 346, 351

musicology, 284, 286–289, 291, 301–302, 328
natives, 4, 314, 317, 320
repositories, 276, 280
revolution, 2, 5, 44, 47–48, 50, 52, 59, 67, 119, 126–127
Disney, 25–26, 30, 32–34, 39, 65, 77, 80, 214, 290, 355
Diva, the, 107
Dirty Dancing The Musical, 7, 75, 84
Doctor Who, 160, 166
Dolan, Jill, 342–343
Dr. Horrible's Sing-Along Blog, 63
Dramaturgy, 10–11, 31, 35, 292, 311–312, 321, 327–328, 345

E

Eisenberg, Daryl, 209–210, 216, 218, 227
EMI, 283, 301–302
Emulators, 265–266
Ensemble, 55, 59, 65–66, 150, 242, 273–275, 281, 286, 337
Equity Chorus Calls /Principal Auditions, 210–211

F

Facebook, 6, 29–30, 32–33, 38, 43, 49, 55, 64–66, 69, 101, 124, 135–136, 140, 173, 178, 208, 210, 212, 214, 216–219, 225–226, 235–236, 250, 262, 273, 275–276, 298, 324–325, 339
Fandom, 8, 36, 39, 49, 120–123, 126, 129, 131–135, 137–138, 140–142, 145, 153, 155, 158, 161, 169, 179, 181, 184, 186, 188, 196, 249
  community, 8, 129–132, 136–137, 160, 188
  competition, 134

culture, 120, 122–123, 130–132, 136, 138, 184, 186, 188
fan art, 8, 129, 134
fanfic, 126, 130
fantagonism, 49
no-object, 145, 158, 161
studies, 121–122
Feingold, Michael, 342, 343
Film adaptations of musicals, 27, 188, 316, 356
First Folio, 276–278, 281
Floppy disks, 10, 264, 275

G
Genius, 120, 125, 142, 319
Geraghty, Lincoln, 160
Ghosting, 7, 74, 82, 84, 87, 254
Ghost The Musical, 7, 75, 78–81, 88–89, 234, 242–243, 245, 247–248
Giddyshaming, 151
Golden Age of Musical Theatre, 77, 88, 309
Goldstar, 103–104, 112
Google, 28, 39, 53, 54, 64, 66–68, 262, 264, 275–276, 294–295, 298, 304, 314
  Drive, 264, 276
  Scholar, 294–295
Grease Live!, 173, 181, 187, 193–196
Grease: You're The One That I Want!, 242–243, 245, 247–248
Guare, John, 321

H
Haimes, Todd, 313–314, 328
Hairspray, 27, 31, 38, 77, 196, 279
Hairspray Live!, 173, 175, 187, 195–196, 199
Hamilton Mixtape, The, 120, 124

Hamlet, 132, 276–277
Hanks, Bailey, 10, 234–235, 246, 250
Hashtags, 36, 190, 218, 357
Hate-watching, 149, 151–152, 167, 174, 184, 187, 190
Hatton, Oona, 344
Heller, Nathan, 334
Hilty, Megan, 146, 152–153, 155, 161–162
Hollywood Fringe Festival, 341–342, 347
Hyper-identities, 212

I
Internet Arcade, 265–266, 280
Internet Dating: The Musical, 53, 68

J
Jenkins, Henry, 7, 121–122, 127, 173, 177, 186
Jobs, Steve, 43, 59–60, 68–69
Jukebox musical, 356

K
Keller, Michael, 271, 273, 281
Kickstarter, 8, 157–158, 163–166
King And I, The, 296, 312, 320, 322–326, 328

L
LaBute, Neil, 344–345
Larson, Jonathan, 10, 49, 264
Legally Blonde, 10, 223, 225, 235, 246–247, 250, 255
Lemon, Brendan, 323, 328
Library of Congress, 264, 276, 280, 327
Like Me: The Social Media Musical, 57, 68

Lincoln Center Theater, 11, 311, 320, 321, 328
Lion King, The, 6, 17, 25–26, 30, 34, 39, 77, 214, 286, 290, 292, 356
Live, 3, 7–9, 12–13, 18, 21, 26–27, 33–36, 44–47, 49, 57–58, 63–65, 67–70, 73–75, 77, 79, 81, 83, 84, 87–88, 96–101, 103–104, 108–110, 112, 120, 122, 124, 128–129, 135–136, 138–141, 145–146, 152, 155, 157–158, 161, 163, 165–166, 173–190, 192–198, 201, 210, 216, 237, 241, 252, 276–279, 281, 292, 293, 302, 319, 323, 331–332, 337, 339, 343, 345, 353, 355–357
    audience, 8, 18–19, 25, 28, 33, 35, 45, 47, 57, 63, 66–67, 75, 77, 83–84, 95–97, 99–101, 103–104, 108, 120–121, 136, 139, 145, 152, 165–166, 173, 175–178, 181–183, 187–188, 193–195, 216, 235–239, 241–243, 276–278, 292, 323
    broadcast, 37, 173–175, 177–178, 180, 182–183, 185, 189–190, 192, 194–196, 216
    liveness, 4–5, 7, 75, 136, 155, 165, 174–179, 181–182, 187, 194, 196–197, 237, 239, 277
    television, 7–9, 21, 37, 44, 75, 139, 145, 161, 166, 173–182, 185, 188, 190–191, 194–196, 234, 236–239, 241–242, 251–252, 355
    theatre, 2–4, 7–9, 11–12, 18–19, 21, 24–28, 34–37, 44–47, 49, 56, 58, 63–64, 67, 68, 73, 75, 76, 81, 83–84, 87–88, 95–97, 100–101, 103–104, 108–109, 121, 124, 131, 136, 138–139, 152, 157, 161, 164, 174, 176–184, 186, 188–189, 193–197, 207, 210, 212, 216, 226–227, 234–239, 251–252, 262, 276–278, 292–293, 302, 331–332, 336–337, 343, 345, 353, 355, 357
    tweeting, 8–9, 51, 108, 174, 177–181, 190–191, 195
LuPone, Patti, 8, 104, 106–107, 113

M

MacAdams, Mikiko Suzuki, 269, 270–271
Mainwaring, Madison, 332, 333
Mashup, 130, 160
McCollum, Kevin, 23, 139
McPhee, Katherine, 146, 152, 155, 157, 161–162
Millennials, 51, 64–65, 69, 85, 212, 223, 314, 317
Mini-musical, 65
Minskoff Theatre, 30, 34, 157, 164
Miranda, Lin-Manuel, 69, 119, 123, 125, 128–129, 136, 141, 221, 223, 251, 277–278, 301
Miranda Sings, 222, 229
Mitchell, Colin, 341–342
Monroe, Marilyn, 145–146, 155, 159, 166
MySpace, 28–29, 67
MyTheatreMates.com, 342

N

Nazareth Brothers, 63–64
Nerds, 44, 60–63, 67, 69
New Instagram: The Musical, 64, 69
Newsies, 32–33, 39, 110, 218
New Yorker, The, 323, 334, 344, 358
New York International Fringe Festival, 55
New York Pops Gala, 162

364 INDEX

New York Public Library, 263–264, 273, 275, 280, 327, 356
New York Times, The, 21, 24–26, 28, 37, 76, 80, 83, 97, 99, 102, 107, 110, 119, 147, 252, 316, 332, 336, 339, 344
Nostalgia, 45–46, 57, 84, 88, 173, 175, 183, 186, 194, 309

O
OMFG! The Internet Dating Musical, 55, 68
On the Twentieth Century, 311–312, 315–319, 328
Operetta, 315
Original Cast Recording, 119
Osnes, Laura, 10, 221, 234, 243–244, 247, 255

P
Peter Pan Live!, 173, 175–176, 179, 181–182, 184, 187–188, 190, 196
Photoshop, 264
Platform Podcasts, 325
Playbill, 18, 22, 24, 38, 60, 97, 102, 107, 125, 128, 134–135, 216, 247–248, 255, 292, 318, 325
Playbill Vault, 318
Postmodern presence, 2, 120, 136, 137
Prince, Harold, 20
Pulitzer Prize, 293

R
Rent, 10, 13, 23–24, 29, 38, 49–50, 123, 196, 218, 264, 293, 296
Rocky The Musical, 7, 75, 77, 81, 83–84, 88–89
Rodgers and Hammerstein, 24–25, 174, 247–248, 294, 312, 321, 323 organization, 24–25, 311, 320, 321
website, 24–25
Roundabout Theatre Company, 11, 311–312

S
Schechner, Richard, 96
School of Rock, 33–34, 39
Screen-to-stage musicals, 4, 6, 73–75, 77, 80, 87–88
Screwball comedy, 315–316
Second Life, 267
Selfie, 49, 65, 222, 356
Seller, Jeffrey, 23, 138
Senft, Theresa, 213, 221, 227
Shakespeare, 30, 267, 276–277, 281, 320, 344, 345
Shipping/Slashing, 126–127
Shuffle Along, 299–300, 304
Situation marketing, 27–28
Smash, 8, 62, 120, 123, 145–153, 155, 157, 159, 161–162, 166–167, 184, 224
Social media, 1, 2, 5–6, 8–11, 13, 18, 28–29, 31–33, 35–37, 44, 48–49, 51–52, 55–57, 66, 68, 100, 112, 119, 121, 123–124, 127–129, 131, 134, 136, 141, 148, 173–174, 177–179, 183, 188, 190, 193–194, 196–197, 207–208, 212–219, 221–223, 226–227, 233–236, 239–240, 250, 252–253, 276, 296–298, 324–325, 327, 333, 343, 351, 356–357
Sociology in the Age of the Internet, 212, 220, 228–229
Sod, Ted, 313, 317, 328
Sound of Music Live!, The, 9, 173, 175, 179, 182–183, 187–189, 194, 196

South Park, 31, 39
Spring Awakening, 28–29, 33
Star Wars, 125, 129–130

T
TalkinBroadway.com, 22
Television, 2, 8, 10, 20, 25, 31, 36, 43–44, 54, 61, 110, 120, 122, 130, 136, 138, 146–148, 150, 160–161, 167, 218, 221, 224, 228, 233–235, 238–248, 252–253, 284, 324, 332–333, 352, 355–356
  audience, 54, 160, 221, 234–235, 238, 240, 244, 246–247, 356
  broadcast of musicals, 8, 25, 31, 37, 173–178, 183–184, 187, 190, 193, 197
  reality, 10, 218, 233–248, 251–253, 333
Theatre Plus, 313
Times Square, 17, 19–20, 26, 80, 353
TKTS, 20, 26
Tommy, 49
Tony Awards, 24, 29, 37, 52, 81, 89, 119, 124, 148, 279, 324
TripAdvisor, 343–344
Tumblr, 64–65, 120, 124, 128–130, 132, 135, 277–279
Twitter, 5–6, 29–32, 49, 51, 58, 64, 66, 101, 103, 107–108, 120, 124, 128, 132, 134–135, 142, 148, 173, 175, 178, 180, 183, 187–192, 197–202, 208, 212, 214, 216–219, 221, 236, 249–250, 255, 276, 298, 303, 324, 325, 342
  followers, 29, 120, 217–218, 249–250
  tweet seats, 108

U
Uncle Tom's Cabin, 323
Underwood, Carrie, 175, 179, 183–185, 198
Upstage Guide, 313–314, 317–318

V
Vaudeville, 267, 281, 353–354
VectorWorks, 269
Vimeo, 276, 279

W
Waitress, 34–35, 39
War Paint, 104, 112
Web of Science, 294
Weiss, Natalie, 215, 225–226, 228
West End, 17, 31, 84, 86, 253, 284, 290, 303, 338
What-If Machine, 285
Wicked, 17, 46, 56, 169, 193, 215, 218, 279, 292, 296, 343
WikiMusical, 57–58, 68
Wikipedia, 57, 149, 293, 298, 314
Williams, Rebecca, 145, 158
Wiz Live!, The, 173–176, 182, 187–196, 200–201
Wolfe, George C., 299–300, 304

Y
A Younger Theatre, 340, 347
YouTubsicals, 47, 63–67, 69

Printed by Printforce, the Netherlands